Emotion and Social Judgments

D0027320

INTERNATIONAL SERIES IN EXPERIMENTAL SOCIAL PSYCHOLOGY
Series Editor: MICHAEL ARGYLE, *University of Oxford.*

Emotion and Social Judgments

Edited by

JOSEPH P. FORGAS
University of New South Wales, Australia

PERGAMON PRESS
Member of Maxwell Macmillan Pergamon Publishing Corporation

OXFORD · NEW YORK · BEIJING · FRANKFURT
SEOUL · SYDNEY · TOKYO

90404684

BF
531
.E4834
1991

U.K.	Pergamon Press plc, Headington Hill Hall, Oxford OX3 0BW, England
U.S.A.	Pergamon Press Inc., Maxwell House, Fairview Park, Elmsford, New York 10523, U.S.A.
PEOPLE'S REPUBLIC OF CHINA	Maxwell Pergamon China, Beijing Exhibition Centre, Xizhimenwai Dajie, Beijing 100044, People's Republic of China
GERMANY	Pergamon Press GmbH, Hammerweg 6, D-6242 Kronberg, Germany
KOREA	Pergamon Press Korea, KPO Box 315, Seoul 110-603, Korea
AUSTRALIA	Maxwell Macmillan Pergamon Publishing Australia Pty Ltd, Lakes Business Park, 2 Lord Street, Botany, NSW 2019, Australia
JAPAN	Pergamon Press, 8th Floor, Matsuoka Central Building, 1-7-1 Nishi-Shinjuku, Shinjuku-ku, Tokyo 160, Japan

First edition 1991

Library of Congress Cataloging-in-Publication Data
Emotion and social judgments: an introductory review/ edited by Joseph P. Forgas.—1st ed.
p.   cm.—(International series in experimental social psychology; [v. 23])
Includes bibliographical references and indexes.
1. Affect (Psychology)   2. Mood (Psychology)
3. Emotions.   4. Social perception.
I. Forgas, Joseph P.   II. Series.
BF531.E4834   1991   302'.12—dc20   90-25908

British Library Cataloguing in Publication Data
Emotion and social judgments: an introductory review.
1. Social judgement
I. Forgas, Joseph P.
153.46

ISBN 0-08-040236-4 Hardcover
ISBN 0-08-040235-6 Flexicover

Front cover illustration by Penny Berry Paterson

Printed in Great Britain by BPCC Wheatons Ltd., Exeter

Contents

List of Contributors

C. R. AHRENS
University of Adelaide, Australia

MICHAEL ARGYLE
Oxford University, UK

SARA M. BAKER
Ohio State University, USA

GORDON H. BOWER
Stanford University, USA

HERBERT BLESS
University of Mannheim, FRG

NYLA R. BRANSCOMBE
University of Kansas, USA

GERALD L. CLORE
University of Illinois at Urbana-Champaign, USA

BRIAN M. COHEN
University of Kansas, USA

CHLOE A. DRAKE
Yale University, USA

KLAUS FIEDLER
University of Giessen, FRG

STEPHANIE A. FISHKIN
Yale University, USA

JOSEPH P. FORGAS
University of New South Wales, Australia

FAITH GLEICHER
Ohio State University, USA

J. M. INNES
University of Adelaide, Australia

MARTIN F. KAPLAN
Northern Illinois University, USA

DIANE M. MACKIE
University of California, USA

PAULA M. NIEDENTHAL
Johns Hopkins University, USA

ANN O'LEARY
Rutgers University, USA

W. GERROD PARROTT
Georgetown University, USA

RICHARD E. PETTY
Ohio State University, USA

PETER SALOVEY
Yale University, USA

NORBERT SCHWARZ
ZUMA, Mannheim, FRG

CAROLIN SHOWERS
University of Wisconsin-Madison, USA

MARTHA S. STRETTON
Yale University, USA

LEILA T. WORTH
Pennsylvania State University, USA

Part 1

Basic Conceptual Orientations

1

Affect and Social Judgments: An Introductory Review

JOSEPH P. FORGAS

University of New South Wales

Contents

How do feelings influence our social perceptions and judgments? This question has been of intense interest to philosophers, artists and scientists, as well as lay people since time immemorial. Surprisingly, the scientific study of affective influences on social judgments is a fairly recent development. Yet a proper understanding of the mechanisms mediating between feeling states and the cognitive processes that are involved in social judgments is also of considerable practical relevance. The accuracy and efficiency of our social perceptions and judgments is of critical importance both in our private and in our working lives. The ability to form accurate and unbiased impressions of others is not only the foundation of effective interpersonal behaviour (Heider, 1958), but is also an important prerequisite for our personal and social adjustment and, ultimately, mental health. Further, the ability to form accurate social judgments is also an increasingly important part of the working lives of many people. In developed industrialized societies an ever increasing proportion of workers are employed in tertiary, service industries, where interpersonal "people skills" are perhaps the most important occupational skills required. During the past several years there has been an explosive growth in research on the role of affective states in social perception, judgments and decisions. This book aims to bring together and integrate the most recent theoretical, empirical and practical developments in this field, in order to present an up-to-date review and integration of how affect impinges on social judgments. Part 1 of the book contains chapters dealing with the basic theoretical framework of research on affect and social judgments; Part 2 includes chapters describing extensions and elaborations; and Part 3 presents contributions that link basic research on affect and social judgments to areas of application.

This introductory chapter in particular has the objective of outlining the historical and theoretical background of interest in affect and cognition, and surveying the future prospects for this exciting field of enquiry.

Affect and Social Judgments: An Historical Overview

The recent emergence of interest in how affective states may influence a variety of cognitive processes (cf. Bower, 1981; Fiedler and Forgas, 1988; Forgas and Bower, 1988; Isen, 1984; Schwarz and Clore, 1988) may only be properly appreciated from an historical perspective. Since its inception, the empirical discipline of psychology operated on the implicit assumption that mental faculties such as affect, cognition and conation can be adequately studied in separation from each other. As Hilgard (1980) argued, this fragmentation of psychology's subject matter originated with German faculty psychology in the eighteenth century, and has been greatly accelerated during the explosive growth of empirical psychology in the twentieth century. The early dominant behaviorist models and the more recent cognitivist orientation that replaced them shared one common characteristic: neither of these two major paradigms attributed much importance to the study of affective processes and reactions. For the radical behaviorist, the study of affect, by definition involving internal processes, was inadmissible. If at all, affect and motivation were often studied in their most trivial manifestations, as aspects of environmentally manipulated drive states, such as hunger or thirst. For the cognitive psychologist, affect was long considered as irrelevant to its subject matter, traditionally defined as the study of essentially cold, rational ideation. At best, affective states were thought of as potentially "disruptive" influences on normal, that is affect-less, cognition.

It is in reaction to this long-assumed myth of affect-less behavior and cognition that during the past ten years or so, a number of influential theorists proposed a re-integration of affect into the mainstream of psychological inquiry. Zajonc (1980), in his influential paper, argued that affective reactions are often primary to, and temporarily precede elaborate cognitive processing, a view that has elicited considerable debate essentially centered on the question of how broadly one should define the domain of "cognition" (Lazarus, 1981, 1984). Others proposed broadly cognitivist conceptualizations of affect, where emotional states and reactions are subsumed as components of a single, integrated cognitive representational system (Bower, 1981; Bower and Cohen, 1982; Isen, 1984). Despite its shortcomings, this cognitive-reductionist view appears to have stimulated the overwhelming majority of recently published research dealing with the interface of affect and cognition, probably because of the existence of a rich experimental tradition in information processing psychology. However, within social psychology there is now growing evidence suggesting that in many everyday social contexts, affect and cognition may be regarded as at least partially independent response systems. Several theorists assume that affective states may fulfill direct informational functions, a position closely related to traditional social psychological formulations, and attribution theory in particular (Schwarz and Clore, 1988).

As in all areas of psychology dealing with affective phenomena, the accurate definition of exactly what is meant by emotion, affect and related terms such as evaluation remains a perennial problem (Frijda, 1986). However, there is a slowly developing consensus providing some clarification of the relationship betwen the most commonly used terms here, such as affect, emotion, evaluation and mood. The term "affect" is often used as a general and inclusive label to refer to both mood and emotion (cf. Petty, Gleicher and Baker, this volume). Some theorists consider that low-level affective reactions of a positive or negative valence arise directly in reaction to a stimulus event, and involve both physiological and phenomenological experiences (Leventhal, 1980) without abstract cognitive antecedents, but with possible informational functions (Clore and Parrott, this volume). A distinction between the terms "emotion" and "mood" is somewhat more problematic. Several theorists have suggested that moods are low-intensity and relatively enduring affective states with no immediately salient antecedent cause and therefore little cognitive content (e.g. feeling good or feeling bad). Emotions in turn are more intense, short lived and usually have a definite cause and clear cognitive content (e.g. annoyance, anger, or fear). Both moods and emotions have informational value. Whereas mood functions as a general, nonspecific positive or negative input that may be easily misattributed to an incorrect cause (Schwarz and Clore, 1988), emotions presumably evolved with specific signalling functions about particular environmental occurrences (Frijda, 1986). There is some evidence that moods have a relatively constant, nonspecific and additive effect on social judgments, while emotions, because of their high cognitive content, are dealt with in a manner similar to other cognitive inputs (Kaplan, this volume). Both of these terms are different from evaluation, an essential component of most attitudes, that may or may not involve affective reactions (see Innes and Ahrens, this volume).

Early Research on Affect and Social Judgments

The currently dominant cognitivist orientation in the domain of affective influences on social judgments represents a relatively recent development. As early as 1940, Razran showed that reactions to socio-political slogans were more favorable when these messages were received by subjects in a positive affective state (while enjoying a free lunch) than in a negative state (while being exposed to unpleasant smells). In the not so distant past, such affective influences on social judgments were typically accounted for in terms of either psychodynamic, or learning and conditioning principles. For example, Feshbach and Singer (1957) used the psychoanalytic concept of "projection" to account for the influence of affective states on social judgments. In this study, male subjects were made fearful through the administration of painful electric shocks, and were then instructed to either express or suppress their feelings, before making social judgments of another person. Results showed that fear resulted in a tendency to "perceive another person as fearful and anxious" and "suppression of fear facilitates the tendency to project fear onto another social object" (p. 286). This interpretation echoes Murray's (1933) even earlier dynamic interpretation of the links between affect and cognition. Several other early studies also demonstrated mood-induced differences in social judgments. In a study by Wehmer and Izard (1962), positive or negative affect was induced in subjects through the manipulated behavior of the experimenter. Subjects in the positive mood condition made more positive judgments of the task and the experimenter and performed better on the task than did subjects in the negative mood condition. In a related study, Izard (1964) used an actress behaving in an enthusiastic, friendly, angry, or fearful manner to induce different affective states in subjects. Subjects in the positive affect conditions performed better on the task, and made more positive judgments of themselves as well as of the actress, than subjects in whom a negative mood had been induced. Wessman and Ricks (1966) found that self-perceptions as well as interest in social activities was positively associated with a person's self-rated mood state over prolonged periods.

Accounts of these effects, consistent with the *Zeitgeist* in psychology at the time, shifted from psychoanalytic to conditioning principles. The Byrne and Clore (1970) model of classically conditioned evaluative responses predicts that reactions to social stimuli are determined by their association with other stimuli capable of eliciting unconditioned affective reactions. Griffitt (1970) found that subjects in whom negative affect has been induced by adverse environmental conditions, such as excessive heat and humidity, made more negative judgments of a target person. Within such a reinforcement–affective framework, "evaluative responses are seen as being determined by the positive or negative properties of the total stimulus situation" (p. 240), through the classical conditioning of evaluative responses. Gouaux (1971) reported mood-induced differences in social judgments following exposure to happy or depressing films, concluding that "interpersonal attraction is a positive function of the subject's affective state" (p. 40). Gouaux and Summers (1973) gave their subjects spurious positive or negative interpersonal feedback to manipulate mood, with essentially similar results. These early experiments provided strong evidence that affective states do have a general and widespread influence on a variety of social judgments, across a number of different judgmental and mood manipulation conditions. However, the theoretical explanations offered for these effects, based on conditioning and associationist principles, were far from conclusive. The conditioning experiments (c.f. Griffitt, Gouaux) relied on the simultaneous presence of affect-eliciting stimuli and the judgmental target, yet it is known from other studies (e.g. Wessman and Ricks, 1966) that preexisting, free-floating mood states can have identical judgmental consequences. Kaplan and Anderson (1973) presented an early critique of the conditioning theory of interpersonal attraction, arguing for an information integration model of affective influences on social judgments instead. Although conditioning and associations can clearly determine evaluative reactions to simpler social stimuli such as words (Staats *et al.*, 1962), as a general theory of mood effects on social judgments the model leaves much to be desired. Paradoxically, it is the psychoanalytic explanation put forward by Feshbach and Singer (1957) that comes closest to contemporary cognitive theorizing, by suggesting that cognition in a sense becomes "infused" with affect. Explaining how this process of "infusion" occurs is precisely what current cognitive models have attempted to do (cf. Bower, 1983, this volume).

Recent Theories of Affect, Cognition, and Social Judgments

It is in theorizing about the role of affect in social judgments that the most striking developments have occurred in recent years. As the accumulation of empirical information reached a "critical mass" in a variety of fields, a slow but inexorable convergence and integration of theories has become apparent in recent years. As is often the case in newly active fields, the similarities and overlaps between models first proposed in isolation from each other have become apparent, and theories first thought of as competing now appear complementary. This convergence of theoretical orientations is a strong feature of many of the contributions to this book. An excellent example of this trend is Bower's chapter, which draws widely from information integration theory, models of judgmental heuristics and social psychological research on judgments in its most up-to-date reformulation of the associative network model. Other chapters, by Branscombe and Cohen, Clore and Parrott, Fiedler, Schwarz and Bless, and others, echo this theoretical eclecticism, suggesting that the emergence of integrative, super-ordinate theories of mood effects on social judgments is an imminent possibility. Such models would need to acknowledge the existence of parallel and complementary information processing strategies, and also pay greater attention to the role of personal, motivational and cultural variables in accounts of mood effects on social judgments.

In contrast to the traditional view that saw affect as either irrelevant to, or at best an intrusion into, normal, affect-less cognitive processing, many of the recent models seek to incorporate affective states as components of an information processing and retrieval system. Models such as Bower's (1981) associative network theory see emotions as capable of indirectly influencing cognition, and eventually social judgments, through selectively facilitating access to related cognitive contents. Other models, derived from social psychological paradigms such as attribution research, give affective states a direct, primary information role (Schwarz and Clore, 1988). In contrast, for some theorists, the central issue is not whether affect or cognition are primary, but how these two distinct sources of information come to be combined in social judgments. This approach is closely based on information integration theory (Anderson, 1974), focusing on the process rather than the content of the affect–cognition interface. Finally, several theorists also focus on the processing strategies used by people as a function of their emotional state. There is now an emerging consensus suggesting that there are at least two alternative processing styles used in social tasks, the first open, construc-tive, creative, and "loose", and the second closed, reconstructive, analyti-cal, and tight (Fiedler, this volume). In fields with the most extensive empirical database, such as research on mood effects on person perception judgments, it now appears that an even larger number of alternative processing strategies are necessary to account for the research findings (see Forgas, this volume). The conditions under which different moods elicit these alternative processing strategies is the focus of active research at the moment.

In summary, four major theoretical positions can be distinguished as accounts of mood effects on social judgments: (1) information storage and retrieval models, based on cognitive research on memory processes, and their various elaborations; (2) attributional or judgmental heuristic models; (3) information integration models; (4) models focusing on alternate pro-cessing strategies and processing capacity variables. These theoretical accounts are by no means mutually exclusive; rather, they represent alterna-tive and often convergent explanations of the role of affect in everyday social judgments. Most current theories of how emotional states come to influence our social judgments also differ in their assumptions about the relationship between affect and cognition. They can be regarded as either separate or interdependent systems, and the primacy of one over the other has con-tinued to be the source of a lively theoretical debate.

Information Storage and Retrieval Theories of Mood Effects on Social Judgments

Several recent models seek to account for emotional influences on social judgments in terms of essentially cognitive, information processing or memory models. Bower (1981, 1983) as well as Isen (1984) proposed that many affective influences on social judgments may be explained in terms of emotional states facilitating the accessing and retrieval of similar or related cognitive categories. The most precise and probably most influential elaboration of this idea has been put forward by Bower (1981), who proposed that

> each specific emotion . . . has a specific node or unit in memory that collects together many other aspects of the emotion that are connected to it by associative pointers . . . In addition, each emotion unit is also linked with propositions describing events from one's life during which that emotion was aroused . . . When activated above a threshold, the emotion unit transmits excitation to those nodes that produce the pattern of autonomic arousal and expressive behaviour commonly assigned to that emotion . . . Activation of an emotion node also spreads activation throughout the memory structures to which it is connected, creating subthreshold excitation (p. 135)

which together with activation from other sources facilitates the retrieval of that information. Within this model, affective states may be thought of as components of a human associative memory system. Through prior associations, affective states become linked to cognitive representations about events, semantic categories and other information. When a mood state is experienced, activation spreads through established pathways to associated categories, leading to the superior accessibility of related constructs.

There are several consequences of this formulation, with implications for social judgments. (1) Memory effects: the model predicts that the recall of information should be facilitated when learning and recall moods match (mood-state-dependent memory). (2) Learning effects: information that is consistent with the prevailing mood state should be better learnt due to the greater availability of related mood-consistent associations (mood-congruent learning). (3) Attention and selective exposure effects: people in a particular mood state should be motivated to pay selective attention to information that is consistent with their prevailing mood state (mood-congruent attention). (4) Associative and interpretational effects: as the interpretation of social information involves top-down, constructive processes (Heider, 1958; Kelly, 1955), temporary moods should influence this process through the greater availability of mood-consistent constructs to be used in associations (mood-congruent associations) and interpretations of ambiguous details. In conjunction, these processes can be expected to have a significant overall impact on social judgments, in the direction of mood-consistent biases. Given that social stimuli such as people are normally extremely complex, consisting of a very intricate information array, much of it indeterminate or ambiguous in character, mood-induced cognitive biases can be expected to play a major role in such judgments. Judges experiencing a positive mood tend to spend more time looking at positive rather than negative information, learn such details better, are more likely to interpret and encode ambiguous information in a mood-consistent manner, remember that information better later on, and tend to interpret the social behaviors of themselves as well as others in a mood-consistent rather than inconsistent manner, according to the cumulative evidence from a growing number of studies (cf. Bower, 1981; 1983; Forgas, this volume; Forgas *et al.*, 1984, in press; Forgas and Bower, 1987, 1988).

Empirical evidence for affect-priming models

There is now strong cumulative evidence supporting the basic postulates of priming models from a variety of domains dealing with learning, memory, attention, and judgmental processes (see Bower, in this volume). This empirical evidence for the basic affect–cognition links postulated by priming models is far from unequivocal, however. Several researchers have failed to find a mood-state dependent memory effect (cf. Bower and Mayer, 1985), and several studies suggest that additional situational and contextual influences often modify mood-priming effects (cf. Branscombe and Cohen, this volume; Fiedler, this volume). Attempts to account for these failures have been less than fully satisfactory, proposing *post hoc* explanations that reduce the falsifiability of the model considerably. Another problem concerns the symmetricity of positive and negative mood effects on cognition as implied by priming models. Several studies report more consistent and enduring mood effects associated with positive rather than negative moods (Forgas *et al.*, 1984; Isen, 1984). These results present a problem for the simple and parsimonious priming principle as originally presented. The universal affect-priming model also does not fit in readily with much of the clinical research demonstrating strong and enduring but self-specific mood effects, as, for example, in depression (Beck, 1976; Ottaviani and Beck, 1988), without similar distortions in not self-relevant judgments. Specific contextual and task variables, such as the target of judgments, or the judgmental dimension used, were also found to interact with the universal priming effect predicted by affect–cognition models (Forgas, in press; Forgas and Bower, 1987; Forgas *et al.*, 1988). It appears now that the simple, universal, and symmetrical cognitive effects associated with moods predicted by priming theories do not reliably occur under all experimental conditions. It has thus become necessary to revise and expand the original theoretical models in order to specify the boundary conditions under which these effects can be expected to occur. We shall look at some of these proposed theoretical elaborations next.

Extensions of the affect-priming models

Mood intensity. Initial reactions to the failure to replicate mood-state-dependent memory effects included the suggestion that only sufficiently strong and intense mood manipulations can be expected to produce such effects (Bower and Mayer, 1985). However, the literature abounds in examples where surprisingly weak mood manipulations were adequate to produce significant weak effects (cf. Isen, 1984), detracting from the plausibility of the intensity explanation.

Causal belonging. Bower (1985) suggested that failure to find mood effects in some studies may be due to the incidental nature of the mood manipulation used. Accordingly, "contiguity alone between the emotion and the event would not be sufficient to produce an association; rather, the subject must perceive the emotion as causally belonging to the event or the materials which give rise to it" (p. 17). The causal association between the affective state and the cognitive material indeed produced the expected memory effect, which may also explain why mood effects are reliably found with autobiographical material (where prior causal associations presumably exist) but not with incidental materials. However, the causal belonging hypothesis has the weakness that it relies on the subject's phenomenological experience of causal association as the critical variable mediating mood effects. Also, several experiments where causal belonging was unlikely to occur, including Bower, Monteiro and Gilligan's (1978) initial two-list learning experiment, have found significant mood effects, detracting from the universality of the causal belonging explanation.

Active vs passive processing. Several authors recently proposed the hypothesis that affective influences on cognitive processes may be limited to occasions when active, constructive, rather than passive, reconstructive, information processing occurs. For example, Fiedler (this volume) in his dual-force model argues that "emotional states will influence cognitive processes to the extent that the cognitive task involves the active generation of new information as opposed to the passive conservation of information given" (pp. 2–3). This model appears consistent with the original emphasis of mood-priming models on productive, generative tasks, and the growing empirical evidence indicating more reliable mood effects on tasks requiring active information transformation, as occurs in social judgments and decisions (cf. Forgas and Bower, 1988) rather than mere information retrieval (cf. Bower and Mayer, 1985).

Universal vs selective priming. Contrary to Bower's (1981) original formulations, the affect-priming model is often assumed to imply that a particular mood state should have a broad, universal infuence on the availability of similarly valenced cognitions. For example, a positive mood state is expected to facilitate the accessing of all positively valenced materials to some extent, and negative moods should increase the likelihood of recall of all negatively valenced cognitive contents. In this form, there are at least two serious problems with the model: (1) with spreading activation to all similarly valenced cognitive contents, a fan effect would rapidly dissipate the priming effects of moods; (2) a further serious problem for the universal priming model is that it predicts relatively context-independent, robust effects: in reality, most judgmental effects have been found to be target and context dependent. As we have seen, negative moods typically lead to more negative judgments of the self but not others, both by normal and by depressed persons. This problem disappears if we assume—as Bower (1981) initially argued—that what mood primes is not all similarly valenced cognitions, but cognitive contents that have been experienced in a similar mood in the past, irrespective of their valence. Thus in a negative mood, both self-deprecatory and other-enhancing cognitions are likely to become more accessible (Forgas *et al.*, in press). This may explain the strong self–other differences found in many studies of mood effects on social judgments in normal as well as in clinical populations (Forgas *et al.*, 1984).

Judgmental ambiguity. The role of affective states on judgments is also dependent on the nature of the judgment (cf. Fiedler, this volume). Some opinions, decisions and judgments are based on often-rehearsed, highly familiar information that has previously been used to arrive at the same conclusion. Such well-rehearsed or "crystallized" judgments are much less likely to be influenced by transient moods than new, ambiguous, or difficult judgments, as noted by Schwarz and Clore (1988). The associative network model can account for this by postulating two alternative avenues for arriving at a social judgment: the retrieval of an already formed, crystallized opinion, or the on-line "calculation" of an opinion. Only the latter process allows for mood-based distortions.

Valence integration. The most recent revision of the associative network model is described in Bower's chapter in this volume. The major change is that the model now specifically includes the provision of a positive and negative valence integration node associated with each judgmental target. That is, positively and negatively valenced information about a judgmental object is "accumulated" and judgments are ultimately determined by the actual balance of positive and negative valences at the time. This version of the model is very similar in its emphasis to classical information integration formulations, such as Anderson's (1974) cognitive algebra. However, by explicitly relying on an associative network framework, the revised model goes beyond information integration principles and is capable of explaining such familiar judgmental effects as primacy and recency, or the persistence of evaluative impressions long after the initial data on which they are based are forgotten. The model implies that mood during original learning (a) influences whether information is interpreted as positive or negative, and (b) focuses attention on, and enhances the learning of mood-consistent details. Additional retrieval effects are predicted at the time of judgment, when mood is expected to activate the congruent valence node, making the recall of mood-consistent information more likely, and biasing the outcome of judgments in a mood-consistent direction.

In summary, the various priming formulations and their elaborations provided perhaps the most influential conceptual framework for exploring emotional influences on social judgments to date. Their influence is probably based on the simplicity and parsimony of their assumptions, and the existence of a rich and stimulating tradition of relevant research on memory and information processing variables. Perhaps the three most notable limitations of these models are that (a) they typically deal with automatic, subconscious processes only, (b) affective variables are assumed to be reducible to components of a cognitive representational system with only indirect rather then direct effects on cognition and judgments, and (c) some of their predictions are not readily open to falsification. Several alternative formulations to account for more direct, conscious, and falsifiable mood effects on judgments have also been developed recently. These will be briefly considered below.

Affect as information: The misattribution model

Several authors suggested that the role of emotions in social judgments is a far more direct one than affect-priming models would imply. Schwarz and Clore (1983, 1988) proposed that temporary affective states may serve as information used by people as a judgment-simplifying heuristic device. When asked to make a social judgment, according to this model, subjects consult their existing mood state to infer their evaluative reactions to the target, and make a judgment accordingly. This model may also be seen as derived from misattribution research: subjects in a sense "misattribute" their existing mood as due to the judgmental target present at the time, instead of its true (and now forgotten) cause. Some experimental evidence suggests that when the true cause of the existing mood is made salient to subjects, their social judgments are no longer influenced by it. This prediction has the advantage of making the model clearly falsifiable, unlike some of the more esoteric mood-priming formulations. To date, several published reports indicate that correctly attributed emotions failed to exert an effect on judgments. However, other articles show that affective states with a clear and salient identifiable cause (for example, following

Velten-type inductions) nevertheless continue to have significant judgmental consequences.

The mood-as-information model differs from affect-priming models in several ways. Whereas for affect-priming theories mood is only an indirect source of information, through its effects on facilitating the recall of other cognitions, for Schwarz and Clore (1988) affective states are just as informative as cognitions, under certain conditions. As Kaplan (in this volume) suggests, there is no fundamental reason why treating affect as a direct source of information would preclude its role in information storage and retrieval as affect-priming models suggest. In fact, in many conditions, there may be no reliable empirical way to distinguish between affect-priming and affect-as-information models, as both make identical predictions of mood-consistent distortions in social judgments. Another difference between mood-as-information and affect-priming models is that the former clearly predict mood effects at the retrieval or judgmental stage only, whereas the mood-priming model also makes strong predictions about encoding, learning, and attention effects. To the extent that such encoding effects are reliably demonstrated in the literature (and there are numerous studies showing such effects; see Forgas and Bower, 1988, for a review), the mood-as-information model appears a less than complete account of mood effects on social judgments. Finally, the two models may also be contrasted in terms of the breadth of range of phenomena they seek to explain. In those terms, the mood-priming model, dealing with mood effects on learning, attention, memory, associations as well as judgments appears a more parsimonious account than the mood-as-information model, which predominantly focuses on judgmental effects only. However, the most recent formulations of the affect-as-information position (Clore and Parrott, this volume; Schwarz and Bless, this volume) tap into the rich tradition of work on judgmental heuristics, and give this model a broader and more general conceptual foundation than was originally the case.

Empirical support for the affect-as-information model comes from several sources (see also Clore and Parrott, this volume; Schwarz and Bless, this volume). The most critical—and admirably falsifiable—implication of the model is that only unattributed emotional states may have judgmental consequences. Schwarz and Clore (1988) report several experiments in which focusing on the source of the affective state led to the disappearance of the judgmental effect. Other evidence, however, is not always consistent with the model. Mackie and Worth (this volume) found that positive mood had a greater facilitating effect on the acceptance of persuasive communication from experts rather than from non-experts, suggesting that mood was unlikely to have been globally used by subjects as information. Rather, different mood-induced processing strategies may account for the findings.

In their most recent reconceptualizations of this model, Schwarz and Bless (this volume) shift the emphasis from judgmental effects to a more general consideration of the information processing consequences of positive and negative affect. According to this view, affective states have a more general informational, signalling function. Positive moods signal that "all is well with the world", resulting in lazy, superficial, heuristic, loose information processing, and a greater tendency to engage in unusual, unorthodox, and creative information processing (Isen, 1984). Negative moods, in contrast, signal problematic, difficult situations, triggering careful, analytic, and "tight" cognitive strategies unlikely to be compatible with creativity. It seems likely that there is an even larger number of alternative processing strategies people may adopt in various situations. In person-perception tasks, for example, at least four different processing strategies may be identified: (1) the direct-access strategy; (2) the substantive processing strategy; (3) the motivated processing strategy; (4) the heuristic processing strategy (see Forgas, this volume, for details).

Affective influences on information processing strategies

The models considered above are essentially information models, primarily dealing with information storage and retrieval, and the availability and interpretation of cognitive content. In recent years, several theorists have looked at the complementary question of how social information, once available, is processed. Several studies indicate that when facing a problem-solving task in a positive mood, people tend to reach a decision more quickly, use less information, tend to avoid demanding, systematic processing of the information, and are more confident about their decisions (Forgas, 1989; Isen, 1984; Isen and Means, 1983; Isen *et al.*, 1982). Unfortunately, relatively little attention has been paid to the processing consequences of dysphoric moods, and what evidence exists suggests a rather complex reaction to dysphoria (Forgas, 1989).

Why should people be reluctant to use more demanding processing strategies when feeling good? Two explanations for this effect were put forward, one cognitive and one motivational in character. According to the cognitive account, positive moods impose greater cognitive strain on attention, memory, and processing capacity in general as greater quantities of positively valenced information become available (Isen, 1984). This may account for the processing differences found between neutral and positive mood, as euphoric subjects engage in shorter, more superficial, and less analytic processing strategies. However, such a cognitive capacity-limit explanation is not a plausible account of negative as against positive mood differences. After all, there is no reason to assume that negative moods do not cause just as great, if not greater, capacity overloads as positive moods are assumed to do. A somewhat different version of this capacity-limitation explanation was recently proposed by Mackie and her colleagues (this volume), suggesting that it is not lack of cognitive capacity *per se*, but attention deficits that underlie the more superficial information processing strategies typically found in positive moods. The second explanation is motivational in character, suggesting that in an elated mood people tend to protect their rewarding affective state by refusing to engage in demanding and effortful cognitive processing if at all possible (Isen, 1984). This motivational explanation is contradicted by evidence from other areas of social psychology suggesting that it is precisely instrumental, effortful activity, such as helping another person, actively seeking out rewarding people, and consciously focusing on rewarding information, that is often used by people in order to maintain and further improve positive moods (Forgas, 1989).

The existing evidence is more consistent with a cognitive capacity-limit than a motivational explanation. Mackie and Worth (this volume) report a series of experiments that suggest that elated subjects, when given an opportunity, are in fact motivated to spend more time reading persuasive messages (presumably to compensate for mood-induced cognitive limits), and seem to engage in systematic rather than heuristic processing under these conditions. Conversely, increasing the motivation of elated subjects to engage in thorough and systematic processing by offering incentives was not sufficient to change processing style, again supporting a cognitive rather than a motivational explanation. It is unfortunate that conditions involving negative affect were not a feature of these studies, as results from positive mood conditions may not necessarily generalize to dysphoric moods.

There is thus converging evidence from a variety of sources suggesting a distinction between at least two different kinds of information processing styles. Clark and Isen (1982) were among the first to introduce the notion of "controlled" and "automatic" processing strategies to account for the aberrant mood effects found in dysphoria. Isen (1984), in a series of studies, found that people in positive moods rely on a different cognitive processing style than subjects in a neutral mood: they are more creative, make more unusual associations, use broader and more inclusive categories, use less information, and reach decisions more quickly. Fiedler (this volume) convincingly argues for a parallel distinction between "productive" and "reproductive" processes, involving the "loosening" and "tightening" of information processing strategies, and suggests that mood effects are most likely to be marked when productive, elaborative and "loose" cognitive processing occurs. Finally, in the persuasion literature Petty and his colleagues (this volume) also proposed a distinction between "central-route" and "peripheral-route" processing styles, finding that the effects of mood on persuasion are mediated by the particular processing style adopted by subjects. These various lines of evidence provide convergent support for the notion that in addition to their influence on information storage and retrieval systems, transient moods also play a major role in invoking alternative information processing styles. The detailed specification of the boundary conditions necessary for these alternative processing styles to occur remains one of the more important tasks for future research.

Affect and Persuasion

The role of affective states in persuasion deserves particular attention. Essentially, a person's reactions to persuasive communication may be thought of in exactly the same conceptual terms as social judgments. In both cases, the recipient of a social stimulus faces the task of evaluating and forming a judgment of a judgmental target. In the case of persuasive communication, the situation differs from other social judgments only to the extent that much is already known about how the characteristics of the sender, the message, and the receiver are likely to influence reactions to the message. Despite considerable interest in persuasive communication for some decades now, the role of affect in persuasion has not been seriously studied, apart from research on fear-arousing messages. Common sense suggests that happy, positive moods are more likely to predispose people towards a receptive frame of mind towards persuasive messages. It is probably for this reason that examples of persuasive communication by salespeople, advertisers or politicians usually involve a determined attempt to instill a positive, happy affective state in the recipients. There is also considerable experimental evidence for the beneficial effects of positive mood on the acceptance of persuasive messages (Dribben and Brabender, 1979; Galizio and Hendrick, 1972; Janis et al., 1965; Razran, 1940).

Recent theoretical accounts of persuasive communication mirror theories of emotional influences on social judgments in focusing on the information processing strategies of subjects. Models such as the Elaboration Likelihood Model (ELM) proposed by Petty and Cacioppo (1986) are in many respects similar to the kind of processing alternatives recently developed in affect–cognition research (cf Fiedler, this volume). Two alternative ways of dealing with persuasive messages have been identified by these authors. The first method entails the careful, detailed and analytic integration of message content and other cognition, when an individual is motivated and able to deal with substantive message contents, also referred to as systematic processing or central-route processing. The second method involves a more superficial, careless and impressionistic processing of persuasive messages, when more attention is perhaps paid to the incidental features of the message (communicator features, attractiveness, etc.) than the quality of the arguments presented. This alternative is also called heuristic or peripheral-route processing (Chaiken, 1980; Petty and Cacioppo, 1981, 1986). Substantive factors, such as the content and quality of a persuasive message are likely to determine its effectiveness when systematic processing occurs, while in heuristic processing other features, such as sender status, likeability, or style, can have a significant effect on judgments of the message. Recent research suggests that people in a good mood may be more likely to adopt a heuristic processing strategy and react to persuasive messages accordingly (Mackie and Worth, this volume; Worth and Mackie, 1987).

Both motivational and cognitive factors may play a role in whether effortful, analytic or superficial, heuristic processing is adopted by a person, and their relative influence is as yet incompletely understood. A suitable test of the cognitive capacity-limit and the motivational mood-preservation accounts is whether elated subjects voluntarily choose to take longer to deal with information when given the opportunity. Evidence showing that they do (cf. Mackie and Worth, 1989) indicates that motivation to avoid stressful processing is not a plausible explanation of processing differences. Manipulations designed to increase subjects' motivation to process information systematically were found to be ineffectual, again supporting a nonmotivational explanation (Worth *et al.*, 1989). However, the results presented here by Innes and Ahrens (this volume) are more consistent with a motivational rather than a cognitive capacity-limit explanation, suggesting that the status of these conflicting models is far from settled. These studies suggest that positive mood is not necessarily always beneficial for persuasive communication. As elated persons are less likely to process messages systematically, positive mood will only be effective to increase persuasion with weak messages and in the presence of helpful heuristic cues such as sender credibility.

Research on mood effects on persuasive communication is one of the most active and promising topics in judgmental research at the moment. Once again, the emerging convergence between models specifically proposed to account for persuasion effects, such as the ELM by Petty and Cacioppo (1981), and the various more general dual-process models developed by mood-cognition researchers (Clark and Isen, 1982; Branscombe and Cohen, this volume; Fiedler, this volume; Isen, 1984) is a most promising development. The inclusion of several contributions from researchers working in the area of persuasive communication here should help to stimulate even closer integration between these areas.

Summary and Overview of the Book

The objective of this book is thus to bring together and survey the current status of research on emotion and social judgments, with a view to identifying the major trends now emerging in this highly active field of research. In selecting contributions for the volume, the aim was to identify the most significant theoretical and practical contributions to the field, in order to highlight similarities in conceptualization and methodology across related areas. The following brief overview provides a general outline of the focus of the different chapters. At the same time, this overview is also designed to highlight complementary and convergent approaches across various research domains in the hope of encouraging further conceptual integration.

The book is organized into three substantive sections. The first section presents basic theoretical contributions from authors who represent distinct conceptual orientations: the affect-priming model (Bower), the affect-as-information model (Schwarz and Bless), the information integration approach (Kaplan), and the dual-force model (Fiedler). In contrast, contributions in the second section extend and integrate theoretical and empirical work from a variety of domains in seeking to present a broader, and perhaps more eclectic and critical, view of how feelings influence social judgments. These contributions expand the judgmental heuristic approach (Clore and Parrott), integrate various fields of research on evaluative judgments (Niedenthal and Showers), link mood effects to other judgmental effects (Branscombe and Cohen), and offer a critique of the individualistic bias inherent in many cognitive theories of mood effects on social judgments (Argyle). The last section of the book presents chapters that are characterized by an integration of well-defined theoretical models and their application in such important areas as judgments of persuasive messages (Petty *et al.*; Mackie and Worth), evaluative judgments about attitudes (Innes and Ahrens), judgments about health and illness (Salovey *et al.*), and person perception judgments (Forgas).

Gordon Bower's contribution introduces the first section. This chapter presents an overview and update of his influential network model, with a revised theoretical formulation to take into account some of the recent empirical evidence. Bower's (1981) paper had a major impact on the field, by systematizing and integrating the available evidence on mood effects on a variety of cognitive processes, summarizing a series of his own experiments in the field, and outlining a comprehensive theoretical model rooted in cognitive models of memory that promised to explain many of the disparate results found in the literature. The present chapter is the most recent in a series of significant updates and modifications of the network model (cf. Bower and Cohen, 1982; Bower and Mayer, 1985). It is in the field of social judgments that the model has received perhaps the most consistent empirical support, despite the existence of a number of competing theories. This is clearly reflected in Bower's contribution here. The revision of the model now proposed involves the addition of a representational node to the associative network, allowing the cumulative integration of positive and negative valences associated with a judgmental target. Although formally this is only a minor change to the model, in practice it makes it possible to account for a variety of findings, such as residual evaluative biases long after the evidence is forgotten, that were difficult to explain by the earlier formulation. Several empirical findings continue to present problems for the network model, such as evidence for nonsymmetrical mood effects and against mood effects at the encoding stage. However, considering the short history of concentrated research in this field, the network model continues to retain its place as perhaps the most general integrative theoretical formulation we have, and Bower's chapter in particular shows a welcome flexibility to deal with new evidence as it becomes available.

Norbert Schwarz and Herbert Bless in their chapter present the most recent formulation of what has become a major alternative theoretical model for conceptualizing mood effects on social judgments. The chapter significantly expands the scope of the original "how do I feel about?" heuristic of Schwarz and Clore (1988) to deal not only with evaluative judgments, but also as a potential explanation of some mood-congruent memory effects. According to this model, unattributed transient moods may be used to make global evaluative judgments about a recall target (for example, childhood), which in turn cues selective evidence to substantiate that judgment. The predictions of this model are generally similar to priming models, but make the strong prediction that only previously unattributed moods should have such memory effects. The chapter also extends the model in another direction, to explain the different processing styles often found to be associated with positive and negative moods. Accordingly, moods act as information to signal states of the world that do or do not require careful processing (Frijda, 1986), resulting in loose, heuristic processing strategies in good moods, and detailed, analytic processing in dysphoria. Schwarz and Bless survey an impressive array of evidence for such assymetrical processing strategies in good and bad moods, associated with narrower attentional focus, more causal explanations, and different organization of information. Their discussion of these issues in terms of a heuristic model serves to link their theorizing with other models (cf. Fiedler, this volume; Isen, 1984; Petty *et al.*, this volume). Schwarz and Bless's account clearly deserves serious empirical study as an alternative explanation of mood-based differences in processing strategies.

A different conceptual approach is offered in Kaplan's stimulating chapter, which argues that as both affect and cognition clearly have an informative function on social judgments, the critical question becomes how information from these two domains is integrated. In seeking an answer to this problem, Kaplan reaches back to Anderson's (1974) information integration model developed as a general model of human social judgments. This approach has its origins in Kaplan and Anderson's (1973) critique of the conditioning explanations put forward to account for emotional influences on attraction judgments by Byrne (1971). Kaplan suggests that the integration of emotion and knowledge in social judgments can be adequately addressed by first establishing common scale values for these disparate sources of information on some substantive dimension, followed by the close analysis of how such scale values are weighted and combined to yield a judgment. Kaplan also summarizes empirical data suggesting that different integration rules may apply in different circumstances. With general undifferentiated moods, judgmental effects may be constant and additive, independent of other information, such as attitude similarity to the judgmental target. In other circumstances, when the emotion has a distinct cognitive content, its influence on judgments may be subject to the same integration rules as apply to other cognitions. The provision of additional information during a group discussion in simulated juries was found to dilute negative mood effects present before the discussion commenced. It seems then that "mood exerts a general halo on judgments that persists in the face of increased cognitive information. Emotion, on the other hand, has specific information properties that are averaged with cognitive information." Kaplan further suggests that moods have a constant effect at the time of judgment, while emotions influence judgments at the encoding stage. The information integration approach offers a simple and parsimonious framework for understanding the way emotional and cognitive information comes to influence social judgments. Individual differences and personality traits may also be accommodated within such a framework, with trait and state emotions predicted to be more situationally volatile, while trait and state moods are expected to be cross-situationally general (cf. Forgas *et al.*, 1984).

In his stimulating chapter, Klaus Fiedler surveys the empirical evidence now available for emotional influences on social cognition and judgments, and points to a number of anomalies suggesting the apparently unstable, situational character of at least some of these effects. He then proceeds to propose an exciting integrative model that is potentially capable of dealing with some of the existing theoretical confusion in the literature, the so-called "dual-force" model. This approach distinguishes between two fundamentally different kinds of cognitive processes: information conservation and information transformation, the first essentially reproductive, the second productive in character. Generally, emotional influences are more marked when productive, transformational processing is involved, as is the case in recall rather than recognition tests, and with ambivalent, self-relevant, unstructured or socially triggered judgmental tasks. Several ingenious experiments are described that support such a "dual-force" formulation. The model predicts differential mood effects, not only as a function of the productive–reproductive character of the task, but also as a function of the particular dependent variable used. Measures requiring constructive, idiosyncratic, or subjective judgments should be more sensitive to mood effects than are constrained, pre-determined judgments. This proposition is again supported by the reported empirical findings, suggesting that the kind of "output" variable collected may itself bias the extent to which emotional influences on judgments are discovered. Fiedler then turns to a consideration of an often neglected issue: what, after all, constitutes an "effective" mood state? He notes that neither intensity, nor the absence of correct attribution is a necessary prerequisite. Instead, the cognitive, thematic priming aspect of the mood manipulation may be most critical, consistent with the dual-force view that it is the active, subjective generation of inferences that is most likely to be subject to mood influences. Taken in its entirety, the dual-force model has much to recommend it as an integrated attempt to reconcile within a single conceptual system some of the more puzzling inconsistencies in the literature. Similar considerations could play a critical role in accounting for affective influences on person-perception judgments (Forgas, this volume).

The second section of the book contains contributions that present an integration and extension of basic theories of mood effects on social judgments. In the first chapter in this section, Gerald Clore and Gerrod Parrott generalize and expand the affect-as-information hypothesis, by developing an integrated conceptual analysis of a broad range of phenomena involving the "infusion" of affect into cognition (cf. Feshbach and Singer, 1957; Murray, 1933). This approach is in a sense a reverse of Ortony *et al.* (1988) influential analysis of emotions as the result of cognitive appraisal; here, it is affect that informs cognition, rather than the other way around. Clore and Parrott suggest that it is not only affect, but also bodily states and cognitive states that have informational effects. Feelings about momentary cognitive states may be misattributed to a mistaken cause the same way as affective states may be misattributed to unrelated judgmental targets. In the second half of this chapter, Clore and Parrott provide a stimulating and up-to-date discussion of the relationship between priming and affect-as-information models, and conclude that the two accounts may be seen as essentially complementary rather than conflicting explanations of a range of affect-related cognitive phenomena. While the priming model emphasizes universal, automatic processes, misattribution models seek to analyze the phenomenological aspects of an actor's experience. In conjunction with Bower's chapter, this contribution presents a strong case for an integration of the various theoretical accounts of mood effects on social judgments, based on mood-priming and mood-as-information models.

The chapter by Paula Niedenthal and Carolin Showers offers a more eclectic and broad theoretical analysis of affective influences on social judgments, emphasizing the stimulus-based character of many affective reactions and experiences. Rather than analyzing affect as a preexisting, or separately manipulated state, their perspective focuses on the close interdependence between various external stimuli and the affective reactions triggered by them. The role of emotional expression as not merely information, but as an affect-eliciting stimulus is considered, followed by a stimulating discussion of the extensive research on evaluative judgments. Niedenthal and Showers suggest that stimulus-based affective reactions may be an important, and largely ignored feature of many kinds of evaluative judgments, potentially relevant to the explanation and linking of such diverse phenomena as research on the physical attractiveness stereotype, pupillometrics, and mood effects on various social judgments. Research on the implicit perception of affective information—such as the facial expression of a target—suggests that affective reactions to stimuli may occur without conscious awareness, and that such reactions have demonstrable effects on social perception and judgments. Assuming that person perception involves either category-based or piecemeal strategies of evaluation (Fiske and Pavelchak, 1986), affective reactions to a target that are inconsistent with the overall evaluation of a category are more likely to trigger piecemeal, bottom-up judgmental strategies. Several empirical studies by the authors described here provide evidence that affective reactions to a target do predispose people towards distinct modes of cognitive processing. One of the central themes of this chapter is its emphasis on a balanced consideration and integration of affect as, on the one hand, a reaction to a stimulus event, and, on the other, as one of the causal antecedents of cognitive responses.

Nyla Branscombe and Brian Cohen begin their chapter with an overview of evidence from social perception research showing that, for a variety of reasons, social perceivers often sacrifice accuracy for efficiency in employing various heuristic and judgment-simplifying devices. Next, they point to the close similarity between the role of stereotypes, and the role of moods as heuristic devices: both involve automatic processing, and both can be controlled by the employment of conscious, motivated processing strategies. It follows that motivational variables may play an important role in controlling or even eliminating mood-based distortions in social judgments, a possibility with important practical implications for social perceivers in everyday life. When subjects are highly involved in a judgmental task, when the judgment is particularly complex and difficult, or when the outcome of a decision has real personal consequences, judges are more likely to use controlled processing strategies, thus limiting mood effects. Indeed, there is evidence that mood effects are less marked when a judgment has personal consequences (cf. Forgas, 1989). Interestingly, these effects again parallel some of the evidence from research with social stereotypes, suggesting that a more global theoretical framework that integrates research on mood effects into a more general conceptualization of judgmental heuristics remains an intriguing possibility. Branscombe and Cohen's chapter provides a useful and stimulating set of suggestions linking research on stereotyping to mood research that makes a significant contribution towards the development of such more integrated models of social perception and judgments.

The majority of the contributions to this volume are characterized by a marked reliance on cognitive information processing models and theories to explain affective influences on social judgments. The preponderance of cognitive models here is representative not only of the state of theorizing in this field, but perhaps also psychology as a whole (Forgas, 1981). It is important to be reminded from time to time that the cognitive paradigm also has important limitations when applied to social phenomena, as is done by

Michael Argyle in his chapter. He argues that intraindividual cognitive processes by definition cannot adequately deal with a variety of social and interpersonal processes. As Argyle suggests, social judgments often involve shared or consensual cognitions, intersubjectivity or "taking the role of the other," as well as many instances of coordinated interpersonal behavior and communication that are difficult or even impossible to reduce to, and explain in terms of, information processing by single individuals. His stimulating chapter serves to remind us of the rich and heterogeneous heritage of social psychology as the discipline most directly concerned with the interdependence of individual and surrounding social systems, a tradition that should continue to stimulate interest in the complementary nature of cognitive, emotional, and interpersonal processes in social judgments.

The third section of the book deals with the integration of well-defined theories and their applications to research on mood effects on social judgments. The first chapter in this section, by Petty, Gleicher, and Baker, introduces the theme of affective influences on persuasive communication. In contrast with other theories of emotional influences on social judgments, Petty and his colleagues propose an essentially situationist formulation, suggesting that the primary influence of affect on judgments of persuasive messages will depend on how motivated subjects are to analytically process the issue-relevant information presented to them ("central-route processing"), instead of relying on simple cues, associations, or heuristic devices to guide their reactions ("peripheral-route processing"). This Elaboration Likelihood Model (ELM) has been markedly successful in accounting for a variety of findings in the literature. Any variable can act as a peripheral or a central cue in different situations, and affect can also serve as an argument or a peripheral cue or an influence on processing strategy. In conditions of high elaboration likelihood, affect may play a direct role as information (e.g. deciding attitudes towards a romantic partner), as also suggested by Clore, Schwarz and others. Alternatively, affect may play an indirect role by priming affect-related materials to be used in judgments and interpretations (cf. Bower, 1981). In the case of low elaboration likelihood, affect serves as a peripheral cue, possibly guiding processing strategies, with positive moods often related to more superficial, careless processing and less attention to argument quality. The second half of the chapter surveys an impressive range of empirical studies strongly supporting the ELM model. Positive affect can have at least three roles in persuasion: as a peripheral cue when subjects are not motivated to analytically process arguments; as a source of bias in thoughts and associations when people are motivated to process arguments; or as a source of disruption when motivation to process is not manipulated. Further work on the precise links between the source and intensity of affect and argument valence is necessary to clarify the information processing consequences of affect in persuasion.

In the next chapter Mackie and Worth also deal with this special aspect of emotional influences on social judgments: the way people evaluate persuasive communications directed at them. Relying on the influential distinction drawn between systematic, effortful, or central-route processing, and effortless, impressionist, or heuristic processing by Chaikin (1980) and Petty and Cacioppo (1981), Mackie and Worth propose that positive moods should lead to more heuristic processing. Their data confirm this pattern. Superficial features, such as communicator expertise, had a greater impact on persuasion in subjects in a good mood than in neutral subjects, while substantive features, such as message quality, had a greater effect on subjects in a neutral mood than on those in a positive mood. But why exactly should elated subjects process persuasive messages less systematically and more heuristically? Explanations of these processing biases are based on cognitive (the assumed greater capacity loads associated with good moods as a larger amount of information is accessed and primed; cf. Isen, 1984), and motivational (the assumed reluctance of good-mood subjects to disrupt their rewarding state by engaging in effortful systematic processing) principles. The first explanation implies that given a choice, subjects should prefer to spend longer examining relevant information to compensate for the mood-induced capacity loss. According to the second, motivational, account, they should do exactly the opposite as they attempt to simplify the task in an effort to safeguard their pleasant mood state. Evidence collected by Mackie and Worth supports the first, capacity-limit, account: when given a chance, elated subjects chose to look longer at messages and processed the information systematically instead of heuristically, and increased motivation was not by itself sufficient to elicit systematic processing in elated moods.

Innes and Ahrens begin their contribution with a discussion of the relevance of the concept of attitude, traditionally thought to comprise affective, cognitive, and conative components, to recent work on affect and cognition, and they suggest that a clearer distinction between affect and evaluation needs to be made in the literature. In particular, the role of affective states in triggering different processing strategies in recipients of persuasive messages is considered, and two experiments involving the factorial manipulation of mood, processing goals and message quality are described. These studies differ from other experiments dealing with mood effects on persuasion in that they explicitly include conditions designed to directly manipulate the processing objectives of subjects, by instigating a "critical" or a "creative" set. The evidence from the first study suggests that people in a positive mood generate just as many thoughts about a persuasive message as people in neutral moods do, indicating the absence of cognitive capacity-limit effects in euphoria. However, positive mood subjects also reacted with more thoughts that were congruent with the valence of the message (for or against) and recalled such details better, suggesting that affect may be a peripheral cue to change motivation to process information, without necessarily affecting cognitive capacity.

Of the many practical consequences of mood effects on social judgments outlined throughout this book, the role of moods on judgments about health and illness are of special importance, as the chapter by Salovey, O'Leary, Stretton, Fishkin, and Drake argues. Although symptoms of illness can, and do, influence mood, there is much to suggest that moods can also have a reverse causal effect on judgments about symptoms. The chapter presents evidence that people in a depressed mood are likely to report more severe and frequent physical symptoms and more discomfort than do happy subjects, and are less likely to believe in their own ability to engage in efficacious health-related behaviors. These judgmental biases are explained by Salovey and his colleagues in terms of three possible mediating mechanisms: mood-congruent memory, mood-dependent attention, and direct mood effects on physiological and immune processes. The arguments developed in the chapter have important implications for health-related behaviors, as well as such applied areas as the validity of health surveys, and some of cognitive and affective processes underlying hypochondriasis.

The final chapter in the book looks at affective influences on person perception, one of the most common and demanding judgmental tasks we undertake. The chapter surveys traditional research on person perception, distinguishing between "constructivist" and "mechanistic" conceptualizations. Next, a multiprocess view of person perception is outlined, suggesting that there are at least four, and possibly more, distinct information processing strategies people employ when making person perception judgments: (1) the direct-access strategy, involving the retrieval of preexisting, crystallized judgments; (2) the substantive processing strategy, involving the on-line processing and interpretation of the available information; (3) the motivated processing strategy, designed to achieve a potentially rewarding judgmental outcome; and (4) the heuristic processing strategy, when subjects seek to simplify and short-circuit the substantive processing of relevant information. The second half of the chapter presents a review of an extensive series of empirical studies demonstrating affective influences on person perception judgments. The evidence shows not only significant and reliable mood biases in such judgments, but also illustrates the role of moods in triggering different information processing strategies.

Social judgments are an essential part of everyday life, and one of the most complex and demanding cognitive tasks we undertake. The contributions to this book present a challenging and stimulating view of the role of affective states in such judgments. It is hoped that the book will indeed amount to more than the sum of its parts, by bringing together and integrating in a single volume the most recent theoretical and applied developments in research on affect and social judgments.

Acknowledgments

Financial assistance from the Australian Research Council, and help by Ms Sandy Morrison in the preparation of this chapter are gratefully acknowledged. Requests for reprints should be sent to Joseph P. Forgas, School of Psychology, University of New South Wales, P.O. Box 1, Kensington 2033, Sydney, Australia.

References

Anderson, N. H. (1974). Cognitive algebra: Integration theory applied to social attributions. In L. Berkowitz (Ed.), *Advances in experimental social psychology*, Vol. 7, New York: Academic Press.

Beck, A. T. (1976). *Cognitive therapy and emotional disorders*. New York: International Universities Press.

Bower, G. H. (1981). Mood and memory. *American Psychologist*, **36**, 129–148.

Bower, G. H. (1983). Affect and cognition. *Philosophical Transactions of the Royal Society, Series B*, **302**, 387–403.

Bower, G. H. (1985). Emotional influences in memory and thinking: Data and theory. In M. S. Clarke and S. T. Fiske (Eds), *Affect and cognition*. Hillsdale, NJ: Erlbaum.

Bower, G. H., and Cohen, P.R. (1982). Emotional influences in memory and thinking: Data and theory. In M. S. Clark and S. T. Fiske (Eds), *Affect and cognition*. Hillsdale, NJ: Erlbaum.

Bower, G. H., and Mayer, J. D. (1985). Failure to replicate mood-dependent retrieval. *Bulletin of the Psychonomic Society*, **23**, 39–42.

Bower, G. H., Montiero, K. P., and Gilligan, S. G. (1978). Emotional mood as a context of learning and recall. *Journal of Verbal Learning and Verbal Behavior*, **17**, 573–585.

Branscombe, N. (1988). Conscious and unconscious processing of affective and cognitive information. In K. Fiedler and J. P. Forgas (Eds), *Affect, cognition, and social behavior*. Toronto: Hogrefe.

Byrne, D. (1971). *The attraction paradigm*. Academic Press, New York.

Byrne, D., and Clore, G.L. (1970). A reinforcement model of evaluation responses. *Personality: An International Journal*, **1**, 103–128.

Chaiken, S. (1980). Heuristic versus systematic information processing and the use of source versus message cues in persuasion. *Journal of Personality and Social Psychology*, **39**, 752–766.

Clark, M. S., and Isen, A. M. (1982). Towards understanding the relationship between feeling states and social behavior. In A. H. Hastorf and A. M. Isen (Eds), *Cognitive social psychology*. New York: Elsevier–North Holland.

Dribben, E., and Brabender, V. (1979). The effect of mood inducement upon audience receptivenss. *Journal of Social Psychology*, **107**, 135–136.

Feshbach, S., and Singer, R. D. (1957). The effects of fear arousal and suppression of fear upon social perception. *Journal of Abnormal and Social Psychology*, **55**, 283–288.

Fiedler, K., and Forgas, J. P. (Eds) (1988). *Affect, cognition and social behavior*. Toronto: Hogrefe International.

Fiske, S. T., and Pavelchak, M. A. (1986). Category-based versus piecemeal-based affective responses: Developments in schema-triggered affect. In R. Sorrentino and E. T. Higgins (Eds), *The handbook of motivation and cognition: Foundations of social behavior*. New York: Guilford.

Forgas, J. P. (Ed.) (1981) *Social cognition: Perspectives on everyday understanding*. London and New York: Academic Press.

Forgas, J. P. (1989). Mood effects on decision-making strategies. *Australian Journal of Psychology*, **41**, 197–214.

Forgas, J. P. (in press). Affective influences on individual and group judgments. *European Journal of Social Psychology*.

Forgas, J. P., and Bower, G. H. (1987). Mood effects on person perception judgments. *Journal of Personality and Social Psychology*, **53**, 53–60.

Forgas, J. P., and Bower, G. H. (1988). Affect in social and personal judgments. In K. Fiedler and J. P. Forgas (Eds), *Affect, cognition, and social behavior*. Toronto: Hogrefe.

Forgas, J. P., Bower, G. H., and Krantz, S. (1984). The influence of mood on perceptions of social interactions. *Journal of Experimental Social Psychology*, **20**, 497–513.

Forgas, J. P., Bower, G. H., and Moylan, S. J. (in press). Praise or blame? Affective influences on attributions for achievement. *Journal of Personality and Social Psychology*.

Forgas, J. P., Burnham, D., and Trimboli, C. (1988). Mood, memory and social judgments in children. *Journal of Personality and Social Psychology*, **54**, 697–703.

Frijda, N. H. (1986). *The emotions*. Cambridge: Cambridge University Press.

Galizio, M., and Hendrick, C. (1972). Effect of musical accompaniment on attitude: The guitar as a prop for persuasion. *Journal of Applied Social Psychology*, **22**, 350–359.

Gouaux, C. (1971). Induced affective states and interpersonal attraction. *Journal of Personality and Social Psychology*, **20**, 37–43.

Gouaux, C., and Summers, K. (1973). Interpersonal attraction as a function of affective states and affective change. *Journal of Research in Personality*, **7**, 254–260.

Griffitt, W. (1970). Environmental effects on interpersonal behavior: Ambient effective temperature and attraction. *Journal of Personality and Social Psychology*, **15**, 240–244.

Heider, F. (1958). *The psychology of interpersonal relations*. New York: John Wiley.

Hilgard, E. R. (1980). The trilogy of mind: Cognition, affection, and conation. *Journal of the History of the Behavioral Sciences*, **16**, 107–117.

Isen, A. M. (1984). Toward understanding the role of affect in cognition. In R. S. Wyer and T. K. Srull (Eds), *Handbook of social cognition*, Vol. 3. Hillsdale, NJ: Erlbaum.

Isen, A. M. and Means, B. (1983). The influence of positive affect on decision making strategy. *Social Cognition*, **2**, 18–31.

Isen, A. M., Means, B., Patrick, R., and Nowicki, G. (1982). Some factors influencing decision-making strategy and risk taking. In M. S. Clark and S. T. Fiske (Eds), *Affect and cognition*. Hillsdale, NJ: Erlbaum.

Izard, C. E. (1964). The effect of role-played emotion on affective reactions, intellectual functioning and evaluative ratings of the actress. *Journal of Clinical Psychology*, **22**, 444–446.

Janis, I. L., Kaye, D., and Kirschner, P. (1965). Facilitating effects of "eating while reading" on responsiveness to persuasive communications. *Journal of Personality and Social Psychology*, **1**, 181–186.

Kaplan, M. F., and Anderson, N. H. (1973). Information integration theory and reinforcement theory as approaches to interpersonal attraction. *Journal of Personality and Social Psychology*, **28**, 301–312.

Kelly, G. A. (1955). *The psychology of personal constructs*. New York: W. W. Norton.

Lazarus, R. A. (1981). A cognitivists's reply to Zajonc on emotion and cognition. *American Psychologist*, **36**, 222–223.

Lazarus, R. A. (1984). On the primacy of cognition. *American Psychologist*, **39**, 124–129.

Leventhal, H. (1980). Towards a comprehensive theory of emotion. In L. Berkowitz (Ed.), *Advances in experimental social psychology*, Vol. 13. New York: Academic Press.

Mackie, D. M., and Worth, L. T. (1989). Processing deficits and the mediation of positive affect in persuasion. *Journal of Personality and Social Psychology*, **57**, 1–14.

Murray, H. A. (1933). The effects of fear upon estimates of the maliciousness of other personalities. *Journal of Social Psychology*, **4**, 310–329.

Ortony, A., Clore, G. L., and Collins, A. (1988). *The cognitive structure of emotion*. New York: Cambridge University Press.

Ottaviani, R., and Beck, A. T. (1988). Cognitive theory of depression. In K. Fiedler and J. Forgas (Eds), *Affect, cognition and social behavior*. Toronto: Hogrefe.

Petty, R. E., and Cacioppo, J. T. (1981). *Attitudes and persuasion: Classic and contemporary approaches*. Dubuque, IA: Wm. C. Brown.

Petty, R. E., and Cacioppo, J. T. (1986). *Communication and persuasion: Central and peripheral routes to attitude change*. New York: Springer.

Razran, G. H. S. (1940). Conditional response changes in rating and appraising sociopolitical slogans. *Psychological Bulletin*, **37**, 481.

Schwarz, N., and Clore, G. L. (1983). Mood misattribution, and judgments of well being.

Informative and directive functions of affective states. *Journal of Personality and Social Psychology*, **45**, 513–523.

Schwarz, N., and Clore, G. L. (1988). How do I feel about it? The informative function of affective states. In K. Fiedler and J. P. Forgas (Eds), *Affect, cognition, and social behavior*. Toronto: Hogrefe.

Staats, A. W., Staats, C. K., and Crawford, H. L. (1962). First-order conditioning of meaning and the parallel conditioning of GSR. *Journal of General Psychology*, **67**, 159–167.

Wehmer, G., and Izard, C. E. (1962). *The effect of self-esteem and induced affect on interpersonal perception and intellective functioning*. Nashville: Vanderbilt University.

Wessman, A. E., and Ricks, D. F. (1966). Mood and personality. *Experimental Aging Research*, **10**, 197–200.

Worth, L. T., and Mackie, D. M. (1987). Cognitive mediation of positive affect in persuasion. *Social Cognition*, **5**, 76–79.

Worth, L. T., Mackie, D. M. and Asuncion, A. G. (1989). Distinguishing cognitive and motivational mediators of the impact of positive mood on persuasion. Unpublished manuscript, Pennsylvania State University, California.

Zajonc, R. B. (1980). Feeling and thinking: Preferences need no inferences. *American Psychologist*, **35**, 151–175.

2

Mood Congruity of Social Judgments

GORDON H. BOWER

Stanford University

Contents

To what extent are social judgments influenced by our emotional state? Since people make many decisions based on their inferences about the character and intentions of others, a better understanding of how our feelings might influence such judgments is of practical and theoretical importance. The collection of papers in this volume attests to the current interest in this topic, and the several contributors suggest somewhat differing answers to the question of how affect influences social judgments.

This chapter reviews an emotion-network theory and associated research showing several domains in which social judgments and choices are influenced in a mood-congruous direction. This is, people who are temporarily (or characteristically) happy or unhappy tend to select impersonal activities as well as social situations which will maintain their mood. People's temporary moods have a strong influence upon their evaluation of strangers, acquaintances, their pro-social behavior, their self-concept, their self-efficacy, their attitudes towards themselves and their possessions. Moods also influence the impact of mood-congruent parts of persuasive messages: happy readers are more influenced by the positive parts of a mixed message,

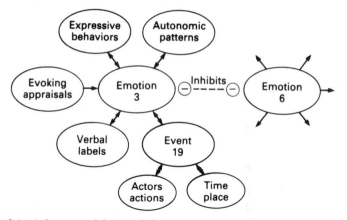

Fɪɢ 2.1   A fragment of the associative network surrounding an emotion node in memory. For example, node 3 might represent sadness and it inhibits emotion 6 for happiness. (Reproduced with permission from Bower, 1981.)

unhappy readers by its negative parts. These evaluation biases are often accompanied by similar memory biases. An amended network theory permits it to explain how someone might remember global evaluations while forgetting the evidence that led to those evaluations.

In 1981 I proposed an associative network theory of how emotions influence cognitions (Bower, 1981). The view is best summarized in Figure 2.1, which depicts an emotion node, say No. 3 is anger or sadness, situated in an associative memory. The presumption is that about six (plus or minus a few) basic emotion nodes are biologically wired into the brain, and that a number of innate as well as learned environmental situations can turn on a particular emotion node. When a particular emotion node is turned on as a result of certain recognition rules, it spreads activation to a variety of indicators, such as characteristic physiological and facial expressions, to memories of events associated with that emotion, and to interpretive rules for classifying the social world. In a later paper, I wrote:

> When emotions are strongly aroused, concepts, words, themes, and rules of inference that are associated with that emotion will become primed and highly available for use by the emotional subject. We can thus expect the emotional person to use top-down or expectation-driven processing of his social environment. That is, his emotional state will bring into readiness certain perceptual categories, certain themes, certain ways of interpreting the world that are congruent with his emotional state; these mental sets then act as interpretive filters of reality and as biases in his judgments.   (Bower, 1983, p. 395).

I also reported in that earlier paper that temporarily induced moods of happiness, sadness, or anger gave rise to a mood-congruent bias in people's free associations, their imaginative fantasies (TAT stories), and their snap judgments of their acquaintances. We found that happy subjects tended to give very charitable, benevolent descriptions of their acquaintances, whereas angry subjects tended to be uncharitable and overcritical in describing their friends. In recent years, a relatively large research literature has accumulated investigating the impact of emotional states on social judgments and choices. This paper provides a selective review of that research.

In reviewing the literature on mood-congruity biases in social judgments, I have been struck by the parallel or similarity between the theory and data in favor of the mood-congruity hypothesis and those in favor of the "cognitive consistency" or dissonance theory of attitude maintenance. According to cognitive consistency theory, having a strongly held attitude on a personally significant topic should predispose one to an interrelated set of biases. These biases include selective exposure to confirmatory information, biased attention to and perception of confirmatory over disconfirmatory evidence, and selective learning and memory for confirmatory information. In my opinion, mood congruity has been demonstrated in a parallel fashion for each of these three types of biases—for selective exposure, attention, and memory.

Selective Exposure to Mood-Congruent Impersonal Situations

We may begin our review by noting some studies in which subjects in a particular mood seem to prefer to be exposed to impersonal, "non-social" situations that are congruent with their mood. Thus, when given a choice, happy or sad subjects prefer to be exposed to happy or sad stimuli, respectively.

A good illustration arose in an experiment by my student Colleen Kelley (reported in Bower, 1983). She induced happy or sad feelings in college students by having them write about some happy or sad experience from their life. Thereafter, as part of a second experiment, they were asked to examine a series of slides of scenes, going at their own pace, dwelling on each scene according to its "intrinsic interest" for them. The slides were a random mixture, half of happy scenes (people laughing, playing, celebrating victories) and half of sad scenes (failures, rejections, funerals, and the aftermath of disasters). Unbeknown to the subjects, Kelley recorded how much time they spent looking at the different types of pictures. She found a mood-congruity effect in the average time subjects spent viewing the pictures. If viewers were happy, they spent more time looking at happy rather than sad scenes (8.3 vs 6.6 s); if they were sad, they spent slightly more time looking at sad rather than happy scenes (8.2 vs 7.9 s). Often subjects were not aware that they were doing this. The result illustrates selective exposure to scenes that agree with the viewer's mood. This difference in exposure time also led to a difference in later recall of the pictures. Happy viewers recalled more happy scenes; sad viewers recalled more sad scenes.

Some experiments by Mark Snyder (personal communication, 1988) make a similar point. His subjects indicated their preferred selections from briefly described movie film clips to review as part of a mock "consumer survey". Subjects made temporarily depressed (by the Velten procedure) chose to look at more somber, serious films than did subjects made temporarily elated. In a second study, sad subjects also selected more sad, nostalgic music to listen to than did happy subjects.

In line with such results, Carson and Adams (1980) found that subjects induced to feel happy or sad reported an increase or decrease, respectively, in the enjoyment they would get from some 300 activities listed in Lewinsohn's Pleasant Events Schedule. When temporarily depressed, people chose fewer activities as "pleasant" and rated them as less enjoyable; when elated, they chose more activities as pleasant and rated them as more enjoyable.

Mark Snyder (personal communication, 1988) confirmed this finding by having temporarily elated or depressed subjects indicate how much time they intended to spend in various activities in the coming weeks. Elated subjects said they planned to spend more time in light-hearted, enjoyable activities; depressed subjects said they planned to spend more time in somber, serious, and solitary activities. These biased choices for future activities nicely mirrored a similar bias observed when elated or depressed subjects recalled the activities they had engaged in over the past several weeks (Snyder and White, 1982).

The loss of interest in social activities is a familiar hallmark of the depressed person. Part of this is surely the consequence of depressed people finding other people far less interesting or "attractive". This effect of mood on attraction was demonstrated long ago by Griffitt (1970) and Gouaux (1971). For example, Gouaux induced elation or depression in college students by having them view a hilarious comedy film or a sad film (about the nation's loss from John Kennedy's death). In a following experiment, these subjects read about another person's opinions on many issues, designed so as to agree with the subject's opinions on 15, 50, or 85% of the issues. They then rated this target person on several scales reflecting positive regard—his likability, intelligence, knowledge, adjustment, and so on. The average composite scores, called "attraction" towards the target person, are plotted in Figure 2.2.

As often found in such studies, subjects were more attracted to others who agree with more of their opinions. Importantly, elated subjects were overall more friendly and open to meeting the target person than were neutral-mood controls, whereas depressed subjects were less attracted to him than were neutral controls. We may think of this outcome in much the same way that Byrne and Clore (1970) did: mood states alter people's expectation of gaining positive versus negative experiences ("reinforcements") from interactions with such a target individual, and the balance of those expectations determines the attraction ratings. By my hypothesis, such expectations should be influenced by subjects' mood-biased remembering of positive

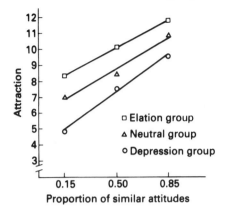

F<small>IG</small> 2.2   Attraction towards a stranger who agrees with 15, 50, or 85% of one's own opinions. Elated or depressed mood causes the attraction to increase or decrease, respectively, from that shown by the neutral mood controls. (Graph from Gouaux, 1971, with permission.)

versus negative experiences with people in their life similar in some respects to the target person. Hence, Gouaux's results follow from the theory.

Selective Exposure to Mood-Congruent Social Situations

The evidence in this category demonstrates that people want to know more about, and to affiliate more with, people who are in a similar mood state. An old bit of folk wisdom is: "Laugh and the world laughs with you; cry and you cry alone." The evidence is quite strong that most of us most of the time prefer the company of happy people and avoid the company of depressed people. However, these choices may arise because we are usually in a moderately good mood. The folk wisdom seems to be wrong when we consider the social choices of depressed or sad people.

A first observation is that depressed people seek out more information about sad people than about happy people (Gibbons, 1986). Moreover, when forced to choose, depressed people prefer to meet and become better acquainted with unfortunate, unhappy people rather than happy people (Wenzlaff and Prohaska, 1989). This supports the old adage that "misery likes company." A significant qualifier, however, is that this attraction is overcome if the target person were unhappy because of having deliberately committed some repugnant, antisocial crime, e.g. injuring someone while driving drunk.

A dramatic demonstration of selective exposure was provided in an experiment by Swann, Wenzlaff, Krull and Pelham (in press). They studied college students who scored very high or very low on the Beck Depression

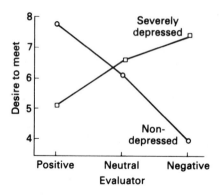

FIG 2.3   Desire to meet a positive, neutral, or negative evaluator by non-depressed compared with severely depressed college students. (Graph drawn from data from Experiment 1 reported by Swann, Wenzlaff, Krull and Pelham, in press, with permission.)

Inventory. Subjects read three different evaluations of themselves supposedly written by evaluators who had examined the subject's answers to a personality test taken earlier. The experimenter composed bogus evaluations so that one was relatively positive, one neutral, and one relatively negative. Subjects were asked to rate which of these three evaluators they would most like to meet and get acquainted with. The results are shown in Figure 2.3. Non-depressed subjects most wanted to meet and get acquainted with the positive evaluator who had the flattering opinion of them, and they wanted nothing to do with their negative evaluator. In contrast, severely depressed subjects said they most wanted to meet and get acquainted with their negative evaluator, the one person who had found the most faults in them and who they could be certain would have an unfavorable opinion about them. This is reminiscent of the script called "Kick me, please" that depressives often use.

A similar example occurred in a study of college roommates by Swann and Pelham (1988). The subjects were freshmen roommates at the University of Texas, Austin, who had been randomly assigned to share a dormitory room. Towards the end of the fall semester, pairs of roommates were assessed for their self-concept and their certainty of it, their private view of their roommate, and their desire to remain with (or change) their roommate the next semester. Students' desire to continue living with a roommate depended on whether the roommate held a positive or negative evaluation of them. However, the nature of this dependence varied according to subjects' self-concept and their confidence in it. People with a confidently positive self-concept were more desirous of keeping a roommate who appraised them positively. Paradoxically, people who held a negative self-concept (and were sure of it) wanted more to continue with a roommate who also held an unfavorable view of them rather than one who held a favorable view of them. Swann and Pelham found a similar relationship in a second study of pairs of college students (not necessarily roommates) who had been friends for a modal time of two years. Students' plans to keep the friendship varied with whether the friend's appraisal of them agreed with their own; paradoxically, as before, students with a negative self-view hoped to maintain a relationship with those friends who had a negative view of them.

Such paradoxical results have several interpretations. One is that people in happy or sad moods prefer to be in living situations that will maintain their mood state. An alternative, and probably more reasonable hypothesis due to Swann (1983), is that people prefer the company of others who will confirm their view of themselves; thus, people who think poorly of themselves will choose to be with others who also think poorly of them. Swann cites much evidence in favor of this self-verification hypothesis: for example, people solicit more feedback when it confirms their self-image, they pay more attention to such feedback, remember it better, and regard it generally as more accurate and credible. People with negative self-views (especially when they are certain of them) follow these laws, even though they will readily admit that it hurts to get negative feedback.

One way perhaps to reconcile these two views (seeking mood-congruous vs self-verifying partners) is to observe that people's prevailing mood is closely related to their reported self-concept. Wessman and Ricks (1966) reported such observations for subjects undergoing natural fluctuations in moods over many days; I have found this with subjects in induced mood states and so have Wright and Mischel (1982). And, of course, it is well known that successes or failures attributed to one's abilities and efforts cause positive or negative feelings, respectively, with corresponding changes in self-esteem and reported self-views (for a review, see D. J. Snyder, 1976). The influence of mood on reports of self-concepts is implied by the mood-priming theory. Associated with a familiar concept like "myself", everyone has a diverse range of conflicting opinions, supporting arguments, memories of behavioral episodes, and contrasting assessments of one's ranking within any number of achievement areas. We may suppose that the memories of negative evaluations we have received are associated with happy feelings they caused, and the memories of received positive evaluations are associated with happy feelings they caused. Hence, by mood-dependent retrieval, a person in a particular mood state will tend to retrieve more of those self-referent opinions that are congruent with (and associatively primed by) that mood. The balance of positive versus negative evaluations that are readily available would thus bias a person's momentary report of his or her "self-concept."

This view implies that associations to our "self-concept" are so diverse, multifarious, and influenced by passing whims ("primes") that our reports are relatively unstable and malleable. This view is hardly unique. For example, in commenting upon the instability of "attitudes," the social psychologist David Snyder had this to say:

One of the most important ways in which this thing [instability] manifests itself is in attitudes towards the self. On some days—everyone has them—a person wonders how anyone as stupid as one's self could have lived this long; on other days, everything seems rosy. . . . I am suggesting that you hold all kinds of attitudes, and the question is how they get activated. Mood is one powerful determinant. Another is environmental stimuli; these stimuli force one to think about only certain sides of a question. . . . Much attitude change results not so much from the act of changing attitudes, but rather of *activating* certain ones. . . . Attitudes are, in fact, less static and stable than most theorists assume; they are dynamic and they change as a function of mood, experience, and the functional requirements of situation and social realities. (Snyder, 1976, pp.265–266).

To continue our reconciliation, while we can accept Swann's hypothesis that people seek out social information that will verify their self-concept, I would note that people's self-concepts are in a causally reciprocal relationship with their prevailing mood. People who have very "negative self-views" as assessed by Swann's test probably also have high scores on the Beck Depression Inventory. Presumably, the Swann and Pelham results could be produced by manipulating a person's self-views indirectly by mood inductions. That would be an interesting experiment to try.

Affiliations Based on Other Affective States

The foregoing section has reviewed studies of social selections by happy and sad people, but has not touched on selections caused by other affective states, such as fear or anger, or motivational states such as created by hunger, pain, or fatigue. We may suspect that people will have some tendency to choose to affiliate with others in a matching affective state, simply because selection among unfamiliar partners is partly determined by perceived similarity of the partner (Byrne, 1969). The well-known studies on affiliation by Schachter (1959) fit within this framework. In those studies, students who had been frightened by the threat of having to endure a series of very painful shocks chose to wait (for the shock experiment to begin) with another subject experiencing the same threat rather than waiting alone or with a subject in another, unrelated, experiment. (These results were qualified by an interaction with the subject's birth-order—which is still not well understood.) In addition to such laboratory studies of affiliation, one may also note the widespread tendency of people with similar problems (and prevailing emotive states) to congregate together spontaneously in self-help support groups such as Alcoholics Anonymous, Narcotics Anonymous, Over-Eaters Anonymous, Gamblers Anonymous, Emotions Anonymous, and support groups for patients dealing with specific illnesses (leukemia, breast cancer, etc.). While Schachter's experimental results provide some support for the hypothesis that people prefer to affiliate with others in a matching affective state, it must be conceded that few explicit tests of it have been carried out.

Processing Variations with Forced Exposure to Affective Stimuli

The experiments reviewed above demonstrate that, depending on their mood, people tend to become interested in or attracted to different activities, different people, stories, movies, and music. This bias seems to occur with temporarily induced moods as well as with long-term character traits, such as depression and hostility. Furthermore, people behave in accordance with their desire for more or less exposure. The consistency or congruity between the mood and the situations that they enter then causes their mood to be maintained.

The results on selective exposure just reviewed can be supplemented by further results showing that even when people are forced to be exposed to an affective social stimulus, their attention to it is heightened or diminished depending on its congruence to their mood. In a study by Forgas and Bower (1987), we found this congruence effect for subjects who had been induced to feel happy or sad before reading a description of a stranger and forming an impression of him. The subjects sat before a computer terminal and presented themselves with a series of statements, each describing some favorable or unfavorable behavior of the stranger. Measuring how long subjects dwelt on the positive versus the negative aspects of the stranger, we obtained the data shown in Figure 2.4.

Two conclusions are warranted. First, subjects in a sad mood took longer than those in a good mood to read and form impressions: this is a common finding. Second, subjects in a good mood dwelt longer on positive aspects of the stranger, subjects in a sad mood dwelt longer on his negative aspects. As you might expect, subjects in a good mood ended up with a more favorable impression of the stranger. Moreover, memory for the stranger's behaviors

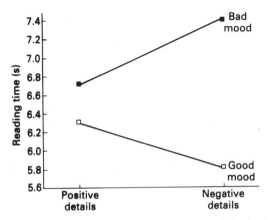

Fig 2.4   Time spent dwelling on positive versus negative behavioral details of the target person depending on the subjects' good or bad mood. (Reproduced from Forgas and Bower, 1987, with permission.)

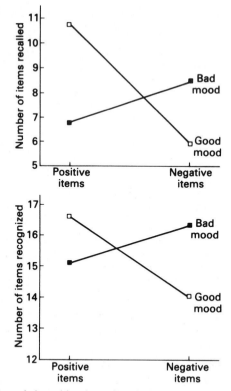

FIG 2.5 Effect of the subjects' good or bad mood during reading upon later memory for positive versus negative items of the target's behaviors, for recall (top) and recognition (bottom) measures. (Reproduced from Forgas and Bower, 1987, with permission.)

showed mood congruence (Figure 2.5): subjects in a good mood remembered his positive details better; subjects in a sad mood remembered his negative details better. This was true for measures of free recall (top of Figure 2.5) and for recognition memory (bottom of Figure 2.5).

Why do unhappy people dwell longer on a target person's negative aspects? The theory says that negative behaviors will be more evocative of other memories in the unhappy reader—he or she will more often be reminded of similar bad behaviors of themselves or other people, and such remindings will take time. As a consequence, these reminiscences create elaborations around the stated negative behaviors, linking them more firmly into familiar material, all of which will promote their later recall. (See Anderson, 1985, for why elaboration promotes memory for the elaborated material.) The process works the same way for pleasant material for happy subjects.

In the Forgas and Bower experiment, subjects formed an impression based only on verbal descriptions of a stranger without meeting him. Baron

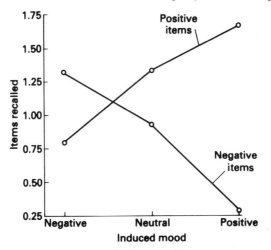

F<small>IG</small> 2.6   Recall of positive versus negative information the applicant gave about himself by interviewers who were feeding in a positive, neutral, or negative mood. (Based on data reported by Baron, 1987, with permission.)

(1987) had subjects develop an impression during a face-to-face interview with a target person. Using bogus feedback about their ability, Baron first induced subjects to feel mildly elated, neutral, or despondent. Each subject then conducted a face-to-face interview with a person who was supposedly applying for a middle-management job, asking him a list of pre-arranged questions in a structured interview. The applicant was in fact a confederate who gave the same canned answers (deliberately mixed and ambivalent) to each interviewer. After the interview, the interviewer rated the job applicant on several traits. As anticipated, compared with neutral interviewers, happy interviewers rated the candidate as more motivated, talented, likable, attractive, and having greater potential for the job. They also said they would hire him. In contrast, the momentarily depressed interviewers rated the applicant considerably worse on all dimensions and were fairly sure they would not hire him. Baron went on to test his interviewers for their later recall of the confederate's canned answers. The results in Figure 2.6 showed mood-congruent recall: happy interviewers recalled more of the positive things the applicant had said about himself; depressed interviewers recalled more of the negative things he had said about himself. Such studies show that in a realistic setting, mood biases could significantly affect the careers of the people and institutions involved.

Mood Variations in the Impact of a Persuasive Message

The results above suggest that the impact of a persuasive message should depend on how its information matches up with the mood of the target

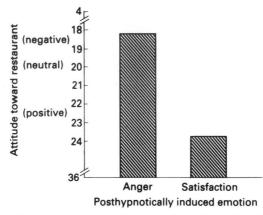

Fɪɢ 2.7 Attitude towards a restaurant by subjects who had been feeling happy or angry at the time they read a mixed review of it. (Reproduced from Calder and Gruder, 1988, with permission.)

audience. Calder and Gruder (1988) arranged several marked demonstrations of this implication. In an initial experiment using a post-hypnotic suggestion, students were made to feel happy or angry as they read a newspaper review of a restaurant. The review contained a mixture of 20 positive and 20 negative statements about the restaurant. Later, after removal of the hypnotic mood, subjects rated the restaurant and recalled the statements of the review as best they could. The evaluative ratings are displayed in Figure 2.7. Subjects who read the review when angry rated the restaurant far more negatively than did the subjects who read it when happy. The two groups also differed somewhat in their relative recall of the negative versus positive statements from the review.

A second experiment by Calder and Gruder differentiated between anger and disgust. Some subjects were induced to feel anger, others to feel disgust, as they read either of two reviews of a restaurant. Along with some common positive information, one review included unfavorable material designed to provoke the customer's anger (e.g. a waiter gives slow service; moreover, he bangs your head with a tray); the other review had material designed to provoke the customer's disgust (e.g. you are seated where you can see the garbage can through the kitchen door and catch bad odors from the kitchen). Later, after the mood was removed, subjects evaluated the restaurant and then recalled as much of the review as they could. The results are shown in Figure 2.8. The attitude ratings (on the left) show that angry readers reacted more negatively and criticized the restaurant more when the review mentioned anger-provoking incidents, whereas readers feeling disgust reacted more negatively to the restaurant when the review mentioned disgusting incidents. The right-hand graph shows mood-congruent recall: disgusted subjects recalled slightly more of the disgust-provoking state-

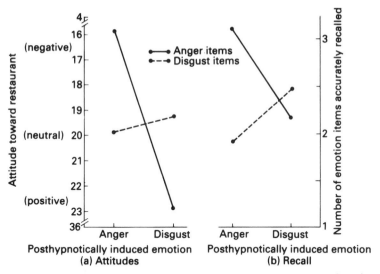

F<small>IG</small> 2.8   On the left, attitude towards a restaurant by angry or disgusted readers of a review that described either anger or disgust-provoking incidents. On the right, recall of the negative statements (anger or disgust-provoking) from the review by subjects who felt angry or disgusted as they read it. The Fs test the interaction of the two variables. (Reproduced from Calder and Gruder, 1988, with permission.)

ments, whereas angry subjects recalled considerably more of the anger-provoking statements.

Mood Influences Current Evaluations

The foregoing review has examined how moods increase a person's exposure to, and processing of, affectively congruent information. I will now briefly review studies showing how mood influences momentary evaluation of objects about which people have a range of diverse, ill-formed opinions. As noted earlier in the discussion of mood influences on reports of self-image, a prevailing mood should prime and make more available those considerations or aspects of an attitude-topic that are congruent with the mood.

In a classic demonstration of this evaluative bias, Isen *et al.* (1978) found that people in a shopping mall who received a small gift reported a few moments later on a consumer survey that their cars and television were working better than did people who had not received that small gift.

A recent demonstration of similar effects was arranged by Forgas and Moylan (1987), who interviewed 980 patrons in cinema lobbies before versus after their seeing films judged to arouse predominantly happy, sad, or aggressive feelings. In the guise of a public opinion survey, patrons took about a minute to rate their mood and their satisfaction with several controversial political figures, the penalties handed out for various crimes (e.g. drunk driving, heroin trafficking), the likelihood of several future prospects, and satisfaction with their personal and work situation. The mood ratings showed that happy and sad movies had significant effects in the expected direction, whereas the violent films (e.g. *Rambo*) had an inconsistent impact upon hostile feelings. Relative to neutral controls, the happy and sad films had a significantly enhancing and depressing influence, respectively, upon the positivity of ratings in all areas. The viewers of aggressive films behaved similarly to the controls except that they advocated more severe punishments for criminals.

Mood Affects Self-Observation and Self-Evaluation

The material reviewed in an earlier section showed that a person's mood influences his or her perception and evaluation of the behavior of others. We also have evidence that mood similarly influences people's observations and evaluations of their own behavior. In an experiment by Forgas *et al.* (1984), subjects in a good or bad mood rated their own behavior every 5 s for prosocial, neutral, or antisocial aspects. They did this by viewing themselves in a social interaction videotaped the day before. People in a happy mood saw themselves (in the video) emitting large numbers of prosocial behaviors, appearing suave, friendly, and competent. People in a sad mood saw themselves as antisocial, withdrawn, socially unskilled, and incompetent. These effects were all "in the eye of the beholder" since objective judges rated the videotaped subjects as displaying about the same levels of positive and negative behaviors. We explained such results by supposing that the perceivers' mood primes into readiness mood-congruent constructs by which they categorize the ambiguous gestures, speech acts, intonation, and body language they view in the videotape.

In related research, Kavanagh and Bower (1985) studied how temporary moods influence one's sense of efficacy or competence in accomplishing a set of tasks. Subjects induced to feel temporarily happy or sad rated the likelihood that they could perform diverse skills at a criterion level—skills in attracting someone of the opposite sex, in forming friendships, in assertively dealing with others, in doing well in intellectual and athletic tasks. We found that relative to control subjects in a neutral mood, happy subjects had an elevated sense of efficacy, whereas sad people had a lowered sense of efficacy. Moreover, these effects prevailed across all content domains. These mood influences are important since we know from Bandura's (1977) research that self-efficacy judgments determine which activities a person will attempt and how long he or she will persist in the face of difficulties. We may explain these effects in terms of mood-congruent availability of the subjects' memories for positive (versus negative) experiences in the questioned activity. Although people's average levels of achievement will differ greatly depending on their history, each of us will have our own private collection of "better" versus "poorer" performances evaluated relative to our own standards in a given domain. Happy or sad mood can then shift the availability of these two sets of memories, thus temporarily biasing the estimate of one's capabilities.

Explaining the Correlation of Judgment and Recall Biases

In the studies by Forgas and Bower (1987) and Baron (1987), we saw that an induced mood caused more processing of mood-congruent material, with a resulting impact on likability judgments as well as biased recall of the evidence. This correlation between selective recall and evaluative bias supposedly resulted from mood-dependent retrieval. The stranger being evaluated was associated with various facts (or beliefs) learned about his behavior, and these were associated in turn with positive or negative evaluations which such behaviors by a stranger would arouse in the perceiver. In judging the stranger when feeling happy or sad, the mood congruent beliefs are advantaged in theory because they lie on intersection points between two memory units, viz. the unit representing the target stranger and the perceiver's current mood state. The beliefs at these intersection points thus gain by the summation of activation from two sources, whereas other relevant beliefs may receive activation from only one source. Hence, these mood-congruent beliefs should be more available than incongruent ones, thus biasing the evaluations.

Although this pattern of biased judgment alongside biased recall should often occur, there is no strict requirement that the two effects must always co-occur. For example, Fiedler *et al.* (1986) found congruent effects of mood on likability judgments but no evidence of mood-congruent biases in recall of information about the target person. This arose especially when the behaviors of the target person were already well organized into a few trait categories. The associative network theory can easily be formulated so that the correlation between judgment and recall biases will be attenuated. We will present such a reformulation in a later section.

Alternative Mechanisms to Explain the Judgmental Bias

A moment's thought suggests several possible mechanisms that might account for mood-congruent biases in judgment in the absence of a mood-selective effect on memory. One possibility is that people integrate their current mood together with the feelings normally evoked by the attitude object; then, confusing the two sources of their summated feelings, people over- or underestimate the positivity of their normal, unbiased attitude towards the object (Schwarz and Clore, 1988). Importantly, according to this hypothesis, when people are made aware of their general mood before they make their judgments, they should be able to *discount* or cancel out these mood influences just as they can discount alternative causes in other attributional judgments. This discounting is not compatible with the mood-priming idea, and it would have difficulty explaining mood-caused biases in judgment even when subjects are quite aware of one source of their current feelings.

A second hypothesis is that people's current highly positive or negative feeling state serves as a beginning "anchor point" on their internal affective scale; then in judging their degrees of positivity towards the attitude object, they insufficiently adjust to compensate for this beginning anchor point (see Tversky and Kahneman, 1974).

A third hypothesis is that the facts or evidence people retrieve from memory (to make a judgment) is not at all biased by mood, but rather the facts so retrieved are *interpreted* in a mood-biased manner as people come to a summary judgment. This interpretive bias can practically always be accomplished by subtly altering the standards by which an event is evaluated, or by emphasizing achievements versus shortcomings (the glass is half-empty versus half-full). For example, the normally hopeful fact that the American government continues to pour millions of dollars into research searching for a medical cure for cancer could be looked upon pessimistically by a depressive as indicating how utterly elusive a cancer cure is, since expenditures to date have turned up so little in the way of cures. A second example from research by Kunda (1987) and Sherman and Kunda (1989) is that the credibility of an essay warning of increasing health risks due to heavy coffee drinking was rated far lower by heavy coffee drinkers compared with non-drinkers.

A fourth hypothesis is the author's associative network theory of mood amended so as to reduce the covariation between mood-related biases in opinion and selective memory. That amended model will be presented in the next section.

I will not attempt a comparative evaluation of these alternative hypotheses. Their evaluation requires special experimental arrangements, most of which have been absent in the literature to date. In passing, however, I would note that the first three hypotheses—integration, anchoring, and interpretation—imply that mood influences on judgments are largely *output* effects, operating at the moment people are making their judgment. As such the hypothesis cannot explain results such as those by Calder and Gruder (reviewed above) in which mood was varied during the subjects' initial exposure to the stimulus material but was removed so that a neutral mood prevailed at the time of judgment. One needs some mechanism for carrying through time a persisting effect on later judgments of what the person felt during the initial intake of information. Of course, this is just what the amended, associative network theory provides. We turn now to describe that theory.

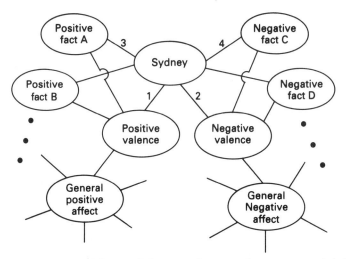

FIG 2.9   Fragment of the associative network representing some person's beliefs ("facts") and evaluations surrounding an attitude object, such as the city of Sydney, Australia. Consideration of each valenced fact about Sydney causes simultaneous activation of, and association between, Sydney and the valence node. Evaluation of a concept depends on its linkages to the positive versus negative valence nodes. See text for fuller description

An Amended Network Model

Figure 2.9 shows an amended model that attenuates the correlation between judgmental biases and recall biases. It shows a fragment of an associative network in which the person is building up a collection of beliefs and evidence about an attitude object or concept, such as the city of Sydney (where this symposium was held). The diagram uses the word "facts" simply as an abbreviation for propositions expressing a person's supported beliefs. Many of the facts we learn about a city are neutral, some are positive, and some are negative regarding its likability. We will suppose that when a positive fact is contemplated, say that Sydney has friendly natives, a central processor causes a small, simultaneous activation of a positive valence node in the emotional system. Thus, as an association is being built up about friendly natives, a parallel association, labelled #1 in the diagram, is also established from Sydney to the positive valence node, simply because of its co-occurrence with the fact. The more important or personally significant a given fact is, the more it will be thought about, resulting in a greater association between it and Sydney, and between Sydney and the positive node, along an associative link such as #1 in Figure 2.9. As each positive fact, such as A or B, is experienced or contemplated, the link (corresponding to #1) to the positive valence node would become stronger. The same strengthening rules apply to the negative facts or beliefs about Sydney, such as C and D; contemplation of *these* strengthens a connection such as that labelled #2 in the diagram, from Sydney to negative valence node.

Before proceeding, let me point out that this amendment to the initial model (of Bower, 1981) is truly trivial. Whereas the earlier model viewed associations as running from the attitudinal object to the belief and thence to the affect, the amended model assumes that the attitudinal object can be associated directly to the affective valence as well, not only via the belief.

At any point in time, when this model person is asked whether it likes Sydney, the control system essentially assesses the difference in strengths of links of type #1 versus #2, to the positive versus negative nodes. This is done by firing off the Sydney node ("thinking of Sydney"), then checking to see how much activation accumulates at the positive versus negative valence nodes. Thus, the model arrives at a summary evaluation that is somewhat related historically to the positive and negative beliefs it holds about the topic.

We have here the ingredients of an algebraic model of attitude and impression formation, much like those of Anderson (1974) and Fishbein and Ajzen (1975). As we add a new belief, we shift the model's impression in the evaluative direction of that belief to a degree depending on its personal significance to the learner. The more facts known about a topic, the less in general will be the impact on the summary judgment due to an additional fact. Because we are dealing here with learned associations, the impact of the facts will reveal a primacy effect and a recency effect both in their recall and in their impact on the judgment. The impression-formation literature shows both primacy and recency effects, depending on specific circumstances.

This model implies that the summary judgment of liking some object such as Sydney can persist long after the model has forgotten *why* it likes it, long after it has forgotten all the detailed, fleeting happenings that contributed to the summary. This is a familiar phenomenon. The model explains it by noting that each small detail may be experienced only briefly, so that the individual associations are weakly established. After suffering decay and interference, these individual memories may not be recalled later, although they may possibly be recognized. In contrast, the association to the positive valence node has been repeatedly boosted by each positive experience about Sydney that occurs, so that the affective association (labelled #1 here) becomes far stronger than any of the individual facts from which it derived its strength. Consequently, this affective association is rapidly accessible and more resistant to forgetting than are the many associations representing individual facts.

A dramatic demonstration of this dissociation between evaluation and memory for supporting evidence occurred in a study of patients with severe memory impairments associated with Korsakoff's syndrome (Johnson *et al.*, 1985). Patients were shown a pair of photographs of neutral male faces and provided descriptions of each man as a likable "good guy" or reprehensible "bad guy." Some days later, when shown each face, these patients were completely unable to recall any specific behavioral facts they had been told about that person. Nonetheless, when asked to judge whether the photograph depicted someone who seemed like a "nice" or "not so nice" person, the patients followed the positive or negative evaluations they had been taught earlier—all the while denying that they had much recollection of what they had been told about the person.

Emotional Influences According to the Amended Model

In terms of this amended model, the subject's emotional state could exert an impact at several places. First, mood during original learning could influence whether particular statements and events are interpreted as positive or negative. Second, mood could increase the person's attention to, and amount of rehearsal of, mood congruent facts, resulting in stronger associations from the attitude object to the fact and to the congruent valence node. By this means, a positive experience occurring in a positive mood would result in greater strength for associations of the type labelled #1 and #3 in this diagram. This would provide a correlation between biases in recall and judgment. Third, the person's mood at the time of judgment, represented here by activation of the "general affect" nodes, can spread and indirectly influence the apparent activation level of the positive versus negative valence nodes attached to the attitude object. This spread would distort the relative valences in a mood-congruent direction. The mood prevailing at the time of judgment may be thought of as elevating or adding a constant of activation to the congruent valence node, thus shifting judgments in that direction. However, this shift is temporary and it will fade as soon as the emotion passes.

Such an effect of retrieval mood on judgment was found by Clore *et al.* (1985). In their experiment, a positive or negative mood was induced before subjects read a somewhat ambiguous description of a person's actions; they then rated him on a number of traits. These initial ratings showed mood-congruent influences. Later, a second mood (same or opposite) was induced and the subjects rated the target person a second time. The results showed that these second ratings were largely dominated by the subjects' second mood, whereas their mood during their original exposure to the information had only a small effect. While the amended model in Figure 2.9 can explain the effect of retrieval mood on judgments, it would still have expected some continuing impact of original encoding mood on the later judgment. These findings by Clore *et al.* deserve replication and extension to check on their robustness.

The amended model has several implications. For example, it implies that the emotional influences will be very widespread, affecting topics far removed conceptually from the specific event, memory, or fantasy that was used to create the mood. This phenomenon was found by Johnson and Tversky (1983) as well as others. Such widespread generalization is expected by this model because it postulates a central pool of positive or negative affect that spreads to some degree to the valence nodes attached to any given topic.

A second implication is that the latency of an affective decision about an attitudinal object will be shorter the greater the dominance of one valence node over the other. Basically, the closer the positive versus negative valence race, the longer subjects will take to make the liking/disliking decision about some object or situation. This relationship between decision latency and extremity of opinion is well known in the survey literature. It was seen again in the Forgas and Bower (1987) experiment discussed earlier: subjects who were feeling happy made faster positive than negative judgments about the target character; subjects who were feeling unhappy made faster negative than positive judgments about him.

An especially interesting extension of these latency predictions concerns the priming of affective judgments (about target words) caused by presenting an attitude-word just before the target. This phenomenon was reported by Fazio *et al*. (1986). In their experiment, the subjects' task was to classify as quickly as possible the positive versus negative valence of words such as *lovely* and *putrid*. Three hundred milliseconds before the target word, a word or phrase signifying a core attitude was briefly presented as a prime. Some of these referred to a subject's positive attitudes (*disarmament*, *tuition cuts*) and some referred to his or her negative attitudes (*Ku Klux Klan*, *racism*). Fazio *et al*. reported facilitation (priming) of decisions about the target word following an affectively congruent prime, and inhibition (slowing relative to controls) of decisions following incongruent primes.

Such results are expected by the theory in Figure 2.9. The affective decision about a target word (*pretty* or *putrid*) is achieved by the word firing its associations to the positive versus negative nodes in memory (see Figure 2.9 for the word *Sydney*). A large class of reaction-time models imply that the time to reach a decision is related to the extent to which the activation at one valence node dominates the other. For instance, one such model views the subject as progressively accumulating activation differences in small time-units until a positive or negative criterion is passed. Whatever the reaction-time model, it is easy to show that a positive attitudinal prime provides a headstart in activation for the decision about a positive target, but a handicap for the eventual decision about a negative target; these influences are reversed for negative attitudinal primes. So, the theory explains these results on attitudinal priming. A qualification is that the priming does not occur when the prime-to-target interval is extended to 1000 ms. However, this effect of interstimulus interval is familiar in studies of priming, and is usually explained in terms of the person attending to other stimuli and thoughts during the longer interval, thus quenching the potency of the experimenter's prime. This may be part of the explanation of a failure to find mood-priming effects on various perceptual and lexical (word–nonword) decisions. For example, Clark *et al.* (1983) found that subjects induced by the Velten method to feel elated or depressed were not faster in making word–nonword decisions about mood-congruent words. This failure could be because such priming tasks require very concentrated, short-lived focusing, and also because no affective information has to be retrieved to make the lexical decision.

Some Complications of the Amended Model

Although this amended model explains some facts, it is clear that several complications must be added. One complication is that the effect of the prevailing mood can be sometimes overridden if people have a strong preformed opinion which they have stored as a stable fact about themselves, just as they can retrieve directly their age, birthday, or marital status. This limitation was noted by Schwarz and Clore (1988). They showed that temporary moods have a greater impact on vague, nebulous evaluations such as one's "satisfaction with life," but only a small effect on well-formed opinions. Presumably, people probably have to estimate their opinion on vague topics using their feelings from the balance in activation of positive versus negative valences. The network theory could handle this difference in the latter case by attaching to the relevant attitude node a proposition expressing one's well-formulated, frequently rehearsed opinion on the topic. This past proposition could then be retrieved when the model is asked for its opinion. This would be like a well-trained Communist spouting the Party line to a political question regardless of how he or she is feeling.

Other research by Schwarz and Clore (1988) that causes difficulties for the model is that suggesting that the impact of a mood on social judgments could be reduced if subjects were led to *discount* their feelings as a way of evaluating the attitude object. This discounting could be reflected in my model by allowing the person a strategic choice of how to arrive at a judgment, either by using the difference in positive versus negative valence, or by retrieving a preformed opinion or set of supporting facts. Later research (Forgas, personal communication, 1989) has not replicated this discounting effect of mood attribution, so we should suspend judgment on the significance and reliability of these effects.

Such complications show that the amended model is incomplete and needs development. Its major problem is that it lacks elegance and parsimony. For example, the model is forced to postulate the existence of two methods for arriving at a judgment, either by direct retrieval of an earlier opinion or by on-line calculation of the valence difference. But the degree to which any given judgment is determined by direct retrieval or by calculation is left to the imagination of the theorist. Another inelegancy is the model's assumption that some *unspecified* amount of activation of a general affect node spreads over to activate the positive or negative valence node attached to a given topic; but the amount of spread is left to the theorist's imagination. Yet it is this spread which determines the extent to which general moods influence judgments about any given attitudinal topic. These two inelegancies are very awkward.

But such inelegancies and indeterminacies are to be expected at this developmental stage for any model aiming to be comprehensive enough to cover the complex pattern of results concerning emotional influences on social judgments. Nonetheless, we may persist in the hope that the field will eventually arrive at a more elegant and powerful theory for explaining these complex and intriguing facts.

Acknowledgments

This research was supported by research grant MH-13950 from the US National Institute of Mental Health, and grant 87-0282A from the US Air Force Office of Scientific Research.

References

Anderson, J. R. (1985). *Cognitive psychology and its Implications*, 2nd edn. New York: W. H. Freeman.

Anderson, N. H. (1974). Information integration theory: A brief survey. In D. H. Krantz, R. C. Atkinson, R. D. Luce, and P. Suppes (Eds), *Contemporary developments in mathematical psychology*, Vol. 2. San Franciso: Freeman.

Bandura, A. (1977). Self-efficacy: Towards a unifying theory of behavior change. *Psychological Review*, **84**, 191–215.

Baron, R. A. (1987). Interviewer's mood and reaction to job applicants: The influence of affective states on applied social judgments. *Journal of Applied Social Psychology*, **17**, 911–926.

Bower, G. H. (1981). Mood and memory. *American Psychologist*, **36**, 129–148.

Bower, G. H. (1983). Affect and cognition. *Philosophical Transactions of the Royal Society of London, Series B*, **302**, 387–402.

Byrne, D. (1969). Attitudes and attraction. In L. Berkowitz (Ed.), *Advances in experimental social psychology*, Vol. 4. New York: Academic Press.

Byrne, D., and Clore, G. L. (1970). A reinforcement model of evaluative responses. *Personality: an International Journal*, **1**, 103–128.

Calder, B. J., and Gruder, C. L. (1988). A network activation theory of attitudinal affect. Unpublished manuscript. Northwestern University; Kellogg Graduate School of Marketing.

Carson, T. P., and Adams, H. E. (1980). Activity valence as a function of mood change. *Journal of Abnormal Psychology*, **89**, 368–377.

Clark, D. M., Teasdale, J. D., Broadbent, D. E., and Martin, M. (1983). Effect of mood on lexical decision. *Bulletin of the Psychonomic Society*, **21**, 175–183.

Clore, G. L., Parrott, W. J. & Wilkin, N. (1985). Does emotional bias occur during encoding or judgment? Paper given at Midwestern Psychological Association Meetings, 1985.

Fazio, R. H., Sanbonmatsu, D. M., Powell, M. C. and Kardes, F. K. (1986). On the automatic activation of attitudes. *Journal of Personality and Social Psychology*, **50**, 229–238.

Fiedler, K., Pampe, H., and Scherf, U. (1986). Mood and memory for tightly organized social information. *European Journal of Social Psychology*, **16**, 149–164.

Fishbein, M., and Ajzen, I (1975). *Belief, attitude, intention, and behavior: An introduction to theory and research.* Reading, MA: Addison-Wesley.

Forgas, J. P. Bower, G. H., and Krantz, S. (1984). The influence of mood on perceptions of social interactions. *Journal of Experimental Social Psychology*, **20**, 497–513.

Forgas, J. P. and Bower, G. H. (1987). Mood effects on person-perception judgments. *Journal of Personality and Social Psychology*, **53**, 53–60.

Forgas, J. P., and Moylan, S. (1987). After the movies: Transient mood and social judgment. *Personality and Social Psychology Bulletin*, **13**, 467–477.

Gibbons, F. X. (1986). Social comparison and depression: Company's effect on misery. *Journal of Personality and Social Psychology*, **51**, 140–148.

Gouaux, C. (1971). Induced affective states and interpersonal attraction. *Journal of Personality and Social Psychology*, **20**, 37–43.

Griffitt, W. B. (1970). Environmental effects on interpersonal affective behavior: Ambient effective temperature and attraction. *Journal of Personality and Social Psychology*. **15**, 240–244.

Isen, A. M., Shalker, T., Clark, M., and Karp, L. (1978). Positive affect, accessibility of material in memory, and behavior: a cognitive loop? *Journal of Personality and Social Psychology*, **36**, 1–12.

Johnson, E. J. and Tversky, A. (1983). Affect, generalization, and the perception of risk. *Journal of Personality and Social Psychology*, **45**, 20–31.

Johnson, M. K., Kim, J. K. and Risse, G. (1985). Do alcoholic Korsakoff's syndrome patients acquire affective reactions? *Journal of Experimental Psychology: Learning, Memory, and Cognition*, **11**, 22–36.

Kavanagh, D., and Bower, G. H. (1985). Mood and self-efficacy: Impact of joy and sadness on perceived capabilities. *Cognitive Therapy and Research*, **9**, 507–525.

Kunda, Z. (1987). Motivated inference: Self-serving generation and evaluation of causal theories. *Journal of Personality and Social Psychology*, **53**, 636–647.

Schachter, S. (1959). *The Psychology of affiliation*. Stanford University Press: Stanford, CA.

Schwarz, N. and Clore, G. L. (1988). How do I feel about it? The informative functions of affective states. In K. Fiedler and J. Forgas (Eds), *Affect, cognition, and social behavior*. Toronto: Hogrefe, pp. 44–62.

Sherman, B. R., and Kunda, Z. (1989). The effect of motivation on the processing of scientific evidence. Poster paper presented at American Psychological Society Convention, June, 1989, Alexandria, VA.

Snyder, D. J. (1976). *Social psychology*. Reading, MA: Addison-Wesley.

Snyder, M., and White, P. (1982). Moods and memories: Elation, depression and the remembering of the events of one's life. *Journal of Personality*, **50**, 149–167.

Swann, W. B. Jr. (1983). Self-verification: Bringing social reality into harmony with the self. In J. Suls and A. G. Greenwald (Eds), *Social psychological perspectives on the self*, Vol. 2. Hillsdale, NJ: Erlbaum.

Swann, W. B. Jr., and Pelham, B. W. (Unpublished manuscript, 1988). Getting out when the going gets good: Choice of relationship partners and the self. University of Texas Psychology Dept.

Swann, W. B. Jr., Wenzlaff, R. M., Krull, D. S. and Pelham, B. W. (in press). Seeking truth, reaping despair: Depression, self-verification, and selection of relationship partners. *Journal of Abnormal Psychology*.

Tversky, A., and Kahneman, D. (1974). Judgment under uncertainty: Heuristics and biases. *Science*, **185**, 1124–1131.

Wenzlaff, R. M., and Prohaska, M. L. (1989). When misery loves company: Depression and responses to others' moods. *Journal of Experimental Social Psychology*, **25**, 220–233.

Wessman, A. E., and Ricks, D. F. (1966). *Mood and personality*. New York: Holt, Rinehart & Winston.

Wright, J., and Mischel, W. (1982). Influence of affect on cognitive social learning person variables. *Journal of Personality and Social Psychology*, **43**, 901–914.

3

Happy and Mindless, But Sad and Smart? The Impact of Affective States on Analytic Reasoning

NORBERT SCHWARZ

ZUMA, Zentrum für Umfragen, Methoden und Analysen, Mannheim

and

HERBERT BLESS

Universität Mannheim

Contents

A growing body of literature indicates that individuals' cognitive performance on a wide variety of tasks may be profoundly influenced by the affective state they are in. While early research on this issue emphasized the disruptive nature of affective states (e.g. Easterbrook, 1959), the accumulating evidence suggests a considerably more complicated picture. Apparently, feeling good and feeling bad may both facilitate and impair cognitive performance, depending on the nature of the task. This chapter will provide a selective review of some of the available evidence, focusing on the impact of affective states on analytic reasoning, and will offer a theoretical framework for the conceptualization of affective influences on information processing.

Specifically, we suggest that *positive moods* are likely to elicit a processing strategy that relies heavily on the use of simple heuristics, and that is characterized by a lack of logical consistency and little attention to detail. Accordingly, positive moods are likely to inhibit performance on tasks that require analytic, detail-oriented strategies. On the other hand, positive moods have also been shown to foster unusual associations, and to be associated with increased creativity. Accordingly, they may be likely to improve performance on creativity-related tasks. In contrast, we suggest that *negative moods* are likely to elicit an analytical mode of information processing that is characterized by considerable attention to detail, careful, step-by-step analysis of the available information, and a high degree of logical consistency, although probably associated with a lack of creativity. Accordingly, they are likely to improve performance on tasks that require analytic processing, but to impair performance on creativity-related tasks. Related hypotheses, based on different theoretical considerations, have been advanced by Isen and colleagues (e.g. Isen *et al.*, 1982), Kuhl (1983), and Fiedler (1988), to whose theorizing the present chapter is indebted.

To begin with the most fundamental issue, we will consider why one might expect that individuals' affective state influences their mode of information processing, before we turn to some selective evidence.

Informative Functions of Affective States

A key element in many theories of emotion is the, often implicit, assumption that "emotions exist for the sake of signaling states of the world that have to be responded to, or that no longer need response and action" (Frijda, 1988, p. 354). Surprisingly, this assumption has received little attention in psychological theorizing about the interplay between affect and cognition. However, a considerable body of recent research on mood effects in evaluative judgment supports the assumption that affective states serve informative functions (see Clore and Parrott, this volume; Schwarz, 1987, 1988; Schwarz & Clore, 1988; for reviews).

Evaluative judgments

Specifically, it has been shown that individuals frequently consult their affective reaction to the judgmental object according to a "How do I feel about it?" heuristic (Schwarz and Clore, 1988) when they are asked to form complex evaluative judgments. In doing so, however, they may misread feelings that were elicited by other causes as affective reactions to the object of judgment, resulting in more positive evaluations in the presence of positive rather than negative feelings. For example, Schwarz and Clore (1983) observed that individuals who were interviewed on sunny days, and who were in a good mood, reported higher happiness and satisfaction with their life as a whole than individuals who were interviewed on rainy days. However, the impact of sunny and rainy days was eliminated when the interviewer, who pretended to call from out of town, asked at the beginning of the interview, "By the way, how's the weather down there?" This finding suggests that respondents did not use their feelings at the time of judgment as a basis for evaluating the quality of their life as a whole when the diagnostic value of their current feelings was called into question. In line with this interpretation, a measure of current mood—assessed at the end of the interview—was correlated more strongly with reports of life-satisfaction when the weather was *not* mentioned, than when it was. This pattern of results is incompatible with models of mood-congruent recall (e.g. Bower, 1981). According to these models, the impact of moods on evaluative judgments is mediated by its impact on the recall of material stored in memory. Note, however, that directing subjects' attention to the weather as a plausible source of their current feelings discredits the informational value of the current feelings themselves, but not the informational value of any positive (or negative) life-events they may recall from memory. Accordingly, this and related findings (cf. Schwarz, 1990; Schwarz & Clore, 1988; for reviews) indicate that affective states may serve informative functions, independently of their impact on the recall of valenced material.

Subsequent laboratory experiments supported this analysis, indicating that the information provided by one's feelings is only used in making evaluative judgments if it is relevant to the judgment at hand, and if its informational value is not called into question. Accordingly, mood effects were not obtained in several studies when subjects were induced to attribute their current mood to a transient, external source (e.g. Schwarz and Clore, 1983; Schwarz et al., 1985). In addition, the impact of affective states was found to decrease as the salience (Collins and Clark, 1989; Strack et al., 1985) or amount (Schwarz et al., 1987b; Srull, 1983, 1984) of other information relevant to the judgment at hand increases, suggesting that the impact of the information that is provided by one's mood varies as a function of the same variables that determine the impact of any other piece of information.

Moreover, several studies demonstrated that global moods may influence a wide variety of evaluative judgments (e.g. Johnson and Tversky, 1983), whereas the information provided by specific emotions appears to be more specific, thus limiting the range of judgments likely to be influenced (e.g. Gallagher and Clore, 1985; Keltner and Audrain, 1988). This reflects that specific emotions have an identifiable cause and a sharp rise time. Moods, on the other hand, may result from a series of mildly pleasant or unpleasant events, none of which needs to be sufficiently intense to produce an emotion by itself, but which collectively leave one in a generalized positive or negative feeling state. Thus, the cause of a mood tends to be more remote in time than the cause of an emotion and tends to be less clearly defined for the experiencer. This is reflected in our use of language that implies specific references for emotions but not for global moods. Thus, we say that we are afraid "of" something and angry "about" something, but that we are "in" a happy or sad mood. Accordingly, the informational value of specific emotions has been found to be limited to its cause, whereas the informational value of global moods is more diffuse, rendering them relevant to a variety of different evaluative judgments. In fact, when subjects are induced to attribute their moods to specific causes—as in the weather experiment described above (Schwarz and Clore, 1983)—its impact on judgments that are unrelated to that source vanishes.

Mood-congruent recall

In addition, the impact of affective states on evaluative judgments may also provide an account for mood-congruency effects in recall. As Higgins and colleagues recently demonstrated, individuals may use previously formed judgments as retrieval cues for reconstructing the information that presumably provided the basis of judgment in the first place (Higgins and Lurie, 1983; Higgins and Stangor, 1988). Applied to the present reasoning, this raises the possibility that individuals' affective state may influence their evaluative judgments, which in turn may serve as mood-congruent retrieval cues, resulting in mood-congruent recall. To use one of Bower's (1981) examples, individuals who are asked to recall events from their kindergarten days may first ask themselves, "Well, kindergarten days. What were they like?". In doing so, they may form a global evaluation that is based on their current mood as described above. Facing the task to report specific episodes, they may then use this global evaluation as a retrieval cue to guide the recall of specific information, resulting in an increased recall—or reconstruction—of mood congruent information.

One important implication of this reasoning is that mood effects on recall should only be obtained under conditions that give rise to mood effects on evaluative judgments in the first place. Accordingly, misattribution manipulations of the type used by Schwarz and Clore (1983) should eliminate the impact of moods on the recall of mood-congruent information from memory. While experimental tests of this possibility are not yet available, it is conceivable that variations in the perceived informational value of one's mood may underlie the inconsistent findings in the mood-congruent memory literature (cf. Blaney, 1986; Bower, this volume).

Affect, Motivation, and Information Processing

However, the informational value of one's affective state may be more fundamental than has been captured in our previous research, which was limited to the impact of moods on evaluative judgments. As many authors pointed out (e.g. Arnold, 1960; Frijda, 1988; Higgins, 1987; Ortony *et al.*, 1988), different affective states are closely linked to different psychological situations. In Frijda's (1988) words, "emotions arise in response to the meaning structures of given situations, [and] different emotions arise in response to different meaning structures" (p. 349). In general, "events that satisfy the individual's goals, or promise to do so, yield positive emotions; events that harm or threaten the individual's concerns lead to negative emotions" (p. 349).

For the purpose of the present argument, we assume that the relationship between emotions and the "meaning structures" that constitute a "psychological situation" (Higgins, 1987) is bidirectional: while different psychological situations result in different emotions, the presence of a certain emotion also informs the individual about the nature of its current psychological situation. At a general level, we may assume that a positive affective state informs the individual that the world is a safe place that does not threaten the person's current goals. That is, positive feelings tell us that our current situation is neither characterized by a lack of positive outcomes, nor by a threat of negative outcomes. Negative affective states, on the other hand, inform the individual that the current situation is problematic, and that it is characterized either by a lack of positive outcomes, or by a threat of negative outcomes. If so, one's affective state could serve as a simple but highly salient indicator of the nature of the situation one is in.

Let us further assume that individuals are motivated to obtain positive outcomes and to avoid negative ones. If so, negative emotions inform the individual that some action needs to be taken, whereas positive emotions may not signal a particular action requirement. Indeed, empirical evidence indicates that different emotions are associated with different states of "action readiness," which are evident in physiological changes (e.g. Lacey and Lacey, 1970; Obrist, 1981) and overt behavior (e.g. Ekman, 1982; Izard, 1977), as well as in introspective reports (e.g. Davitz, 1969; Frijda, 1986, 1987). In Frijda's (1988) words, "emotions exist for the sake of signaling states of the world that have to be responded to, or that no longer need response and action" (p. 354).

What are the implications of these considerations for information processing?

The use of processing strategies

Their significance for information processing derives from the assumption that different psychological situations, which are reflected in different affective states, require different information processing strategies. If positive affective states inform the individual that his or her personal world is currently an OK place, the individual may see little need to engage in cognitive effort, *unless* this is required by other currently active goals. In pursuing these goals, the individual may also be willing to take some risk, given that the general situation is considered safe. Thus, simple heuristics may be preferred to more effortful, detail-oriented, judgmental strategies; new procedures and possibilities may be explored; and unusual, creative associations may be elaborated. Accordingly, the thought processes of individuals in a positive affective state may be characterized by what Fiedler (1988) has called "loosening," using a term introduced by Kelly (1955).

If negative affective states inform the individual about a lack of positive, or a threat of negative, outcomes, the individual may be motivated to change his or her current situation. Attempts to change the situation, however, initially require a careful assessment of the features of the current situation, an analysis of their causal links, and explorations of possible mechanisms of change and their potential outcomes. Moreover, individuals may be unlikely to take risks in a situation that is already considered problematic, and may therefore avoid simple heuristics as well as novel solutions. Accordingly, their thought processes may be characterized by what Fiedler (1988) termed "tightening."

In summary, these considerations suggest that individuals' thought processes are tuned to meet the requirements of the psychological situation that is reflected in their feelings. To the extent that affective states are directly experienced and likely to receive considerable attention (Zajonc, 1980), a link between affective states and cognitive processes could be highly adaptive by shortcutting the need for time-consuming interpretations of situational processing requirements.

This assumption has interesting implications for individuals' thoughts about the affect eliciting situation, as well as for their performance on unrelated tasks. In the present chapter, we will focus on the key prediction, namely that positive moods decrease and negative moods increase the use of detail-oriented, analytical processing strategies. A more extended discussion of the implications of this line of argument for phenomena of memory, learning, and selective attention is provided by Schwarz (1990).

Event-Related Thoughts: Affective States as Elicitors of Attributional Activity

As a first hypothesis, we may assume that individuals in a negative affective state will be more likely to focus their attention on features of the situation that elicited their feelings. In fact, a large body of literature indicates a narrowing of attentional focus under negative affect (e.g. Easterbrook, 1959). As a recent example, Wegner and Vallacher (1986) observed that failures to obtain a desired outcome are more likely to elicit attention to details of one's action strategy than successful actions. Similarly, individuals in a depressed mood were found to pay more attention to the features of a given situation, resulting in a more detailed and accurate representation, and more adequate contingency judgments, than individuals in an elated mood—a phenomenon that has become known as "depressive realism" (see Ruehlman et al., 1985 for a review). In a related vain, Forgas et al. (1990) observed that causal attributions for achievement only reflected a self-serving bias if subjects were in a good or a non-manipulated mood, but not if they were in a bad mood.

As a second hypothesis, we may assume that individuals in a negative affective state are more likely to engage in causal reasoning about the affect-eliciting event than individuals in a positive affective state. Such an asymmetry has repeatedly been observed in the attribution literature. Specifically, it has been found that negative events, which elicit negative feelings, are more likely to trigger causal explanations than positive events (e.g. Abele, 1985; Schwarz and Clore, 1983; Schwarz, 1987). For example, Schwarz (1987, Experiment 9) observed that college students who were asked to describe a positive or a negative life-event were more likely to provide unelicited causal explanations for negative (38%) than for positive (18%) events. Moreover, if a causal explanation was offered, it was provided earlier in the description if the event was negative (specifically, after 10.2 words), than if the event was positive (after 41.0 words), suggesting that causal explanations are more accessible in the cognitive representation of negative rather than positive events.

However, these data are difficult to interpret due to a natural confounding of valence and expectancy: as many attribution theorists have noted, unpleasant events are seen as less likely than pleasant ones in everyday life. Accordingly, the subjective probability of the event and its hedonic quality are naturally confounded. The unexpectedness of an event, however, has been found to trigger causal explanations in its own right (see Hastie, 1984, for a review). It is therefore unclear whether persons in a negative mood think more analytically because the event that made them feel sad was unexpected, or whether a person's affective state has a genuine impact on causal reasoning in its own right that is independent of the expectedness of the affect-eliciting event.

To isolate the contribution of both variables, Bohner et al. (1988) conducted a laboratory experiment that provided independent manipulations of the subjective probability of an event and its hedonic valence. Subjects in their study received either success or failure feedback about their performance on an ostensible "professional skills test." In addition, the subjective probability of success was varied by informing subjects that either 23% or 77% of a comparable student population met the criterion. Following success or failure feedback, subjects were asked to write down everything that came to mind, and finally provided a direct rating of the intensity with which they tried to explain their test result.

Manipulation checks indicated that the manipulation of subjects' expectations regarding success or failure was successful. Moreover, subjects who received success feedback reported being in a significantly better mood than subjects who received failure feedback, and their self-reported affective state showed no impact of the *a priori* likelihood of success. Thus, subjects' performance expectations and their feelings as a function of outcome were efficiently manipulated.

As expected, these manipulations produced pronounced main effects of the valence of the outcome on measures of causal reasoning: specifically, subjects' reported thoughts about the testing situation, as well as about the test result, contained more causal explanations when they had experienced a negative event (failure; M's = 35% and 21%, respectively) than when they had experienced a positive event (success; M's = 12% and 5%, respectively), independent of the *a priori* probability of the outcome. In addition, subjects reported a higher intensity of causal reasoning after negative than after positive feedback. Additional correlational analyses indicated that the number of causal explanations reported, as well as the intensity ratings, increased with increasing negativity of subjects' current affective state.

In summary, these findings indicate that subjects were more likely to explain a negative event that elicited negative feelings, than to explain a positive event that elicited positive feelings. Given that the expectancy of the outcome was held constant, these findings demonstrate that the valence of the event, and its accompanying affective reaction, is a determinant of the degree of causal reasoning in its own right.

At a more general level, Holyoak and Nisbett (1988) observed that "people make inferences only when there is some triggering condition. An event or relationship must be problematic, unexpected, or at least interesting, before people begin to make inferences" (p. 61). The present argument holds that experiencing negative feelings may be one of the conditions that inform individuals that an event or relationship is "problematic," and may thus serve as a triggering condition for processing styles that are likely to deal successfully with problematic situations.

Generalization to Other Tasks

While the preceding discussion pertained to subjects' reasoning about the situation that elicited the affective state to begin with, we will now turn to the more intriguing possibility that the impact of affective states may *generalize to other tasks* that individuals work on while in that state. Why might such a generalization occur?

If we assume that analytic reasoning is helpful in handling negative situations, it would be highly adaptive if the negative affective states that accompany them increased the cognitive accessibility of relevant procedural knowledge. This would increase the speed with which the adequate procedures could be applied to the negative situation. Moreover, it would decrease response competition between various applicable procedures, thus reducing the likelihood that other potentially applicable, but less effective, procedures would be selected.

However, any mechanism that increases the accessibility of analytic procedures to facilitate their application to the effect-eliciting situation, would also increase the accessibility of the same procedures *per se*, resulting in a higher likelihood that they are applied to *any* task to which they are applicable. Accordingly, we should find that subjects in a bad mood are more likely to apply analytic processing strategies in cognitive tasks that they work on while in that mood than subjects in an elated mood. Evidence from diverse areas of research supports this assumption (see Schwarz, 1990, for a review). In the present chapter, we will focus on the impact of moods on the organization of information and the role of moods in the processing of persuasive communications.

Moods and the organization of information

As Isen (1984) observed, "positive affect results in an organization of cognitive material, such that either more or broader, more integrated, categories" are used (p. 535). For example, items that are not generally considered good exemplars of a category (e.g. "cane" as a member of the category "clothing"), were more likely to be assigned to that category by subjects in an elated than by subjects in a non-manipulated mood (Isen *et al.*, 1986). Similarly, subjects in an elated mood were found to sort stimuli into fewer groupings, again suggesting the use of broader categories.

Evidence for the assumption that different affective states are associated with different styles of organizing information is also provided by Bless *et al.* (1989). In their studies, different affective states were crossed with memory- and impression-set instructions in two person-memory experiments. Specifically, subjects in positive, neutral, or negative moods read behavioral descriptions representing four different trait categories (e.g. intelligent, friendly) that were presented in a random order. Subjects were either instructed to remember these behaviors (memory set) or to form an impression about the person who had performed them (impression set). After working on a filler task. Subjects were asked, in a neutral mood, to recall as many behaviors as possible.

Replicating Hamilton *et al.* (1980a,b), subjects in a neutral mood recalled more behaviors under impression- than under memory-set instructions. As predicted, the increased recall under impression-set instructions was mediated by a higher amount of clustering under impression-set than under memory-set instructions, again replicating the findings of Hamilton *et al.* (1980a,b). However, the recall of subjects in positive as well as negative moods was *not* affected by instructions. The amount of recall provided by these subjects under either impression- or memory-set instructions was as high as the recall provided by subjects in a neutral mood under impression-set instructions. This effect was obtained for behaviors of positive and of negative valence, independently of whether the valence of the behaviors was varied in a between subject design (Experiment 1) or a within subject design (Experiment 2).

Moreover, memory- or impression-set instructions did not affect the amount of clustering obtained under either positive or negative moods, in contrast to their impact under neutral mood. Rather, the amount of clustering under both mood conditions was found to be solely a function of subjects' affective state. Specifically, the recall protocols of subjects in a positive mood showed a degree of clustering that was as *high* as for neutral mood subjects under impression-set instructions, independent of the instructions that positive mood subjects received. In contrast, the amount of clustering shown by subjects in a negative mood was as small as for neutral mood subjects under memory-set instructions, again independently of the instructions that negative mood subjects received. Thus, subjects in a positive mood showed increased, and subjects in a negative mood showed decreased, clustering, independent of the experimental instructions.

Given that subjects in a positive and a negative mood showed equal recall performance, despite differential clustering, it can be assumed that their recall was mediated by different processes. Specifically, this pattern of findings suggests that the recall performance of subjects in a positive mood was facilitated by their high degree of clustering, paralleling the findings obtained under neutral mood/impression-set conditions. Subjects in a negative mood, on the other hand, showed as little clustering as subjects under neutral mood/memory-set conditions, but still recalled as much material as subjects who showed a high degree of clustering. In line with the above assumptions, this suggests that subjects in a negative mood processed the incoming information in a more effortful and detail-oriented manner. Accordingly, the narrower focus of attention under negative mood, resulting in narrower categorizations, inhibited the organization of the material, as indicated by the low clustering scores, whereas the effortful learning of the material facilitated subjects' recall performance.

Consistent with these conclusions, Sinclair (1988) observed that subjects' mood mediated their performance on a simulated personnel appraisal task. Specifically, subjects in a negative mood considered more information in making performance appraisals than subjects in a positive mood, with subjects in a nonmanipulated mood again falling in between. More importantly, the performance appraisals provided by depressed subjects corresponded more closely to the number of positive or negative behaviors presented, than did the performance appraisals provided by elated subjects, suggesting that elated subjects may "form sweeping global impressions," whereas depressed subjects may "assess more facts and make more discrete judgments" (p. 39).

In combination, the reviewed results suggest that individuals' affective states influence the organization of information. Negative affective states facilitate the use of a detail-oriented processing style that is characterized by a narrow focus of attention, narrow categorization, and a low degree of clustering, even under conditions that are known to facilitate clustering under neutral mood. In contrast, positive affective states elicit the use of processing strategies that are characterized by wider categorizations and a high degree of clustering, even under conditions that are known to interfere with clustering under neutral mood.

Moods and the processing of persuasive communications

The conclusion that individuals in a bad mood are more likely to spontaneously engage in effortful, detail-oriented analytic processing strategies than individuals in an elated mood is further supported by research on the impact of affective states on the processing of persuasive communications (cf. Bless et al., 1989; Bless et al., 1990; Mackie and Worth, 1989; Schwarz et al., in press; Worth and Mackie, 1987). As a large body of research in the elaboration likelihood paradigm of persuasion demonstrated, a message that presents strong arguments is more persuasive than a message that presents weak arguments—provided that the recipient is motivated, and able, to process the content of the message (cf. Petty and Cacioppo, 1986a,b, for reviews). If the recipient does not engage in a careful processing of the message's content, on the other hand, the advantage of strong over weak arguments is eliminated.

Several studies explored the impact of moods on recipients' spontaneous processing strategies. In one of these studies (Bless et al., 1990), subjects were asked to provide a vivid report of a pleasant or an unpleasant life-event, to induce a good or bad mood. As part of a purportedly independent second study, concerned with language comprehension, they were subsequently exposed to a tape-recorded communication that presented either strong or weak arguments in favor of an increase in student services fees. Finally, their attitudes toward an increase in student services fees and their cognitive responses to the message were assessed.

As expected, the results showed a significant interaction of mood and argument quality. Subjects in a bad mood reported more favorable attitudes toward an increase in student services fees when they were exposed to strong arguments than when they were exposed to weak arguments. Subjects in a good mood, on the other hand, were equally persuaded by strong *and* by weak arguments, and reported a moderately positive attitude independent of the quality of the arguments. This suggests that subjects in a good mood may have been less likely to elaborate the content of the message than subjects in a bad mood.

This conclusion is supported by an analysis of subjects' cognitive responses. Specifically, subjects who were put in a bad mood generated a higher proportion of favorable and a lower proportion of unfavorable thoughts in response to the strong arguments than in response to the weak arguments, reflecting a high degree of systematic elaboration of the message. The cognitive responses generated by subjects in a good mood, on the other hand, did not vary as a function of message quality, suggesting that the occurrence of favorable and unfavorable thoughts under good mood was independent of the content of the message. Additional data indicated that subjects in a good mood only paid attention to the quality of the arguments when they were explicitly instructed to do so (Bless *et al.*, 1990, Experiment 1) or when they were provided with unlimited time for argument processing (Mackie and Worth, 1989), whereas individuals in a bad mood did so spontaneously. On the other hand, introducing a distractor task that interfered with subjects' processing of the message reduced the advantage of strong over weak arguments for bad mood subjects, but not for good mood subjects—further suggesting that subjects in a good mood did not spontaneously engage in message processing to begin with (Bless *et al.*, 1990, Experiment 2).

In combination, these findings support the hypothesis that the impact of mood on persuasion is mediated by its impact on subjects' processing strategies. While subjects in a bad mood spontaneously elaborate the content of the message according to what Petty and Cacioppo (1986a,b) call a "central route" of persuasion, subjects in a good mood seem unlikely to do so (see Schwarz *et al.*, in press, for a review).

Creative problem solving

While the above research suggests an increased use of analytical reasoning strategies under bad mood, it has also been observed that individuals in a good mood perform better at creative problem-solving tasks than individuals in a bad mood. For example, they were found to be better at solving Dunker's candle problem, and to generate more unusual associations (Isen *et al.*, 1982, 1985). We propose that both the increase of analytical reasoning under bad moods and the increase of creative reasoning under good moods, reflects the impact of affective states on individuals' motivation and the accessibility of relevant procedural knowledge.

If positive affective states inform the individual that no particular action is required by the current situation, they are unlikely to activate any specific procedure. Accordingly, no response hierarchy that is tuned to the current situation may be elicited, and different procedures may be equally accessible. If so, individuals in a good mood may be more likely to access a diverse range of procedural, semantic, and episodic knowledge than individuals in a bad mood. The combination and application of diverse knowledge, however, is exactly what we usually consider to be at the heart of creative problem solving. Moreover, persons in a good mood may be less likely to consciously constrain themselves, because their affective state informs them that their current environment is safe, thus allowing them to take the risk that is associated with novel solutions.

Individuals in a bad mood, on the other hand, may be more constrained, both at the level of access to diverse knowledge and at the level of their willingness to engage in risky novel solutions, in a situation that is already defined as problematic. As a result, they are likely to perform less well on creative problem solving tasks, but better on analytical tasks, than individuals in an elated mood.

Conclusions

In summary, the considerations offered in the present chapter, and the limited evidence that bears on them, suggest that individuals' affective state may influence their style of information processing (see Fiedler, 1988; Isen, 1987; Kuhl, 1983, for related claims and Schwarz, 1990, for a more extended treatment). These influences may be conceptualized by considering the informative functions of affective states and their implications for individuals' inferences about the nature of their psychological situation (Frijda, 1988; Higgins, 1987). If negative emotions inform the individual about a threat of negative or a lack of positive outcomes, they may activate procedural knowledge that is relevant to the handling of these problematic situations. This procedural knowledge may therefore be more accessible in memory, increasing the likelihood that the respective procedures will be applied to other tasks to which they are applicable while the individual is in a negative affective state. Moreover, individuals in a negative state may appreciate opportunities to distract themselves from this state by concentrating on other tasks, in particular if the event that elicited their bad feelings cannot be changed, as is typical of the experimental manipulations used in affect and cognition research. In addition, individuals in a bad mood may be motivated to avoid risky novel solutions in a situation that is already characterized as problematic. As a result, one finds that individuals are more likely to use effortful, detail-oriented, analytical processing strategies spontaneously when they are put in a bad rather than in a good mood, but that their reasoning is characterized by a lower degree of originality, creativity, and playfulness.

Positive affective states, on the other hand, inform the individual that the current environment is a safe place. Accordingly, individuals in a good mood may be more likely to take risks and to use simple heuristics in information processing. Moreover, they may have better access to a variety of procedural knowledge, given that no specific procedure is activated to cope with the current situation. In combination, this may facilitate the higher creativity that has been observed under elated mood, but may inhibit the spontaneous use of effortful analytic processing strategies, unless they are required by other active goals.

Do these arguments imply that we should expect to find mood-induced differences in processing style under all conditions? Obviously not. To the extent that handling the negative situation itself binds a considerable degree of subjects' cognitive capacity, performance on unrelated tasks should be impaired, despite better accessibility of relevant knowledge. Similarly, if individuals are not motivated to work on a task to begin with, as is frequently the case under severe depression, any potential advantage of processing style cannot be observed. Moreover, other currently active goals (cf. Srull and Wyer, 1986) may override the impact of affective states, as has been demonstrated in the Bless et al. (1990) studies reviewed above. Note, however, that the present theorizing implies that it should be easier to induce individuals in a good mood to use an analytic processing style than to induce individuals in a bad mood to use a heuristic style. If positive feelings inform us that no action is needed, overriding this message due to other action requirements poses no problem. In contrast, if negative feelings inform us about current problems, ignoring this message would not be adaptive. Accordingly, one may expect that the impact of negative feelings on processing style is more immune to the influence of other variables than the impact of positive feelings. Obviously, future research should address these plausible limitations, and should employ cognitive tasks with well-understood processing requirements.

For the time being, however, we note that the informative functions approach to the interplay of affect and cognition (Schwarz, 1990) provides a heuristically fruitful framework for conceptualizing the impact of affective states on evaluative judgments (cf. Clore and Parrott, this volume; Schwarz, 1987; Schwarz and Clore, 1988) and on individuals' spontaneous choice of processing strategies. Most importantly, the basic assumption that affective states may serve informative functions is clearly in line with a long tradition of theorizing about the nature of emotions (cf. Frijda, 1986, 1987, for reviews), and it invites an explicit consideration of what the specific information is, that may be provided by different moods and emotions. One may expect that current explorations of the conditions that give rise to different emotions (e.g. Higgins, 1987; Oatley and Johnson-Laird, 1987; Ortony et al., 1988; Weiner, 1985), as well as research on people's knowledge about their emotions (e.g. Stein and Levine, 1987), will result in a more precise understanding of their respective informational value. In principle, one may assume that affect-elicited cognitive tuning is more functional for an organism, the more closely different types of emotions correspond to different situational requirements. If so, future insights into situational determinants of emotions are likely to allow more precise specifications of the processing requirements that are signaled by different affective states, providing a theoretical basis for more specific predictions about the impact of different moods and emotions on strategies of information processing.

Acknowledgments

The reported research was supported by grants Schw 278/2 and Str 264/2 from the Deutsche Forschungsgemeinschaft to Norbert Schwarz and Fritz Strack, and a fellowship from the DAAD to Herbert Bless. Stimulating discussions with Gerd Bohner, Jerry Clore, Tory Higgins, Tom Ostrom, Fritz Strack, and Bob Wyer are gratefully acknowledged. Address correspondence to Dr. Norbert Schwarz, ZUMA, P.O. Box 12 21 55, D-6800 Mannheim, Germany.

References

Abele, A. (1985). Thinking about thinking. Causal, evaluative and finalistic cognitions about social situations. *European Journal of Social Psychology*, **15**, 315–332.

Arnold, M. B. (1960). *Emotion and personality*, Vol. 1,2. New York: Columbia University Press.

Blaney, P. H. (1986). Affect and memory: A review *Psychological Bulletin*, **99**, 229–246.

Bless, H., Bohner, G., Schwarz, N. and Strack, F. (1990). Mood and persuasion: A cognitive response analysis. *Personality and Social Psychology Bulletin*, **16**, 331–345.

Bless, H., Hamilton, D. L., and Mackie, D. M. (1989). Mood effects on the organization of person information. Unpublished research.

Bless, H., Mackie, D. M., and Schwarz, N. (1989). Mood effects on encoding and judgmental processes in persuasion. Manuscript under review.

Bohner, G., Bless, H., Schwarz, N., and Strack, F. (1988). When do events trigger attributions? The impact of valence and subjective probability. *European Journal of Social Psychology*, **18**, 335–345.

Bower, G. H. (1981). Mood and memory. *American Psychologist*, **36**, 129–148.

Collins, J., and Clark, L. (1989). Mechanisms of meaning. University of Illinois: Unpublished manuscript.

Davitz, J. R. (1969). *The language of emotion*. New York: Academic Press.

Easterbrook, J. A. (1959). The effect of emotion on cue utilization and the organization of behavior. *Psychological Review*, **66**, 183–201.

Ekman, P. (1982). *Emotion in the human face*. New York: Cambridge University Press.

Fiedler, K. (1988). Emotional mood, cognitive style, and behavior regulation. In K. Fiedler and J. Forgas (Eds), *Affect, cognition, and social behavior*. Toronto: Hogrefe.

Forgas, J. P., Bower, G. H., and Moylen, S. J. (1990). Praise or blame? Mood effects on attributions for success and failure. *Journal of Personality and Social Psychology*, **59**, 809–818.

Frijda, N. H. (1986). *The emotions*. London: Cambridge University Press.

Frijda, N. H. (1987). Emotions, cognitive structure, and action tendency. *Cognition and Emotion*, **1**, 235–258.

Frijda, N. H. (1988). The laws of emotion. *American Psychologist*, **43**, 349–358.

Gallagher, D., and Clore, G. L. (1985). Effects of fear and anger on judgments of risk and blame. Paper presented at the meetings of the Midwestern Psychological Association, Chicago, (May).

Hamilton, D. L., Katz, L. B., and Leirer, V. O. (1980a). Organizational processes in impression formation. In R. Hastie, T. M. Ostrom, E. B. Ebbessen, R. S. Wyer, D. L. Hamilton, and D. E. Carlston (Hrsg.), *Person memory: The cognitive basis of social perception*. Hillsdale, NJ: Erlbaum, 1980.

Hamilton, D. L., Katz, L. B. and Leirer, V. O. (1980b). Cognitive representation of personality impressions: Organizational processes in first impression formation. *Journal of Personality and Social Psychology*, **39**, 1050–1063.

Hastie, R. (1984). Causes and effects of causal attribution. *Journal of Personality and Social Psychology*, **46**, 44–56.

Higgins, E. T. (1987). Self-discrepancy: A theory relating self and affect. *Psychological Review*. **94**, 319–340.

Higgins, E. T., and Lurie, L. (1983). Context, categorization, and memory: The "change-of-standard" effect. *Cognitive Psychology*, **15**, 525–547.

Higgins, E. T., and Stangor, C. (1988). A "change-of-standard" perspective on the relations among context, judgment, and memory. *Journal of Personality and Social Psychology*, **54**, 181–192.

Holyoak, K. J., and Nisbett, R. E. (1988). Induction. In R. J. Sternberg and E. E. Smith (Eds). *The psychology of human thought*, pp. 50–91. Cambridge: Cambridge University Press.

Isen, A. M. (1984). The influence of positive affect on decision making and cognitive organization. In T. Kinnear (Ed.), *Advances in consumer research*, Vol. 11, pp. 530–533. Provo, UT: Association for Consumer Research.

Isen, A. M. (1987). Positive affect, cognitive processes, and social behavior. In L. Berkowitz (Ed.), *Advances in experimental social Psychology*, Vol. 20, pp. 203–253. New York: Academic Press.

Isen, A. M. and Daubman, K. A. (1984). The influence of affect on catgorization. *Journal of Personality and Social Psychology*, **47**, 1206–1217.

Isen, A. M., Daubman, K. A., and Gorgolione, J. M., (1986). The influence of positive affect on cognitive organization. In R. Snow and M. Farr (Eds), *Aptitude, learning and instruction: Affective and conative processes*. Hillsdale, NJ: Erlbaum.

Isen, A. M., Means, B., Patrick, R., and Nowicki, G. (1982). Some factors influencing decision making strategy and risk-taking. In M. S. Clark and S. T. Fiske (Eds), *Affect and cognition: The 17th Annual Carnegie Mellon Symposium on Cognition*. Hillsdale, NJ: Erlbaum.

Izard, C. E. (1977). *Human emotions*. New York: Plenum Press.

Johnson, E., and Tversky, A. (1983). Affect, generalization, and the perception of risk. *Journal of Personality and Social Psychology*, **45**, 20–31.

Kelly, G. (1955). *The psychology of personal constructs*. New York: Norton.

Keltner, D., and Audrain, P. (1988). Moods, emotions, and well-being judgments. Unpublished manuscript: Stanford University.

Kuhl, J. (1983). Emotion, Kognition und Motivation—II. *Sprache und Kognition*, **4**, 228–253.

Lacey, J. I., and Lacey, B. C. (1970). Some autonomic nervous system relationships. In P. Black (Ed.), *Physiological correlates of emotion*, pp. 205–227. New York: Academic Press.

Mackie, D. M., and Worth, L. T. (1989). Cognitive deficits and the mediation of positive affect in persuasion. *Journal of Personality and Social Psychology*, **57**, 27–40.

Oatley, K., and Johnson-Laird, P. N. (1987). Towards a cognitive theory of emotions. *Cognition and Emotion*, **1**, 29–50.

Obrist, P. A. (1981). *Cardiovascular psychophysiology*. New York: Plenum Press.

Ortony, A., Clore, G. L., and Collins, A. (1988). *The cognitive structure of emotions*. London: Cambridge University Press.

Petty, R. E., and Cacioppo, J. T. (1986a). The elaboration likelihood model of persuasion. In L. Berkowitz (Ed.), *Advances in Experimental Social Psychology*, Vol. 19, pp. 124–203. Orlando: Academic Press.

Petty, R. E., and Cacioppo, J. T., (1986b). *Communication and persuasion: Central and peripheral routes to attitude change*. New York: Springer.

Ruehlman, L. S., West, S. G., and Pasahow, R. J. (1985). Depression and evaluative schemata. *Journal of Personality*, **53**, 46–92.

Schwarz, N. (1987). *Stimmung als Information: Untersuchungen zum Einfluß von Stimmungen auf die Bewertung des eigenen Lebens*. Heidelberg: Springer.

Schwarz, N. (1988). Stimmung als Information. Zum Einfluß von Stimmungen auf evaluative Urteile. *Psychologische Rundschau*, **39**, 148–159.

Schwarz, N. (1990). Feelings as information. Informational and motivational functions of affective states. In R. Sorrentino and E. T. Higgins (Eds), *Handbook of motivation and cognition*, Vol. 2, pp. 527–561. New York: Guilford Press.

Schwarz, N., Bless, H., and Bohner, G. (in press). Mood and persuasion: affective states influence the processing of persuasive communication. In: M. Zanna (Ed.) *Advances in Experimental Social Psychology*, Vol. 24, New York: Academic Press.

Schwarz, N., and Clore, G. L. (1983). Mood, misattribution, and judgments of well-being:

Informative and directive functions of affective states. *Journal of Personality and Social Psychology*, **45**, 513–523.

Schwarz, N., and Clore, G. L. (1988). How do I feel about it? Informative functions of affective states. In K. Fiedler and J. Forgas (Eds), *Affect, cognition, and social behavior*. Toronto: Hogrefe.

Schwarz, N., Kommer, D., and Lessle, N. (1987). Covariation perception as a function of mood states. Unpublished manuscript: University of Heidelberg.

Schwarz, N., Servay, W. and Kumpf, M. (1985). Attribution of arousal as a mediator of the effectiveness of fear-arousing communications. *Journal of Applied Social Psychology*, **15**, 74–78.

Schwarz, N. Strack, F. Kommer, D. and Wagner, D. (1987). Soccer, rooms and the quality of your life: Mood effects on judgments of satisfaction with life in general and with specific life-domains. *European Journal of Social Psychology*, **17**, 69–79.

Sinclair, R. C. (1988). Mood, categorization breadth, and performance appraisal: The effect of order of information acquisition and affective state on halo, accuracy, information retrieval, and evaluations. *Organizational Behavior and Human Decision Processes*, **42**, 22–46.

Srull, T. K. (1983). Affect and memory: The impact of affective reactions in advertising on the representation of product information in memory. In R. Bagozzi and A. Tybout (Eds.), *Advances in consumer research*, Vol. 10. Ann Arbor, MI: Association for Consumer Research.

Srull, T. K. (1984). The effects of subjective affective states on memory and judgment. In T. Kinnear (Ed.), *Advances in consumer research*, Vol. 11, pp. 530–533. Provo, UT: Association for Consumer Research.

Srull, T. K., and Wyer, R. S. (1986). The role of chronic and temporary goals in information processing. In R. M. Sorrentino and E. T. Higgins (Eds), *Handbook of motivation and cognition: Foundations of social behavior*. New York: Guilford Press.

Stein, N. L., and Levine, L. J. (1987). Thinking about feelings: The development and organization of emotional knowledge. In R. E. Snow and M. J. Farr (Eds), *Aptitude, learning, and instruction: Conative and affective processes*, Vol. 3, pp. 165–197. Hillsdale, NJ: Erlbaum.

Strack, F., Schwarz, N., and Gschneidinger, E. (1985). Happiness and reminiscing: The role of time perspective, mood, and mode of thinking. *Journal of Personality and Social Psychology*, **49**, 1460–1469.

Wegner, D. M., and Vallacher, R. R. (1986). Action identification. In R. M. Sorrentino and E. T. Higgins (Eds.), *Handbook of motivation and cognition: Foundations of social behavior*. New York: Guilford Press.

Weiner, B. (1985). An attributional theory of achievement motivation and emotion. *Psychological Review*, **92**, 548–573.

Worth, L. T., and Mackie, D. M. (1987). Cognitive mediation of positive affect in persuasion. *Social Cognition*, **5**, 76–94.

Zajonc, R. B. (1980). Feeling and thinking: Preferences need no inferences. *American Psychologist*, **35**, 151–175.

4

The Joint Effects of Cognition and Affect on Social Judgment

MARTIN F. KAPLAN

Northern Illinois University, USA

Contents

Events can simultaneously produce cognition and affect. Social judgment is a joint product of both. In the literature, all possible relationships between cognition and affect have been proposed. One view is that affect has precedence and influences cognition by distortion, producing selective attention to information, or cueing and priming stored cognitions. Bower (1981, this volume) proposes an associative network model in which emotions are the nodes of the network; emotional cues facilitate retrieval of information. Another view is that affect is influenced by cognitions which give meaning to undifferentiated emotional arousal (see, for example, Schachter and Singer, 1962). Disputing this widely held conclusion, Anderson (1989) suggests that evidence that the interpretation of emotion always requires cognitive structuring is faulty. A third view is that the two are "under the control of separate and partially independent systems that can influence each other in a variety of ways . . . both constitute independent sources of effects in information processing" (Zajonc, 1980).

The question of whether one or the other is more basic (see Zajonc, 1984) may not be pertinent to an understanding of the contribution of cognition and affect to social judgment if we adopt Anderson's (1989) and Schwarz and Clore's (1983, 1988) proposal that both serve as relevant sources of information about the target person. According to Schwarz and Clore, affective states inform us of our reactions to others, and thus have the same conceptual status as cognitions in contributing to our judgments. The Schwarz and Clore formulation descends from an earlier assertion by Kaplan and Anderson (1973) that affect-inducing events (e.g. reinforcements) are sources of information in the same manner as are cognitive events. Schwarz and Clore extended the earlier Kaplan and Anderson assertion by specifying the manner by which affect informs: it is a shorthand way of informing us about our reaction to the person. People use the most readily available information for judgment, and one's momentary affective state is readily available. Kaplan and Anderson had in mind a more direct informative function whereby the affect tells us something about the nature (e.g. pleasing or not) of the person and the social interaction. Both conceptions view affect as informing about qualities of the other person; the former suggests that this information is mediated by the subjective emotional experience.

The various treatments of affect and cognition seem to revolve around different views of whether the two operate by means of a single or separate process systems, and within the system(s), different views of the role of affect in judgment. For Bower (1981) and Isen *et al.* (1982), emotional cues facilitate retrieval of similar cognitive memories ("mood-congruent" retrieval). Branscombe (this volume) suggests that under some conditions affect may also interfere with information processing. In addition to this role as a mediator of information processing, Anderson (1989), Kaplan and Anderson (1973) and Schwarz and Clore (1988), suggest that affect is itself information, and not only a mediator for retrieval. Schwarz and Clore assign a particularly salient role to affective states: they are judgment-simplifying devices used when conditions favor automatic processing (see also Branscombe, 1988).

Treating affect as a source of information does not preclude its role in information storage and retrieval as detailed in the associative network model (Bower, 1981). Affect may serve both as a source of information about the target person *and* as a facilitator in storing and retrieving prior cognitions. Once affect-assisted material is retrieved and available, the next stage addresses the question of how this material is integrated with contemporaneous cognitions and informative emotions into a social judgment.

Many studies show affect, i.e. moods and emotions, to influence judgments of others, the self, and life in general. Taking the view that affect serves the same informative end result as cognition by invoking thoughts relevant to the judgment, we are faced with the important question of how affects and cognitions aggregate to produce judgment. That is, how does a mood or emotional state combine with systematically varied cognitive information, whether it is contemporaneous or retrieved from prior storage? This question, central to more purely cognitive treatments of social judgment (e.g. Anderson, 1989; Kaplan, 1975), has been lost in the debate over whether affect, cognition, or neither is primary. Perhaps another reason the integration question has been ignored is hinted at in the Bower and Branscombe chapters in this volume: feelings and thoughts *seem* so different, so much like apples and oranges. But the differential experience of affect and cognition does not preclude treating them in the same conceptual system (see Anderson, 1989; Branscombe, 1988; Schwarz and Clore, 1988). In the case of cognitive stimuli, judgments are multiply determined. If emotional stimuli are also informative, they contribute to the multiple causation of judgment within the same process, and thus a prime though neglected question becomes how are these multiple stimuli, whether from cognitive and emotional sources, integrated into judgment? This issue is the subject of this chapter.

Integration of Affect and Cognition

Most early studies of affect arousal and social judgment (e.g. Gouaux, 1971; Gouaux and Summers, 1973; Griffitt, 1970) did not ask the integration question. This is largely because they did not consider affective states as informative, but instead interpreted their effects by a classical conditioning model (Byrne *et al.*, 1973) wherein positive and negative affect are internal stimuli which are conditioned to previously neutral social stimuli (persons) when the latter are contiguously paired with the source of the affect. Kaplan and Anderson (1973) rejected a reinforcement-conditioning model as too narrow for social judgment, and instead proposed a cognitive integration interpretation for these early studies, which treats emotional stimuli the same as cognitive stimuli, reducing both to their scale values for the judgment (see below for a more detailed exposition). A similar cognitive interpretation is implied in Schwarz and Clore's treatment (1988, this volume), though they are unclear with respect to the process of integration.

In order to capture the process by which elements are combined into a judgment, the elements must first be represented by a common property. This is important to the Schwarz and Clore model, for how do we combine two vastly different elements—emotion and knowledge—even if they serve a similar function? The means is the *scale value*, or the evaluation of that element on the dimension of judgment. If, for example, the dimension being judged is the person's likability, any piece of information, whether a cognitive belief about the person or an emotional feeling aroused by or in the presence of the person, can be represented by the value of that information on a quantitative likability dimension. The knowledge that person X is a fan of Gershwin's music has a likability value just as does the good feeling in my stomach when I see her. Given this common scale value metric, it is possible to integrate such disparate elements as hot flushes due to sexual arousal, warm feelings upon seeing a smile, and cold knowledge of musical tastes.

Each piece of information also has a weight, which refers to the effective importance in contributing to the overall judgment. For example, were I considering inviting person X to a concert, information about her musical tastes would carry more weight than information about my state of sexual arousal.

Finally, we take into account the integration rule. This is the algebraic function, empirically derived, that describes how the weighted scale values are combined. This function is often, though not exclusively, a weighted average of the scale values.

In addressing the integration question empirically, I will turn to two studies I conducted several years ago. While originally aimed at different issues, they are relevant to the question before us. Before turning to the studies, it is useful to consider a distinction between moods and emotions posed by Schwarz and Clore (1988). Moods are characterized as general feelings having indiscriminate effects on judgment (much like "halo" effects). Emotions are more distinctive, have an identifiable cause, are of relatively short duration, and have specific effects on judgment. We will see that, as Schwarz and Clore suspect, these variants of affect have different effects on judgment.

Two experiments on the integration of affect and cognition

In the first study (Kaplan, 1981), positive or negative moods were induced by having subjects listen to a radio broadcast casually turned on by the experimenter while they were completing some innocuous forms. The broadcast appeared to be an editorial feature (or in the case of the control condition, some emotionally neutral music) embedded in a musical program. In actuality, the manipulation consisted of one of three tapes which defined the mood condition. One broadcast was of emotionally neutral, popular music (*control condition*). Another broadcast was a commentary on humankind by a radio columnist in which the wicked deeds in human history were recounted. People were painted as nasty creatures who are responsible for the cited misfortunes (*negative mood condition*). The third broadcast mentioned adversities similar to the second, but was optimistic about people, showing how the human race always perseveres in the face of adversity and overcomes the difficulties posed by a cruel world to triumph in the end. People in this condition were depicted as good and just (*positive mood condition*). The reader familiar with Ma Joad's optimistic speech at the end of the novel *Grapes of Wrath* will grasp the flavor of this condition. After the broadcasts, subjects were exposed to a confederate who professed attitudes either similar or dissimilar to those of the subject on either three or six topics. The attitudes were communicated via an intercom under the pretext that we were studying opinion polling procedures, and we wanted to see whether procedures could be improved and candor enhanced by having the pollster also share his own attitudes on the issues. Attitudes were constructed so that the other person (the "pollster") either agreed or disagreed with the subject on two-thirds of either three or six issues representing a broad range of topics. The subject first read an assertion into the intercom (e.g. "there should be one national presidential primary rather than the present system of several statewide primaries"), then reported his/ her agreement or disagreement, and finally gave three statements supporting that position. The pollster then did the same for that issue; the supportive statements were gleaned from relevant attitude scales. The subject was led to believe that communication was with an actual person in the next room, via intercom, but actually a tape of the pollster's responses was played on the intercom. This process of reporting attitudes and supportive statements, first by the subject and then by the pollster, was repeated for all three (or six) issues. Subsequently, subjects responded to a questionnaire about the polling in which were embedded several items assessing the subject's liking for the pollster. Ten subjects appeared in each cell of the mood (control, negative, positive) by agreement (2/3, 1/3) by number of issues (3, 6) design.

We were not startled to find that liking for the confederate was affected both by induced mood and attitude similarity. We were also unsurprised, though pleased, to find a set-size effect, that is, that liking or disliking was more extreme for six attitudes than for three. What did surprise was that set-size (six versus three) did not interact with induced mood. If mood-as-information is averaged with cognitive information, the effect of mood should decrease with an increase in the amount (three versus six) of the latter. But it did not; the mood effect remained constant. More about this soon.

The second study was of a simulated jury decision (Kaplan and Miller, 1978). In a realistic courtroom setting, juries of 12 subjects each served in reenacted trials. Two basic cases were enacted: one in which the evidence favored the defendant, and the other in which it favored the prosecution. Jurors were told that we were reenacting actual trials, and were investigating whether mock juries that were given shortened trials, in which the less essential testimony was eliminated, would duplicate the verdicts of real juries. Juries were led to believe at the outset that the experiment would last less than an hour. This promise was true only for the control condition. In three other conditions, the trial was lengthened (and juror frustration deepened) by annoying delays, redundancy, and theatrics. Conditions differed as to whether the source of the frustration/delay was the defense attorney, the prosecutor, or neutral parties (judge and experimenter). After trial, jurors individually reached a verdict and decided on *degree* of apparent guilt, and then deliberated to a group decision on these judgments. Two findings are interesting. First, the affect induced by annoying conditions produced more negative judgments of the defendant (compared with controls) *before* deliberation, but only when the source of annoyance was the defense attorney or the judge. This suggests a cognitive property to the emotion that links it with specific sources. Second, emotional arousal had no effect on judgments made *after* deliberation, that is, verdicts and degree-of-guilt judgments of the juries that were annoyed by the prosecutor or judge converged to the levels of the control juries in both the incriminating and exonerating cases. This suggests that the added information provided by discussion reduced the effect of negative emotional information, as it would in information averaging.

Together, the two studies tell something about the combination of affective and cognitive elements. In the radio study, an undifferentiated mood was invoked, and it had general, additive effects on judgment. That is, increasing the amount of cognitive information did not decrease the mood effect. In the jury study, a more specific emotion was induced: annoyance with a trial participant. Schwarz and Clore (1988) suggest that specific emotions invoke thoughts relevant to the judgment. Such emotions should therefore be integrated in the same manner as cognitions, i.e. averaged. And they were, in the sense that increasing the amount of other information by means of deliberation decreased the contribution of affect.

This interpretation of the studies extends Schwarz and Clore's (1988) differentiation between mood and emotion to the process of their integration with cognitive stimuli in social judgment. Mood exerts a general halo on judgment that persists in the face of increased cognitive information. Emotion, on the other hand, has specific informational properties that are averaged with cognitive information. To speculate a bit, mood may have its effect at the time of judgment, in that it is added as a constant to whatever judgment would have been reached from other information. This conflicts with Bower's (1981) conclusion that mood activates specific knowledge components. But if this were so, and if these knowledge elements are integrated into judgment, why are they added, and not averaged as any other knowledge? The first study described here suggests that mood behaves differently than emotion when integrated with cognitive knowledge of the target person. Emotion, on the other hand, may have its effect at the encoding stage, since its informativeness is linked to a specific source, and it obeys the same combination rule as other encoded cognitive information.

The two studies differ not only in the arousal of undifferentiated mood versus specific emotion, but may also differ in the sheer intensity of emotional arousal. It may be that where affective intensity is high, cognitive elements, that is, information about the target person, would have less impact and information set size would produce negligible effects (as found in the radio study). It is difficult to calibrate the affective intensity across studies since different assessments were made. In the radio study, subjects in the negative condition reported more negative feelings about the experiment on a rating scale, and in the jury study subjects expressed extreme annoyance in experimental conditions in a postexperimental interview. Though the two degrees of affective intensity cannot be directly compared, it is plausible that greater arousal was present in the jury study where distressful conditions were more personally relevant. However, it was in this study that that information set size had an effect, ruling out an interpretation based solely on greater intensity attenuating the effect of added information. It appears, instead, that the *quality* of arousal, rather than the *quantity*, affects the interaction of affective and cognitive elements in the directions observed in the two experiments. A more definitive answer awaits a study which co-varies intensity and type of arousal (mood or emotion) in the same paradigm and measures intensity with a common metric.

A Methodological Note

Findings suggest a means to differentiate between general and cognitively mediated effect: one can observe whether their effects can be modified by increased relevant information about the target person. The effects of specific emotions are more likely to be reduced by increased information set size. The use of a set-size strategy has another benefit as well. It can diagnose the relative strength of induced emotional states. For example, Forgas and Bower (1988) found that positive mood induction had a greater effect than negative induction on social judgments. This is a step toward answering the integration question, but it is not conclusive since weight of any element is relative to that of other elements and is best determined by comparing the effect of one component to others with which it is being combined. It may be, for example, that one induction manipulation was simply stronger than another, or that moods and social judgments were measured on scales with different origins or intervals, or that as Forgas suggests, social norms toward positive public expression may come into play.

A strategy to test whether positive moods are more impactful on social judgments would be to co-vary the amount of cognitive information, the scale value of the information, and the mood induction. The paradigm would require the construction of several sets of stimuli, equivalent to one another in mean value of positivity or negativity but varying in the number of descriptors. For example, one target is described by two positive traits, another by four positive traits, and another by six traits, the three sets equated for mean positive value. The same pattern would be followed for sets of negative traits so that the positive and negative sets are equivalent in extremity, that is, the positive sets are each as extremely positive in the normative value of component descriptors as is the extremity of the negative sets (see Kaplan, 1972, for examples). Persons who have been subject to emotional induction would be asked to judge targets described by these sets.

Emotional states, as initial impressions, are averaged with the value of the information (Kaplan, 1975, 1976) leading to a number of consequences. First, increased set size (i.e. from two to four to six descriptors) would produce a greater increase in the polarity of judgments of sets opposite in valence to that of the induced emotion, compared to same-valence sets. That is, if positive emotion has been induced, the increase in negativity of judgment as one progresses from two to four to six negative descriptors would be greater than the increase in positivity of judgment from two to four to six positive descriptors, and the reverse for negative emotional induction. Second, the relative difference in set-size polarity between emotion congruent and incongruent sets would vary with the intensity of the emotion. More intense arousal should produce greater polarization of the opposite valence sets, and less polarization of the same valence sets, compared with less intense arousal. For example, if induced positive arousal has been more intense (Forgas and Bower, 1988), the increment in negative judgment by positively aroused subjects when negative stimulus information is increased should be greater than the increment in positive judgment by negatively aroused subjects given an increase in positive information. And conversely, positively aroused subjects should show *less* set-size polarization for positive information sets than would negatively aroused subjects for negative information sets. Were negative and positive emotions equally intense, set-size polarization for arousal-congruent information would be equivalent for both induction groups, as would polarization for arousal-incongruent information. Thus, such a set-size strategy can potentially assess whether one emotional state is more intense than another.

Affect in the Form of Dispositional Traits

Treatment of affect in social judgment need not be limited to temporally induced mood and emotional *states*. Affect may also be represented by more enduring *traits*. This distinction is similar to Bower's (1981) study of depression as a mood and as a long-term state. I have dealt with these in the form of general judgmental predispositions, e.g. a tendency to evaluate others in a positive or negative way (Kaplan, 1975, 1976). At first glance, these judgmental dispositions may seem to qualify as *moods*, but they may also be reasonably considered to be emotions, with specific informational referents. Congruent with the latter form of affect, dispositions are identified by asking people to indicate their beliefs about the traits possessed by "people in general." The beliefs are indexed by having subjects select characteristics they believe to be possessed by "typical" others from a checklist containing normatively positive, neutral, and negative characteristics (Kaplan, 1976). This dispositional checklist appears to assess a relatively stable trait characteristic, yielding a test–retest correlation of 0.63 for scale scores, as well as obtaining a good split-half reliability coefficient (0.78) (Kaplan, 1976). Consistent with findings in the jury study and with our analysis of emotional *states* as forms of information, *trait* dispositions are averaged with cognitive information in forming social judgments. The impact on judgment of one's disposition decreases as either the *weight* or *amount* of cognitive information about the target increases (Kaplan, 1975). Thus, affect considered as a trait interacts with cognitive information in a manner similar to emotional states.

These findings extend to jury decision making. Parallel to the study of juror emotional *states* described earlier, when juror *dispositional traits* toward leniency or stringency are identified, e.g. by use of trait measures such as Authoritarianism, and the Attitude toward Punishment of Criminals Scale, they too are averaged with cognitive information about the defendant. That is, dispositions for leniency or stringency have less impact on juror verdicts when trial evidence is strong (i.e. reliable) (Kaplan, 1982).

It is notable that affective traits obey the interactionism rule for personality variables (Ekehammar, 1974; Ender and Magnusson, 1976). The impact of affective dispositions on social judgments depends on the strength and amount of information about the target, implicating a personality by situation interaction. The same interaction was true for affect as an induced state when the state was specific to the target, but not when it was in the form of a general mood. Thus, global moods may act more as generalized personality variables, exerting a consistent effect on social judgments across situations whereas trait and state emotion effects vary with the situation. Maybe that is why moods are often labeled "halos"!

Concluding Remarks

Social judgments are affected by multiple determinants. Several cognitions and one or more affective states may jointly affect a single judgment. A central question is how the multiple determinants combine to produce social judgments. The question is more easily approached when we consider that both affective states and cognitions inform us about the target person. Affect can take the form of more or less temporary states (moods, emotions) or more long-term dispositional traits. Asking how affective and cognitive information are integrated leads to the interesting possibility that moods and emotions are processed differently, though both can still be considered as sources of information and thus possess scale value and weight, and are subject to integration rules (though perhaps different rules). Observing how affective states and traits are combined with cognitive information that systematically varies in scale values, weights, and amount can shed light on different forms of affect, and on the relative impact of different affective states and traits.

References

Anderson, N. H. (1989). Information integration approach to emotions and their measurement. In R. Plutchik and H. Kellerman (Eds), *Emotion: Theory, research, and experience*, Vol. 4, pp. 133–186. New York: Academic Press.

Bower, G. H. (1981). Mood and memory. *American Psychologist*, **36**, 129–148.

Branscombe, N. (1988). Conscious and unconscious processing of affective and cognitive information. In K. Fiedler and J. P. Forgas (Eds), *Affect, cognition, and social behavior*, pp. 3–24. Toronto: Hogrefe.

Byrne, D., Clore, G. L., Griffitt, W., Lamberth, J., and Mitchell, H. E. (1973). When research paradigms converge: Confrontation or integration? *Journal of Personality and Social Psychology*, **28**, 313–320.

Ekehammar, B. (1974). Interactionism in personality from a historical perspective. *Psychological Bulletin*, **81**, 1026–1048.

Ender, N. S., and Magnusson, D. (1976). Toward an interactional psychology of personality. *Psychological Bulletin*, **83**, 956–974.

Forgas, J. P., and Bower, G. H. (1988). Mood effects on person perception judgments. *Journal of Personality and Social Psychology*, **54**, 697–703.

Gouaux, C. (1971). Induced affective states and interpersonal attraction, *Journal of Personality and Social Psychology*, **20**, 37–43.

Gouaux, C., and Summers, K. (1973). Interpersonal attraction as a function of affective state and affective change. *Journal of Research in Personality*, **7**, 254–260.

Griffitt, W. (1970). Environmental effects on interpersonal behavior: Ambient effective temperature and attraction. *Journal of Personality and Social Psychology*, **15**, 240–244.

Isen, A. M., Means, B., Patrick, R., and Nowicki, G. (1982). Some factors influencing decision-making strategy and risk taking. In M. S. Clark and S. T. Fiske (Eds), *Affect and cognition*, 243–261. Hillsdale NJ: Erlbaum.

Kaplan, M. F. (1972). The modifying effect of stimulus information on the consistency of individual differences in impression formation. *Journal of Experimental Research in Personality*, **6**, 213–219.

Kaplan, M. F. (1975). Information integration in social judgment: Interaction of judge and information components. In M. F. Kaplan and S. Schwartz (Eds) *Human judgment and decision processes*, pp. 139–171). New York: Academic Press.

Kaplan, M. F. (1976). Measurement and generality of response dispositions in person perception. *Journal of Personality*, **44**, 179–194.

Kaplan, M. F. (1981). State dispositions in social judgment. *Bulletin of the Psychonomic Society*, **18**, 27–29.

Kaplan, M. F. (1982). Cognitive processes in the individual juror. In N. L. Kerr and R. M. Bray (Eds). *The psychology of the courtroom*, pp. 197–220. New York: Academic Press.

Kaplan, M. F., and Anderson, N. H. (1973). Information integration theory and reinforcement theory as approaches to interpersonal attraction. *Journal of Personality and Social Psychology*, **28**, 301–312.

Kaplan, M. F., and Miller, L. E. (1978). Reducing the effects of juror bias. *Journal of Personality and Social Psychology*, **36**, 1443–1455.

Schachter, S., and Singer, J. (1962). Cognitive, social, and physiological determinants of emotional state. *Psychological Review*, **65**, 379–399.

Schwarz, N., and Clore, G. L. (1983). Mood, misattribution and judgments of well-being: Informative and directive functions of affective states. *Journal of Personality and Social Psychology*, **45**, 513–523.

Schwarz, N., and Clore, G. L. (1988). How do I feel about it? The informative function of affective states. In K. Fiedler and J. P. Forgas (Eds) *Affect, cognition, and social behavior*. Toronto: Hogrefe.

Zajonc, R. B. (1980). Feeling and thinking: Preferences need no inferences. *American Psychologist*, **35**, 151–175.

Zajonc, R. B. (1984). On the primacy of affect. *American Psychologist*, **39**, 117–123.

5

On the Task, the Measures and the Mood in Research on Affect and Social Cognition

KLAUS FIEDLER

University of Giessen

Contents

It seems that recent research on affect and cognition has shifted away from the theoretical clarification of basic issues towards applications in social and clinical psychology. Basic theoretical concepts and empirical phenomena such as *mood congruency* or *state-dependent learning* are taken for granted as approved principles to be applied or transferred into other paradigms such as *self-efficacy* (Kavanagh and Bower, 1985), *close relationships* (Bradbury and Fincham, 1987), *persuasion* (Petty; Schwarz, this volume), *social-cognitive development* (Forgas *et al.*, 1988), and as much as ever, of course, *depression research* (Ingram, 1984). This clearly testifies to the fruitfulness of the affect-cognition approach and the impact it has had on diverse fields of modern psychology.

Unfortunately, the empirical evidence for the "classical" mood effects on memory, person judgment and social interaction is not that unequivocal. For instance, consider the general principle of mood congruency (Bower *et al.*, 1981; Isen *et al.*, 1978), that is, the selective processing of pleasant information under good mood and unpleasant information under negative mood in memory and social judgment tasks (Isen, 1984). On the one hand, there are several failures to replicate mood congruency under conditions expected to produce this basic phenomenon (Bower and Mayer, 1985; Hasher *et al.*, 1985; Mecklenbrauker and Hager, 1984). On the other hand, the theoretical attempts to account for such unexpected results are often unsatisfactory, resting on *ad hoc* or *post hoc* assumptions. It is commonly accepted by now that affective states do *not* have an influence under all task conditions. However, our *a priori* knowledge of the exact conditions under which cognitive processes will reflect emotional processes is still remarkably meager.

An attempt to figure out the crucial moderator variables in the mood and cognition literature may well end in confusion. For instance, we are told that failures to demonstrate mood-congruent memory may reflect too weak a mood manipulation (Mayer and Bower, 1985), suggesting mood intensity as a central moderator. At the same time, however, we are surprised by the apparent weakness and incidental nature of affective events that often suffice to produce the same cognitive effects as hypnosis and clinical depression (Isen *et al.*, 1978; Schwarz and Clore, 1988). We learn about the asymmetrically stronger mood congruency effect of positive as opposed to depressed mood (Isen, 1984, 1985), but at the same time we find the most important application in the field of depression. On the theoretical level, mood-selective cognition is explained in terms of activation in an associative network spreading out from an active mood node to associated cognitions (Bower and Cohen, 1982; Singer and Salovey, 1988) so that we think of an automatic (neurological) process that should be hard to control or influence voluntarily. However, we hardly feel much dissonance when we hear about motivated processes which counteract the associative processes [e.g. avoidance of negative contents in depressed mood to improve one's mood state (Isen, 1984)].

In spite of these critical allusions, I am not going to portray a pessimistic picture of the affect and cognition literature. Rather, I shall present a theoretical perspective from which many unexpected or seemingly inconsistent findings may be explained and become intelligible. This perspective, which is loosely called a *dual-force* model and which is described in more detail elsewhere (Fiedler, 1990), will be outlined in the first section of this article. It leads to the central working hypothesis that emotional states will influence cognitive processes to the extent that the cognitive task involves the active generation of new information as opposed to the passive conservation of information given. Also I provide a brief synopsis of empirical findings that can be accounted for by this working hypothesis. Afterwards, I try to develop and illustrate some implications that this perspective has regarding *mood-sensitive task characteristics, effective mood manipulations* and different *dependent measures* used to capture emotional influences. Accordingly, the remaining three sections are devoted to the task, the measures, and the mood in research on affect and social cognition. I discuss some relevant evidence, provide some new findings and point out some nontrivial implications that may be tested in future research.

Two Forces: Mere Conservation and Active Transformation

A few terminological conventions are helpful in explaining the dual-force perspective. Let us define a "cognitive process" as a translation from an information input to an output. Without loss of generality, any cognitive process can thus be conceived as involving two components or interacting forces, namely, *information conservation* and *active transformation*. As a precondition to all further processing, the stimulus input first has to be conserved (e.g. an image on the retina or a spoken sentence in short-term memory). Conservation is therefore necessary for the explication of a cognitive process, but not sufficient, because we would not experience a "process" nor could it be measured if no transformation or change of the input were involved. The transformation of the input into the output requires that the input be somehow related to other information, typically older knowledge (concepts, schemata, scripts), in memory. It is important to note the psychological asymmetry of conservation and transformation, the former being a premise of the latter. Moreover, conservation is a passive function whereas transformation involves active change and the creation of something new, leaving more degrees of freedom for subjective influences in the second component. My basic assumption is, therefore, that affective (as well as other motivational) influences take their primary effect on the active transformation component.

If mood influences would function on the conservation stage, this would roughly correspond to the *filter* metaphor of mood influences. According to the present perspective, however, mood effects on cognitions are not due to selective filtering in the conservation stage. Rather, the present account might be called a *generation* theory of mood effects, suggesting that mood states have their impact on whatever new information is actively generated. Note that, after all, an emotional state is a force within the subject; what the subject adds to or generates out of the input information in the course of mental transformations (judgments, decisions, imaginations, attributions) should therefore be most sensitive to subject states.

At the empirical level, this basic theoretical assumption can be translated into a generic working hypothesis giving rise to many testable predictions. This hypothesis states that mood influences on *productive* tasks (emphasizing active transformation more than conservation) are more pronounced than mood effects on *reproductive* tasks (which give much weight to conservation). The terms "reproductive" and "productive" refer to task characteristics in much the same way as "conservation" and "active transformation" refer to cognitive operations. Different tasks can be compared on the productive–reproductive dimension regarding the relative weight they give to the basic cognitive components. Whenever the ordinal positions of two tasks on this dimension are unequivocal, the theory predicts that the more productive task is more mood-sensitive than the task closer to the repro-ductive end. If tasks differ in too many respects to be ordered on the dimension, then no predictions can be derived.

The working hypothesis does not presuppose, to be sure, that *any and all* cognitive tasks can be represented on the same unidimensional productive-ness scale. Strong empirical tests are possible even if only *some* task characteristics or experimental manipulations are unequivocally related to the productive–reproductive distinction. For instance, there should be general agreement that free recall is a more productive task than cued recall, or even recognition, when all other aspects (stimulus material, time inter-vals, subjects, etc.) are held constant. Memory for ill-structured material is more productive than memory for highly prestructured material, other factors being equal. Similarly, memory-based judgments involve more production (active transformation, inferences, evaluations) than a memory test alone. Therefore, mood effects should be more pronounced with free recall than cued recall or recognition (Bower and Cohen, 1982; Gerrig and Bower, 1982), when the stimulus material is unstructured (Ellis, 1985; Fiedler and Stroehm, 1986), and social judgments may sometimes be more sensitive to mood effects than memory tests (Mayer and Salovey, 1988; Fiedler *et al.*, 1986).

Of course, there are also some less obvious, albeit equally interesting, predictions, for instance, that memory for pictures is less susceptible to mood influences than memory for symbolic (verbal) material if the view can be maintained that the representation of pictures in memory involves more (analogous) conservation and less active transformation than verbal stimuli. A plausible argument could also be that the productive nature of any cognitive task increases with self-reference, because self-reference means enrichment with evaluative reactions and a complex network of self-related knowledge (Brown and Taylor, 1986; Rogers *et al.*, 1977). Ego involvement, indeed, is essential to many spontaneous reactions and judgmental activi-ties. While these "predictions" are more plausible than logical, admittedly, they may be nevertheless of heuristic value.

Table 5.1 provides a summary of relevant empirical findings. The left column comprises a list of empirical conclusions which are related to the distinction of productive and reproductive tasks, and some pertinent refer-ences are given on the right. Many inconsistencies in the research literature and failures to obtain expected results may be explained or understood as an example of the moderator effects summarized in the table.

Let us now consider some new evidence, or reconsider some familiar evidence, against the background of this theoretical framework. The em-phasis here is placed on the heuristic impact of the dual-force approach rather than contrasting it with other conceptions. Nevertheless, while

TABLE 5.1   Summary of implications of a dual-force approach

Implication*	Sample reference
Recall test performance should be more susceptible to mood influences than recognition	Bower and Cohen (1982) Forgas *et al*. (1988) Gerrig and Bower (1982)
Ambivalent stimuli may be more mood-sensitive than evaluatively unambiguous material	
Self-related information facilitates rich encoding and deep processing and should therefore be mood-sensitive	Blaney (1986) Brown and Taylor (1986) Forgas, Bower, and Moylan (1990)
Memory-based *judgments* may reflect mood states more than measures of memory	Fiedler *et al*. (1986) Mayer and Salovey (1988)
Social instigation of mental activities such as in a *group discussion* may enhance mood congruity	Forgas (1990)
Motivated processes, in general, may override the associative proximity of mood and congruent information	Blaney (1986)
In particular, the motive for mood repair may inhibit the active processing of unpleasant information, causing an *asymmetry* for positive and negative mood	Isen (1984)
Unstructured material is more likely to reflect mood influences than highly structured material	Fiedler and Stroehm (1986) Ellis *et al*. (1984)
Self-generated information should enhance mood congruency.	Fiedler *et al*. (submitted)
Inhibition of mental *activity* (by drugs or pathological state) may eliminate mood congruency.	

*The critical features which are supposed to foster active, generative processes are printed in italic type.

alternative conceptions may also *account for* certain findings, the dual-force model is superior at *predicting* most of them.

Judgmental Activities Involved in Memory Tasks

When applying the above theoretical framework, the *minimal* experimental design has to include at least three factors pertaining to (a) the subject's mood, (b) the valence of the stimuli, and (c) the productive versus reproductive nature of the task. This is exactly the design we obtain if mood influences are examined within the so-called *generation effect* paradigm. The

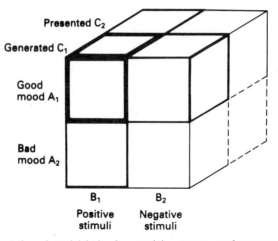

Fɪɢ 5.1   A three-factorial design for examining memory performance as a function of mood (factor A), stimulus valence (B) and active participation (C). The diameter of cell borders indicates the hypothesized memory strength.

generation effect (Gardiner and Hampton, 1985; Graf, 1982; Slamecka and Graf, 1978) refers to the general memory advantage of self-generated over received information as operationalized, for instance, by the comparison of words that have to be actively generated during learning (e.g. "accident" to be inferred from "-c--d-nt") versus words that simply have to be read. Despite some controversies on the theoretical explanation of the generation effect, there is wide agreement that memory for self-generated information is enhanced, and that this has important implications for applied disciplines. Furthermore, however, the underlying paradigm is ideally suited for testing the impact of mood on active judgmental operations during encoding. Thus, while judgments are usually treated as a consequence of memory (biases), the roles are reversed in the generation effect paradigm.

It is instructive to consider the different main effects and interactions that are possible in the three-factorial design depicted in Figure 5.1. It is interesting to recognize that all three main effects as well as all four interactions are either already well established or at least afford plausible hypotheses. As mentioned above, the main effect for factor C is usually called a *generation effect*. The main effect of the stimulus valence factor (B) is known as a *repression effect* (Bock, 1980; Zeller, 1950), that is, a general tendency to remember more pleasant than unpleasant information. Although somewhat forgotten and not always obtained (especially when negative stimuli are more salient), the repression effect exists as a potential bias obtained repeatedly. Finally, at least in recall measures, performance is often enhanced in a positive mood and reduced in a depressed mood (Ellis and Ashbrook, 1988; Strömgren, 1977); this main effect for factor A may be termed a *depression* effect.

The common *mood-congruency* effect (Bower, 1981; Riskind, 1983) amounts to an A × B interaction, and the present working hypothesis that mood congruency is enhanced for productive tasks corresponds to the A × B × C three-way interaction. In other words, the A × B congruency effect should be more pronounced for C_1 and C_2. There are good reasons, however, to suspect that repression will also be reinforced in a generation task, yielding a B × C interaction, and that the depression effect due to the general advantage of good mood will be more apparent for an active generation task, leading to an A × C interaction. These established or hypothesized effects are represented in Figure 5.1 in such a way that performance increases from the right back bottom (the dashed cell) of the cube to the left front top (the bold cell).

Such an asymmetry in a 2 × 2 × 2 design reflecting the dominance of one single cell (i.e. the left front top cell) implies that three basic effects combine in a *multiplicative* fashion: performance is maximal when mood is positive *and* the stimuli are pleasant *and* the task is a productive one. However, the three effects do not simply add up but reinforce each other: The generation effect is assumed to reinforce the repression effect and the depression (mood) effect is assumed to reinforce the repression and the generation effect. It then seems worthwhile to further pursue the question if there is really empirical support for the postulated effects.

Mood congruency and generation

Our first attempt to demonstrate a mood × valence × generation interaction in accordance with our working hypothesis originates in a preliminary experiment by Fiedler and Fladung (1989). As in all other studies to be reported, positive versus negative mood was manipulated using an approved procedure based on the imagination of a happy or sad life experience in a relaxed situation (cf. Fiedler, 1985, 1988; Fiedler and Stroehm, 1986). The effectiveness of the manipulation was checked by having "blind" judges rate the affective quality of the subject's associations to ambiguous cue words. The stimulus material in this experiment consisted of evaluatively positive or negative verbs (e.g. love, hate, abhor, help, hurt, etc.), which all describe interpersonal behaviors. Apart from the mood manipulation, there were three different task conditions. Subjects in the *productive* condition did not see any stimulus words but were asked to generate as many interpersonal verbs as they could from their lexical memory. In two *reproductive* conditions, participants were presented with all the verbs generated by the last two subjects in the productive condition (one from each mood group), after which a free-recall test was administered. Either the encoding mood or the retrieval mood was manipulated in

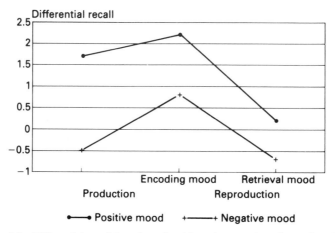

Fɪɢ 5.2   Differential recall (number of positive minus number of negative stimuli recalled) as a function of different memory tasks.

these two conditions. As shown in Figure 5.2, mood congruency is most pronounced for the productive condition, suggesting that actively generating evaluative verbal material is more susceptible to emotional influences than reproducing a list from episodic memory.

This first experiment has several shortcomings. First of all, memory performance had to be computed in terms of the absolute number of recalled items because proportions cannot be determined in the productive condition. Secondly, the interaction in Figure 5.2 was only marginally significant. And in the third place, the productive and reproductive conditions differ in too many respects to be directly comparable. In particular, the productive task has an idiosyncrasy advantage because subjects can select "their own" words. Nevertheless, the overall congruency effect is strong, and the demonstration is included here because the direct comparison of production and reproduction has some face validity.

The generation effect literature (cf. Slamecka and Graf, 1978) suggests how the methodology can be improved. To equate the information and the general task situation in all conditions, all participants should have to learn an experimentally controlled stimulus list. However, only part of the stimuli should appear in complete format while the remaining stimuli should have to be actively generated on the basis of incomplete fragments. This method allows the participants to generate part of the information and at the same time eliminates the idiosyncrasy advantage and maintains experimental control over the stimulus information.

In a recent experiment by Fiedler *et al.* (submitted), this improved methodology was employed. Participants were presented with a list of cue words followed by a target word of similar meaning (e.g. abhor → detest). All targets were either positive or negative in valence. Half of the cue-target

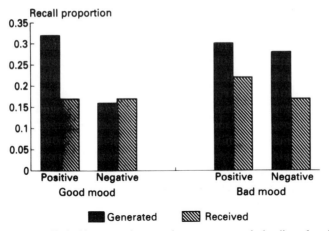

FIG 5.3   Recall of self-generated or experimenter-presented stimuli as a function of mood and valence.

pairs was presented fully; on the remaining trials, several letters of the target word were replaced by dashes and subjects had to infer the target. Note that the mood manipulation was administered immediately before the encoding phase, because it is at this time that the judgmental activity takes place.

The results appear in Figure 5.3. Mood congruency is not observed unless semantic judgments during encoding support the intrusion of mood influences. In addition to the critical three-way interaction involving mood × valence × encoding task, the generation and repression main effect are also significant. The most important conclusion from this pattern of results is that mood effects on recall are mediated by mood-congruent judgments during encoding.

Perhaps the most cogent evidence we have obtained up to now for the mood × valence × generation interaction stems from an experiment by Fiedler and Drommershausen (submitted), although it deviates from the typical generation paradigm. The underlying assumption here was that one main generative activity in many memory tasks consists of the construction of high-order encoding units from the singular stimuli. In particular, participants were presented with different sets of ten photographs each and were asked to form picture-stories from whatever subset of pictures they liked. The photographs portrayed either pleasant or unpleasant scenes. Immediately before the picture-story construction task, a positive or negative mood state was induced using the approved procedure. While the stimulus pictures were given by the experimenter, the story themes, as the main organizing units in memory, had to be actively created by the participants themselves. Thus, the subset of pictures that was incorporated into the stories was enriched with thematic associations and a link to the subject's "own" story theme, whereas the memory code of the remaining (excluded) pictures should not have included that self-generated component. Therefore, the mood congruency effect was predicted to be enhanced for, or perhaps confined to, the integrated subset of pictures. This prediction is obviously borne out by the results portrayed in Figure 5.4.

Thus, there is already some supportive evidence for the postulated three-way interaction, although strong experimental evidence is still rather scarce. It should also be noted that the highest three-way interaction in an asymmetric $2 \times 2 \times 2$ pattern with a single outstanding cell is often obscured by the ANOVA model, which displaces part of the effect into the main effects and lower interactions (cf. Rosenthal and Rosnow, 1985). Empirically, this means that sufficient statistical power is required to replicate and substantiate the postulated three-way interaction.

Repression, depression, and generation

Having treated the major (and most complex) prediction at some length, a few comments are in order regarding the lower-order effects in the design of Figure 5.1. There should be general agreement about the main effects. The generation effect is well documented in recent literature (Gardiner, 1988) and need not be reviewed here. Also, the general impairment of memory under depressed mood is well established and hardly debatable (Weingartner *et al.*, 1981). The repression effect has not received much attention in recent years, but it is also well alive. Although a meta-analysis has not been done to my knowledge, a synopsis of all relevant experiments would presumably indicate a general advantage of positive over negative information, at least in free recall. However, the evidence is somewhat mixed because the saliency or extremity of negative information may

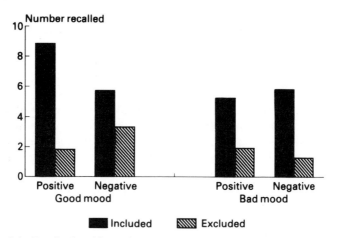

FIG 5.4   Recall of positive and negative pictures that have been included in, or excluded from, higher-order encoding units during positive or negative mood states.

counteract repression and sometimes lead to better recall of negative stimuli (e.g. Forgas *et al.*, 1988).

Little direct empirical support is available for the two-way interactions, apart from the familiar depression × repression effect known as mood congruency. However, the remaining two interactions are not only of heuristic interest but provide further empirical tests of the contention that all three effects combine multiplicatively.

The hypothesized depression × generation effect suggests greater impairment under depressed mood with productive tasks and is neatly illustrated in a recent article by Ellis and Ashbrook (1988). Although these authors use different terms, referring to productive tasks as "demanding," the evidence they present is compatible throughout with the present hypothesis. For instance, Ellis *et al.* (1984) investigated the influence of elaborative encoding on memory decrement under depressed mood and found greater decrement for contextually rich sentences requiring inferential and judgmental activity during encoding.

Another piece of evidence from our own research may be mentioned here. In a generation experiment in which the mood state at the time of retrieval was manipulated, the superiority of self-generated over received information was confined to the positive mood condition (Fiedler *et al.*, submitted). This finding may be of interest because it suggests a motivational component in the generation process.

Finally, the generation × repression hypothesis states that self-generated information should tend to be particularly positive. Although this prediction was hardly addressed directly, it is consistent with some subsidiary findings. For instance, the strongest effect in the picture-story experiment above was that positive pictures were much more likely to be incorporated into the stories than negative pictures, regardless of the subjects' mood. Also, in the verb-production condition of the Fiedler and Fladung (1989) experiment, positive verbs were more frequent than negative verbs, although the lexicon is somewhat biased in the opposite direction.

The Impact of Different Dependent Measures

A generally neglected issue in research on affect and cognition is the systematization of dependent measures, although many methodological tools are available from cognitive psychology, such as reaction-time and latency measures (Sternberg, 1969), the method of memory judgment (Hintzman, 1976), structural analyses of free recall protocols (Tulving, 1968), or the signal-detection methodology (Banks, 1970). The majority of studies employ some variant of a memory test or judgmental measures (Forgas and Bower, 1987), while behavioral measures were only occasionally used in the context of altruism (Aderman 1972; Bierhoff, 1988; Isen, 1970) or decision making (Isen *et al.*, 1982). However, many potentially interesting measures such as chronometric analyses, the ordinal positions in recall protocol, frequency judgments of pleasant and unpleasant information, or the forced recall of only positive or negative information were rarely considered, if at all. It is interesting to note, parenthetically, that some of these measures would be crucial for testing the common associative network account (Bower, 1981; Teasdale, 1983) which implies, for instance, that mood-congruent items should appear in clusters at the beginning of free-recall protocols. This seems to follow from any reasonable assumption about the way in which activation spreads in a semantically organized network. In our own research, we have routinely tested this hypothesis and virtually never found an accumulation of mood-congruent items in the first part of recall protocols. Thus, a more differentiated analysis of dependent measures would undoubtedly be of advantage.

In particular, the dependent measure determines in part the productive or reproductive nature of the experimental task. The general implication from our working hypothesis states that mood influences should be more apparent with dependent measures that leave many degrees of freedom for constructive memory, idiosyncratic selection and subjective judgments. This is completely in line with the aforementioned observation that mood effects on memory are almost never obtained with recognition tests but only with recall measures—typically, free recall, which leaves the most freedom for active search and construction (Bower and Cohen, 1982; Fiedler, 1990). Indeed, free recall may be considered as a means of communication or social judgment (Schuurmans and Vandierendonck, 1985).

Direct empirical support for this prediction is less frequent than the common agreement about it might suggest. The problem is that positive evidence for (free) recall and negative evidence for recognition are usually obtained in different studies using different manipulations and materials. Nevertheless, the asymmetry of outcomes is so impressive that the recall–recognition difference seems hardly debatable. Moreover, in two of our own experiments (e.g. Fiedler and Fladung, 1989, mentioned above), we included both measures in the same session but found mood congruency to be confined to free recall.

Mood effects need not disappear in recognition if productive task elements are built into a recognition test. For instance, a (nontrivial) prediction from the present account is that mood effects on recognition should be obtained if recognition involves, say, the presentation of blurred pictures or subliminal stimuli to be inferred by active (re)construction (cf. Postman and Brown, 1952).

Similarly, a cued-recall task, to be mood sensitive, would only have to be unrestrictive and invite active processes. In this regard, one might argue that many judgment tasks may be considered a productive version of cued recall. For example, if the stimuli consist of social behavior descriptions, the cues in a cued-recall memory test might be category labels such as "sociability," "altruism," "tolerance," and the same cues typically serve as scale labels in judgment tasks. The only difference is that cued-recall instructions emphasize the *specific* items associated with cues, whereas judgment tasks ask for an *abstract* (evaluative) summary of the associated information. The latter task invites interpretation and evaluation and it is no surprise, therefore, that memory-based judgments, conceived here as a productive variant of cued recall, are a highly sensitive measure of mood influences (Mayer and Salovey, 1988).

Any reluctance to accept a judgment task as an indicator of memory should be weighted against the adequacy of traditional memory tests. It is highly questionable whether a free-recall test will provide something like a copy of current memory contents, and there is hardly a real-life analogue to a free-recall test. Granting that memory is constructive in nature and its character is ever-changing, a memory test which says "now pour out all that you know" appears to be quite unrealistic. Moreover, it seems doubtful that this kind of test would reflect the sample or "snapshot" of memory which mediates complex cognitive processes such as judgments or decisions. Less exhaustive and more productive measures of memory which leave more degrees of freedom for subjective editing may afford more suitable means of grasping that aspect of memory which is utilized in the course of judgment formation. However, such measures should also be particularly prone to mood influences. A study by Fiedler and Fladung (1987) on the impact of mood on persuasion (see also Petty, this volume) may illustrate this point.

Participants listened to a videotaped discussion about the virtues and vices of a polygamous as opposed to a monogamous lifestyle. One of the two female discussants consistently argued in favor of polygamy while the other person argued for the opposite position. There was no hostility in the discussion, and the *pro* and *contra* arguments were matched for contents, so that one *pro* and one *contra* argument always referred to the same topic (e.g. "Polygamous relationships are more honest" but "the motive is egotism, however, not honesty"). Prior to the video communication, either a positive or a negative mood was induced. Results confirmed the general assumption that subjects in an elated mood state would be more susceptible to *pro* arguments favoring polygamy, while negative mood subjects should tend to agree with the more conservative arguments against polygamy.

However, not all the dependent measures were equally sensitive. There were two measures of memory for the arguments and two measures of attitude change. Only the less exhaustive, less constrained dependent measures reflected the influence of mood and the systematic relationship between memory and attitude change. Peformance on a free-recall test, for example, was not affected by the mood manipulation, presumably because the recall of coherent texts is too much determined by the internal structure to allow for mood effects (Ellis, 1985). Moreover, the thematic matching of *pro* and *contra* arguments may have prevented selective recall, because once a *pro* item is recalled the associated *contra* item is likely to be recalled, too. However, a second measure of "edited recall" was included which consisted of the retelling of the essential arguments to some other person. Note that this task leaves considerable freedom for mood-sensitive processes such as editing decisions or implicit judgments. In fact, the mood manipulation had an effect on this measure, with subjects in a good mood "recalling" more *pro* arguments than subjects in a bad mood.

Moreover, the number of *pro* minus *contra* arguments in this less restrictive measure turned out to be a better predictor of attitude change ($r = 0.49$) than the corresponding free-recall measure ($r = 0.35$), suggesting that edited recall is closer to the memory sample which actually determines persuasion. Most impressive, however, is the result for another, indirect, measure of persuasion. In addition to the rating scale measure of attitude change (referred to above), which may demand self-consistency and which may be too direct for subjects to admit that they are influenced on such an ego-involving topic, a more indirect (or projective) measure was included. Participants anticipated that they would have to engage in a discussion themselves and were asked to choose if they would like to argue for or against polygamy and to indicate the reasons for their choice. An indirect persuasion measure derived from their choice and explanation correlated $r = 0.39$ with selectivity in free recall and as high as $r = 0.75$ with the edited-recall measure. As it seems, less restrictive measures are not only mood-sensitive but also capture the way in which "edited memory" mediates social cognitive processes.

At the other extreme, a kind of "forced recall" could be utilized in such a way that people in a good or bad mood are forced to remember only positive or only negative information. Such a restrictive task reduces the subject's freedom to search in a mood-congruent direction and should therefore reduce the impact of mood. Forced recall, as well as the use of pay-offs for processing pleasant versus unpleasant information, may be an appropriate means of testing whether people *are not able* to or simply *not willing* to process mood-incongruent information. While the signal-detection methodology may be utilized to this purpose in a recognition paradigm (Zuroff *et al.*, 1983), forced processing of mood-congruent or mood-incongruent information may help to extend the logic of signal detection analyses to recall and social judgment tasks. If mood effects reflect response biases, they should be eliminated, or at least reduced, by deliberate instructions or pay-offs that act against mood congruency.

To conclude, this section on different dependent measures was intended to emphasize the dependency of emotional influences on the way in which the output of cognitive processes is prompted or assessed. Some evidence was presented to show that it is worthwhile to pay more attention to the dependent measures, and some open questions were raised. Assuming that affect operates on the active or generative components of cognitive processes, mood influences should be most apparent for unrestrained measurement procedures that leave much freedom for subjective strategies and selectivity. This is in fact what the available evidence suggests. Moreover, the present account, which may be termed a motivational account after all, suggests that cognitive effects of mood will turn out to depend on whether pay-offs or motivational forces reinforce or inhibit mood influences on active or generative processes. Perhaps the most prominent example of such motivated processes is the familiar finding of more congruency for positive than negative mood (cf. Isen, 1984).

Characteristics of an Effective Mood State

Having discussed the most sensitive task conditions and dependent measures, the question remains as to what constitutes an effective mood manipulation with maximal impact on memory and judgment. What are the crucial aspects of an emotional treatment which are most likely to guide the active transformation of given information in a mood-congruent direction? Is it the intensity of the emotion (Mayer and Bower, 1985), or distinct arousal patterns (Clark, 1982)? Or is it essential that the mood state is not attributed to an external source (Schwarz and Clore, 1988)? some empirical support is available for all these factors, which, solely for logical reasons, have to be relevant. Thus, if the intensity of an emotion decreases *ad infinitum*, any effect must vanish at some point. Likewise, the assumption of emotional arousal patterns can hardly be falsified altogether.

However, more remarkable than the potential relevance of these factors is the empirical conclusion that none of these factors can be considered a *necessary* condition for mood to take effect on social cognition. Thus, although several authors (e.g. Singer and Salovey, 1988) argue for the intensity principle, there is no systematic meta-analysis of empirical results to support this suggestion. On the contrary, it is often surprising how weak a mood manipulation can be and still suffice to influence cognition (Isen *et al.*, 1978; Johnson and Tversky, 1983; Schwarz and Clore, 1988). With regard to arousal, mood effects have also been shown to occur independently of excitation and even in deep relaxation (e.g. Fiedler and Stroehm, 1986).

If mood influences the active phases of cognitive processing, indeed, one would not necessarily expect highly intense emotions to exert the strongest effect. Too extreme an emotional state may even interfere with cognitive activity, as in the case of severe depression. An investigation with hospitalized depressed patients (Fiedler *et al.*, 1989) may be interpreted in this way. Depressed patients were presented with the same picture-story task as in the aforementioned study by Fiedler and Drommershausen. The results deviated markedly from the same investigation with normal subjects. First, these patients were very passive in the story-construction task and composed very incoherent stories lacking continuity. Second, there was a strong tendency of depressives to avoid negative contents, that is, a preference to select positive pictures for the stories, to judge the contents of the pictures to be more positive than in the pretest and to recall positive pictures, especially in the morning when they were most depressed. This need not contradict the common finding that depressives are biased toward the negative (Derry and Kuiper, 1981) which is usually obtained with memory for autobiographic or self-related material. In fact, the same patients did show such a negativity effect in a memory test for life experiences. However, the lack of a congruency effect with the pictures seems to reflect motivated processes as well as their general passivity during encoding, which may have prevented their depressive mood from determining the story themes.

Admittedly, this is but one piece of preliminary evidence, and no systematic evidence is available on the effects of extreme mood states. However, somewhat more conclusive evidence can be presented for the reverse argument, namely, that very weak mood treatments suffice to produce "mood" selectivity. In fact, "moods" as local and weak as a single stimulus may be potent enough to produce a congruity effect, as illustrated in the following couple of recent studies conducted by Fiedler *et al.* (1990).

In these studies, we refrained from the usual mood manipulation altogether. Instead, participants were presented with pleasant or unpleasant photographs projected on the wall and were asked to associate one concept or event that was somehow related to the background photograph. On one half of the trials, they were instructed to infer a stimulus that matched the valence of the picture (congruent condition), and on the remaining trials they were to infer nonmatching (incongruent) stimuli. Free recall of the self-generated stimuli was then examined as a function of the valence of the background pictures (positive versus negative) and the matching manipulation (congruent versus incongruent).

Instead of a continuous mood state persisting over the whole session, this operationalization only involves an affective encoding context (i.e. the photographs) that changes as rapidly as the stimuli and that is no more intense than pictures used as stimuli in other experiments. Would a congruency effect be obtained nevertheless? Or would even an *incongruency* effect be obtained because the generation of incongruent stimuli requires more cognitive effort (cf. Horton, 1987)? In fact, the results show a strong congruency effect (Figure 5.5), suggesting that no personally involving or stable or intense mood state is necessary for the congruency effect to occur.

We wondered whether the inferiority of the incongruency condition was simply due to the fact that it was difficult or impossible to think of affective mismatches. Therefore, we repeated the experiment with somewhat altered material and a slightly different procedure, including verbal labels for the background pictures, thus rendering incongruent generations easier. The strong congruency effect was replicated, however (see Figure 5.5, Experiment 2).

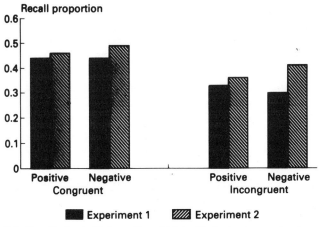

Fig 5.5   Recall of verbal information which is affectively congruent or incongruent with positive or negative background pictures.

If these findings are valid, then the crucial aspect of an effective mood treatment may lie in the thematic or cognitive priming component of the mood manipulation, which provides an encoding (or decoding) context for thematically related material. For instance, being confronted in the mood manipulation with themes like success, happy experiences, praise and a positive self-concept, or laughter and jokes may prime positive memories regardless of whether the phenomenological experience of an emotion is really involved. According to this view, the cognitive concomitants of an emotional experience may be responsible for the cognitive consequences, rather than the emotional experience itself. While little evidence is available to test this speculative view, it would certainly fit into the dual-force model; after all, it is the active process of generation and inference, which should profit most from the activation of an appropriate semantic context.

Two kinds of mood manipulation suggest themselves for testing this priming hypothesis, namely, mood induced by music and by facial muscle activities. Music may be very effective as a mood treatment, and yet it may lack the same semantic priming component as other mood treatments. Rather, music may be assumed to induce "pure" mood which is less clearly related to successful or happy scripts in memory. Indeed, the most disappointing negative finding we ever obtained in our own experiments was with a music treatment (popular versus atonal music) and pictures as stimuli. The pictures had been successfully used in other experiments, the experimental power was high (sample size = 96) and the manipulation was very effective according to the mood check. However, no sign of mood selectivity was obtained. The only plausible explanation for this null finding is that this kind of mood induction is not effective.

On the other hand, when subjects are instructed to produce facial muscle reactions that resemble emotion expressions, mood effects can be obtained, even when demand characteristics are controlled for (Strack *et al.*, 1988) and even though facial feedback does not involve an apparent semantic priming component. Moreover, such mood states induced by facial feedback have been shown to affect memory (Laird *et al.*, 1982). Other evidence suggests, however, that some direct priming effect of expressive patterns on cognition remains even when mood is controlled statistically (Riskind, 1983). In any case, it seems fair to conclude that semantic priming does not appear to be the only factor. On the other hand, there is sufficient evidence to suggest that an effective mood manipulation need not create a truly experienced emotional state in a phenomenological sense.

Concluding Remarks

Starting from the premise that cognitive processes can be decomposed into two stages, conservation and active transformation, the central assumption was introduced that emotional states act primarily on the second stage. In operational terms, productive tasks which encourage judgments and active generation of new information should be more susceptible to mood effects than reproductive tasks which give more weight to conservation. The viability of this general working hypothesis was illustrated and discussed with respect to the tasks, the measures, and the mood manipulations usually employed in research on affect and cognition. Some recent evidence was presented, suggesting that mood effects are most pronounced when the task requires active generation and when the dependent measures leave freedom for active processes, and that an effective mood manipulation need not be intense or ego involving. Rather, the crucial aspect seems to be that the manipulated state provides an efficient context for inferential and judgmental activities.

Many predictions derived from this framework can be tested in a minimal design that allows for the interaction of three factors or effects: repression, depression, and generation (cf. Figure 5.1). Thus, there is a general bias towards positive mood, for pleasant material, and for self-generated information; but these effects do not just add up—they reinforce each other in a multiplicative fashion. Such an approach sheds some new light on familiar issues and raises new issues as well. On the one hand, empirical inconsistencies and failures to replicate emotion effects under certain conditions can be explained. On the other hand, completely new hypotheses can be derived within this framework and tested in future research, in which manipulations of the task, the measures and the mood should play a major role.

The theoretical position advocated here may be considered a motivational account of the affect–cognition interface, as opposed to an automatic processing position or an assumption of permanently wired affective structures in semantic memory. Perhaps the main advantage of a motivational account is that it allows for volitional and motivated influences which are difficult to handle within an associative network approach (Bower and Cohen, 1982) or a cognitive capacity model (Ellis and Ashbrook, 1988). One testable, although neglected, implication of the motivational position states that emotional effects on cognition are not unconditional but can be erased by incentives, pay-off manipulations, and task instructions.

To the extent that the dual-force approach emphasizes motivated processes, it may be particularly suited for explaining mood influences on social as opposed to merely cognitive processes. To give but one example, the intriguing finding that positive mood may enhance the polarizing effect of group discussions (Forgas, 1990) is difficult to explain by purely associative principles. However, considering group discussions as a social variant of generative activity, the present approach offers a plausible interpretation at least. Social processes may thus turn out to be an especially rich domain of the dual-force model.

A final comment pertains to an intriguing issue in the affect–cognition literature which is usually treated separately from the congruency effect or the impact of mood on social judgment and behavior. When people are in a good mood, they prefer heuristic problem-solving strategies and show improved performance on creative tasks, whereas people in a bad mood prefer more systematic strategies and show improvement on tasks requiring assiduity and discipline. There is, by now, a good deal of converging evidence to support this contention (Fiedler, 1988; Isen et al., 1982). With reference to Figure 5.1, this phenomenon need not be treated as independent of congruency and its behavioral consequences. If positive mood is assumed to foster not only the generation of positive material (i.e. a mood × valence × generation interaction in Figure 5.1) but the generation process in general (i.e. a mood × generation interaction), then the enhanced creativity of people in a good mood can be accounted for. Indeed, the kind of creativity which gains from good mood (cf. Isen et al., 1985; Isen and Means, 1983) is characterized by the same generative activities that have been emphasized throughout this chapter.

As it seems, then, the suggested framework may help to account for various phenomena including the asymmetry of positive and negative affect, the special importance of the self or the interaction with task characteristics. Whether the model has much predictive power in addition to its *post hoc* integrative value cannot yet be determined, but some promising evidence is already available. In any case, the model is a reminder to keep the basic principles in mind, along with the social and clinical applications, and to strive for more experimental control over the task, the measures, and the moods.

References

Aderman D. (1972). Elation, depression, and helping behavior. *Journal of Personality and Social Psychology*, **24**, 91–101.

Banks, W. P. (1970). Signal detection theory and human memory. *Psychological Bulletin*, **74**, 81–99.

Bierhoff, H. W. (1988). Affect, cognition and prosocial behavior. In K. Fiedler and J. P. Forgas (Eds), *Affect, cognition, and social behavior*. Toronto: Hogrefe.

Blaney, P. H. (1986). Affect and memory: A review. *Psychological Bulletin*, **99**, 229–246.

Bock, M. (1980). Angenehme und unangenehme Erfahrungen aus gedächtnispsychologischer Sicht—Bilanz einer 80jährigen Forschung. *Psychologische Beiträge*, **22**, 280–292.

Bower, G. H. (1981). Mood and memory. *American Psychologist*, **36**, 129–148.

Bower, G. H., and Cohen, P.R. (1982). Emotional influences in memory and thinking: Data and theory. In M. S. Clark and S. T. Fiske (Eds), *Affect and cognition*. Hillsdale, NJ: Erlbaum.

Bower, G. H. Gilligan, S. G., and Monteiro, K. P. (1981). Selectivity of learning caused by affective states. *Journal of Experimental Psychology: General*, **110**, 451–473.

Bower, G. H., and Mayer, J. D. (1985). Failure to replicate mood–dependent retrieval. *Bulletin of the Psychonomic Society*, **23**, 39–42.

Bradbury, T. N., and Fincham, F. D. (1987). Affect and cognition in close relationships: Towards an integrative model. *Cognition and Emotion*, **1**, 59–87.

Brown, J. D., and Taylor, S. E. (1986). Affect and the processing of personal information: Evidence for mood-activated self-schemata. *Journal of Experimental Social Psychology*, **22**, 436– 452.

Clark, M. S. (1982). A role for arousal in the link between feeling states, judgments, and behavior. In M. S. Clark and S. T. Fiske (Eds), *Affect and cognition*. Hillsdale, NJ: Erlbaum.

Derry, P. A., and Kuiper, N. A. (1981). Schematic processing and self-reference in clinical depression. *Journal of Abnormal Psychology*, **90**, 286–297.

Ellis, H. C. (1985). On the importance of mood intensity and encoding demands in memory: Commentary on Hasher, Rose, Zacks, Sanft, and Doren. *Journal of Experimental Psychology: General*, **114**, 392–395.

Ellis, H. C. and Ashbrook, P. W. (1988). Resource allocation model of the effects of depressed mood states on memory. In K. Fiedler and J. P. Forgas (Eds), *Affect, cognition, and social behavior*. Toronto: Hogrefe.

Ellis, H. C., Thomas, R. L., and Rodriguez, I. A. (1984). Emotional mood states and memory: Elaborative encoding, semantic processing, and cognitive effort. *Journal of Experimental Psychology: Learning, Memory and Cognition*, **10**, 470–482.

Fiedler, K. (1985). Zur Stimmungsabhängigkeit kognitiver Funktionen. *Psychologische Rundschau*, **36**, 125–134.

Fiedler, K. (1988). Emotional mood, cognitive style, and behavior regulation. In K. Fiedler and J. P. Forgas (Eds), *Affect, cognition, and social behavior*. Toronto: Hogrefe.

Fiedler, K. (1990). Mood-dependent selectivity in social cognition. In W. Stroebe and M. Hewstone (Eds), *European review of social psychology*, Vol. 1. New York: Wiley.

Fiedler, K., Asbeck, J., and Nickel, S. (1990). Congruity and congruency. Unpublished research, University of Giessen.

Fiedler, K., and Drommershausen, B. (submitted). Mood congruency and higher-order encoding.

Fiedler, K., Gerlach, A., Stroehm, W., and Braun, G. (1989). Depression and memory: Some unexpected findings. Unpublished research. University of Giessen.

Fiedler, K., and Fladung, U. (1987). Emotionale Stimmung, Selbstbeteiligung, und Empfänglichkeit für persuasive Kommunikation. *Zeitschrift für Sozialpsychologie*, **18**, 169–179.

Fiedler, K., and Fladung, U. (1989). Mood congruence in productive and reproductive memory. Unpublished research, University of Giessen.

Fiedler, K., Nickel, S. and Asbeck, J. (submitted). Mood and the generation effect.

Fiedler, K., Pampe, H., and Scherf, U. (1986). Mood and memory for tightly organized social information. *European Journal of Social Psychology*, **16**, 149–164.

Fiedler, K., and Stroehm, W. (1986). What kind of mood influences what kind of memory: The role of arousal and information structure. *Memory and Cognition*, **14**, 181–188.

Forgas, J. P. (1990). The effects of group discussion on mood-based distortions in social judgments. *European Journal of Social Psychology*, **20**, 441–453.

Forgas, J. P. and Bower, G. H. (1987). Mood effects on person perception judgments. *Journal of Personality and Social Psychology*, **53**, 53–60.

Forgas, J. P., Bower, G. H., and Moylan, S. J. (1990). Praise or blame? Mood effects on attribution for success and failure. *Journal of Personality and Social Psychology*, **59**, 809–818.

Forgas, J. P., Burnham, D. K., and Trimboli, C. (1988). Mood, memory, and social judgments in children. *Journal of Personality and Social Psychology*, **54**, 697–703.

Gardiner, J. M. (1988). Generation and priming effects in word-fragment completion. *Journal of Experimental Psychology: Learning, Memory and Cognition*, **14**, 495–501.

Gardiner, J. M. and Hampton, J. A. (1985). Semantic memory and the generation effect: Some tests of the lexical activation hypothesis. *Journal of Experimental Psychology: Learning, Memory and Cognition*, **11**, 732–741.

Gerrig, R. J., and Bower, G. H. (1982). Emotional influences on word recognition. *Bulletin of the Psychonomic Society*, **19**, 197–200.

Graf, P. (1982). The memorial consequences of generation and transformation. *Journal of Verbal Learning and Verbal Behavior*, **21**, 539–548.

Hasher, L., Rose, K. C., Zacks, R. T., Sanft, S., and Doren, B. (1985). Mood, recall, and selectivity effects in normal college students. *Journal of Experimental Psychology: General*, **114**, 104–118.

Hintzman, D. L. (1976). Repetition and memory. In G. H. Bower (Ed.), *The psychology of learning and motivation*, Vol. 10. New York: Academic Press.

Horton, K. D. (1987). The incongruity effect in memory for generated targets. *Journal of Experimental Psychology: Learning, Memory and Cognition*, **13**, 172–174.

Ingram, R. E. (1984). Toward an information-processing analysis of depression. *Cognitive Therapy and Research*, **8**, 443–478.

Isen, A. M. (1970). Success, failure, attention and reactions to others: The warm glow of success. *Journal of Personality and Social Psychology*, **15**, 294–301.

Isen, A. M. (1984). Toward understanding the role of affect in cognition. In R. S. Wyer and T. K. Srull (Eds), *Handbook of social cognition*, Vol. 3, Hillsdale, NJ: Erlbaum.

Isen, A. M. (1985). Asymmetry of happiness and sadness in effects on memory in normal college students: Comment on Hasher, Rose, Sanft, Zacks, and Doren. *Journal of Experimental Psychology: General*, **114**, 388–191.

Isen, A. M., Johnson, M. M. S., Hertz, E., and Robinson, G. F. (1985). The effects of positive affect on the unusualness of word associations. *Journal of Personality and Social Psychology*, **48**, 1413–1414.

Isen, A. M., and Means, B. (1983). The influence of positive affect on decision making strategy. *Social Cognition*, **2**, 18–31.

Isen, A. M., Means, B., Patrick, R., and Nowicki, G. P. (1982). Some factors influencing decision-making and risk taking. In M. S. Clark and S. T. Fiske (Eds), *Affect and cognition*. Hillsdale, NJ: Erlbaum.

Isen, A. M., Shalker, T. E., Clark, M., and Karp, L. (1978). Positive affect, accessibility of material in memory, and behavior: A cognitive loop? *Journal of Personality and Social Psychology*, **36**, 1–12.

Johnson, E. J., and Tversky, A. (1983). Affect, generalization, and the perception of risk. *Journal of Personality and Social Psychology*, **45**, 20–31.

Kavanagh, D. J., and Bower, G. H. (1985). Mood and self-efficacy: Impact of joy and sadness on perceived capabilities. *Cognitive Therapy and Research*, **9**, 507–525.

Laird, K. A., Wegner, J. J., Halal, M., and Szegda, M. (1982). Remembering what you feel: The effects of emotion on memory. *Journal of Personality and Social Psychology*, **42**, 646–657.

Mayer, J. D., and Bower, G. H. (1985). Naturally occurring mood and learning: Commentary on Hasher *et al. Journal of Experimental Psychology: General*, **114**, 396–403.

Mayer, J. D., and Salovey, P. (1988). Personality moderates the interaction of mood and cognition. In K. Fiedler and J. P. Forgas (Eds), *Affect, cognition, and social behavior*. Toronto: Hogrefe.

Mecklenbrauker, S., and Hager, W. (1984). Effects of mood on memory: Experimental tests of mood-state-dependent retrieval hypothesis and of a mood-congruity hypothesis. *Psychological Research*, **46**, 355–376.

Postman, L., and Brown, D. R. (1952). The perceptual consequences of success and failure. *Journal of Abnormal and Social Psychology*, **47**, 213–221.

Riskind, J. H. (1983). Nonverbal expressions and the accessibility of life experience memories: A congruence hypothesis. *Social Cognition*, **2**, 62–86.

Rogers, T. B., Kuiper, N. A., and Kirker, W. S. (1977). Self-reference and the encoding of personal information. *Journal of Personality and Social Psychology*, **35**, 677–688.

Rosenthal, R., and Rosnow, R. L. (1985). *Contrast analysis: Focused comparisons in the analysis of variance*. Cambridge: Cambridge University Press.

Schuurmans, E., and Vandierendonck, A. (1985). Recall as communication: Effects of frame of anticipation. *Psychological Research*, **47**, 119–124.

Schwarz, N., and Clore, G. L. (1988). How do I feel about it? The informative function of affective states. In K. Fiedler and J. P. Forgas (Eds), *Affect, cognition, and social behavior*. Toronto: Hogrefe.

Singer, J. A., and Salovey, P. (1988). Mood and memory: Evaluating the network theory of affect. *Clinical Psychology Review*, **8**, 211–251.

Slamecka, N. J., and Graf, P. (1978). The generation effect: Delineation of a phenomenon. *Journal of Experimental Psychology: Learning, Memory and Cognition*, **4**, 592–604.

Sternberg, S. (1969). Memory-scanning: Mental processes revealed by reaction time experiments. *American Scientists*, **57**, 421–457.

Strömgren, L. S. (1977). The influence of depression on memory. *Acta Psychiatrica Scandinavia*, **56**, 109–128.

Strack, F., Martin, L. L., and Stepper, S. (1988). Inhibiting and facilitating conditions of the human smile: A nonobstructive test of the facial feedback hypothesis. *Journal of Personality and Social Psychology*, **54**, 768–777.

Teasdale, E. (1983). Affect and accessibility. *Philosophical Transactions of the Royal Society of London, Series B*, **302**, 403–412.

Tulving, E. (1968). Theoretical issues in free recall. In T. R. Dixon and D. L. Horton (Eds), *Verbal behavior and general behavior theory*. Englewood Cliffs, NJ: Prentice-Hall.

Weingartner, H., Cohen, R. M., Murphy, D. L., Martello, J., and Gerdt, C. (1981). Cognitive processes in depression. *Archives of General Psychiatry*, **38**, 42–47.

Zeller, A. F. (1950). An experimental analogue of repression—I. Historical summary. *Psychological Bulletin*, **47**, 39–51.

Zuroff, D. C., Colussy, S. A., and Wielgus, M. S. (1983). Selective memory and depression: A cautionary note concerning response bias. *Cognitive Therapy and Research*, **7**, 223–232.

Part 2

Integrations and Extensions

6

Moods and Their Vicissitudes: Thoughts and Feelings as Information

GERALD L. CLORE

University of Illinois at Urbana-Champaign

and

W. GERROD PARROTT

Georgetown University

Contents

> The object [is] . . . the most variable thing about an instinct. . . . It may be changed many times in the course of the vicissitudes the instinct undergoes [and] . . . a highly important part is played by this capacity for displacement in the instinct.   (Freud, 1915, p. 65)

In 1915, Freud published an essay entitled, "Instincts and their Vicissitudes." In it he proposed that instinctual (i.e. affective) energy often changes the object (i.e. idea) to which it is attached in order to achieve its aim of being expressed. Although this chapter is based on a cognitive rather than a psychodynamic model, it concerns the analogous observation that the affective experience of mood is often similarly fickle in its object of attachment.

Freud's underlying model was that repression involved the splitting of instinctual energy from an unacceptable idea so that it could not reach consciousness. This objectless energy could still achieve expression, however, by attaching itself to an associated but harmless idea, which would then be propelled into consciousness. Having been originally associated with an important idea, however, the repressed energy would sometimes be large in quantity, so that it would drive the harmless idea into consciousness with inappropriate force. This can be seen, said Freud, in obsessive–compulsive disorders, when a person becomes intensely preoccupied with a seemingly meaningless idea or action. Through such techniques as hypnosis or free association, the goal of therapy was to trace the symbolic link to the unconscious idea so that it could be expressed and the patient could be relieved of his or her symptoms.

The model discussed here also seeks to explain how an initially modest idea can become inappropriately extreme by inheriting objectless affect. In this case too, the problem stems from the fact that one can be unaware of the true source of one's affective state. The affective value of an object can then become inflated by the affective experience from this irrelevant source. And, as in the Freudian case, the cure for such distortion is to reestablish awareness of the true cause of the affective experience.

In the present chapter, this model will be extrapolated from the domain of affective experience to the domain of cognitive experience more generally. We shall attempt to show that the mood-as-information model (Schwarz and Clore, 1983, 1988) can serve as a more general model of judgment in which various kinds of cognitive experience act as information. The chapter is divided into three parts. The first reviews the mood-as-information hypothesis as such. The second applies the hypothesis to feelings that are not affective in nature. And the third further generalizes the hypothesis beyond feelings to other features of cognitive and affective experience, including thoughts and the self-perception of affective expressions.

Mood as Information

Consider the following questions: "Are you still angry?"; "Aren't you ashamed of yourself?"; "Are you enjoying the movie?" These questions ask directly about a person's feelings and can only be answered by using introspection. A related class of questions asks for affective appraisals of external objects: "How much should the defendant be blamed?"; "How well did the job candidate do?" A relevant source of data for answering these questions is to hold the object of the question in mind and to assess one's momentary affective reaction. That is, to ask oneself, "How do I feel as I consider the object of judgment?"

We shall argue that affective experience plays a more central role in everyday judgment and decision-making than has previously been realized. Its role has not been appreciated, perhaps because consulting one's momentary experience is more or less inseparable from making such judgments. Recent research shows, however, that judgments can be disentangled from the affective experiences on which they are sometimes based. The usual technique involves introducing extraneous affective experiences and arranging for these to be misattributed as reactions to the object being judged (Clore, 1985; Schwarz and Clore, 1983, 1988).

The research is somewhat similar in concept to Zillman's studies of excitation transfer (e.g. Cantor, Bryant, and Zillman, 1974) and to Zanna and Cooper's (1976) experiments on the arousal component of dissonance. However, Zillman was primarily concerned with the central role in judgment played by general, undifferentiated arousal, and the goal of Zanna and Cooper's studies was to show that feelings of tension are necessary components of dissonance phenomena. Our own use of the misattribution paradigm has focused on the implications of Wyer and Carlston's (1979) suggestion that a generally overlooked function of affective states is that they provide information or feedback to the experiencer that can be used in subsequent information processing.

The basic premise of this "informational hypothesis" is that just as emotional expressions convey emotional information to other people, emotional experience conveys such information to oneself. Emotional experience serves as feedback from the appraisal system, signifying or confirming that a situation is personally significant. This view has some rather Jamesian aspects—that we are informed about the significance of events by our own affective reactions to them. But whereas James argued for a direct link between events in the world and emotional reactions, we would insist on interposing between events and emotions a cognitive analysis wherein the personal significance of the events is appraised.

Ortony, Clove, and Collins (1988) have recently proposed a theory that treats emotions as the results of cognitive appraisals. The theory maps the structure of emotions in terms of the cognitive variables that differentiate one emotion from another, and that make emotional experiences intense or mild. The present proposal, on the other hand, is about the vicissitudes of emotions once produced—about emotional function. In particular, we shall be concerned with the function of the experiential aspect of emotion. The working assumption is that the output of affective processes includes distinctive experiences that indicate how important an event is and in what way it is important. Such emotional experiences serve as information for judgment and decision-making processes.

Several different kinds of observations support such an informational approach to the relationship between mood and judgment. The most important is the observation that emotions do not seem to bias people's judgment unless they make appropriate attributions for their experience. For example, Schwarz and Clore (1983) telephoned subjects on rainy days and sunny days to ask about their life satisfaction. We found people to be more satisfied with their lives on sunny days than on rainy days. We also found that respondents were in a more positive overall mood on sunny days,

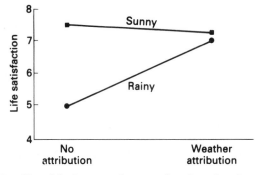

FIG 6.1   Mean life satisfaction scores for respondents interviewed on rainy or sunny days when weather is or is not made salient as a source of their mood states (Schwarz and Clore, 1983).

and we hypothesized that the effect of weather on ratings of life satisfaction was mediated by subjects' misattributions of their mood-based feelings. Evidence for this hypothesis comes from the fact that we were able to disrupt the effect of weather on judgments of life satisfaction simply by mentioning the weather; that is, by making a possible external cause of their feelings salient. After respondents implicitly attributed their moods to the weather they were still in a better mood on sunny than on rainy days, but their life satisfaction judgments no longer differed, as shown in Figure 6.1. Making an external attribution for one's feeling does not appear to influence the feelings themselves but only their interpretation.

The attributional explanation contrasts with the more commonly encountered explanation for the effect of mood on judgment based on cognitive priming. Stemming from the landmark studies by Isen (e.g. Isen, 1984) and by Bower (e.g. Bower, 1981), the basic argument is that one can think of moods as having some properties in common with semantic concepts that are represented in a semantic network in memory. When activated, moods and semantic concepts tend to stimulate related memories and concepts, which are then more likely to enter consciousness. Thus, a positive mood might lead to pervasive optimism because the good mood node is at least weakly associated in the network with all other positive memories and concepts. Schwarz and Clore interpreted their results as support for an informational hypothesis rather than a cognitive-priming hypothesis, because priming is supposed to be an automatic cognitive process. There is no *a priori* reason to assume that such automatic and unconscious priming processes should depend on subjects' conscious attributions about their momentary affective experience.

The results of this study were replicated in a laboratory experiment with a different mood induction. Subjects spent 15 minutes writing a detailed description of a happy or a sad event in their recent past, and the results showed that subjects who had written about a happy event were in a better mood than those who had written about a sad event. Later they answered the same life satisfaction questions used in the previous study, and those who were in a happy mood rated themselves as more satisfied with their life as a whole than did sad subjects. In addition, however, the salience of a possible external cause for subjects' feelings was varied. The experiment was conducted in a small and unusual sound-proof room with its own ventilation and lighting system. Before they began, half of the subjects were given reason to think that the room might make them feel tense. They were told that other subjects had reported that being in the sound-proof room made them feel tense after a period of time. To lend credibility to this story, subjects were asked to fill out a questionnaire about the room, the lighting, the ventilation, etc. As in the weather study, making salient a plausible external cause for subjects' feelings short-circuited the mood effect, as shown in Figure 6.2. These subjects misattributed their sad feelings to the room, and were therefore less likely to read them as an indication of how they felt about their life as a whole. As before, the moods reported by subjects in this external attribution group did not differ from the moods reported by other subjects, but their implicit understanding of these momentary affective experiences did differ. The gist of the hypothesis, then, is simply that the proximal cue for many kinds of affective judgments is the information provided by one's feelings as one considers the object of judgment. As in this study, the hypothesis suggests that the primary determinant of whether or not mood influences a particular judgment is the degree to which the information one gleans from that momentary affective experience seems relevant to the judgment to be made. The limiting case of relevance is when the experience is seen as a reaction to (is attributed to) the object of judgment. A variety of

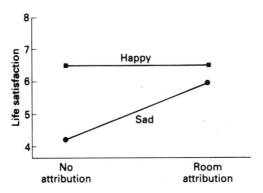

FIG 6.2   Mean life satisfaction scores after a sound-proof room has or has not been made salient as a possible cause of feelings of tension for happy and sad subjects (Schwarz and Clore, 1983).

other studies have also been conducted that have led us to believe that the informational view is a powerful hypothesis. Since those studies have been discussed elsewhere (Schwarz and Clore, 1988), we shall now turn to the second theme of the paper.

Bodily and Cognitive States as Information

The same ideas may apply to experiences other than affective experiences. Consider, for example, the physical feelings of hunger, thirst, and tiredness. They also may serve as data for answering relevant questions. In these cases, the relevant questions might include: "Shall I go to lunch?"; "Are you thirsty?"; "Are you tired?" etc. The primary basis for answering such questions is whether or not one feels hungry, thirsty, or tired. Just as momentary affective feelings appear to provide data for affective judgments, momentary physical feelings may provide information for judgments about bodily states. In addition to affective and bodily feelings, however, there are also other kinds of feelings, including what might be called "cognitive feelings." Like affective and bodily feelings, these momentary cognitive feelings also seem to serve an informative function in that they provide data for certain cognitive and metacognitive judgments. The terms "cognitive judgments" and "cognitive feelings," are intended to refer to judgments and feelings about knowing, being confused, being certain, and so on. Again, the evidence comes largely from studies of misattribution.

In a recent pair of experiments (Clore and Parrott, 1987), we studied the misattribution of cognitive feelings of uncertainty and confusion. As part of a hypnosis demonstration for a large audience, we administered a standard group test of hypnotic susceptibility. During the hypnosis we gave subjects a guided fantasy designed to induce feelings of uncertainty and confusion. In one experiment these were feelings of confusion induced by having subjects vividly imagine listening to a lecture on computer programming. In an unselected group, most people turn out not to be highly hypnotizable. These low-hypnotizable subjects served as a control group. They were compared with the highly hypnotizable subjects who served as the experimental group. These hypnotizable subjects reported more feelings of confusion than the low-hypnotizable, control subjects. For half of the subjects in both groups, hypnosis was made salient as the cause of their feelings after they awoke, and for half of the subjects no explanation for the feelings was made salient. These conditions formed a 2 × 2 design in which high versus low hypnotizability was crossed with instructions that made the cause of their momentary feelings of uncertainty either salient or not. They were then given a short Rudyard Kipling poem to read and were asked to rate how well they understood it and how well they thought they could explain what the author had in mind.

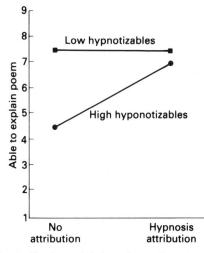

Fig 6.3   Mean self-ratings of their understanding of a poem made by high and hypnotizable subjects after a fantasy inducing them to feel uncertain (Clore and Parrott, 1987).

As shown in Figure 6.3, the low-hypnotizable subjects, who did not generate strong feelings of uncertainty in the first place, felt that they understood the poem reasonably well. The highly hypnotizable subjects generally did report feelings of uncertainty, but those in the condition in which external causes for their feelings (the hypnosis) had been made salient thought they understood the poem well. By contrast, the highly hypnotizable subjects in the condition in which feelings of uncertainty remained unexplained, were significantly less sure that they had understood the poem.

This experiment was later replicated in a different setting with a different fantasy. The new fantasy was written to see if feelings of uncertainty that did not involve confusion would have the same effect. The guided fantasy used in the replication was about feelings of uncertainty experienced when trying to decide between two equally attractive apartments to rent. The results were the same. These experiments suggest, therefore, that one function served by feelings is to inform the experiencer about his or her own state. In this case the feelings were metacognitive feelings, and the state was the subject's state of knowledge. The proximal cue for determining whether one understands something, we would suggest, is often a "feeling of understanding" or a sense of comprehension.

There are other examples in which "cognitive feelings" or experiential aspects of cognitive processes appear to play a similar role. For example, Jacoby and Dallas (1981) studied subjects' abilities to recognize words they had seen on a previous study list as a function of whether the words were rare or common. They found that rare and common words were both readily recognized when subjects had seen them earlier. Also, in the case of rare words, subjects could accurately detect which ones had not been presented. In the case of common words, however, subjects frequently said they recognized them, even when they had never been presented. They were apparently fooled by the experience of familiarity (caused by the commonness of the words) into thinking they had seen them earlier in the experiment. They misattributed to recency of exposure the sense of familiarity that actually came from frequency of exposure.

A related logic can be seen in Tversky and Kahneman's (1974) proposals about the availability heuristic. The availability heuristic is intriguing because it focuses on the phenomenology rather than the content of cognition. Tversky and Kahneman show, for example, that judgments about the likelihood of events in a particular class are often based on the ease with which relevant examples come to mind. When one finds it easy to imagine a given scenario or to retrieve a given instance, one is likely to judge the scenario or the event as more likely or more frequent than scenarios that are less easy to imagine. Tversky and Kahneman suggest that people may assess the risk of heart attack among middle-aged men, for example, by recalling instances of heart attacks among their acquaintances, or they may gauge the possibility of a given business venture failing based on the ease of imagining various difficulties it could encounter.

The key to the availability heuristic is the experience of ease with which an example of a particular category comes to mind. When an instance comes to mind easily, this experience of ease sometimes does reflect the fact that frequent instances in the world have made examples more common in memory. But such a rule is also subject to error, in that we are generally unable to say whether the experience of ease results from the frequency of the event or from an irrelevant property of the event that made it salient. That is, the heuristic is error prone because the subjective experience that serves as data for the implicit inference is, like the other examples we have cited, subject to misattribution.

A recent incident in one of the authors' experience also illustrates the role of "cognitive feelings" in perceptual experience and plausible inference. This example involves the experience of novelty. It occurred when a friend who had just returned from sabbatical leave drove past a familiar building that had been re-landscaped during his absence. The presence of new hedges and the addition of some other features in the re-landscaped scene made the usual view seem rather different, and the friend commented, "Oh, they've built a new building on this site." He had in fact seen the same building on that site many times before, but the new peripheral details created a strong feeling or sense of novelty, and since the building was still the most salient aspect of this scene, he naturally concluded that the building was new.

A related and more familiar example is the feeling of unfamiliarity one gets when a friend shaves off his beard. Because people tend to perceive faces as unanalyzed gestalts, such changes often give rise only to a general sense of novelty. They may attribute this experience to the first thing they notice about the beardless friend. As a result they may ask if he has changed glasses or gotten a haircut. As Jacoby (1988) points out, the meaning and effect of such experiences of novelty depend on the attributions that one makes.

The research on feelings of knowing by Nelson (Nelson, Leonesio, Landwehr, and Narens, 1986) and others (e.g. Wellman, 1977) is similar in its implications. That research suggests that when one is asked whether one knows the answer to some question, the proximal cue for answering the question is a "feeling of knowing." When a plausible answer does not appear immediately, the "feeling of knowing" turns out to be an accurate predictor of whether or not one will later be able to recognize the correct answer. Our point is that these effects in the metacognitive domain are essentially the same as those from our research in the affective domain in which affective feelings are often the proximal cues for answering evaluative questions or questions about liking.

This handful of studies and examples indicates the critical role played by implicit inferences about one's momentary cognitive experience. All involve misattribution. But this is not intended to be a paper fundamentally concerned with misattributions and errors. Focusing on error is useful to the extent that it offers a window through which to view normal functioning. Misattribution is interesting in the same way that disease is interesting to a biologist or irregularity in the terrain is interesting to a geologist. The psychological outcropping represented by misattributed feelings allows us to see beneath the usually undisturbed surface of human judgment and decision making. What it affords is a view of the parallel roles played in ordinary functioning by the phenomenology of cognition and the phenomenology of emotion.

Primed Thoughts as Information

We have reviewed the implications of an informational interpretation of the effects of mood on evaluative judgment, and we have extended the hypothesis to cover the role of what might be called "cognitive feelings" on judgments about knowing. A third set of implications of the mood-as-information approach concerns the informational value of primed thoughts. The mood-as-information hypothesis suggests that it is the experience of mood and what subjects implicitly infer from that experience that accounts for the role of mood in judgment. In this section we shall argue that part of the experience of happy, sad, or angry moods is that one has happy, sad, or angry thoughts, and that the mood-as-information hypothesis is no less applicable to this component of the mood experience. First, however, let us consider the sufficiency of the priming hypothesis as an explanation.

As indicated earlier, the most prominent explanation for the effect of mood on cognitive processes in the current literature is some version of the priming hypothesis (e.g. Bower, 1981; Clark, 1982; Isen, 1984; Isen *et al.*, 1978). Within this view, mood inductions are thought of as playing the role of cognitive priming manipulations, so that whenever moods influence judgments, one should expect to find that the nonemotional cognitive content of the induction also shows priming effects. The evidence, however, has not always been consistent with this expectation. Several experiments have shown clear evidence for mood effects in the absence of any evidence of nonaffective cognitive priming in studies where a priming interpretation demands both to be present (e.g. Clore *et al.*, 1983; Johnson and Tversky, 1983). These studies cast doubt on priming as the sole mechanism for mood effects.

Another tenet of the priming hypothesis is that mood effects are mediated by subjects; *interpretations* of ambiguous situations. The hypothesis predicts that mood activates mood-congruent memories or concepts about a situation, and that, to the extent that the situation is open to interpretation, these activated concepts may then bias interpretations. In one study testing this idea, however, strong mood effects were found to occur even when situations were designed to be evaluatively unambiguous and did not, therefore, lend themselves to varied interpretations (Schwarz *et al.*, 1985).

Finally, it is notable that studies of priming in the social cognition literature (e.g. Massad *et al.*, 1979; Srull and Wyer, 1979) typically find that priming manipulations have their effects on judgment only at the encoding stage of processing, when stimulus materials are first interpreted. When introduced later, at the output stage, attempts at priming generally have no effect on judgment at all. We have looked for a comparable pattern of effects using mood manipulations as the priming stimulus, but they are not to be found. Unlike the pattern in nonemotional priming studies, mood effects can be shown even when mood is not induced until the time of judgment, well after the stimulus materials had been read and processed (e.g. Clore *et al.*, 1987). Such data suggest that mood may often exercise its influence on judgment not by coloring one's initial interpretation of the stimulus at the encoding stage, but by affecting one's evaluation of the interpreted information. In fact, this effect should be seen regardless of whether the evaluation occurs early during encoding or later at the output or rating stage, but the effects often appear to be on subjects' evaluation rather than their interpretation of the materials. These results are consistent with predictions of the mood-as-information hypothesis. Indeed, the results of each of the studies reviewed above—finding mood effects without corresponding non-mood priming effects, finding mood effects with unambiguous stimuli, and finding mood effects when mood is induced at the output stage—are all consistent with the mood-as-information hypothesis. The hypothesis conceptualizes affective experience as a source of (sometimes misleading) information. It predicts that mood can bias social perception even when judgments are made long after the stimulus has been interpreted. All that is required is for the person to encounter unattributed affective reactions at the time of making evaluative judgments. In several studies, therefore, mood effects occurred in situations that should not have produced priming effects and did not occur in situations that should have produced priming. Such findings suggest that the influence of mood on judgment in these studies may not have been due to cognitive priming.

While the results of some studies of mood and judgment do not appear to depend on priming, moods surely do spark mood-congruent thoughts and memories. Bower (1981) and Forgas and Bower (1988) cite a number of studies that show such priming effects of mood, and the phenomenon is also consistent with much of our everyday experience with mood. In what way then are an informational view and a priming view at odds, if at all? As can be seen in Figure 6.4, the two hypotheses are actually relevant to somewhat

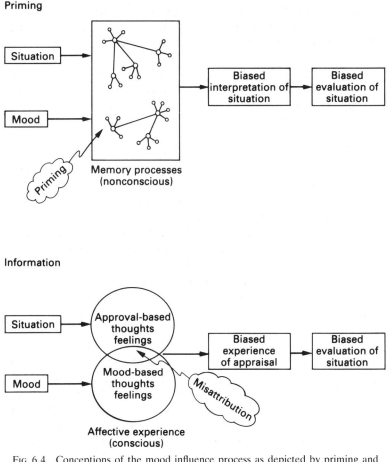

Fɪɢ 6.4   Conceptions of the mood influence process as depicted by priming and mood-as-information theories.

different questions, because they focus on different parts of the judgment process. Priming is believed to be automatic, to involve the unconscious activation of mood-congruent memories and concepts, and to exert its influence on interpretations of incoming information. By contrast, the processes involved in the mood-as-information hypothesis are believed to involve the conscious experience of mood-related reactions and to depend on implicit attributions about their source. These hypotheses may at first seem irreconcilable. One relies on unconscious, automatic processes, and the other focuses on the effects of the conscious experience of emotion, effects that are not believed to be automatic but that depend on how individuals understand their own experience.

As Figure 6.4 suggests, however, these explanations may not be incompatible. They may simply be describing different ends of the same elephant. As shown in the figure, the domain of the priming hypothesis is the fact that moods are likely to activate mood-congruent thoughts at the time of input, while the domain of the information hypothesis is the fact that, at output, the thoughts and feelings of good and bad moods are indistinguishable from the thoughts and feelings of having appraised some situation as good or bad. The priming explanation thus stresses the role of retrieval in making biased information available for encoding ambiguous situations. The informational explanation stresses the constructive processes necessarily involved in any experience-based judgment. They thus appear to complement each other. Nevertheless, an implication of the information view is that the mechanisms generally appealed to in priming studies in the social cognition literature are, by themselves, insufficient to explain even standard priming effects, let alone mood effects. Priming explanations must be supplemented with what might be called a "thoughts-as-information" corollary. From this perspective, one can see that, like mood effects, the standard priming effect on judgment depends on an implicit misattribution of primed cognitions. That is, subjects must take the thoughts that occur to them as reactions to the stimulus to be judged rather than as a consequence of the priming manipulation. As we shall see, the existing literature is consistent with such an idea.

Consider ordinary nonemotional priming studies in the social cognition literature. To obtain priming effects, subjects in such experiments must surely see the primed concept as a reaction to the object of judgment. If they saw this mental event as having a different source (as due to the prior priming task, for example), it seems likely that they would not show priming effects. A close reading of the relevant literature suggests that this is the case. Priming seems to be successful only when it is done in a subtle manner, only when subjects do not isolate the priming manipulation as a separate event in episodic memory. For example, the terms used as primes are sometimes exposed subliminally so that subjects are not fully aware of having seen them (Bargh and Pietromonaco, 1982). They have also been presented as background stimuli in a Stroop task (Higgins *et al.*, 1977) or embedded in other apparently irrelevant tasks (Srull and Wyer, 1979). If the concept to be primed is simply mentioned to subjects without disguise, priming effects tend not to occur. Perhaps this is because when introduced with subtlety the concepts primed in semantic memory are not tied to a particular event in episodic memory. They remain episodically unconstrained and free to be misattributed as part of the cognitive reaction to the stimulus to be judged. In contrast, if the activated concepts were seen clearly as belonging to the priming task, then it would not be misattributed and would not influence judgment.

Relevant data come from an ingenious study by Martin (1986) (see also Lombardi et al., 1987). He did not present the primes subliminally or embed them in another task; he presented them quite explicitly, in a manner that would usually be ineffective. but in that study, priming was effective because he manipulated the perceived relevance of the primed concept in another way. The priming task was one in which subjects wrote paraphrases of four happy or sad Velten mood-induction statements. Half of the subjects believed they were going to respond to eight statements and half expected only four. After four statements, subjects were given an ambiguous paragraph to read and rate. The paragraph was the familiar "Donald" paragraph from Higgins et al. (1977). For the subjects who believed they would respond to eight statements, reading the Donald paragraph after completing only four was seen as an interruption. They expected to return to the initial (priming) task later, so that the primed material continued to seem relevant. But the other subjects, who had expected only four sentences, believed that they had now completed the initial (priming) task. These subjects presumably saw the priming task as a distinct and separable episode from the subsequent judgment task, and as a result the usual priming effect did not occur. The fact that priming influenced judgment only when the priming task was not perceived as a separate and completed event suggests that priming effects ordinarily depend on misattributions. That is, they depend on the perception that the primed thought is really part of their momentary reaction to the stimulus to be judged rather than that it is due to the prior priming task. What Martin's study shows is that subjects are most likely to make such tacit misattributions when primed concepts are episodically unconstrained, and that they are unlikely to do so when priming tasks stand out as distinct and separable (episodically constrained) events.

These proposals do not raise questions about whether or not priming is an automatic process. Presumably it is. Rather, they focus on what happens to material once it is primed. Analogously, they do not raise questions about the necessity of experiencing sad feelings during sad moods. Rather, the emphasis is on what happens to the thoughts and feelings once elicited. The question is, under what conditions do primed thoughts and mood-based feelings each exercise an influence on later judgments? We are suggesting that the conditions for one may also be the conditions for the other.

Emotional thoughts and emotional feelings are, of course, closely linked. The thoughts present in consciousness when in a depressed mood, for example, are as much a part of one's affective reaction as are the dysphoric feelings (see Parrott, 1988, for an extended discussion of the role of cognitive content in emotional experience). Distinctive facial, postural, and other bodily expressions also typify some affective states, and the processes that govern the influence of thoughts and feelings may also govern the role of feedback from such bodily expressions of emotion. All of these can be viewed as cues that convey to oneself information about one's own momentary relationship to the world. In this sense, self-perceived affective reactions are part of a feedback system analogous to the pain system (except that the physical events that trigger the pain system in the first place do not require the kind of cognitive interpretation that emotional processes typically involve). Our point is that affective feedback involves emotional feelings (Schwarz and Clore, 1983), emotional thoughts (Isen *et al.*, 1978), and even the self-perceived aspects of emotional expressions (Strack *et al.*, 1988), and the same processes govern the use of information from all of these sources.

The current proposal represents a kind of phenomenological position, in that the emphasis is on interpretation of momentary conscious experience. It contrasts, therefore, with the more common focus on emotion as a primitive response system, characterized by automaticity and irrationality. This is not to deny that emotions may involve automaticity, irrationality, or primitive mechanisms, but rather that, by themselves, such processes cannot explain the effect of emotion on human judgment. A critical role is played by subjects' assumptions, perceptions, and attributions about their experience of their own reactions. This attributional emphasis also contributes to the phenomenological flavor of this position. Invoking "attributional processes" sometimes brings to mind an individual engaged in explicit deliberations about the causes of events, but that is not intended here. It is well to remember that Heider (1958), to whom we owe the emphasis on attribution in contemporary social psychology, was a gestalt psychologist. He was concerned, for example, with the principles underlying visual illusions and the principles whereby objects in close proximity might be seen as a unit. It is in that context that attributions are to be understood, as unanalyzed perceptions of causal belongingness. The attributional emphasis locates the effects of mood within people's momentary experience of their emotions and within their understanding of (or parsing of) that experience. Good evidence exists about the role of such attributions in mediating the effect of emotional feelings on judgment, and the suggestion here is that this evidence is equally applicable to emotional thoughts. The claim, then, is that such belongingness relations, or tacit attributions, provide the glue whereby emotional experiences influence judgment.

Summary

The effects of mood on judgment often depend on a perception that the affective experience accompanying a mood state is occasioned by the to-be-judged stimulus. In other words, mood bias often involves a misattribution of mood-based experience as appraisal-based experience (Schwarz and Clore, 1983, 1988). This model predicts that the potentially troublesome effects of mood on judgment can be eliminated by increasing the salience of possible external causes of the experience (e.g. the weather, a sound-proof room, hypnosis, etc.). Affective reactions that appear to be due to such purely external causes will seem irrelevant to the object of judgment, so that no bias results. It was emphasized that the attributions involved are not the results of extended deliberations about causation, but are implicit perceptions concerning which other aspect of one's experience *belongs with* the emotional experience. Such perceptions of belongingness can be created or disrupted by encouraging subjects to segment or punctuate their experience in appropriate ways, so that the affect does or does not appear to be relevant to the object of judgment.

The role played by the experience of affective cues in providing affective information is the same as the role played by the experience of bodily reactions in providing information about physical states (e.g. hunger or thirst). And these, in turn, are not essentially different from the role played by the experience of cognitive cues (e.g. feeling confused, finding that something comes to mind easily) in providing information about one's state of knowledge. These observations led to the hypothesis that the same attributional and parsing principles that are at work when affective states influence evaluative judgment (discussed in the first part, "Mood as information") also operate in the domain of nonaffective cognitive experience (discussed in the second part, "Bodily and cognitive states as information"). Thus, the experience of novelty or familiarity appears to influence relevant judgments only when an appropriate attribution is made about the cause of the experience.

In the third part, ("Primed thoughts as information"), we proposed that the same principles also apply to the experience of particular cognitive content. That is, a passing thought should influence judgment only when appropriate attributions are in place, i.e. that the thought is part of one's reaction to the object of judgment. In priming experiments, of course, this attribution is false, since the primed thoughts are actually due to a (necessarily subtle) priming manipulation. The effects of social cognitive priming studies, therefore, also depend on implicit attributions or perceptions of belongingness. This is presumably true whether or not the material primed is affective or nonaffective in nature. One advantage of this view is that it suggests that explanations of mood effects on judgment based on the priming of mood-consistent cognitive content (e.g. Bower, 1981; Isen *et al.*,

1978) may not be incompatible with explanations based on mood as information (e.g. Schwarz and Clore, 1983, 1988). It also suggests, however, that focusing on priming and activation alone is not a complete account of such mood effects. What is critical is the informativeness of affective experiences—experience that involves distinctive thoughts, distinctive feelings, and in some cases distinctive expressions and actions. When, for example, we experience our own feelings of fright, our own thoughts of impending calamity, and the trembling in our own voices, we are informed about (or receive confirmation of) the nature and intensity of our fear. This is a rather Jamesian view, which we have combined with Freud's observation that affect is easily displaced to irrelevant ideas. In an information processing context, these ideas intersect to focus attention on the informativeness of affective, bodily, and cognitive experience in the construction of (sometimes biased) judgments.

Acknowledgments

Support for this project was provided by the National Science Foundation in the form of a research grant (BNS 83-18077) and by a research training grant from The National Institute of Mental Health (MH 15140). The authors also benefited from comments on the manuscript by Leonard Martin, Andrew Ortony, and Norbert Schwarz.

References

Bargh, J. A., and Pietromonaco, P. (1982), Automatic information processing and social perception: The influence of trait information presented outside of conscious awareness on impression formation. *Journal of Personality and Social Psychology*, **43**, 437–449.
Bower, G. H. (1981). Mood and memory. *American Psychologist*, **36**, 129–148.
Cantor, J. R., Bryant, L., and Zillman, D. (1974). The enhancement of human appreciation by transferred excitation, *Journal of Personality and Social Psychology*, **30**, 812–821.
Clark, M. S. (1982). A role for arousal in the link between feeling states, judgments, and behavior. In M. S. Clark and S. T. Fiske (Eds), *Affect and cognition*. Hillsdale, NJ: Erlbaum.
Clore, G. L. (1985). The cognitive consequences of emotion and feeling. Presented at the American Psychological Association, Los Angeles.
Clore, G. L., and Parrott, W. G. (1987). Cognitive feelings and metacognitive judgments. Unpublished manuscript, University of Illinois.
Clore, G. L. Parrott, W. G., and Wilkins, N. (1987). Mood effects and stage of processing evaluative information. Unpublished manuscript, University of Illinois at Urbana-Champaign.
Clore, G. L., Schwarz, N., and Kirsch, J. (1983). Generalized mood effects on evaluative judgments. Paper presented at the Midwestern Psychological Association, Chicago.
Forgas, J. P. and Bower, G. (1988). Affect in social and personal judgments. In K. Fiedler and J. Forgas (Eds) *Affect, cognition, and social behavior*, pp. 183–208. Toronto: Hogrefe.
Freud, S. (1915). Instincts and their vicissitudes. Reprinted in E. Jones (Ed.) (1959), *Sigmund Freud: Collected papers*, Vol. 4. New York: basic Books.
Heider, F. (1958). *The psychology of interpersonal relations*. Hillsdale, NJ: Erlbaum.
Higgins, E. T., Rholes, W. S. and Jones, C. R. (1977). Category accessibility and impression formation. *Journal of Experimental Social Psychology*, **13**, 141–154.
Isen, A. M. (1984). Toward understanding the role of affect in cognition. In R. S. Wyer and T. K. Srull (Eds), *Handbook of social cognition*, Vol. 2. Hillsdale, NJ: Erlbaum.
Isen, A. M., Shalker, T. E., Clark, M., and Karp, L. (1978). Affect, accessibility of material in

memory, and behavior: A cognitive loop? *Journal of Personality and Social Psychology*, **36**, 1–11.

Jacoby, L. L. (1988). Memory observed and memory unobserved. In U. Neisser and E. Winograd (Eds), *Remembering reconsidered: Ecological and traditional approaches to the study of memory*. Cambridge: Cambridge University Press.

Jacoby, L. L., and Dallas, M. (1981). On the relationship between autobiographical memory and perceptual learning. *Journal of Experimental Psychology: General*, **110**, 306–340.

Johnson, E. J. and Tversky, A. (1983). Affect, generalization, and the perception of risk. *Journal of Personality and Social Psychology*, **45**, 20–31.

Lombardi, W. J., Higgins, E. T., and Bargh, J. A. (1987). The role of consciousness in priming effects on categorization: Assimilation versus contrast as a function of awareness of the priming task. *Personality and Social Psychology Bulletin*, **13**, 411–429.

Martin, L. L. (1986). Set/reset: Use and disuse of concepts in impression formation. *Journal of Personality and Social Psychology*, **51**, 493–504.

Massad, C. M., Hubbard, M., and Newtson, D. (1979). Perceptual selectivity: Contributing process and possible cure for impression perseverance. *Journal of Experimental Social Psychology*, **15**, 513–532.

Nelson, T. O., Leonesio, R. J., Landwehr, R. A., and Narens, L. (1986). A comparison of three predictors of an individual's memory performance: The individual's feeling of knowing versus the normative feeling of knowing versus base rate item difficult. *Journal of Experimental Psychology*, **12**, 279–287.

Ortony, A., Clore, G. L., and Collins, A. (1988). *The cognitive structure of emotion*. New York: Cambridge University Press.

Parrott, W. G. (1988). The role of cognition in emotional experience. In W. J. Baker, L. P. Mos, H. V. Rappard, and H. J. Stam (Eds), *Recent trends in theoretical psychology*, pp. 327– 337. New York: Springer.

Schwarz, N., and Clore, G. L. (1983). Mood, misattribution, and judgments of well-being; informative and directive functions of affective states. *Journal of Personality and Social Psychology*, **45**, 513–523.

Schwarz, N., and Clore, G. L. (1988). How do I feel about it? The informative function of mood. In K. Fiedler and J. Forgas (Eds), *Affect, cognition, and social behavior*. Toronto: Hogrefe.

Schwarz, N., Robbins, M., and Clore, G. L. (1985). Explaining the effects of mood on social judgment. Paper presented at the Midwestern Psychological Association, Chicago.

Srull, T. K., and Wyer, R. S., Jr. (1979). The role of category accessibility in the interpretation of information about persons: Some determinants and implications. *Journal of Personality and Social Psychology*, **37**, 1660–1672.

Strack, R., Martin, L. L., and Stepper, S. (1988). Inhibiting and facilitating conditions of the human smile: A nonobtrusive test of the facial feedback hypothesis. *Journal of Personality and Social Psychology*, **54**, 768–777.

Tversky, A., and Kahneman, D. (1974). Judgment under uncertainty: Heuristics and biases. *Science*, **185**, 1124–1131.

Wellman, H. M. (1977). Tip of the tongue and feeling of knowing experiences: a developmental study of memory monitoring. *Child Development*, **48**, 13–21.

Wyer, R. S., Jr., and Carlston, D. E. (1979). *Social cognition, inference, and attribution*. Hillsdale, NJ: Erlbaum.

Zanna, M. P., and Cooper, J. (1976). Dissonance and the attribution process. In J. Harvey, W. K. Ickes, and R. F. Kidd (Eds), *New directions in attribution research*, Vol. 1 Hillsdale, NJ: Erlbaum.

7

The Perception and Processing of Affective Information and its Influences on Social Judgment

PAULA M. NIEDENTHAL

Johns Hopkins University

and

CAROLIN SHOWERS

University of Wisconsin-Madison

Contents

> Finally, old Sally started coming up the stairs, and I started down to meet her. She looked terrific. She really did. The funny part is, I felt like marrying her the minute I saw her. I didn't even *like* her, and yet all of a sudden I felt like I was in love with her and wanted to marry her. I swear to god I'm crazy. I admit it.
> Holden Caulfield in *The Catcher in the Rye* (J. D. Salinger, 1951)

> Certain features of the object which the subject does not consciously perceive are nevertheless physically affecting his body, and though he may be unable to report upon these internal happenings, they are nevertheless affecting his conscious appraisal of the object.
> Henry Murray (1933)

The antecedents of social judgment are so numerous as to make the prediction of an individual's impression of another person, or change in the impression over time, a frustrating exercise. As illustrated by Holden Caulfield in the above quotation, in some situations an individual's reaction to another person can be contradictory to a previous one, or can seem inexplicable even to the individual. There are a variety of contemporary cognitive models which may in part explain Holden's experience (Uleman and Bargh, 1989). However, Murray's (1933) suggestion that affective reactions may contribute to the content of social perception and social judgment provides the intellectual basis for the present chapter. We depart from Murray's psychoanalytic notions of the source and aim of the affective reaction, but concur that although both cognitive and affective processes are omnipresent in social perception and judgment, affective ones may exert effects independently of those processes identified as cognitive. Rather than offer a new definition of affect or posit special affective mechanisms, we suggest that a concern with affect primarily (1) broadens the scope of information thought to be utilized by the social perceiver, (2) shifts the focus from aspects of the descriptive content to the valence of social judgment, and (3) calls for attention to be paid to how the perception and processing of affective information fits, as well as does not fit, in current models of social judgment.

There are three main sections of the chapter. In the first we define affective reaction. We then locate this type of reaction in social perception by reviewing research that suggests that affective reactions are sometimes elicited by features of the typical object of social perception, namely, other people. We close the section by examining several areas of research that indicate that affective reactions have effects on specific kinds of social judgments: judgments of liking and attractiveness and evaluations of behaviors and attributes.

In the remainder of the chapter, we report findings from our laboratories that highlight some of the important features of affective processes in social perception and judgment. Specifically, in the second section, we present evidence that people can *implicitly perceive* affective stimuli as indicated by their influences on concurrent cognitive processes. In the final section, we examine how affective processes may influence the cognitive ones that form the basis of social judgment. We point to the possible effects of affective reactions on both category-based and piecemeal evaluation processes (Fiske and Neuberg, 1990). Finally, we discuss the possibility that affective reactions exert their influences on judgment via the (re)organization of information in memory.

Affective Information in Social Perception

Affective reactions defined

The concern here is with low-level affective reactions. Such reactions have been described by Leventhal (1980) and by Zajonc (1980) as basic feelings of positivity or negativity that are attached to perception of a stimulus event. The reaction involves changes in visceral, autonomic, and expressive processes (Leventhal, 1984). These aspects of affect are summarized cogently by de Charms (1968/1983): "Affect is to be understood as an emotional response with physiological and phenomenological correlates aroused or elicited by certain stimulus conditions in the environment" (p. 63).

Affective reactions may be mediated by the matching of basic visual features, or patterns, of the event to their corresponding mental representations; and this connection may be learned (Leventhal, 1980), or innate (Ekman and Friesen, 1975; LeDoux, 1986). It is assumed that higher-order cognitive processes, or the transformation of an internal or external event into propositional knowledge [cf. *analytic cognition*, (Buck, 1985); *abstract cognition* (Leventhal, 1984)], are not necessary antecedents of low-level affective reactions.

Finally, affective reactions are assumed to be functional. They are thought to serve as a cue to the approachability (or pleasantness) of the stimulus event [cf. *spontaneous communication*, (Buck, 1984, 1988; Tomkins, 1962)]. Consistent with other recent suggestions that affective reactions can be conceptualized as "information" about the environment (Ortony *et al.*, 1988; Clore and Parrott, this volume), we refer to the class of stimuli that recruit immediate innate or learned affective reactions as *affective information*.

Affective reactions and other affect constructs

The distinction between affective reaction and constructs such as *mood, emotion*, and *evaluation* can be made on a number of different dimensions.

Mood. Moods are relatively protracted feeling states that affect a variety of cognitive and behavioral responses (Clark and Isen, 1982; Isen, 1984, 1987; Singer and Salovey, 1988). In contrast, affective reactions are momentary responses that should primarily influence the transformation of the affect-eliciting stimulus itself into conscious experience. Thus, mood and affective reaction differ in their duration and in the pervasiveness of their effects on other on-going processes (Isen, 1984).

Emotion. Affective reactions also differ from emotions. This distinction may be made in terms of their necessary antecedents. As noted earlier, affective reactions are thought to be elicited by the nature of an external stimulus. Emotions, on the other hand, are held to arise when a discrepancy exists between an individual's appraisal of an event and his or her expectations of it (Frijda, 1986; Lazarus, 1984). Emotions are also equated with conscious experience, while affective reactions may proceed without demanding attentional resources. According to Izard (1984), "the level of awareness for feelings varies with the intensity of the feelings, with low-intensity feelings operating more in terms of filtering and focusing perceptual–cognitive processes and high intensity feelings dominating consciousness by gating out information irrelevant to the emotion and the related coping behaviors." (p. 28). This suggests that affective reactions and emotion may have qualitatively distinct perceptual and cognitive consequences.

Evaluation. A final, related construct, evaluation, is typically equated with purer forms of cognition. Both the processes by which evaluation is computed (Fiske and Neuberg, 1990) and by which evaluation is represented internally (Breckler and Wiggins, 1989) are held to involve largely cognitive-propositional processes. Evaluations can be retrieved at will as when a person is asked whether he or she likes the Red Sox. Willful retrieval of an affective reaction is unlikely to yield veridical results (Breckler and Wiggins, 1989; Zajonc and Markus, 1984).

Expressions of emotion as affective information

Emotional expression is thought to be one of the most powerful types of affective information (Buck, 1984, 1988; Izard, 1977). There is considerable cross-cultural agreement about the meaning of facial expressions (Ekman, 1973; Ekman *et al.*, 1987); and infants possess a well-developed capacity to discriminate among emotional expressions (Field *et al.*, 1982; Schwarz *et al.*, 1985). Few studies have explicitly sought to demonstrate the affect-eliciting quality of facial expression in the laboratory; however, findings from studies with different aims indicate that perception of an emotional expression involves an immediate (congruent) affective reaction.

Social referencing refers to the idea that infants interpret situations by attending to the facial expression of the primary caretaker (Campos, 1983; Campos and Sternberg, 1981). For example, an infant may avoid a stimulus of which a parent expresses fear. This suggests that infants possess the capacity to interpret emotional expressions. However, the manner in which facial expressions are internally transformed by the infant is not clear. One possibility is that the perception of facial expression produces mimicry in infants (Meltzoff and Moore, 1977) and that a congruent affective reaction is a consequence of the mimicry (Adelmann and Zajonc, 1987; Zajonc *et al.*, 1987). The affective reaction itself may motivate appropriate action.

Additional evidence that the perception of emotional expression recruits a congruent affective reaction comes from research in which expressive faces are employed as conditioned stimuli (CS) (Dimberg and Ohman, 1983; Lanzetta and Orr, 1980). In one study, subjects' autonomic responses were conditioned to pictures of facial expressions of fear or happiness using shock as the unconditioned stimulus (UCS). The magnitude and rate of acquisition of the conditioned response were greater when fear faces, compared with happy faces, served as the CS. Apparently, facial expressions are associated with externally valid classes of events in memory; fear and electric shock are compatible events whereas happiness and shock are not. This study also provided evidence for the primary affect-eliciting properties of facial expressions. Emotional expressions are potent enough releasers of affective reactions to be resistant to conditioning to a UCS that itself elicits a conflicting feeling; emotional expressions may therefore be considered one type of UCS (Lanzetta and Orr, 1980). As Zajonc (1986) has noted, "If smiling has subjectively felt pleasurable after effects, then the reproduction of another person's smile is *in itself* pleasurable and, therefore, reinforcing" (p. 14).

Results of a few studies that have examined the physiological processes that accompany perception of emotional expression lend further support to this argument. Dimberg (1982) showed that electromyographic (EMG) activity in the zygomatic muscle increases during perception of smiling faces and activity in the corrugator muscle increases during perception of angry faces. The presence of minute facial muscular, and particularly autonomic, responses, does not count as conclusive evidence for the affect-eliciting potential of facial expression. However, in combination with work demonstrating the presence of certain EMG patterns during emotional imagery and feeling states (Cacioppo *et al.*, 1986), it seems reasonable to conclude that emotional expressions can elicit a reaction congruent in valence (though probably not intensity or duration) in a perceiver (Lanzetta *et al.*, 1976).

We might now accept the proposition that facial expression elicits affective reactions in perceivers. Research on the influences of this and other types of affective information on social judgment is reviewed next.

Is there a role for affect in social judgment?

Clearly, individuals' feelings about other people accompany their judgments, evaluations, and impressions of them (Schneider *et al.*, 1979). That initial affective reactions to a target also directly influence the processes by which judgments are generated is less widely accepted. In this section, we survey some of the experimental research that suggests that affective reactions influence social judgment. While most of this work does not rule out strictly cognitively mediated processing, findings range from those which seem merely to suggest an important role for affect in social judgment (e.g. studies of evaluative inconsistency and physical attractiveness), to those which provide more "pure" demonstrations of affective influence (e.g. studies of pupillary dilation and mood).

Evaluative inconsistency. Osgood *et al.*, (1957) were struck by the centrality of the evaluative dimension in judgments of objects and persons. Although the evaluative dimension appeared to explain the greatest part of the variance in subjects' judgments, Osgood and his colleagues did not ask whether the cognitive processes or information structures involved in evaluative judgments differed in kind from those associated with descriptive judgments. Recent research on person memory supports the hypothesis that independent cognitive structures exist for descriptive and evaluative person representations, respectively (Gordon and Wyer, 1987; Srull and Wyer, 1989). Wyer and Gordon (1982) provide evidence that individuals attempt to resolve evaluatively inconsistent information about a target by forming more associative links among items of information. This does not appear to be the case for descriptively inconsistent information.

Why is it that evaluative inconsistency is more likely to promote cognitive elaboration than is descriptive inconsistency? One possibility is that the tension of conflicting affective reactions to evaluative inconsistencies motivates the integration of information within the existing structure. Alternatively, evaluative inconsistency may simply be perceived to be of greater importance, and deserving of more energy toward resolution. In either case, since affective reactions to targets may conflict with the evaluative tone of descriptive information, they are likely to contribute to the strong influence that evaluative inconsistency has on the organization of information about others, as well as the independent evaluative representations that are sometimes formed.

Physical attractiveness. Physical attractiveness facilitates positive judgments, ranging from liking for dance partners (Walster *et al.*, 1966), to judgments of happiness, success, and other positive personality attributes (Dion *et al.*, 1972), to decreased blame for criminal behavior (Sigall and Ostrove, 1975). The explanations for these findings have traditionally been couched in cognitive terms. Labels such as *stereotype, bias* or *halo* are used, suggesting that the feature "attractive" serves as a higher-order cue to associated positive material in semantic memory. Rarely have researchers explicitly considered the role that affect plays in the general praise of attractive others, however (Berscheid, 1982). It is possible that the attribute attractive is a positive judgment produced to match the quality of a positive affective reaction to an attractive person. This role of affect in the attractiveness "stereotype" is suggested by the fact that judgments of attractiveness are highly unstable and can change if the perceiver's affective reaction to the target is manipulated. For example, judgments of attractiveness have been altered by elevating the arousal of the perceiver, as in the "wobbly bridge" study by Dutton and Aron (1974) (see also Clark *et al.*, 1983) and by altering the interpersonal "warmth" of the target (Nisbett and Bellows, 1977).

Results of another study also suggest that the attractiveness stereotype might be more generally considered a consequence of positive affect. Mueser et al., (1984) obtained three pictures of fifteen female models in which the models expressed joy, a neutral emotion, and sadness. Different subjects saw one of the three pictures of each model and rated her attractiveness. Results indicated that the models were perceived as less attractive in their "sad" pictures compared with their "neutral" and "happy" ones. Further, these results were obtained even when subjects attempted to compensate for the influence of emotional expression. As Mueser et al. pointed out, a positive affective reaction to a target may lead a perceiver to form positive judgments of that target, *one of which is that the target is attractive.*

Pupillary dilation. Perceivers react positively to other people whose pupils are dilated and more negatively to people with constricted pupils (Hess, 1975; Jones and Moyel, 1971; Stass and Willis, 1967). Results of two recent experiments indicate, further, that this cue affects the valence of a perceiver's judgments of the target person, at least in the absence of other information (Niedenthal and Cantor, 1986). Two slides of each of eight models (four males, and four females) were obtained for use in the study. One of the slides showed the model with dilated pupils and the other with constricted pupils (Figure 7.1). Two sets of slides were then constructed. Each set included slides of four of the models with dilated pupils and four with constricted pupils; two slides of the same model were, of course, never members of the same set. Subjects were exposed to one set of slides. As each slide was presented, subjects heard short personality profiles of the prototypic member of a positive or negative social category. A positive profile, of a *generous mother*, was "She does charity work, is inventive, has warm, soft hands, and supports social programs." A negative profile, of a *scheming politician*, was "He tries to con people, is ambitious, wears tailored suits, and likes being in the spotlight." Subjects rated the likelihood that the profile accurately described the target. Results showed that subjects rated profiles of positive, compared with negative, types of people as more likely to describe targets with dilated pupils. Profiles of negative types of people were rated as more likely to describe targets with constricted pupils.

One alternative interpretation of these results is that individuals with constricted pupils "fit" negative social categories better than positive categories, and that the opposite is true of persons with dilated pupils. The attribute "beady eyes" may be diagnostic of membership in a negative category. However, in this and related studies (Flade and Lindner, 1979), subjects were unaware of the dilation manipulation. Furthermore, this rudimentary cue has been shown to elicit affect on other nonverbal, and physiological, measures (Kirkland and Smith, 1978; Simms, 1967).

Mood. Although we have distinguished stimulus-based affective reaction from mood, mood state has been shown to exert an influence on a wide range of cognitive processes involved in social judgment (see Clark and Williamson, 1989; Mayer and Salovey, 1988; for recent reviews). Forgas, Bower, and their colleagues have investigated the effects of mood on social judgment. In one study they found that adults who had been placed in experimentally induced happy and sad moods spent more time reading mood-consistent, compared with mood-inconsistent, information about target individuals (Forgas and Bower, 1987). Happy and sad moods also facilitate the interpretation of videotaped behaviors in a mood-consistent manner (Forgas *et al.*, 1984). In both of these studies, subjects' judgments about the targets were mood-consistent in valence and their recall of mood-consistent information was superior to mood-inconsistent information. Results of prior studies by Gouaux (1971) and Griffitt (1970) also suggest that positive mood is associated with increased attention to the positive features of others.

In the domain of self-perception, Salovey and Birnbaum (1989) found that mood influences individuals' attention to their own physical symptoms and estimated vulnerability to health problems in the future (see also Salovey *et al.*, this volume). Again, mood-consistent findings were obtained, with happier subjects feeling less discomfort and greater efficacy regarding the alleviation of symptoms than those in sad moods. The effect of mood upon the accessibility of features of the self-concept seems to be a robust one (Mischel *et al.*, 1976; Salovey and Singer, 1989), though the effect may be moderated by personality factors (Mayer and Salovey, 1988).

Presumably, the processes by which mood affects social judgment are similar to those which may be triggered by affective reactions to a target. In either case, an interest in affect and its consequences for information processing shifts the focus of research in person perception to emphasize different aspects of the perceptual and interpretive processes, and calls for attention to the consequences of implicitly perceived affective information.

Focus on the Perception of Affective Information: Implicit Perception

Individuals can and do control the consequences of their affective reactions to other people so long as they are aware that there is an affective reaction to control or they are aware of the cue that elicited the affect (Buck,

FIG 7.1   Target with dilated and constricted pupils.

1983). An example of control is the substitution of a socially or societally appropriate facial expression for one that seems unexpected or inappropriate (Hochschild, 1979). However, affective information may also be perceived implicitly (Niedenthal, 1990; Robles *et al.*, 1987) and the consequences in this case may be less likely to be controlled. *Implicit perception* is inferred when stimuli that are demonstrably outside of conscious awareness exert reliable influences on on-going perceptual and cognitive processes (Kihlstrom, 1989). The effects of implicit perception of information are of considerable importance in understanding social judgment (Lewicki, 1986) and social interaction (Neuberg, 1988). As Bargh (1989) has suggested, the results of processes instigated by undetected information may feel more veracious than those instigated by consciously perceived events.

Empirical evidence for the implicit perception of (verbal) affective information comes from the work of Greenwald and his colleagues. In one study (Greenwald *et al.*, 1989) a positive or negative word (prime) was presented to subjects' nondominant eye. The prime was rendered undetectable by the presentation of a pattern mask to the dominant eye; a procedure called *dichoptic pattern masking*. The mask was followed by a second word (target) and subjects reported whether the target word had a positive or negative meaning. Results showed that the speed with which subjects reported the affective meaning of the target word was related to the valence of the prime. When prime and target were inconsistent in affective meaning, response latencies were significantly longer than when prime and target were affectively consistent. This suggests that the valence of the prime had been implicitly perceived via processes that interfered with the processing of information of a different valence (see also Fazio *et al.*, 1986).

Recently, Niedenthal (1988, 1990) reported evidence that individuals implicitly perceive emotional expressions. Specifically, she demonstrated that undetected facial expressions could serve as a cue to the identity of a spatially and temporally linked detectable stimulus. Subjects were exposed to 20 slides of a novel cartoon character (the target). Each target was immediately preceded by a very brief presentation of a slide of a human face expressing either joy or disgust. This procedure, in which a second detectable slide masks (prevents detection of) a prior slide, has been termed *metacontrast* (Dixon, 1981). Later, subjects discriminated targets from distractor cartoons, and response latencies to identification were recorded. Type of emotion expressed by undetected faces on discrimination trials varied, however. On half of the trials, for both targets and distractors, the face expressed an emotion which was consistent with that expressed by the faces paired with the target cartoons during learning (affect-consistent trials). On the remaining trials, for each type of stimulus, a face expressing an inconsistent emotion was presented (affect-inconsistent trials). If the undetectable faces were associated with the visual target stimulus initially, then "target" responses should be faster on affect-consistent compared with affect-inconsistent trials. Results of the experiment confirmed this expectation: target stimuli were identified more quickly as such when the affective information present in the context was consistent in valence with the previous affective information.

The experiment just described provides some evidence for the implicit perception of facial expression of emotion and its influences on the speed of identification of a stimulus. However, the experiment provides no evidence for the idea that these stimuli elicited affective reactions in perceivers. It is possible that the structural features of one type of facial expression (joy) served as a cue to identification of targets and the structural difference of the affect-inconsistent faces (disgust) was sufficient to inhibit identification. A second experiment was conducted to provide evidence for a role of affective reaction in the observed effect.

In this study (Niedenthal, 1991), subjects saw slides of faces of 12 different female targets expressing neutral emotion over two blocks of learning trials. Target slides were paired with undetectable slides of scenes which sometimes contained people, but which did not depict expressions of joy or disgust. The scenes had been shown in pretesting to elicit joy or disgust reactions. Meanwhile, the slides used to elicit consistent and inconsistent affect on discrimination trials were not the affect-inducing scenes, but the faces of joy and disgust used in the previous study-slides that were structurally different from the scene slides. In spite of this difference in the structure of the affective information, subjects still made target responses faster on affect-consistent compared with affect-inconsistent trials. The effect was strongest in the disgust condition (in which disgusting scenes were paired with the women's faces on learning trials). Thus it seems that affective reactions themselves can come to serve as cues to the identity of external stimuli such as human faces.

If implicit perception of affective information involves affective reactions in perceivers, it is possible that those reactions influence not only perception (as evidenced by influences on identification) but also social judgment (the valence of attributes that are assigned to the target, for example). Judgments of an affect-consistent valence could be produced because the affective reaction cues affect-consistent information in memory (Isen, 1984) or because people are motivated to provide verbal justifications for their affective reactions (Bartlett, 1932). This idea was tested in an experiment in which novel cartoons were paired with undetectable faces that expressed either joy or disgust in metacontrast (Niedenthal, 1990). Subjects assigned to the joy condition formed a more positive impression of the cartoon as indicated by their use of positive and negative attributes to describe the cartoons. Subjects in the disgust condition formed a somewhat more negative impression of the cartoons. Thus, it appears that even subtle affective reactions, elicited by implicitly perceived affective information, may influence both social perception and the quality of social judgment.

Focus on the Processing of Affective Information: Category-Based and Piecemeal Evaluation, and Organization by Affect

It has been argued that affective reactions exert effects on the valence of social judgments; but the processes by which the effects obtain remain unspecified. In the following sections, we consider the possible role of affect in a model of evaluation developed by Fiske and her colleagues (Fiske and Neuberg, 1990; Fiske and Pavelchak, 1986). This model holds that perceivers typically try to match the known features of a target person to readily accessible, familiar social categories. If categorization is successful—the target matches a category well—the perceiver applies the global evaluation of that category to the target. To the extent that a target is not successfully categorized, the perceiver must effortfully combine the valences of each known feature of the target in a piecemeal fashion to form an overall evaluation. For example, if Ronald has liked most tennis players he has met, and he meets Francine, who says she is a tennis player, Ronald will evaluate Francine positively. On the other hand, if Ronald learns that Francine possesses the attributes friendly, stingy, angry, and talented—a set of attributes that does not fit a social category easily—he will combine his evaluation of each attribute incrementally to form a global one. Although this model (as stated) is highly cognitive, in the following sections we consider how affective reactions might influence both *category-based* and *piecemeal* modes of evaluation.

Influences on categorization. When processing is category-based (for example, a label such as "tennis player" is explicitly known), affective reactions to stimulus-based features may still influence the perceived goodness-of-fit of the target to the category. As described above, affective reactions to a target induced by pupillary dilation have been shown to increase the perceived descriptiveness of affect-consistent personality profiles (Niedenthal and Cantor, 1986, Experiment 1). Similar results were obtained when affective reactions were manipulated through implicit perception of emotional expressions (Niedenthal, 1990, Experiment 2). These studies suggest that social categorization is more successful when affective reactions to a target match the overall evaluation of the category. When affective reactions to a target are inconsistent with the valence of the category which offers the best fit to descriptive information, the inconsistency may motivate greater cognitive activity to maintain the descriptively plausible categorization. Alternatively, the perceiver may attempt to resolve the inconsistency by creating a new affectively-consistent subcategory (Fiske and Neuberg, 1990).

Influences on piecemeal processing. Under piecemeal conditions (when no category label is available), affective reactions may influence information processing in many of the same ways that cognitive expectations have been shown to. For example, just as expectations influence the interpretation of ambiguous information about a target (Darley and Gross, 1983), affective reactions may bias interpretation of information to be affectively consistent; affective reactions may also enhance recall of consistent information (Isen *et al.*, 1978); and they may motivate the elaboration of affectively inconsistent information (time permitting) which will be well-remembered if elaboration is successful (cf., Hastie, 1980, on processing of schema-incongruent events). We propose that such affect-based influences may potentially occur *independently* of any cognitive expectancies that are formed. Just as mood has been shown to have special effects on memory and judgment (Isen and Means, 1983), affective reactions may influence interpretations, recall, and even judgment heuristics.

Affective influences on organization. Whether evaluation is produced in piecemeal or category-based fashion, affective reactions may exert their influence via the reorganization of information in working memory. Increasingly, evidence suggests a relationship between affective states and cognitive organization. Isen (1987) argues that positive mood is associated with a "complex cognitive content," characterized by the activation of a wide range of thoughts organized in a broader, more integrated, and more flexible fashion, compared with organization in neutral or negative mood states. Positive mood subjects have been shown to rate weak exemplars of a category as better members of that category than neutral mood controls. And the effect obtains for both social (Isen *et al.*, 1990) and nonsocial (Isen and Daubman, 1984) material. In a recent study, positive mood subjects formed fewer categories of items in a sorting task, yet recognized more different ways of grouping items, implying increased use of both differentiated and integrative thought (see Isen and Daubman, 1984; Isen, 1987; for discussion). Moreover, Murray *et al.* (1990) found that positive mood subjects recognized both more similarities and more differences between target persons than did neutral mood subjects.

Recent research by Showers (1989) examined the relationship between mood and the organization of affectively laden information, namely, positive and negative knowledge about the self. Measures of cognitive organization used in that work assess the extent to which an individual's knowledge about the self is evaluatively integrated (i.e. negative information is linked to and integrated with more positive features of the self) or evaluatively compartmentalized (i.e. negative information is closely associated with other negative information). The results of three studies demonstrate correlational relationships between evaluative organization and individual's mood (i.e. level of depression), and global self-evaluation. However, it is not clear whether mood states influenced the organization and reorganization of affect-laden information, or whether moods reflect the impact of evaluative organization on judgments about the self.

Similarly, the organization of information about others may be influenced by affective reactions *and* contribute to effects on social judgments. Studies by Niedenthal and Showers (in preparation) used measures of cognitive organization to examine processing differences that may result from affective reactions to a target as compared with cognitive expectancies. Although cognitive expectancies may facilitate increased attention to and elaboration of inconsistent information (given sufficient processing time; Hastie and Kumar, 1979), affective reactions may tend to bias judgments via selective attention to affectively consistent information (Forgas and Bower, 1987) and via biased interpretations of information (Forgas *et al.*, 1984). In other words, individuals with a positive cognitive expectancy may be prone to process subsequent positive and negative information about a target in an integrative fashion as they attempt to resolve the apparent inconsistencies between their positive expectations and the information they receive. In contrast, individuals who have an initial positive *affective reaction* to a target may be more likely to compartmentalize positive and negative information, because that type of organization allows them to attend selectively to affectively consistent information and to ignore or devalue inconsistent items.

In two studies, Niedenthal and Showers manipulated subjects' interpretive set for a target by eliciting either an affective reaction or a cognitive expectancy. The "affect" groups were shown one of two sets of slides of the target (Leslie). The slides in each set were similar; however, there were differences in Leslie's facial expressions (she was either smiling or displaying neutral expression), which elicited different affective reactions in pretest subjects. Subjects assigned to the cognitive expectancy ("description") groups read either positive or neutral personality descriptions of Leslie constructed from pretest subjects' impressions of the slides. Next, subjects in all four groups read the same (randomly presented) positive, negative, and neutral statements about Leslie's social behavior under impression-formation instructions. Finally, after a distractor task, subjects recalled the statements about Leslie and rated her on scale anchored by positive and negative personality attributes (e.g. friendly–unfriendly).

Analyses examined subjects' tendency to organize information about Leslie according to its positive or negative valence, and the extent to which that organization predicted the valence of attribute judgments. The measure of organization was the conditional probability of recalling a positive statement about Leslie following recall of a different positive statement. Similar measures were calculated for recall of negative and neutral statements. In both studies, subjects in the positive description condition were most likely to organize the information they recalled about Leslie in an integrative fashion. (There were no differences in the average numbers of positive, negative, or neutral statements recalled.) Moreover, organization of information predicted subjects' impressions of Leslie. Integrative organization by the positive description group was associated with less positive impressions both in comparison with the positive affect condition and as assessed by the within-cell correlation between organization and valence of impression. It appears that integrative processing was associated with increased attention to and greater weighting of negative statements in the subjects' judgments. In the positive affect condition, subjects did not integrate positive and negative information and also retained a positive impression of Leslie.

Consistent with the findings of Showers' self-concept research, for subjects in the neutral description condition of this experiment, a positive relationship between integrative organization and positive impression was observed. In this case, attention to positive and negative statements would not have been biased by prior expectations (or contrast effects), and so integrative processing may simply reflect the successful resolution of inconsistencies.

Affective reactions and cognitive expectancies appear to promote distinct modes of information processing. Individuals who hold specific cognitive expectancies may be motivated to confront inconsistencies with integrative processing of subsequent information. In contrast, affective reactions may guide attention to and bias interpretations of individual pieces of information without motivating integrative processing.

Concluding Remarks

In this chapter we tried to broaden the class of information believed to influence social perception and social judgment to include those stimuli that elicit affective reactions, even when implicitly perceived. We argued that affective reactions, like other types of information, can guide the identification of social targets; contribute to the goodness-of-fit of such targets to plausible social categories; and influence evaluations of target individuals. In considering the processes by which these effects obtain, we suggested that an affective reaction, like mood, might serve as a cue to affectively laden material in memory, or that an affective reaction might simply motivate verbal justification. In addition, we presented some evidence that affective reactions serve to motivate a particular organization of the separate pieces of descriptive information learned about a target. These organizational processes may then mediate global evaluation.

In conclusion, we end on a cautionary methodological note: when conducting research on the influences of affective reaction on social judgment, it is tempting to point to the dependent measure of interest (e.g. valence of social judgment) as both the interesting outcome of an affective reaction, *and* as the validation of the affective reaction itself. In future research, demonstration that a stimulus-base cue has elicited an affective reaction should be independent of the demonstration that an affective reaction is associated with changes in concurrent perceptual and cognitive processes.

Acknowledgments

Preparation of this chapter was supported by funds from BRSG S07 RR0741 and grants # BNS-8919755 from the National Science Foundation and R29 MH4811-O1A1 from the National Institute of Health awarded to Paula M. Niedenthal.

The authors wish to thank Joseph Forgas, John D. Mayer, Steven Neuberg, and Peter Salovey for their helpful comments on a previous draft of this chapter. Address correspondence either to Paula M. Niedenthal, Department of Psychology, Johns Hopkins University, 34th and Charles Streets, Baltimore, MD, 21218; USA, or to Carolin Showers, Department of Psychology, University of Wisconsin, 1202 W. Johnson Street, Madison, WI, 53706, USA.

References

Adelmann, P. K. and Zajonc, R. B. (1987). Facial efference and the experience of emotion. *Annual Review of Psychology*, **40**, 249–280.

Bargh, J. A. (1989). The power behind the throne of judgment: Varieties of automatic influence in social perception and cognition. In J. S. Uleman and J. A. Bargh (Eds), *Unintended thought: Limits of awareness, intention and control*. New York: Guilford Press.

Bartlett, F. (1932). *A study in experimental social psychology*. New York: Cambridge University Press.

Berscheid, E. (1982). Attraction and emotion in interpersonal relationships. In M. S. Clark and S. T. Fiske (Eds), *Affect and cognition: The 17th annual Carnegie symposium on cognition*. Hillsdale, NJ: Erlbaum.

Breckler, S. J. and Wiggins, E. C. (1989). On defining attitude and attitude function: Once more with feeling. In A. R. Pratkanis, S. J. Breckler, and A. G. Greenwald (Eds), *Attitude structure and function*. Hillsdale, NJ: Erlbaum.

Buck, R. (1983). Emotional development and emotional education. In R. Plutchik and H. Kellerman (Eds), *Emotion: Theory, research, and experience*, Vol. 2. New York: Academic Press.

Buck, R. (1984). *The communication of emotion*. New York: Guilford Press.

Buck, R. (1985). Prime theory: An integrated view of motivation and emotion. *Psychological Review*, **92**, 389–413.

Buck, R. (1988). The perception of facial expression: Individual regulation and social coordination. In T. R. Alley (Ed.), *Social and applied aspects of perceiving faces*. Hillsdale, NJ: Erlbaum.

Cacioppo, J. T., Petty, R. E., Losch, M. E., and Kim, H. S. (1986). Electromyographic activity over facial muscle regions can differentiate the valence and intensity of affective reactions. *Journal of Personality and Social Psychology*, **50**, 260–268.

Campos, J. (1983). The importance of affective communication in social referencing: A commentary on Feinman. *Merrill-Palmer Quarterly*, **29**, 83–87.

Campos, J., and Sternberg, C. (1981). Perception, appraisal, and emotion: The onset of social referencing. In M. Lamb and L. Sherrod (Eds), *Infant social cognition*. Hillsdale, NJ: Erlbaum.

Clark, M. S., and Isen, A. M. (1982). Toward understanding the relationship between feeling states and social behavior. In A. Hastorf and A. M. Isen (Eds), *Cognitive social psychology*, New York: Elsevier North–Holland.

Clark, M. S., Milberg, S., and Ross, J. (1983). Arousal cues arousal-related material in memory: Implications for understanding effects of mood on memory. *Journal of Verbal Learning and Verbal Behavior*, **22**, 633–649.

Clark, M. S., and Williamson, G. M. (1989). Moods and social judgments. In H. Wagner and A. Manstead (Eds), *Handbook of social psychophysiology*. Chichester: Wiley.

Darley, J. M., and Gross, G. R. (1983). A hypothesis-confirming bias in labeling effects. *Journal of Personality and Social Psychology*, **44**, 20–33.

de Charms, R. (1983). *Personal causation*. Hillsdale, NJ: Erlbaum, (first published 1968).

Dimberg, U. (1982). Facial reactions to facial expressions. *Psychophysiology*, **19**, 643–647.

Dimberg, V., and Ohman, A. (1983). The effects of directional facial cues on electrodermal conditioning to facial stimuli. *Psychophysiology*, **20**, 160–167.

Dion, K. K., Berscheid, E., and Walster, E. (1972). What is beautiful is good. *Journal of Personality and Social Psychology*, **24**, 285–290.

Dixon, N. F. (1981). *Preconscious processing*. New York: Wiley.

Dutton, D. G., and Aron, A. P. (1974). Some evidence for heightened sexual attraction under conditions of high anxiety. *Journal of Personality and Social Psychology*, **30**, 510–517.

Ekman, P. (1973). Cross-cultural studies of facial expression. In P. Ekman (Ed.), *Darwin and facial expression: A century of research in review*. New York: Academic Press.

Ekman, P., and Friesen, W. V. (1975). *Unmasking the face*. Englewood Cliffs, NJ: Prentice-Hall.

Ekman, P., Friesen, W. V., O'Sullivan, M., Chan, A., Diacoyanni-Tarlatzis, I, Heider, K., Krause, K., LeCompte, W. A., Pittcairn, T., Ricci-Bitt, P. E., Scherer, K., Tomita, M., and Tzavaras, A. (1987). Universals and cultural differences in the judgments of facial expressions of emotion. *Journal of Personality and Social Psychology*, **53**, 712–717.

Fazio, R. H., Sanbonmatsu, D. M., Powell, M. C., and Kardes, F. R. (1986). On automatic activation of attitudes. *Journal of Personality and Social Psychology*, **50**, 229–238.

Field, T. M., Woodson, R., Greenberg, R., and Cohen, D. (1982). Discrimination and imitation of facial expressions by neonates. *Science*, **218**, 179–181.

Fiske, S. T., and Neuberg, S. L. (1990). A continuum model of impression formation from category-based to individuating processes: Influences of information and motivation on attention and interpretation. In M. P. Zanna (Ed.) *Advances in experimental social psychology* (Vol. 23). New York: Academic Press.

Fiske, S. T., and Pavelchak, M. A. (1986). Category-based versus piecemeal affective response: Development in schema-triggered affect. In R. M. Sorrentino and E. T. Higgins, (Eds), *The handbook of motivation and cognition: Foundations of social behavior*. New York: Guilford Press.

Flade, A., and Lindner, G. (1979). Die Rolle der Pupillengrosse bei der Wahnung von Personen. *Zeitschrift fur Experimentelle Angewandte Psychologie*, **26**, 436–447.

Forgas, J. P., and Bower, G. H. (1987). Mood effects on person-perception judgments. *Journal of Personality and Social Psychology*, **53**, 53–60.

Forgas, J. P., Bower, G. H., and Krantz, S. (1984). The influence of mood on the perception of social interaction. *Journal of Experimental Social Psychology*, **20**, 497–513.

Frijda, N. H. (1986). *The emotions*. Cambridge: Cambridge University Press.

Gordon, S. E., and Wyer, R. S., Jr. (1987). Person memory: Category-set-size effects on the recall of a person's behavior. *Journal of Personality and Social Psychology*, **53**, 648–662.

Gouaux, C. (1971). Induced affective states and interpersonal attraction. *Journal of Personality and Social Psychology*, **20**, 37–43.

Greenwald, A. G., Klinger, M. R., and Lui, T. J. (1989). Unconscious processing of dichoptically masked words. *Memory and Cognition*, **17**, 35–47.

Griffitt, W. (1970). Environmental effects on interpersonal behavior: Ambient effective temperature and attraction. *Journal of Personality and Social Psychology*, **15**, 240–244.

Hastie, R. (1980). Memory for behavioral information that confirms or contradicts a personality impression. In R. Hastie, T. M. Ostrom, E. B. Ebbeson, R. S. Wyer, D. L. Hamilton, and D. E. Carlston (Eds), *Person memory: The cognitive basis of social perception*, Hillsdale, NJ: Erlbaum.

Hastie, R. and Kumar, P. A. (1979). Person memory: Personality traits as organizing principles in memory for behavior. *Journal of Personality and Social Psychology*, **37**, 25–38.

Hess, E.H. (1975). *The tell-tale eye*. New York: Litton.

Hochschild, A. R. (1979). Emotion work, feeling rules and social structure. *American Journal of Sociology*, **85**, 551–575.

Isen, A. M. (1984). Toward understanding the role of affect in cognition. In R. S. Wyer and T. K. Srull (Eds), *Handbook of social cognition*, Vol. 3. Hillsdale, NJ: Erlbaum.

Isen, A. M. (1987). Positive affect, cognitive processes, and social behavior. In L. Berkowitz (Ed.), *Advances in experimental social psychology*, Vol. 20. New York: Academic Press.

Isen, A. M., and Daubman, K. A. (1984). The influence of affect on categorization. *Journal of Personality and Social Psychology*, **47**, 1206–1217.

Isen, A. M., and Means, B. (1983). The influence of positive affect on decision-making strategy. *Social Cognition*, **2**, 18–31.

Isen, A. M., Niedenthal, P. M., and Cantor, N. (1990). An influence of positive affect on social categorization. Unpublished manuscript, Johns Hopkins University and Cornell University.

Isen, A. M., Shalker, T. E., Clark, M., and Karp, L. (1978). Affect, accessibility of material in memory and behavior: A cognitive loop? *Journal of Personality and Social Psychology*, **36**, 1–12.

Izard, C. E. (1977). *Human emotions*. New York: Plenum Press.

Izard, C. E. (1984). Emotion-cognition relationships and human development. In C. E. Izard, J. Kagan, and R. B. Zajonc (Eds), *Emotion, cognition, and behavior*. Cambridge: Cambridge University Press.

Jones, Q. R., and Moyel, I. S. (1971). The influence of iris color and pupil size on expressed affect. *Psychometric Science*, **22**, 126–127.

Kihlstrom, J. F. (1989). Implicit cognition and the cognitive unconscious. Paper presented at a symposium on Implicit Cognition, Meetings of the Society for Philosophy and Psychology, Tucson, AR, April 1989.

Kirkland, J., and Smith, J. (1978). Preferences for infant pictures with modified eye-pupils. *Journal of Biological Psychology*, **20**, 33–34.

Laird, J. D. (1984). The real role of facial response in the experience of emotion: A reply to Tourangeau and Ellsworth, and others. *Journal of Personality and Social Psychology*, **47**, 909–917.

Lanzetta, J. T., Cartwright-Smith, J., and Kleck, R. E. (1976). Effects of nonverbal dissimulation on emotional experience and autonomic arousal. *Journal of Personality and Social Psychology*, **33**, 354–370.

Lanzetta, J. T., and Orr, S. P. (1980). Influence of facial expressions on the classical conditioning of fear. *Journal of Personality and Social Psychology*, **39**, 1081–1087.

Lazarus, R. S. (1984). Thoughts on the relations between emotion and cognition. In K. S. Scherer and P. Ekman (Eds), *Approaches to emotion*. Hillsdale, NJ: Erlbaum.

LeDoux, J. E. (1986). Neurobiology and emotion. In J. E. LeDoux and W. Hirst (Eds), *Mind, and brain: Dialogues in cognitive neuroscience*. New York: Cambridge University Press.

Leventhal, H. (1980). Toward a comprehensive theory of emotion. In L. Berkowitz (Ed.), *Advances in experimental social psychology*, Vol. 13, pp. 139–207. New York: Academic Press.

Leventhal, H. (1984). A perceptual motor theory of emotion. In K. S. Scherer & P. Ekman (Eds), *Approaches to emotion*. Hillsdale, NJ: Erlbaum.

Lewicki, P. (1986). *Nonconscious social information processing*. New York: Academic Press.

Mayer, J. D., and Salovey, P. (1988). Personality moderates the interaction of mood and cognition. In K. Fiedler and J. Forgas (Eds), *Affect, cognition and social behavior*. Toronto: Hogrefe.

Meltzoff, A. N., and Moore, M. K. (1977). Imitation of facial and manual gestures by human neonates. *Science*, **198**, 75–78.

Mischel, W., Ebbeson, E., and Zeiss, A. (1976). Determinants of selective attention about the self. *Journal of Counselling and Clinical Psychology*, **44**, 92–103.

Mueser, K. T., Grau, B. W., Sussman, S., and Rosen, A. J. (1984). You're only as pretty as you feel: Facial expression as a determinant of physical attractiveness. *Journal of Personality and Social Psychology*, **46**, 469–478.

Murray, H. A. (1933). The effects of fear upon estimates of the maliciousness of other personalities. *Journal of Social Psychology*, **4**, 310–329.

Murray, N., Sujan, H., Hirt, E. R., and Sujan, M. (1990). The influence of mood on categorization: A cognitive flexibility hypothesis. *Journal of Personality and Social Psychology*, **59**, 411–425.

Neuberg, S. L. (1988). Behavioral implications of information presented outside of conscious awareness: The effect of subliminal presentation of trait information on behavior in the prisoner's dilemma game. *Social Cognition*, **6**, 207–230.

Niedenthal, P. M. (1988). Automatic affective responses guide person perception. Presented at Symposium on Nonconscious Processing of Affect. Meetings of the American Psychological Association, Atlanta, GA, 12–16 August.

Niedenthal, P. M. (1990). Implicit perception of affective information. *Journal of Experimental Social Psychology*, **26**, 505–527.

Niedenthal, P. M. (1991). Affective reactions in social perception. Unpublished manuscript, Johns Hopkins University.

Niedenthal, P. M., and Cantor, N. (1986). Affective responses as guides to category-based inferences. *Motivation and Emotion*, **10**, 217–232.

Niedenthal, P. M., and Showers, C. (in preparation). Influence of affective reactions on the organization of information about others.

Nisbett, R. E., and Bellows, N. (1977). Verbal reports about casual influences on social judgment: Private access versus public theories. *Journal of Personality and Social Psychology*, **35**, 613–624.

Ortony, A., Clore, G. L., and Collins, A. (1988). *The cognitive structure of emotion*. New York: Cambridge University Press.

Osgood, C. E., Suci, G. J., and Tannenbaum, P. H. (1957). *The measurement of meaning*. Urbana: University of Illinois Press.

Robles, R., Smith, R., Carver, C. S., and Wellens, A. R. (1987). Influences of subliminal visual images on the experience of anxiety. *Personality and Social Psychology Bulletin*, **13**, 399–410.

Salovey, P. and Birnbaum, D. (1989). Influence of mood on health-relevant cognitions. *Journal of Personality and Social Psychology*, **57**, 539–551.

Salovey, P., and Singer, J. A. (1989). Mood congruency effects in recall of childhood versus recent memories. *Journal of Social Behavior and Personality*, **43**, 99–120.

Schneider, D. J., Hastorf, A. H., and Ellsworth, P. C. (1979). *Person perception*. Reading, MA: Addison-Wesley.

Schwartz. G. M., Izard, C. E., and Ansul, S. E. (1985). The five-month-old's ability to discriminate facial expressions of emotion. *Infant Behavior and Development*, **8**, 65–77.

Showers, C. (1989). The organization of positive and negative components of the self. Paper presented at the meeting of the Midwestern Psychological Association, Chicago, 4–6 May.

Sigall, H., and Ostrove, N. (1975). Beautiful but dangerous: Effects of offender attractiveness and nature of the crime on juridic judgment. *Journal of Personality and Social Psychology*, **31**, 410–414.

Simms, T. M. (1967). Pupillary response of male and female subjects to pupillary difference in male and female picture stimuli. *Perception and Psychophysics*, **2**, 553–555.

Singer, J. A., and Salovey, P. (1988). Mood and memory: Evaluating the network theory of affect. *Clinical Psychology Review*, **8**, 211–251.

Srull, T. K. and Wyer, R. S. (1989). Person memory and judgment. *Psychological Review*, **96**, 58–83.

Stass, J. W., and Willis, F. N. (1967). Eye contact, pupil dilation, and personal preference. *Psychonomic Science*, **7**, 375–376.

Tomkins, S. S. (1962). *Affect, imagery, and consciousness*, Vol. 1. New York: Springer.

Uleman, J. S., and Bargh, J. A. (1989). *Unintended thought: Limits of awareness, intention and control*. New York: Guilford Press.

Walster, E., Aronson, V., Abrahams, D., and Rottmann, L. (1966). Importance of physical attractiveness in dating behavior. *Journal of Personality and Social Psychology*, **4**, 508–516.

Wyer, R. S., Jr., and Gordon, S. E. (1982). The recall of information about persons and groups. *Journal of Experimental Social Psychology*, **18**, 128–164.

Zajonc, R. B. (1980). Feeling and thinking. Preferences need no inferences. *American Psychologist*, **35**, 151–175.

Zajonc, R. B. (1986). The face as a primary instrument of social process. Presented at the symposium "Social Psychology and the Emotions," Maison des Sciences de l'Homme, Paris, 5–9 January.

Zajonc, R. B., Adelmann, P. K., Murphy, S. T., and Niedenthal, P. M. (1987). Convergence in the physical appearance of spouses. *Motivation and Emotion*, **11**, 335–346.

Zajonc, R. B., and Markus, H. (1984). Affect and cognition: The hard interface. In C. E. Izard, J. Kagan, and R. B. Zajonc (Eds), *Emotions, cognition, and behavior*. Cambridge: Cambridge University Press.

8

Motivation and Complexity Levels as Determinants of Heuristic Use in Social Judgment

NYLA R. BRANSCOMBE and BRIAN M. COHEN

University of Kansas

Contents

Throughout our lives, we make thousands of social judgments—Did I enjoy that party? Am I satisfied with my income? How do I feel about a particular political candidate? Is he attractive? Will she make a good roommate? How much do I like my new colleague? Not only do we face questions like these daily, but most of us have little problem providing acceptable and relatively quick answers. Yet we probably pay scant attention to what sources of information we actually use and how we arrive at such judgments. Without a good reason for doing so, we typically do not attempt to identify and partition all the sources of information used in making these judgments. If asked to explain how and why we arrived at a particular judgment, we are likely to point to properties of the target or event being judged. Few people would admit to, or are even aware of, using their own emotional state as a means of making a judgment, and people are, if anything, even more reluctant to admit that they might make judgments based solely on culturally acquired group-level stereotypes (Crosby *et al.*, 1980; Darley and Gross, 1983; Karlins *et al.*, 1969).

Most people believe that their judgments are veridical, and the result of a thoughtful, rational process. Clearly, one way of arriving at social judgments is to consider all relevant target information, and to process this information through some sort of controlled cognitive analysis (cf. Anderson, 1974). Presumably, such a process would provide the perceiver with a relatively accurate judgment, perhaps even allowing the perceiver access to how it was accomplished. Even under these circumstances, however, when a judgment is computed, moods and stereotypes can still potentially exert a biasing effect by determining what information is accessible and therefore used in forming the judgment. An alternative to this time- and effort-consuming processing route is available and it involves the use of heuristics that can shorten and simplify the judgment task. This latter view, which paints perceivers as "cognitive misers," has guided much social perception research (Fiske and Taylor, 1984).

A great deal of research has now demonstrated that for many judgments perceivers are willing to sacrifice accuracy for efficiency. Or, because of time and processing constraints, people cannot prevent themselves from making such a trade-off, even if they might wish to do otherwise. Clearly, valuable time would be unnecessarily spent if we considered all of the relevant factors every time we made a judgment. Social stereotypes are a well-studied example of such judgment-simplifying devices that allow people a means of predicting others in a complex and busy world (Fiske, 1982; Hamilton and Trolier, 1986; Taylor, 1981). Similarly, in the emotion and social judgment literature we see this same portrait of the human judge—people using their current mood state as a heuristic device for arriving at judgments (Blaney, 1986; Forgas and Bower, 1988a; Isen, 1984; Schwarz and Clore, 1988).

An Integration of the Stereotyping and Mood Research Literature

Thus far, work on mood state effects and research on the influence of stereotypes in social judgment has not been well integrated. This state of affairs is an obvious omission when one considers that both bodies of work are concerned with the same fundamental issue—when people use affect as a heuristic in social judgment and decision making. We will attempt to draw this work together and show that the use of either of these heuristic devices occurs under the exact same set of conditions—when the information processing strategy that the perceiver employs is relatively automatic in nature. By the same token, the likelihood of *not* using either of these heuristic strategies is also determined by the same set of variables—those that encourage a more controlled processing strategy—primarily motivational or goal-related components.

Social perceivers may allow both of these sources of target-irrelevant information to influence their impressions for a variety of reasons. First, social perception, as opposed to physical perception, involves targets that are inherently ambiguous and need considerable effort to evaluate systematically (cf. Asch, 1946; Heider, 1958). Furthermore, there are few criteria for deciding if one's social judgments are correct or not (Kruglanski, 1989). Therefore, because social perception tasks are complex and necessarily inferential, information located outside the target and within the perceiver is especially likely to bias judgments (Forgas and Bower, 1988b).

Both moods and stereotypes influence judgments precisely because people are unaware of their influence. If made aware of the potential role that a mood state or a stereotype could play in judgment, the impact of these factors is decreased (cf. Darley and Gross, 1983; Devine, 1989; Schwarz and Clore, 1988). In fact, there are numerous social clichés that are repeated in order to remind, or make people aware of, potential external and automatic influences on social judgment. In terms of mood influences, we are admonished to avoid making financial decisions during times of grief in recognition that such judgments may be later regretted when no longer in that state. Similarly, people are reminded not to use their physical appearance stereotypes in judging other people with the phrase "don't judge a book by its cover." Well-socialized adults—but not children, who lack the culturally acquired controlled processing strategies (see Basow, 1980; Cialdini and Kenrick, 1976) can forgo their reliance on these well-practiced inference rules and avoid their biasing effects. So, the impact of moods and stereotypes is exhibited primarily when awareness of their likely influence is not present, when the judgment task is relatively complex, and when motivation to overcome their effects is absent (Fiske, 1989).

Theoretical Explanations of Social Judgment Biases

Both moods (Bower, 1981) and stereotypes (Devine, 1989) can influence social judgments in an automatic manner. That is, stereotype-consistent attributes and mood-congruent information is involuntarily made accessible for a short period of time following activation. Bower's (1981) extension of the associative network theory of memory (Anderson and Bower, 1973) suggests that moods activate concepts in memory that have been previously associated with that mood. Such information, mood-congruent and stereotype-consistent information, is then more consciously accessible and likely to be used when forming a judgment. Many theories of social cognition similarly acknowledge the powerful role that accessible information of any sort plays in judgment (Higgins *et al.*, 1977; Tversky and Kahneman, 1973; Wyer and Srull, 1981).

Although this effect occurs automatically, Bower (Bower and Cohen, 1982; Forgas and Bower, 1988a) and others who have proposed similar models (Clark and Isen, 1982; Teasdale, 1983) have suggested that social, cultural, and motivational factors may override these automatic effects. Overriding these automatic accessibility effects occurs when people consciously search for mood-inconsistent or stereotype-inconsistent information on which to base a judgment. If such a secondary search does not occur, then even if the heuristic approach is avoided and a judgment is computed, the information used in the computation may still be biased. The most accessible information will be used, without a good reason for expending additional cognitive effort. Yet, if the effort is expended, these automatic effects may be avoided. For example, people are often motivated to relieve a negative mood state that they may be in, so instead of persevering with the negative aspects of a social target or situation, the perceiver may search for positive features or actions that would help alleviate the negative mood. This may explain the consistent asymmetry of results in social judgment research found for perceivers in good versus bad moods (Forgas, 1989; Isen, 1984). Another well-known social norm is the convention of politeness prohibiting unprovoked negative evaluations of strangers. Application of this norm has been used to explain why depressed judges rate others' behavior less negatively than they rate their own behavior (Forgas *et al.*, 1984; Roth and Rehm, 1980). Thus, our view accords motivation the capability of overriding automatic stereotype-based and mood-based influences on social judgments, under certain conditions, just as conscious expectancies can override automatic processes in nonaffective semantic tasks (Neely, 1977).

Use of stereotypes and moods as a heuristic can be overcome if their potential effects are noted by the perceiver and thereby avoided. When the validity of the current mood state is questioned by directing subjects' attention to it (Schwarz and Clore, 1983), or when the true source of the feeling is salient (Zillmann, 1978), then people will avoid using this factor as a simplifying strategy—its relevance for judgment, in effect, is discounted. Stereotypes can be similarly avoided or discounted if stereotype-inconsistent information is made highly accessible (Locksley *et al.*, 1980), if perceiver inferences and the target's actual attributes are clearly separable (Slusher and Anderson, 1987), or if it is patently obvious to the subject that he or she is being "forced" to employ a stereotype because specific target information is absent (Darley and Gross, 1983).

Schwarz and Clore (1988) claim that this discounting effect is in opposition to the predictions of the associative network model, and explain mood-consistent judgment by arguing that perceivers misattribute their affective reaction from the mood-inducing stimulus to the judgmental target. However, a different look at the Schwarz and Clore results suggests that they are not necessarily inconsistent with the associative network model. It may be that a given mood state activates mood-congruent attributes of a target, but since the perceiver knows that the mood should be discounted, the perceiver also discounts the mood-congruent attributes. In effect, the perceiver, as a consequence of discarding the value of this heuristic makes an unbiased judgment.

Evidence that automatically accessed information is similarly discounted and corrected for when the biasing agent is pointed out to the subject, however subtly, comes from Martin's (1986, 1989) two-stage set/reset theory of social-priming effects. According to Martin, if people are made aware that a primed social category may influence their judgment of a target, they discount the information that is associated with the primed category and make judgments without using the accessible category, or sometimes even in the opposite direction of the activated category. Consistent with this idea, Devine (1989) found that low-racist individuals who do not personally endorse the stereotype, if given sufficient time for controlled processing, report less stereotypic judgments than high-racist individuals who do endorse the automatically accessed stereotype. Stereotype-consistent reactions were, however, obtained for both high- and low-racist persons when there was insufficient time for conscious attentional employment of personal beliefs.

It is thus our position that moods and stereotypes affect social judgments in two ways: (a) by automatically and unconsciously activating mood-consistent or stereotype-consistent target attributes, and through their greater accessibility, this information comes to bias the resulting judgment; and (b) by using the affective tag itself as a judgmental shortcut to avoid examining target information at all. Both effects can be reduced by the presence of motivational variables that encourage more thorough processing of the target information, and by the knowledge that one's preexisting stereotype or mood may inappropriately bias the judgment. This is not to say that the means by which these variables operate to change information processing strategies are necessarily available to the perceiver's consciousness *per se*. The increased voluntary control produces only the subjective feeling that effort is being expended and that the perceiver is trying to be careful in forming a judgment.

Mediators of Heuristic Use in Social Judgment: Level of Involvement and Degree of Complexity

This chapter argues for a set of conditions where people may use a more controlled information processing strategy before reporting a judgment. When this occurs, they may forgo the heuristic-based judgment route and expend considerable effort and attention to arrive at a complex, and perhaps more accurate, judgment that has stronger links to the information at hand than the lazy perceiver image implies. In order to explicate the conditions where more effortful processing is likely, we need to consider the role of motivation and goal or task complexity. Little by little, motivation has been finding its way back into our theories of social cognition (cf. Neuberg and Fiske, 1987; Sorrentino and Higgins, 1986). How people process information when they are not particularly motivated may be quite different from the processes involved when motivational variables are present. In fact, much past research has demonstrated that motivational arousal is a critical

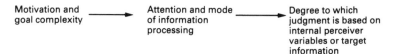

Fig 8.1   Model of the influence of motivational and cognitive processes on the relative use of internal and external information in social judgment

determinant of how much effort people are willing to expend in performance of many different types of tasks (Brehm and Self, 1989).

The specific motivational factor of concern in this chapter is *personal involvement*. As a number of attitude change investigators have shown (Johnson and Eagly, in press; Petty and Cacioppo, 1984), high personal involvement with an issue does motivate people to engage in message-relevant thinking, whereas low involvement results in persuasion due to more peripheral or message-extraneous factors. Personal involvement in a social judgment task may therefore initiate socially learned controlled processes involving target-relevant thinking.

The second factor that may influence one's information processing strategy consists of goal-related variables, specifically the *complexity of the judgmental goal or the judgment task*. As with motivation, people may process information differently when the judgment is simple as opposed to when it is difficult (Wyer and Carlston, 1979). Simple judgmental tasks not only allow the perceiver to attend to the individuating attributes of a target, but also permit the perceiver the cognitive capacity to take into account social norms regarding the appropriateness of reporting certain judgments, and to access all of the judgment-relevant information available, not just mood-congruent or stereotype-consistent information.

As suggested above, conditions that induce a more controlled method of information processing result in judgments that are more closely related to the target information and less influenced by internal perceiver variables. Specifically, in this chapter we will show that high levels of motivation, induced through the perceiver's involvement with the target, and low levels of goal or task complexity can induce or allow controlled attentional processing, which in turn determines the degree to which a judgment is based on internal perceiver variables (either a mood state or a stereotype stored in memory) or observable individuating target information. Figure 8.1 graphically illustrates the chain of events that we are hypothesizing.

Evidence that Motivation Determines Mood and Stereotype Use

Consider first the role of motivation in the use of moods in social judgments. When a person is asked to judge someone or something, and he or she does not care about it, there is no expectation of meeting the target person, and the judgment basically has no personal consequences, then it would be a most inefficient use of cognitive resources for the person to spend time and effort attending to and integrating the presented information. Many of the mood and social judgment studies that have been conducted have involved precisely these conditions of low personal involvement.* That is, when the judgment has no consequences for the perceiver [such as subjects who are asked to rate various consumer products while walking through a shopping mall (Isen *et al.*, 1978)], when the consequences that stem from a decision are hypothetical rather than actual (Isen and Patrick, 1983), or when the judgment required concerns another person and there is no expectation of meeting or interacting with the person being evaluated [they are hypothetical people presented on paper or are just personally irrelevant (Forgas and Bower, 1987)], mood states influence judgment.

In an attempt to assess whether higher levels of motivation would alter the information processing strategy employed, and consequently decrease the perceiver's use of their mood when making social judgments, personal involvement in the task has been directly manipulated (Branscombe, 1988). When subjects were not expecting to meet and interact with the target person they were to judge we, as previous investigators, have found mood-congruent effects, with intensity of the mood correlating with judgments of the target. In contrast, when subjects were anticipating interaction with a target, mood effects were decreased and mood state ratings no longer correlated with judgments of the target. In these conditions, effects of the actual information about the target were much stronger and more complicated, with memory for the information about the target correlating with the judgment formed. This suggests that attention to the actual information about the target was determining subjects' judgments, when subjects were motivated to attend to it because of personal involvement. In the same vein, we have also found that subjects spend considerably longer reading and examining information about a target when they expect to have to explain their opinion to another person, relative to when there is no such expectation. Hence, individuals clearly can devote more effort to processing the specific information given about a target, if motivated to do so. Such attention to individuating information, in turn, produces a more complex and integrated impression of the target (see also Tetlock and Kim, 1987).

Use of social stereotypes as the basis of judgment can also be seen as another affectively based simplifying judgment heuristic that perceivers employ when they are *not* motivated to engage in controlled processing.

---

*This is not intended as a criticism of the experimental procedures employed in the research discussed here. Such conditions may be an accurate reflection of reality. People in their daily lives are often too busy to become highly involved in many of their judgment tasks. In fact, in terms of frequency, it is possible that heuristic-based processing may be more the rule than the exception. We are simply suggesting that given a different set of conditions than those employed in these studies, then mood state effects might be attenuated or eliminated.

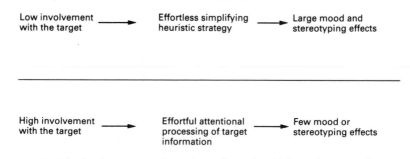

Fig 8.2   Involvement as a determinant of perceivers' information processing

Gilbert *et al.* (1988) and Fiske and Neuberg (1990) argue that when judging another person people first make inferences involving abstract generalizations, frequently based on category membership. People then adjust their judgments, as they receive individuating information about the target. This latter process requires both the cognitive resources to make a more individuated judgment and heightened motivation to do so. Given the motivation, judges work beyond the initial category-based impression towards a more individuated impression based on the target information.

Motivation to attend to, and use, the presented individuating information has been induced in a variety of ways. When the target to be judged is relevant to the perceiver's goals (Brewer, 1988), when the target has consequences for the perceiver's well-being because of outcome dependency (Fiske and Neuberg, 1990; Sherif *et al.*, 1961), when we want to be accurate or fair because we value a nonprejudiced identity (Branscombe and Smith, 1990; Devine, 1989), when we do not wish to be seen as foolish or closed-minded (Fiske, 1989) or when we anticipate public scrutiny of our judgments (Kruglanski and Freund, 1983), then the use of category membership information as a heuristic is reduced or even eliminated. As shown in Figure 8.2 motivation in the form of personal involvement greatly determines the mode of information processing, and the strategy employed in turn determines the degree to which internal perceiver variables in the form of mood states or stereotypes influence social judgment.

Evidence that Goal or Task Complexity Determines Mood and Stereotype Use

Goal or task complexity does not necessarily influence people's willingness to employ an attention-demanding controlled processing strategy as does personal involvement, although it can. Rather, goal or task complexity primarily influences people's ability to effectively focus on target information, consider socially learned judgmental norms, and to form a well-integrated judgment. Mackie *et al.* (1989) have demonstrated that when the complexity of the judgment task is increased by making the individuating target attributes less accessible, there is an increased tendency to simply make stereotype-consistent estimates rather than use the target information.

Complexity in social judgment can, however, arise in a number of ways. First, the target of judgment can be complex; that is, not inherently positive or negative, or easily diagnosed as such. Most social targets are complex in this sense. People consist of a complicated combination of positive and negative attributes. As stated above, it may be just this complexity that makes social targets prime victims of heuristic-based judgments (Forgas and Bower, 1988b). When making a judgment it is virtually impossible to incorporate all of the potentially relevant attributes, thus the information that is first brought into consciousness may disproportionately influence the judgment, with one's mood or stereotype influencing what is accessible.

Second, the judgment task itself can be more or less complex. Different judgment tasks may require the judge to incorporate more or less information into the judgment. What information to consider, and how much of it should be used, is especially unclear in self-related judgments (Schwarz and Strack, 1985). Task complexity can be also altered by the goal of the judgment, the consequences that may follow from it, or the ease with which certain behaviors and traits are diagnosed and validated (cf. Rothbart and Park, 1986). In addition, complexity can differ as a function of individual differences in the perceiver. Individuals differ in the degree to which they consistently perceive and organize person information in a complex fashion (cf. Linville, 1982), possibly rendering them more susceptible to heuristic-based processing as a consequence.

Situational demands can alter the complexity of the judgment task. Situational factors such as time pressures (Fiske and Neuberg, 1990) or distractions (Gilbert *et al.*, 1988) away from the target can increase judgment difficulty, thus permitting fewer cognitive resources to be allotted to the target's individuating characteristics. As a whole, when the goal or judgment task is expected to be, or actually is, relatively simple and situational demands are low, then perceivers can allocate their attention to the individuating target information, reducing the likelihood of both mood and stereotyping effects. On the other hand, when the goal or task is complex in any of the senses described above, a heuristic that would simplify the judgment is particularly likely to be employed.

Consider first the evidence for the impact of complexity on the use of moods in social judgment. Schwarz and his associates (Schwarz and Clore, 1988; Schwarz and Strack, 1985) present data indicating that when people are asked to make judgments that are difficult or ambiguous, such as how satisfied they are with their lives, then mood-congruent judgments are observed. When, however, the judgment that is required is considerably less complex, such as how happy they are with their work, then mood effects disappear. It may be that all of the relevant information is simply more accessible for these simpler judgment tasks, producing the reduction in bias. Or, as we hypothesize, when the task is reasonably simple, then people are more willing and able to engage in a controlled processing strategy involving the retrieval from memory relevant information to compute a judgment, rather than just relying on the simpler heuristic strategy of using their mood state.

Expectations concerning the complexity of the judgment task similarly influence people's employment of stereotypes. For example, Bodenhausen and Lichtenstein (1987) presented subjects with very complex information from a jury transcript. When the subjects processed the trial information with a simple goal in mind—to make a trait judgment—then they were able to avoid using stereotypes in forming their judgments. On the other hand, when given that same trial information and an expectation that they would be required to make a much more complex judgment—one of guilt or innocence—then they did not employ as thoughtful a processing strategy but used stereotypes as a means of simplifying the judgment process.

Situational demands that force perceivers' attention away from the target can also increase complexity (cf. Mackie *et al.*, 1989). People who are cognitively involved elsewhere should not have a lot of difficulty characterizing the target based on stereotypes, although their ability to make corrections based on the individuating information should be diminished (Fiske and Neuberg, 1990). It follows then that people whose attention is directed inwardly toward self-regulation of their overt behavior (a task requiring a significant amount of cognitive resources), should display an impairment at the attribute integration stage. Gilbert *et al.* (1988) found that persons who were required to monitor their own actions by not looking at the words appearing at the bottom of a video screen were, in fact, less able to employ individuating situational constraint information than were persons not so required.

Omoto and Borgida (1988) found that white male subjects who expected to date a black woman made more stereotypic judgments of the target person than did men who thought they were just going to informally interact with her. The cross-race dating subjects' attention was allocated elsewhere (inwardly) rather than toward the target. Self-reports of anxiety and behavioral measures of self-focused attention both indicated that subjects who anticipated a cross-racial date were in fact not focusing on the target. When people think more about themselves, either to regulate their actions or because of anxiety that is aroused by the situation, then they will have fewer cognitive resources to allocate to judging the target, increasing the likelihood of stereotype-based judgments. That is, they will be forced to rely on a judgment-simplifying heuristic.

As summarized in Figure 8.3, goal or task complexity determines the

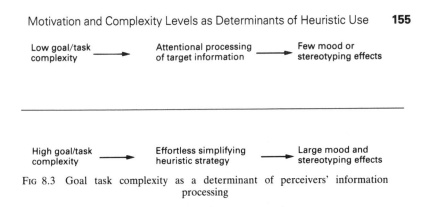

FIG 8.3   Goal task complexity as a determinant of perceivers' information processing

degree to which mood states and stereotypes influence social judgments. It should be noted that the impact of goal/task complexity is opposite to that of personal involvement. Complexity increases the likelihood of heuristic processing and personal involvement decreases the likelihood that people will resort to such judgment-simplifying strategies. What the research from these two literatures reviewed above reveals is essentially two independent sets of main effects. What is not known at this point is whether level of personal involvement and level of goal/task complexity exert interactive effects on the mode of processing and consequently the likelihood that people will employ heuristics. Figure 8.4 summarizes the effects that have been demonstrated concerning people's use of these two affective strategies and the research that remains to be done. Both moods and stereotypes can

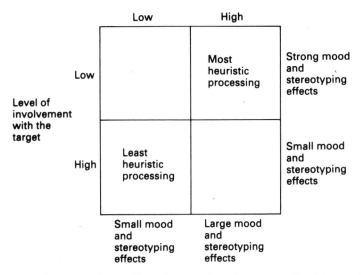

FIG 8.4   Summary of research to date on the role of motivational factors in influencing stereotype-based and mood-based social judgment

serve judgment-simplifying roles, and both are used under similar conditions, yet we do not know which would take precedence or how use of theses two heuristic devices might combine. The problem of how a judgment-simplifying device is selected requires additional research. Below we outline several of the most promising possibilities.

Directions for Further Research on Heuristic Selection

The first alternative is that whichever simplifying device is most salient or intense will be employed. From this perspective, if the mood is strong but the stereotype is weak, then mood effects would predominate. Or, if the stereotype is held particularly strongly or is highly salient but the mood state is weak, then stereotype effects might be anticipated to be strongest. Several investigators (Forgas and Bower, 1988a; Ortony *et al.*, 1988) have, however, advanced theoretical reasons for why this alternative in the mood case is unlikely to be true. The more salient the mood state, the more likely it is to be attributed to a specific cause, making it less likely to influence judgments in general, due to discounting as discussed earlier. Similarly, Darley and Gross (1983) find that if a stereotype is too salient people avoid using it. On the other hand, when the obviousness of the stereotype is diluted by presenting stereotype-irrelevant information, then stereotype-consistent judgments do occur.

Another possibility is that the two heuristic strategies will simply combine in an additive fashion. Hence, if a perceiver is in a bad mood and the applicable stereotype is negative then the impression formed will be more negative than if either the stereotype or mood state were incompatible, in this example positive. The theoretical mechanism here would be some sort of affective summation process, where both sources of affect—the stereotype and the current mood state—combine. The affect resulting from two sequential emotional states has been shown to operate in this manner, at least when the two states are temporally close (Branscombe, 1985).

The third possibility centers on the notion that stereotypes are multidimensional, with the valence of those dimensions often being opposite (Deaux and Lewis, 1984). Take the example of gender stereotypes. Men are perceived as instrumental, which is a socially positive dimension, but they are also perceived as not expressive, which is socially negative. The stereotype for women is, of course, opposite. What may happen is that the perceiver's current mood state may determine which dimension of the activated stereotype is employed. When the male stereotype is accessible and the perceiver is in a positive mood state, it may lead people to exaggerate the application of the positive dimension of that stereotype. Conversely, when in a negative mood, the negative stereotype component may exert a stronger effect. In both cases the stereotype is influencing the judgment but the current mood state is determining which component of the stereotype is used. That is, moods can make one component more accessible and hence likely to be used over another.

Erber (in press) reports a study that is consistent with this notion. When two trait categories are descriptive of a target, the mood-congruent category is used in judgment formation while the mood-incongruent category is ignored. The mood-stereotype link may, however, go beyond increasing accessibility of the mood-consistent stereotypic component to direct attention to mood-consistent category information available in the environment. Forgas and Bower (1987) report that people do spend more time reading and thinking about mood-congruent person information. It is not known yet whether, if given a choice of only stereotypic information, people will solicit or attend to the stereotype component that is mood-congruent over the equally available mood-incongruent stereotypic information. We predict that this would be the case.

The final possibility that we will suggest links the mood and stereotype literatures directly with work on category accessibility. Mood states, because of their time dependency, may be fruitfully thought of as temporary sources of accessibility. Stereotypes, because of their early development and the frequency with which they are practiced, may be conceptualized as information that is chronically accessible. If this is the case, then it is possible that the likelihood of employing either moods or stereotypes as judgment-simplifying devices may depend greatly on time. Bargh *et al.* (1988) have shown that temporary sources of accessibility exert their effects early on, but following a time delay, more chronic sources of accessibility come to dominate judgment. This work suggests then that when two simplifying devices such as moods and stereotypes are both available, moods may predominate early on but stereotypes may quickly come to be the favored judgment-simplifying device.

Resolving this complex issue of which judgment shortcut mechanism will be employed when both are available, and the processes determining their joint operation, will require considerable additional research. We have suggested here some of the most likely possibilities that should be examined. More importantly, the motivational and goal-related conditions that determine how information will be processed, and consequently when mood states or stereotypes will or will not play a role in social judgment, were shown to be identical. Linking the literatures on mood effects and stereotyping effects on social judgment should lead to increased theoretical integration concerning the interplay of affective and cognitive processes under various motivational conditions.

Acknowledgment

Preparation of this chapter was assisted by a New Faculty Grant from the University of Kansas to the first author. Portions of this manuscript are based on an invited presentation given at the meeting of the Midwestern Psychological Association in May 1989. Many thanks to Bob Wyer for the stimulating discussions that encouraged my thinking on these issues, and to Ralph Erber, Joe Forgas, and Yechiel Klar for their helpful comments on an earlier draft of the manuscript. Correspondence should be addressed to Nyla R. Branscombe, Department of Psychology, University of Kansas, Lawrence, KS 66045, USA, or to NYLA @ UKANVM via bitnet.

References

Anderson, J. R., and Bower, G. H. (1973). *Human associative memory*. Washington, DC: Winston.

Anderson, N. H. (1974). Information integration theory: A brief survey. In D. H. Krantz, R. C. Atkinson, R. D. Luce, and P. Suppes (Eds), *Contemporary developments in mathematical psychology*, Vol. 2. San Francisco: Freeman Press.

Asch, S. E. (1946). Forming impressions of personality. *Journal of Abnormal and Social Psychology*, **41**, 258–290.

Bargh, J. A., Lombardi, W. J., and Higgins, E. T. (1988). Automaticity of chronically accessible constructs in person × situation effects on person perception: It's just a matter of time. *Journal of Personality and Social Psychology*, **55**, 599–605.

Basow, S. A. (1980). *Sex–role stereotypes: Traditions and alternatives*. Monteray, CA: Brooks/Cole.

Blaney, P. H. (1986). Affect and memory: A review. *Psychological Bulletin*, **48**, 229–246.

Bodenhausen, G. V., and Lichtenstein, M. (1987). Social stereotypes and information processing strategies: The impact of task complexity. *Journal of Personality and Social Psychology*, **52**, 871–880.

Bower, G. H. (1981). Mood and memory. *American Psychologist*, **36**, 129–148.

Bower, G. H. and Cohen, P. R. (1982). Emotional influences in memory and thinking: Data and theory. In M. S. Clark and S. T. Fiske (Eds), *Affect and cognition*. Hillsdale, NJ: Erlbaum.

Branscombe, N. R. (1985). Effects of hedonic valence and physiological arousal on emotion: A comparison of two theoretical perspectives. *Motivation and Emotion*, **9**, 153–169.

Branscombe, N. R. (1988). A model for predicting the effects of mood and informational factors on social judgment. Paper presented at the meeting of the International Congress of Psychology, Sydney, Australia.

Branscombe, N. R., and Smith, E. R. (1990). Gender and racial stereotypes in impression formation and social decision-making processes. *Sex Roles*, **22**, 627–647.

Brehm, J. W., and Self, E. A. (1989). The intensity of motivation. *Annual Review of Psychology*, **40**, 109–131.

Brewer, M. B. (1988). A dual process model of impression formation. In T. K. Srull and R. S. Wyer, Jr. (Eds), *Advances in social cognition*, Vol. 1. Hillsdale, NJ: Erlbaum.

Cialdini, R. B., and Kenrick, D. T. (1976). Altruism and hedonism: A social development perspective on the relationship of negative mood state and helping. *Journal of Personality and Social Psychology*, **34**, 907–914.

Clark, M. S., and Isen, A. M. (1982). Toward understanding the relationship between feeling states and social behavior. In A. H. Hastorf and A. M. Isen (Eds), *Cognitive social psychology*. New York: Elsevier/North-Holland.

Crosby, F., Bromley, S., and Saxe, L. (1980). Recent unobtrusive studies of black and white discrimination and prejudice: A literature review. *Psychological Bulletin*, **87**, 546–563.

Darley, J. M., and Gross, P. H. (1983). A hypothesis-confirming bias in labeling effects. *Journal of Personality and Social Psychology*, **44**, 20–33.

Deaux, K., and Lewis, L. L. (1984). The structure of gender stereotypes: Interrelationships among components and gender label. *Journal of Personality and Social Psychology*, **46**, 991–1004.

Devine, P. G. (1989). Automatic and controlled processes in prejudice: The role of stereotypes and personal beliefs. In A. R. Pratkanis, S. J. Breckler, and A. G. Greenwald (Eds), *Attitude structure and function*. Hillsdale. NJ: Erlbaum.

Erber, R. (in press). Affective and semantic priming: Effects of mood on category accessibility and inference. *Journal of Personality and Social Psychology.*

Fiske, S. T. (1982). Schema-triggered affect: Applications to social perception. In M. S. Clark and S. T. Fiske (Eds), *Affect and cognition.* Hillsdale, NJ: Erlbaum.

Fiske, S. T. (1989). Examining the role of intent: Toward understanding its role in stereotyping and prejudice. In J. S. Uleman and J. A. Bargh (Eds), *Unintended thought: the limits of awareness, intention, and control.* New York: Guilford Press.

Fiske, S. T., and Neuberg, S. L. (1990). A continuum of impression formation, from category-based to individuating processes: Influences of information and motivation on attention and interpretation. In M. P. Zanna (Ed.), *Advances in experimental social psychology,* Vol. 23. New York: Academic Press.

Fiske, S. T., and Taylor, S. E. (1984). *Social cognition.* New York: Random House.

Forgas, J. P. (1989). Mood effects on decision making strategies. *Australian Journal of Psychology,* **41,** 197–214.

Forgas, J. P., and Bower, G. H. (1987). Mood effects on person perception judgments. *Journal of Personality and Social Psychology,* **53,** 53–60.

Forgas, J. P., and Bower, G .H. (1988a). Affect in social and personal judgments. In K. Fiedler and J. Forgas (Eds), *Affect, cognition, and social behavior.* Toronto: Hogrefe.

Forgas, J. P., and Bower, G. H. (1988b). Affect in social judgments. *Australian Journal of Psychology,* **40,** 125–145.

Forgas, J. P., Bower, G. H., and Krantz, S. E. (1984). The influence of mood on the perception of social interaction. *Journal of Experimental Social Psychology,* **20,** 497–513.

Gilbert, D. T., Krull, D. S., and Pelham, B. W. (1988). Of thoughts unspoken: Social inference and the self-regulation of behavior. *Journal of Personality and Social Psychology,* **55,** 685–694.

Hamilton, D. L., and Trolier, T. K. (1986). Stereotypes and stereotyping: An overview of the cognitive approach. In J. Dovidio and S. L. Gaertner (Eds), *Prejudice, discrimination, and racism.* New York: Academic Press.

Heider, F. (1958). *The psychology of interpersonal relationships.* New York: Wiley.

Higgins, E. T., Rholes, W. S., and Jones, C. R. (1977). Category accessibility and impression formation. *Journal of Experimental Social Psychology,* **13,** 141–154.

Isen, A. M. (1984). Toward understanding the role of affect in cognition. In R. S. Wyer, Jr., and T. K. Srull (Eds), *Handbook of social cognition,* Vol. 3. Hillsdale, NJ: Erlbaum.

Isen, A. M., and Patrick, R. (1983). The effect of positive feelings on risk-taking: When the chips are down. *Organizational Behavior and Human Performance,* **31,** 194–202.

Isen, A. M., Shalker, T. E., Clark, M., and Karp, L. (1978). Positive affect, accessibility of material in memory, and behavior: A cognitive loop? *Journal of Personality and Social Psychology,* **36,** 1–12.

Johnson, B. T., and Eagly, A. H. (in press). The effects of involvement on persuasion: A meta-analysis. *Psychological Bulletin.*

Karlins, M., Coffman, T. L., and Walters, G. (1969). On the fading of social stereotypes: Studies in three generations of college students. *Journal of Personality and Social Psychology,* **13,** 1–16.

Kruglanski, A. W. (1989). *Lay epistemics and human knowledge.* New York: Plenum Press.

Kruglanski, A. W., and Freund, T. (1983). The freezing and unfreezing of lay-inferences: Effects of impressional primacy, ethnic stereotyping, and numerical anchoring. *Journal of Experimental Social Psychology,* **19,** 448–468.

Linville, P. W. (1982). Affective consequences of complexity regarding the self and others. In M. S. Clark and S. T. Fiske (Eds), *Affect and cognition.* Hillsdale, NJ: Erlbaum.

Locksley, A., Borgida, E., Brekke, N., and Hepburn, C. (1980). Sex stereotypes and social judgment. *Journal of Personality and Social Psychology,* **39,** 821–831.

Mackie, D. M., Hamilton, D. L., Schroth, C. J., Carlisle, B. F., Gersho, L. M., Meneses, L. M., Nedler, B. F., and Reichel, L. D. (1989). The effect of induced mood on expectancy-based illusory correlation. *Journal of Experimental Social Psychology,* **25,** 524–544.

Martin, L. L. (1986). Set/reset: Use and disuse of concepts in impression formation. *Journal of Personality and Social Psychology,* **51,** 493–504.

Martin, L. L. (1989). Automatic and controlled processes in context effects. Paper presented at the meeting of the Midwestern Psychological Association, Chicago.

Neely, J. H. (1977). Semantic priming and retrieval from lexical memory: Roles of inhibition-less spreading activation and limited-capacity attention. *Journal of Experimental Psychology: General*, **106**, 226–254.

Neuberg, S. L., and Fiske, S. T. (1987). Motivational influences on impression formation: Outcome dependency, accuracy-driven attention, and individuating processes. *Journal of Personality and Social Psychology*, **53**, 431–444.

Omoto, A. M., and Borgida, E. (1988). Guess who might be coming to dinner? Personal involvement and racial stereotypes. *Journal of Experimental Social Psychology*, **24**, 571–593.

Ortony, A., Clore, G. L., and Collins, A. (1988). *The cognitive structure of emotions*. New York: Cambridge University Press.

Petty, R. E., and Cacioppo, J. T. (1984). The effects of involvement on responses to argument quantity and quality: Central and peripheral routes to persuasion. *Journal of Personality and Social Psychology*, **46**, 69–81.

Roth, D., and Rehm, C. P. (1980). Relationship among self-monitoring processes, memory, and depression. *Cognitive Therapy and Research*, **4**, 149–157.

Rothbart, M., and Park, B. (1986). On the confirmability and disconfirmability of trait concepts. *Journal of Personality and Social Psychology*, **50**, 131–142.

Schwarz, N., and Clore, G. L. (1983). Mood, misattribution, and judgments of well-being: Informative and directive functions of affective states. *Journal of Personality and Social Psychology*, **45**, 513–523.

Schwarz, N., and Clore, G. L. (1988). How do I feel about it? The informational function of affective states. In K. Fiedler and J. Forgas (Eds), *Affect, cognition, and social behavior*. Toronto: Hogrefe.

Schwarz, N., and Strack, F. (1985). Cognitive and affective processes in judgments of well-being: A preliminary model. In H. Brandstadter and E. Kirchler (Eds), *Economic psychology*. Linz, Austria: Trauner.

Sherif, M., Harvey, O. J., White, B. J., Hood, W. E., and Sherif, C. W. (1961). *Intergroup conflict and cooperation: The Robber's Cave experiment*. Norman, OK: University of Oklahoma.

Slusher, M. P., and Anderson, C. A. (1987). When reality monitoring fails: The role of imagination in stereotype maintenance. *Journal of Personality and Social Psychology*, **52**, 653–662.

Sorrentino, R. M., and Higgins, E. T. (1986). *Handbook of motivation and cognition: Foundations of social behavior*. New York: Guilford Press.

Taylor, S. E. (1981). A categorization approach to stereotyping. In D. L. Hamilton (Ed.), *Cognitive processes in stereotyping and intergroup behavior*. Hillsdale, NJ: Erlbaum.

Teasdale, J. D. (1983). Negative thinking in depression: Cause, effect, or reciprocal relationship? *Advances in Behavior Research and Therapy*, **5**, 3–25.

Tetlock, P. E. and Kim, J. I. (1987). Accountability and judgment processes in a personality prediction task. *Journal of Personality and Social Psychology*, **52**, 700–709.

Tversky, A., and Kahneman, D. (1973). Availability: A heuristic for judging frequency and probability. *Cognitive Psychology*, **5**, 207–232.

Wyer, R. S., and Carlston, D. E. (1979). *Social cognition, inference, and attribution*. Hillsdale, NJ: Erlbaum.

Wyer, R. S., and Srull, T. K. (1981). Category accessibility: Some theoretical and empirical issues concerning the processing of social stimulus information. In E. T. Higgins, C. P. Herman and M. P. Zanna (Eds), *Social cognition: The Ontario Symposium*, Vol. 1. Hillsdale, NJ: Erlbaum.

Zillmann, D. (1978). Attribution and misattribution of excitatory reactions. In J. Harvey, W. Ickes, and R. F. Kidd (Eds), *New directions in attribution research*, Vol. 2. Hillsdale, NJ: Erlbaum.

9

A Critique of Cognitive Approaches to Social Judgments and Social Behavior

MICHAEL ARGYLE

Oxford University

Contents

The Rise and the Limitations of Cognitive Social Psychology

Cognitive social psychology (CSP) has become one of the dominant approaches to social psychology. However it is mainly about internal cognitive processes, decisions, and attributions, and not about actual social behavior, ongoing social interaction, or real-life judgments. It is inevitably about the thoughts, memories, and other cognitive activities of one person, not two. The hard-line version of CSP sees social behavior and judgments as a kind of rational problem solving, performed by computer-like processes in the head. This position is largely a man of straw attacked by many, believed by few, but the textbook by Fiske and Taylor (1984) comes close to it. However even they admit that: "The Social perceiver has been viewed as somewhat of a hermit, isolated from the social environment. Missing from

161

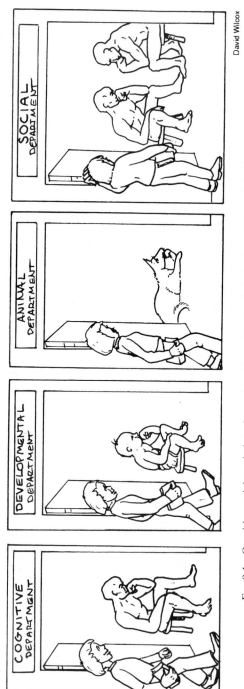

FIG 9.1 Cognitive social psychology (reproduced from *The Psychologist*, July 1988, p. 296 with permission).

much research in social cognition have been other people in a status other than that of a stimulus" (p. 416). (See Figure 9.1.)

By "cognitive" I shall refer to those processes for which subjects have some subjective awareness and are able to give some kind of verbal account. This definition is in tune with the ideas of Harré and Secord (1972), for example, who regard such accounts as the most important kind of data. I am aware that some cognitive psychologists use cognition in an extended sense, to include the conscious routines inferred to be responsible for riding a bicycle, for example, but this has not been the practice in social psychology.

A number of limits to the scope of CSP have already become familiar. (1) Fishbein and Ajzen (1975) supposed that behavior can be predicted from intentions, but Bentler and Speckart (1979) found that while behavior is partly predictable from intentions, it is also partly predictable from past behavior and from attitudes, independently of intention. For example, health-related behavior (such as taking exercise) was more predictable via this second route. Subjects said they were going to work harder, take more exercise, stop smoking, etc., but often failed to do so; to predict their actual behavior, past behavior had to be taken into account (Figure 9.2). (2) In another relevant analysis, Zajonc (1980) argued that emotion, not cognition, may be the primary reaction to social stimuli, and indeed, that cognition and affect may be generated quite independently from external stimuli. (3) Nisbett and Wilson (1977) documented many areas in which subjects are unable to provide accurate reports about the cognitive processes which could explain their behavior, or where these cognitive explanations are simply mistaken, as in cases of subliminal perception and unawareness of the true causes of behavior. This evidence provides a serious challenge to the Harré and Secord (1972) doctrine that the best way to explain social behavior is to seek

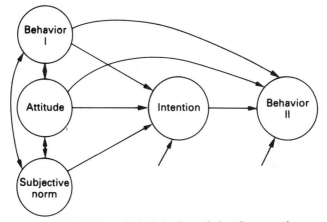

FIG 9.2 A model of the attitude–behavior relation incorporating previous behavior. (From P. M. Bentler and G. Speckart, 'Models of attitude–behavior relations', *Psychological Review*, **86** (1979), 455. Copyright 1979 by the American Psychological Association. Reprinted with permission.)

introspective verbal "accounts" from participants. (4) The prisoners' dilemma game is an example of CSP which *does* involve two subjects—except that they are isolated, in different rooms. The level of "cooperative" behavior found is typically 50–60%, but is much higher than this if realistic interpersonal communication is allowed, or if there is already some relationship, like marriage or friendship, between the players (Colman, 1982).

Two Additional Cognitive Hypotheses

In this chapter I want to show that, although cognitive processes do play an important role in social behavior and judgments, there are several aspects of social interaction and social judgments which operate quite differently. First, however, I want to suggest two extensions to CSP which will take us some way towards analyzing social interaction, further, for example, than the prisoners' dilemma game.

Interactors and judges need shared cognitions

For two people to interact or to form social judgments, it is suggested they need to have some shared cognitions. An important example is the need for shared vocabulary and information in conversation. Two individuals cannot converse unless there are some words which have similar meanings for them. In addition, they need some shared knowledge or information, since utterances depend on this, and add something new to it. "The new is vested in the old," i.e., a sentence contains new information but it only makes sense if existing shared information is referred to, as "There's a message for you on BITNET" (said to me by Ann, my secretary). In the course of a conversation, for example, in a tutorial or seminar, there is a build-up of shared information, and utterances are uttered which would have been impossible at the beginning of the session (Clark, 1985; Rommetveit, 1974). In this way new meanings and knowledge are generated in every interaction, which form the raw material for later social judgments and behavior.

Another example concerns the need to share perceptions of the nature of a social situation, including the rules which should be followed, the behavior allowed, and the goals to be sought. Symbolic interactionists have emphasized the joint construction of social situations, the need to negotiate an agreed definition. It is necessary to agree whether one is playing tennis, squash, or ping-pong, or no game is possible. However most situations are familiar (like tennis), and the rules, moves, and goals are defined already. All that really remains is to agree on the "spirit" or manner of play, i.e. how serious, aggressive, and so on. The model of games can be applied to all social situations, since they too have their rules, moves, and goals, and often their physical setting as well (Argyle *et al.*, 1982). We studied the rules for situations commonly entered by Oxford psychology students, and asked

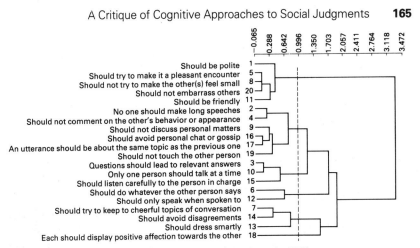

FIG 9.3   Clusters of rules (Argyle *et al.*, 1979)

subjects to rate the importance of a number of rules for each situation. There was a high level of agreement about the rules for each. Figure 9.3 shows a cluster analysis: rules are clustered together if they apply to the same situations. The first cluster of rules applied to all situations, the last cluster to parties. Such a shared understanding of social rules and social situations is once again fundamental to effective interpersonal behavior and judgments—yet contemporary CSP has little or nothing to say about how such shared understanding is achieved.

Another example of the need for *shared* cognitions is self-presentation. People may send all manner of grandiose or exotic signals and information about themselves, but this may not influence judgments by others unless they accept it. Self-presentation has to be negotiated, and an agreed compromise reached on how each person will be perceived (Goffman, 1956). Self-presentation is a cooperative activity *par excellence*, not reducible to the isolated cognitive activity of a single individual as CSP assumes.

Shared cognitions not only make social interaction and social judgments possible, they also have positive effects—for example, leading to people liking each other more. Many studies have shown that people like those with similar opinions, beliefs, and attitudes, and also people with similar personal constructs (Duck, 1973).

Interactors and judges need to take account of the cognition of others

This is sometimes known as "taking the role of the other" (TRO), "role-taking," or "intersubjectivity." The need for TRO is most obvious in the case of language, where a sender must take account of the capacities and interests of the receiver. In fact, people vary their verbal messages considerably, depending on whether they are addressing an expert, a child, a dog, etc. (Krauss, 1987). A recipé for successful conversation, which has some empirical support, is provided by Grice's (1975) cooperative principle— "make your conversational contribution such as is required, at the stage at which is occurs, by the accepted purpose or direction of the talk exchange in which you are engaged." Utterances should be, and usually are, constructed so that they will have a planned impact on other people; this entails considering carefully what they know already, what they would understand, what arguments will appeal to them, and so on.

A further area in which TRO is important is politeness. There have been several formulations of how politeness is achieved; one is provided by the top cluster in Figure 9.3 from our study of situational rules. Leech (1983) proposed that the key to politeness is in maxims such as *tact*—minimize cost to other and maximize benefit to other; *modesty*—minimize praise to self and maximize praise of other; and *generosity*—minimize benefit to self and maximize cost to self. All of this involves careful consideration of the other's point of view before social judgments or social interaction occurs.

The extent of TRO can be regarded as a component of social competence. O'Keefe and Delia (1985) showed a developmental sequence in the construction of persuasive messages. The highest type emphasized advantages to the other, and attempted to find a common plan of action. Taking into account the emotional state of the recipient of persuasive communications may be essential for its effectiveness, as several chapters in this book argue.

Failures of TRO are commonly found in mental patients. Blakar (1985) ran experiments in which two people discussed routes using what they thought were copies of the same map; schizophrenic subjects had great difficulty discovering that the two maps were in fact different. In our own work using social skills training with adult neurotics, we found that extreme egocentricity was very common in these patients; some had no interest at all in the point of view of another interactor (Trower *et al.*, 1978). It is possible that this is the most central of the various deficits in the social behavior of lonely and other socially unskilled people. Inability to take the role of others may be one of the major causes of inaccurate or suboptimal social judgments in many everyday situations.

Extra-cognitive Aspects of Social Interaction and Judgments

We now turn to several aspects of social interaction and judgments which cannot be accounted for by cognitive factors, even when the two additional hypotheses have been included.

Physiological factors in nonverbal communication

There are a number of aspects of social interaction where there is no cognitive process responsible but where the physiological basis is well known. The study of nonverbal (NV) communication provides some interesting examples. Why do people smile and frown? Because they have faces, with facial muscles, which are operated by the facial nerve. The facial nerve is activated partly by lower brain areas, for spontaneous emotions, and partly by the motor cortex, for deliberate expression and reflecting the effects of socialization. The first of these routes is not under conscious control, though the second one is, and the actual expression shown is a synthesis of the two inputs, often containing "leakage" of true feelings. Further aspects of the physiology of facial expression can explain why the left-hand side of the face is more expressive, and why women are better decoders than men. On the decoding side, some NV signals are received without conscious awareness, such as pupil dilation. Physiological factors are also needed to explain the functioning of other NV signals—for example, why right-handed people gesture mainly with their right hands, while left-handed people use both, and the special patterns of gesture found in patients with different kinds of brain damage. The accurate perception and judgment of such nonverbal displays cannot be reduced to purely cognitive processes, particularly when one considers the very complex social rules that are involved (cf. Forgas, 1987; Forgas *et al.*, 1983).

The development of social performance in children

Children show an interest in and a capacity for social behavior and social relationships and social judgments at a very early age, before their cognitive powers have developed, and these skills increase rapidly in the course of interaction in the family and with peers.

Early social responsiveness. Soon after birth, infants are responsive to faces, and face-like masks, and to female voices, they can send some basic signals, notably crying and cooing. They can cooperate in at least one basic form of interaction, i.e. finding the mother's breast and sucking; there is an element of turn-taking over the sucking, in that mother is quiet during active sucking and more active when the baby is quiet. "It can now be accepted that the infant is in a number of ways preadapted to interact with other people" (Schaffer, 1984, p. 34).

At 8 weeks infants are particularly interested in people, and mothers enjoy the experience of mutual gaze. "At two months the infant possesses an intricate mechanism for inter-personal understanding, which develops well in advance of the cognitive mechanisms for dealing with physical objects" (Bruner and Sherwood, 1981). Murray and Trevarthen (1985) found that infants of this age are happy to watch their mothers over CCTV, but not at all happy to watch an earlier clip of her behavior: they want to interact. Cohn and Tronick (1988) coded mother's and baby's behavior in 1 sec units and found that each was responsive to the other's behavior, though the mother was the more responsive.

Early attachment. This is definitely noncognitive in character, and all the mechanisms which have been put forward to explain it have invoked more primitive biological processes. Attachment occurs in some species of animals and in humans, and is difficult to prevent. An evolutionary explanation is generally accepted in terms of obtaining food and protection. There are, however, different kinds of attachment, as Ainsworth *et al.* (1978) have shown, and secure attachment, following a warm relationship, is a source of sociability and cooperativeness by the age of 12–18 months (Sroufe, *et al.*, 1983).

Again infants appear to be prepared to enter the relationship; moreover, infant and mother seem to share the same program, like two people doing a waltz (Stern, 1977). The mechanism by which attachment takes place is not agreed: it could be imprinting, conditioning, or "psychobiological attunement," whereby the mother acts as a homeostatic device to regulate the infant's mood. Following Harlow's experiments, no-one now thinks that simple instrumental learning via food reward is all that is involved, and no one has so far offered a complete cognitive theory.

However it works, attachment is unlike other kinds of learning, in that it lasts more or less for ever, without need of further reinforcement. While it is universal in relation to the main caretaker, usually the mother, it also applies to some extent to siblings, and later in life to romantic love.

Early cooperative play. Piaget (1932) explained the growth of cooperative play during the years 7–10 in terms of the growing cognitive ability to see the point of view of others, and hence to be able to negotiate and follow the rules of marbles and other games. However, cooperative play occurs long before such role-taking powers have developed. Infants play with mothers at dolls' tea parties at 12 months, and cooperate with older siblings in fantasy play by 18 months. There is a sharp increase in cooperative play at age 3 (Parten, 1932), and between 3 and 7 elaborate games of doctors and patients, travelling, cooking, etc. are enacted (Garvey, 1977). Dunn (1988) describes the various kinds of cooperation which these games require, including role reversal, negotiation, sharing moods and actions, and cooperating in familiar scripts and scenarios. As we have argued, these interactive skills also form the basis of competent social interaction and judgments of others in later life.

Turn-taking. We shall describe shortly the great accuracy with which adults synchronize their utterances. This synchrony is acquired very early in life. At 8 weeks, mother and infant usually make simultaneous social signals, like vocalizations. From about 6 months turn-taking improves: the infant becomes silent while mother is speaking, she responds to his vocalizations as if they were contributions to a dialogue, and by 12 months quite good turn-taking is established (Snow, 1977). Interaction sequences with mother are first established by games like "peek-a-boo" and "round and round the garden like a teddy bear"; by 12 months the child is not just a recipient but can initiate the sequences. These games may be how children learn turn-taking, reciprocity, and the other skills needed for social interaction (Bruner, 1977).

Early helping behavior. It is generally assumed that helping behavior in adults is mediated by a state of empathy with the person in need of help (e.g. Batson, *et al.*, 1987). It might be expected that help would not be found in children until they are able to empathize, at age 7–8 according to Piaget. However, the correlation between empathy and help is weak for young children (Grusec and Lytton, 1988). Furthermore, helping is found so early that neither cognition nor learning can play much part. Empathy and helping behavior are observed in children at an early age, so early that learning can play little role in this. Newborn infants, 2 days old, will cry in response to tapes of a child crying. However, this is probably not a response to another's distress, but more a kind of emotional contagion, perhaps based on similarity to own crying. But this may be the beginning of the empathic response. They begin to interpret facial expressions in terms of emotions between 6 and 12 months, and check back on mother's emotional reactions when they are uncertain.

The child is particularly responsive to mother's moods, since the two of them are in a kind of symbiotic biological relationship, and the child does not have a clear sense of differentiation of the self from others. Several lines of research show that infants are not "fundamentally egocentric organisms," but are "highly responsive in non-egocentric ways to the socio-emotional expressions of others, and are motivated to use these expressions in their ongoing transactions with the surround" (Thompson, 1987, p. 122).

In a number of studies, nursery school children have been asked why they had helped or shared; by 4 they often referred to the needs of others. However, this was not the only reason that they gave; they also did these things simply as part of enjoyable social behavior with friends (Dunn, 1988). This was also the conclusion of Rheingold (1982) who found an increasing amount of cooperation and help with parents between 18 and 30 months, for example over household jobs. They did this to enjoy the companionship, and the use and recognition of skills.

The detailed analysis of interaction sequences

The sequence of verbal and nonverbal signals in social interaction is intricate and fast-moving, so much so that interactors or judges normally have little idea of what is going on, though study of a slowed-down video afterwards can give us a good idea.

Turn-taking. The synchronizing of utterances in adults is amazingly accurate: pauses between utterances are often less than the normal reaction time of 0.15–0.20 s, interruptions are few, and often intended to help the other complete a sentence. Until quite recently, no one knew how this synchrony was achieved, but now we do know. Kendon (1967) found that a long, "terminal," gaze is usually made just before the end of a long utterance, and when it is not made there is a longer pause before the other replies, showing that such pauses act as full-stop signals. Beattie (1983), however, found that terminal gazes only worked in this way if the level of gaze was quite low and he found that falling pitch contour was another important end of utterance signal. Returning hands to rest at the end of an utterance is another such signal, and keeping hands in the air usually prevents others from breaking in. Finally, the grammatical structure provides information about the coming end of an utterance; Slugoski (1985) found this was more important than falling pitch.

Back-channel signals. The activity of the individual in the "listener" role plays an essential role in social interaction. Back-channel signals convey two main kinds of information. First they may be "listening behavior," simply indicating attention to the other, and willingness to listen further. Secondly, they provide feedback, indicating whether he or she understands, agrees, etc., with what has just been said. We showed how a speaker looks up just before the end of a long utterance; this is precisely when such feedback information is needed, and the face is the main region from which it is sought. Other back-channel signals are sent by posture, showing interest, boredom, or disagreement (Bull, 1987), and by vocalizations like "uh-huh" and "really?". Over the telephone the only possible back-channel signals are vocal, and so more of these are used (Argyle, 1988).

The importance of interactional synchrony. I believe that synchrony at a micro level of analysis, is one of the foundations of social interaction and accurate social perception and judgments, and that it is achieved by close cooperation between interactors. We have seen that interactors normally succeed in synchronizing their utterances and taking turns with some accuracy, and that this is achieved partly by the sending and receiving of small number of NV cues. We have seen how back-channel signals are picked up by a pattern of gaze which enables them to be received when needed. There are other examples of this cooperation and coordination by interactors: often listeners speak, not to interrupt but to help the speaker; often interactors copy each other's moves, both verbal and nonverbal, e.g. adopting similar postures or gestures, as in "movement mirroring" (Kendon, 1970). This coordination is achieved in several ways: each interactor reinforces certain behavior on the part of the other, usually quite unconsciously; and each imitates the other, if they like him or her, but if an interactor becomes aware of this he or she stops doing it. It is possible to manipulate the degree of mirroring of bodily movements experimentally, by giving different instructions to confederates. If this is done, subjects like more a confederate who copies their movements (Dabbs, 1969). In experiments where subjects were asked to sit in chairs which produced congruent postures, they liked each other more. And postural congruence is interpreted by observers as a sign of rapport.

However, there is some controversy over the time-scale at which this bodily coordination takes place. Several early investigations claimed to have found a "gestural dance" at a very fine time scale of 1/24 s or less. In dancing there is very close coordination and near-simultaneous movement, but this is assisted by the music and by the learnt, often-repeated program. Boxing is perhaps a closer analogy, and here too each responds to the other, apparently at speeds greater than the normal reaction time (Stern, 1977). However, no statistical evidence was provided by earlier research workers to show that this was more than a chance phenomenon. McDowall (1978) filmed a group of six people, three of them friends, at 8 frames per second, recording 18 parts of the body for 1000 frames. He studied synchrony in any of 18 parts of the body for each dyad; only one out of 57 such comparisons showed above chance synchrony. It is possible that these people did not know each other well enough for the gestural dance to have taken off, or that it only works in groups of two, not groups of six. However, this study has caused doubts over whether the gestural dance exists at the split-second level of timing. Rosenfeld (1981) concludes that while there is a gestural dance, it is at the level of utterances and phonemic clauses. Whatever is the case, it is hard to see how the kinds of cognitive processes studied by cognitive social psychologists could help us to understand such micro-levels of interpersonal perception and behavior.

The limited role of cognition in socially skilled behavior. There is no question that cognitive factors, such as following plans, goals, rules, and cognitive structure of all kinds, are important for social interaction and judgments. It would not be possible to play or understand cricket without knowing the main rules and how to win, or without mastering such concepts as "not-out," "declare," etc. Social behavior is like such games in many

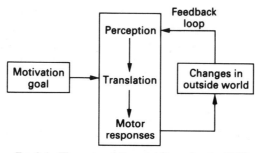

Fɪɢ 9.4   The motor skill model (from Argyle, 1969)

ways. Social behavior, like most games, requires skilled cooperative performance, and the model of a motor skill can be applied to both (Figure 9.4).

Motor skills have a hierarchical structure, and perhaps riding a bicycle is a
simpler example than cricket. The larger goal, e.g. cycling to work, leads to
a conscious plan, which is affected by known rules of the road, and
knowledge of geography—it is entirely cognitive. However, riding the
bicycle without falling off is at a much lower, more automatic, less conscious
level of skill. Trying to think about how it is done can result in falling off. On
the other hand, skills training, including social skills training, often involves
a period of conscious attention to lower levels of performance—e.g. how to
look and smile properly, though this awareness is usually shortlived, and
conscious attention returns to focus on the goals of encounters, not the
minutiae of performance (Argyle, 1983).

Social relationships

Again there is no question of the importance of cognitive factors in social
relationships and our perceptions and judgments about them. Our own work
on rules showed that for every relationship there is a set of informal rules
which it is widely believed should be followed, and which if broken often
lead to a collapse of the relationship (Argyle and Henderson, 1985). It was
found by La Gaipa and Wood (1981) that disturbed adolescent girls who had
no friends also had inadequate concepts of friendship, and had not appreciated the importance of commitment and concern for the other. However,
there are several aspects of relationships which cannot be explained in
cognitive terms.

Do people understand relationships? To some extent of course people
know very well what is meant by friends, parents, workmates, and the rest.
However, Burnett (1986) asked subjects in detail, using a variety of
methods, what they thought the differences were between, for example
"friends" and "sisters," and she found a very low level of awareness of the

key features. Subjects found this task difficult, it made them uncomfortable or embarrassed, especially in the case of male subjects, and they showed a superficial understanding, mindlessness rather than thoughtfulness or expertise. Nevertheless, most of them succeed in handling a range of relationships, apparently without the need to understand them.

The nature of love. Most psychological theories of love have supposed that it is based on receiving rewards, or achieving an equitable balance of rewards. And there is no doubt that love relationships are extremely rewarding. However, the subjective experience of love is rather different: it focuses on concern for the other person, and the importance of intimacy with them, as intrinsically important goals (McClelland, 1986). It was found by McAdams (1988) that people in love had high scores on a projection test for "need for intimacy." It was found that this measure predicted intimate behavior, and McClelland speculates that intimacy is based on noncognitive right hemisphere activation. Love is often said to be irrational, and so in many ways it is. Shaver and Hazan (1988) produced evidence to show that secure, avoidant, and anxious/ambivalent attachment to mother lead to similar kinds of attachment to romantic partners later.

Why friends are a source of joy. There is extensive evidence that friends are judged to be an extensive source of positive emotions, indeed the most common source (Scherer *et al.*, 1986). But what is the explanation? One possibility is that friends are reinforcing: they smile and send other positive nonverbal signals to each other, to express and sustain the relationship. Kraut and Johnston (1979) found that friends did smile a lot at one another at the bowling alley, 47% of the time after a hit, and 28% of the time after a miss—but not at the skittles. Another explanation is that friends typically engage in agreeable leisure activities together. Table 9.1 shows the ratios of frequency of engaging in various activities with friends and with a whole range

TABLE 9.1   *Distinctive activities shared with friends*

mean ratio	1.26 : 1
Activities above this ratio	
Dancing	2.00
Tennis	1.67
Sherry party	1.63
Joint leisure	1.60
Pub	1.63
Intimate conversation	1.52
Walk	1.50

Argyle and Furnham, 1982.

of relationships, i.e. it shows the activities most characteristic of friendship. All of these activities are enjoyable ones, so that an explanation of the joy experienced when with friends is that they do such nice things together. A final speculation is that the experience of closely synchronized interaction is intrinsically rewarding, the result of evolutionary pressures favoring cooperation. We saw above that synchrony of bodily movements leads to liking, and is probably enjoyable. A number of leisure activities with friends involve closely synchronized behavior—dancing, singing and other music, many forms of sport. None of these processes can be readily reduced to the kind of individual intrapsychic cognitive variables that contemporary social psychologists are so interested in.

The Limits of Cognitive Approach to Applied Social Psychology

The application of cognitive approach emphasizes the roles of education, correct beliefs, and generally teaching people sensible, rational behavior. A great deal can be done in this way, but there are whole areas where it does not work.

Health behavior

As we have argued, people often do not follow their intentions and cognitions in a number of spheres, of which health behavior is one. Health beliefs certainly affect health behavior in some areas—getting 'flu injections, having polio vaccinations, health check-ups, and going to the dentist (Taylor, 1986). However, two areas of health behavior which are notoriously difficult to change by cognitive rational methods are smoking and drinking. A number of ingenious forms of behavior therapy are more successful, including aversion therapy for alcohol, and continuous smoking in a small, ill-ventilated room, while concentrating on the negative effects of smoking. Social support, e.g. in AA, and public commitment helps, as can some social skills training, e.g. to deal with the anxiety to which alcohol is a reaction (Taylor, 1986).

The processes whereby health behavior affects health are not accessible to introspection, and appear to operate through a more primitive mechanism. For example, social support evidently strengthens the immune system, so that stressful events have less effect on health (Jemmott and Locke, 1984), perhaps by avoiding the damaging biological effect of negative emotions such as anxiety and depression. A recent development is the discovery of physiological "toughness," a capacity to resist the effects of stress on health, which is built up by exercise, and other sources of physiological stress, including cold (Dienstbier, 1989).

Social skills training (SST)

The earliest attempts to train people in social skills used lecture or other familiar educational methods, and were very unsuccessful as assessed by follow-up studies. Many of us regarded social behavior as a kind of motor skill, and were aware that other motor skills, such as cycling or swimming, cannot be taught by lectures or reading books. So educational methods, relying on purely cognitive processes, were abandoned for the time being. However, some success was later reported in the training of cross-cultural skills, for example to work abroad, using educational methods like the Culture Assimilator (Fiedler *et al.*, 1971). In some other areas of SST it has become clear that there is a lot which can be taught in this way. For marital and other relationship training, the rules can be taught, as can an enhanced understanding of the relationship (Argyle and Henderson, 1985).

Most SST uses role-playing, combined with modelling, explanation, and feedback, both oral and from video playback. This kind of training includes some cognitive elements, and some learning by practice and experience. It also involves verbal labeling of what is not normally attended to, and temporary focusing of attention on aspects of behavior which are normally automatic, as described earlier.

Intergroup problems

These are perhaps the most urgent problems to which social psychology might make a contribution. The main methods suggested so far have been racial education and propaganda, both of which have had rather limited success; they affect cognitions more than feelings or behavior.

Sheer frequency of interaction has a lot more effect, if it is under the right conditions, such as equal status and cooperative activities (Stephan, 1985). The precise mechanism producing these changes is not known; it may be partly cognitive, e.g. increased knowledge and understanding of the other group, though we have just seen that this often does not produce liking. Another possibility is that some kind of skill learning takes place, i.e. learning to communicate and interact with members of the other group. Experience of cooperation towards shared goals appears to be particularly important, as suggested by the success of the "jig-saw classroom" method, devised by Aronson *et al.* (1978) for reducing racial prejudice in American school children.

Success has also been obtained by various kinds of intercultural training. These include some cognitive components, from books and lectures. They also include partly noncognitive elements, such as role-playing with members of the other culture, watching films, and simply meeting members of the other culture (Argyle, 1981).

Conclusion: The Many Sides of Social Interaction and Judgments

Cognition plays important roles in social behavior and judgments, but cannot explain everything. And interactors need to have shared cognitions and take account of the cognitions of others. People are not always aware of, and cannot provide adequate accounts of, the causes of their behavior and judgments in a variety of fields.

We have described several examples of social phenomena involving social judgments which are, partly at least, independent of cognitive processes—nonverbal communication, social behavior of infants, interaction sequences like turn-taking, response to back-channel signals, interactional synchrony, aspects of social skills performance. Social relationships are also partly irrational and outside cognition. A number of applied problems can be tackled better by recognition of the noncognitive components—aspects of health behavior, social skills training, and problems of intergroup behavior. In the context of the present volume, these arguments and examples should provide a useful illustration of the limitations of the currently dominant information processing paradigm as it applies to social judgments. Future work in this important field should increasingly recognize the complementary nature of cognitive emotional, and social variables as they come to influence interpersonal behavior and judgments.

References

Ainsworth, M. D. S., Blehan, M. C., Waters, E., and Wall, S. (1978). *Patterns of attachment.* Hillsdale, NJ: Erlbaum.

Argyle, M. (1969). *Social interaction.* London: Methuen.

Argyle, M. (1981). Inter-cultural communication. In M. Argyle (Ed.), *Social skills and work.* London: Methuen.

Argyle, M. (1983). *The psychology of interpersonal behavior*, 4th edn. Harmondsworth: Penguin.

Argyle, M. (1988). *Bodily communication*, 2nd edn. London: Methuen.

Argyle, M., and Furnhan, A. (1982) The ecology of relationships: choice of situation as a function of relationship. *British Journal of Social Psychology*, **21**, 259–262.

Argyle, M., Furnham, A. and Graham, J. A. (1982). *Social situations.* Cambridge: Cambridge University Press.

Argyle, M., Graham, J. A., Campbell, A., and White, P. (1979). The rules of different situations. *New Zealand Psychologist*, **8**, 13–22.

Argyle, M., and Henderson, M. (1985). *The anatomy of relationships.* London: Heinemann; Harmondsworth: Penguin.

Aronson, E., Stephen, C., Sikes, J., Blaney, N., and Snapp. M. (1978). *The jigsaw classroom.* Beverly Hills, CA: Sage.

Batson, C. D., Fultz, J., and Schoenrode, P. A. (1987). Adults' emotional reactions to the distress of others. In N. Eisenberg and J. Strayer (Eds), *Empathy and its development.* Cambridge: Cambridge University Press.

Beattie, G. W. (1983). *Talk: an analysis of speech and non-verbal behavior in conversation.* Milton Keynes: Open University Press.

Bentler, P. M., and Speckart, G. (1979). Models of attitude–behavior relations. *Psychological Review*, **86**, 452–464.

Blakar, R. M. (1985). Towards a theory of communication in terms of preconditions: a conceptual framework and some empirical explorations. In H. Giles and R. N. St. Clair

(Eds), *Recent advances in language, communication and social psychology*. London: Erlbaum.

Bretherton, I., McNew, S., and Beeghly-Smith, M. (1981). Early person knowledge as expressed in gestural and verbal communications: When do infants acquire a "theory of mind"? In M. E. Lamb and L. R. Sherrod (Eds), *Infant social cognition*. Hillsdale, NJ: Erlbaum.

Bruner, J. S. (1977). Early social interaction and language acquisition. In H. R. Schaffer (Ed.) *Studies in mother-infant interaction*. London: Academic Press.

Bruner, J. S., and Sherwood, V. (1981). Thought, language and interaction in infancy. In J. P. Forgas (Ed.), *Social cognition*. London: Academic Press.

Burnett, R. (1986). Conceptualization of personal relationships. D.Phil. thesis, Oxford.

Bull, P. (1987). Posture and posture. Oxford: Pergamon.

Clark, H. H. (1985). Language use and language users. In G. Lindzey and E. Aronson (Eds), *Handbook of Social Psychology*, 3rd edn. New York: Random House.

Clark, H. H., and Clark, E. V. (1977). *Psychology and language*. New York: Harcourt Brace.

Clarke, D. D. (1983). *Language and action*. Oxford: Pergamon.

Colman, A. M. (1982). *Game theory and experimental games*. Oxford: Pergamon Press.

Cohn, J. F., and Tronick, E. Z. (1988). Mother-infant face-to-face interaction: influence is bidirectional and correlated to periodic cycles in either partner's behavior. *Development Psychology*, **24**, 386–92.

Dabbs, J. M. (1969). Similarity of gestures and the structure of the nonverbal communication of emotion. *Journal of Personality*, **45**, 564–584.

Dienstbier, R. A. (1989). Arousal and physiological toughness: implications for mental and physical health. *Psychological Review*, **96**, 84–100.

Duck, S. (1973). *Personal relationships and personal constructs*. Chichester: Wiley.

Dunn, J. (1988). *The beginnings of social understanding*. Oxford: Blackwell.

Fiedler, F. E., Mitchell, R., and Triandis, H. C. (1971). The culture assimilator: An approach to cross-cultural training. *Journal of Applied Psychology*, **55**, 95–102.

Fishbein, M. and Ajzen, I. (1975). Belief, attitude, intention and behavior: *An introduction to theory and research*. Reading, MA: Addison-Wesley.

Fiske, S. T., and Taylor, S. E. (1984). *Social cognition*. Reading, MA: Addison-Wesley.

Forgas, J. P. (1987). The role of physical attractiveness in the interpretation of facial expression cues. *Personality and Social Psychology Bulletin*, **13**, 478–489.

Forgas, J. P., O'Connor, K., and Morris, S. L. (1983). Smile and punishment: the effects of facial expression on responsibility attribution by groups and individuals. *Personality and Social Psychology Bulletin*, **9**, 587–596.

Garvey, C. (1977). *Play*. London: Open Books.

Goffman, E. (1956). *The presentation of self in everyday life*. New York: Doubleday Anchor Books.

Grice, H. P. (1975). Logic and conversation. In P. Cole and J. L. Morgan (Eds) *Syntax and semantics, Vol. 3, Speech acts*. New York: Academic Press.

Grusec, J. E., and Lytton, H. (1988). *Social development*. New York: Springer.

Harlow, H. F. and Harlow, M. K. (1965). The affectional systems. In A. M. Schrier, H. F. Harlow and F. Stollnitz (Eds) *Behavior of nonhuman Primates*, Vol. 2. New York: Academic Press.

Harré, R., and Secord, P. F. (1972). *The explanation of social behaviour*. Oxford: Blackwell.

Jemmott, J. B., and Locke, S. E. (1984). Psychosocial factors, immunology mediation, and human susceptibility to infectious diseases: How much do we know? *Psychological Bulletin*, **95**, 78–108.

Kendon, A. (1967). Some functions of gaze direction in social interaction. *Acta Psychologica*, **26**, 22–63.

Kendon, A. (1970). Movement coordination in social interaction: some examples considered. *Acta Psychologica*, **32**, 1–25.

Krauss, R. M. (1987). The role of the listener: Addressee influence on message formulation. *Journal of Language and Social Psychology*, **6**, 81–98.

Kraut, R. E., and Johnston, R. E. (1979). Social and emotional messages of smiling: An ethological approach. *Journal of Personality and Social Psychology*, **37**, 909–917.

La Gaipa, J. J., and Wood, H. D. (1981). Friendship in disturbed adolescents. In S. Duck and

R. Gilmour (Eds), *Personal relationships*, Vol. 3, *Personal relationships in disorder*. London: Academic Press.

Leech, G. N. (1983). *Principles of pragmatics*. London: Longman.

McAdams, D. P. (1988). Personal needs and personal relationships. *In* S. Duck (Ed.), *Handbook of personal relationships*. Chichester: Wiley.

McClelland, D. C. (1986). Some reflections on the two psychologies of love. *Journal of Personality*, **54**, 334–353.

McDowall, J. J. (1978). Interactional synchrony: a reappraisal. *Journal of Personality and Social Psychology*, **36**, 963–975.

Murray, L., and Trevarthen, C. (1985). Emotional regulation of interactions between two-month olds and their mothers. In T. M. Field and N. A. Fox (Eds), *Social perception in infants*. Norwood, NJ: Ablex.

Nisbett, R. E., and Wilson, T. D. (1977). Telling more than we can know: Verbal reports on mental processes. *Psychological Review*, **84**, 231–259.

O'Keefe, B. J., and Delia, J. G. (1985). Psychological and interactional dimensions of communication development. In H. Giles and R. N. St. Clair (Eds), *Recent advances in language, communication and social psychology*. London: Erlbaum.

Parten, M. B. (1932). Social participation among preschool children. *Journal of Abnormal and Social Psychology*, **27**, 243– 69.

Piaget, J. (1932). *The moral judgment of the child*. London: Routledge & Kegan Paul.

Rheingold, H. L. (1982). Little children's participation in the work of adults, a nascent social behavior. *Child Development*, **53**, 114–25.

Rommetveit, R. (1974). *On message structure: A framework for the study of language*. London: Wiley.

Rosenfeld, H. M. (1981). Whither interactional synchrony? In K. Bloom (Eds.), *Prospective issues in infancy research*. New York: Erlbaum.

Schaffer, H. R. (1984). *The child's entry into a social world*. London: Academic Press.

Scherer, K. R., Walbott, H. G., and Summerfield, A. (1986). *Experiencing Emotion*. Cambridge: Cambridge University Press.

Shaver, P. R. and Hazan, C. (1988). A biased overview of the study of love. *Journal of Social and Personal Relationships*, **5**, 473–501.

Slugoski, B. R. (1985). Grice's theory of conversation as a social psychological model. D.Phil. thesis, University of Oxford.

Snow, C. E. (1977). The development of conversation between mothers and babies. *Journal of Child Language*, **4**, 1–22.

Sroufe, L. A., Fox, N. G. and Pancake, V. R. (1983). Attachment and dependency in developmental perspective. *Child Development*, **54**, 1615–1627.

Stephan, W. G. (1985). Intergroup relations. In G. Lindzey and E. Aronson (Eds), *Handbook of Social Psychology*, 3rd edn, Vol. 2. New York: Random House.

Stern, D. (1977). *The first relationship*. Cambridge, MA: Harvard University Press.

Taylor, S. E. (1986). *Introduction to health psychology*. New York: Random House.

Thompson, R. A. (1987). Empathy and emotional understanding: The early development of empathy. In N. Eisenberg and J. Strayer (Eds), *Empathy and its development*. Cambridge: Cambridge University Press.

Trevarthen, C. (1980). The foundation of intersubjectivity: Development of interpersonal and cooperative understanding in infants. In D. R. Olson (Ed.), *The social foundations of language and thought*. New York: Norton.

Trower, P., Bryant, B. and Argyle, M. (1978). *Social Skills and Mental Health*. London: Methuen.

Zajonc, R. B. (1980). Feeling and thinking: Preferences need no inferences. *American Psychologist*, **35**, 151–175.

Part 3

Theories and Applications

10

Multiple Roles for Affect in Persuasion

RICHARD E. PETTY, FAITH GLEICHER, and SARA M. BAKER

Ohio State University

Contents

Introduction

The major goal of this chapter is to describe a new and potentially integrative approach for understanding the role of affect in attitude formation and change. The idea that attitudes have affective as well cognitive and behavioral foundations has a long history in the social and behavioral sciences (Allport, 1935; McGuire, 1969) and is currently undergoing a renaissance in interest (e.g. Breckler and Wiggins, 1989; Millar and Tesser, 1986; Petty *et al.*, 1988a; Wilson *et al.*, 1989). Importantly, previous approaches to studying the role of affect in persuasion have tended to focus on the "one true process" by which affect determines attitudes, with different theorists emphasizing different processes (e.g. classical conditioning; cognitive priming; see Forgas and Bower, 1988, for a review). In contrast, our approach begins with the assumption that affect can influence attitudes in multiple ways in different situations. This assumption is a critical one in the Elaboration Likelihood Model of persuasion (ELM) (Petty and Cacioppo, 1981, 1986a).

In brief, the ELM holds that affect (like any other variable) can influence attitudes in the following ways: (a) by serving as an argument or item of issue-relevant information, (b) by functioning as a simple cue, (c) by influencing the extent of information processing activity, or (d) by influencing the type of thoughts that come to mind. The specific role in which a variable serves is influenced by the overall elaboration likelihood (how generally motivated and able recipients are to process the issue-relevant information that is presented). For example, in situations where the elaboration likelihood is quite low, a variable such as affect can influence attitudes by serving as a simple cue, increasing the favorability of the attitude when the mood is pleasant, but decreasing the favorability of the attitude when the mood is unpleasant. In other situations, affect influences attitudes in different ways. The ELM has been successful in accounting for a variety of source, message, and recipient variables in previous research and integrating what had appeared to be conflicting findings (Petty and Cacioppo, 1986b).

Diversity of initial findings on the effects of affect

The accumulated research on affect and persuasion over the past several decades has clearly indicated that individuals' evaluations of people, objects, and issues can be influenced by their feelings, moods, and emotions whether or not the affect is actually relevant to the attitude object under consideration. Many early empirical demonstrations revealed that evaluations of words, people, political slogans, and persuasive communications could be modified by pairing them with a variety of affect-producing stimuli. For example, when attitude objects were associated with pleasant food (Janis et al., 1965; Razran, 1940), a comfortable room (Griffitt, 1970), a happy movie (Forgas and Moylan, 1987), or the termination of electric shock (Zanna et al., 1970), subjects expressed more favorable evaluations than when the attitude objects were associated with unpleasant odors, a hot room, a sad movie, or the onset of electric shock (see Petty et al., 1988b, for a review).

Although the vast proportion of research on affect and attitudes is generally consistent with the reasonable proposition that positive affective experiences and states tend to be associated with enhanced persuasion and more favorable attitudes, whereas negative affective states tend to be associated with reduced persuasion and less favorable attitudes (see McGuire, 1985), important exceptions to this principle exist (see Petty et al., 1988). Notably, some research has shown that negative affect can be associated with increased persuasion and positive affect with reduced persuasion. For example, an early study by Weiss and Fine (1956) showed that subjects who had been angered by an insulting experimenter were more likely than subjects who had been complimented to agree with a message calling for more punitive treatment of juvenile delinquents.* Perhaps the most notable instances in which negative moods have produced more favorable attitudes reside in the vast literature on fear appeals (see Rogers, 1983). Importantly, the conditions under which these different effects are likely to occur and the processes underlying them are only beginning to attract significant conceptual and empirical attention.

The complex and conflicting findings observed for affect present a situation similar to that which has existed for many other variables in the persuasion literature. For example, although the existing literature shows that increasing source credibility mostly increases persuasion, some investigations have demonstrated a reversal or no effect of credibility on attitudes. A complete understanding of the role of affect in persuasion requires an overall conceptual framework that accounts for the diverse effects of affect and other variables, and specifies the *processes* by which these variables modify attitudes.

Conceptualization and assessment of affect

Before presenting an analysis of the role of affect in persuasion, it is useful to distinguish affect from the constructs of "attitude" and "arousal." In this chapter we use "affect" as a superordinate construct to encompass emotions and relatively transient moods and feelings. Attitudes, on the other hand, refer to global and enduring (i.e. stored in long-term memory) *evaluations* of attitude objects (cf., Fazio, 1986).† A person's general evaluations or attitudes can be based on a variety of behavioral, affective, and cognitive experiences, and are capable of guiding behavioral, affective and cognitive responses. Thus, a person may come to like a new breakfast cereal because she or he just bought it ("If I bought it, I must like it"—behavioral influence), because a recently viewed commercial with pleasant music induced feelings of warmth (affective influence), or because the information in the commercial about the health benefits of consuming the product were persuasive (cognitive influence). An implication of this is that two global evaluations of an object, issue, or person that are identical when assessed on an overall favorable–unfavorable scale may be based on quite different experiences and may have quite different implications (Millar and Tesser, 1986).

Affective states may be viewed as having at least two components—

---

* Angered subjects also tended to agree less with a message advocating a more lenient foreign policy toward countries that disagreed with US policy toward China.

† Ephemeral, transitory, or self-presentational expressions of global evaluation would not be considered expressions of attitudes because they would not be reliable and enduring. Of course, the notion of an "enduring" attitude is a relative concept. That is, attitudes can endure for varying lengths of time. For example, attitudes based largely on exposure to simple cues tend to endure for a shorter period of time than attitudes based on extensive issue-relevant thinking (Petty and Cacioppo, 1986b).

intensity (how strong is the affect) and direction (is it positive or negative). Elevations in the intensity of affective states may be associated with increments in physiological (autonomic, cortical) arousal, but arousal is neither a requirement for nor a reliable indicator of affect. Affective states that are evoked by mildly pleasant and unpleasant stimuli can be accompanied by primitive expressions of emotion that are detectable even in the absence of diffuse autonomic arousal (see Cacioppo and Petty, 1987), and autonomic activity has been shown to accompany cognitive as well as affective responses (e.g. Lacey *et al.*, 1963). Although complete understanding of the role of affect in persuasion will require examination of both the intensity and the valence of affective states, in this chapter our focus is on valence rather than intensity.

The Elaboration Likelihood Model of Persuasion

Now that affect has been distinguished from the attitude (evaluation) and arousal concepts, we briefly describe the Elaboration Likelihood Model of persuasion and the manner in which it deals with affect. The ELM represents an attempt to integrate the many seemingly conflicting findings in the persuasion literature under one conceptual umbrella by specifying a finite number of ways in which source, message, recipient, context, and other variables have an impact on attitude change (Petty and Cacioppo, 1981; 1986b). The ELM is based on the notion that people want to form correct attitudes (i.e. those that will prove useful in functioning in one's environment) as a result of exposure to a persuasive communication, but there are a variety of ways in which a reasonable position may be adopted.

The most effortful procedure for evaluating an advocacy involves drawing upon prior experience and knowledge to carefully scrutinize and elaborate the issue-relevant arguments in the persuasive communication along the dimensions that are perceived central to the merits of the attitude object. According to the ELM, attitudes formed or changed via this *central route* are postulated to be relatively persistent, predictive of behavior, and resistant to change until they are challenged by cogent contrary information along the dimension or dimensions perceived central to the merits of the object. People attempting this effortful cognitive activity have been characterized as engaging in "systematic" (Chaiken, 1987) or "mindful" processing (Palmerino *et al.*, 1984).

Importantly, it is neither adaptive nor possible for people to exert considerable mental effort in processing all of the persuasive communications to which they are exposed. Indeed, people often act as "lazy organisms" (McGuire, 1969) or "cognitive misers" (Taylor, 1981). This does not mean that people never form attitudes when motivation and/or ability to scrutinize a message are low. Rather, the model holds that attitudes may be changed as a result of relatively simple associations (as in classical conditioning; Staats and Staats, 1958), identifications (Kelman, 1961); inferences (as in self-perception; Bem, 1972), or heuristics (such as "experts are correct"; Chaiken, 1987) in these situations. Attitudes formed or changed by this *peripheral route* are postulated to be relatively less persistent, resistant, and predictive of behavior.

The discussion so far highlights two ways in which variables can have an impact on persuasion. Variables can serve as persuasive *arguments*, providing information as to the central merits of an object or issue, or they can serve as simple *cues*, allowing favorable or unfavorable attitude formation in the absence of a diligent consideration of the true merits of the object or issue. Two other ways in which a variable can have an impact on persuasion are by (a) affecting the *extent of argument elaboration* (i.e. the intensity with which the person thinks about and evaluates the central merits of the issue-relevant information presented) and (b) affecting the direction of any *bias in elaboration* (i.e. are the thoughts biased in a positive or negative direction; Petty and Cacioppo, 1990).

The ELM holds that as the likelihood of elaboration is increased (whether the thinking is relatively objective or biased), the quality of the issue-relevant arguments presented has a greater impact on attitudes. As the likelihood of elaboration is decreased, however, peripheral cues become more important. That is, when the elaboration likelihood is high, the central route to persuasion dominates, but when the elaboration likelihood is low, the peripheral route takes precedence. There are, of course, many variables capable of moderating the route to persuasion. Some variables, such as personal relevance (Petty and Cacioppo, 1979b), personal responsibility (Petty *et al.*, 1980), and an individual's level of "need for cognition" (Cacioppo and Petty, 1982b) determine one's overall *motivation* to process issue-relevant arguments. Other variables, such as message repetition (Cacioppo and Petty, 1989) and distraction (Petty *et al.*, 1976) determine a person's overall *ability* to process issue-relevant arguments. Finally, some variables affect information processing activity in a relatively objective manner, whereas others may introduce a systematic bias to the information processing. For example, telling a highly involved audience that a message is specifically attempting to persuade them motivates active resistance and counterarguing (Petty and Cacioppo, 1979a).

One of the most important features of the ELM, is that it holds that any one variable can serve in multiple roles. That is, a variable can serve as a persuasive argument in some situations, act as a peripheral cue in others, and affect the intensity of thinking or the direction of processing bias in still other contexts. For example, in separate studies, source attractiveness has: (a) served as a simple peripheral cue when it was irrelevant to evaluating the merits of a consumer product (a typewriter) and subjects were not motivated to process the issue-relevant arguments (Haugtvedt *et al.*, 1988); (b) served as a message argument when it was relevant to evaluating the merits of a product (a new shampoo) and the elaboration likelihood was high (Petty and Cacioppo, 1980); and (c) affected the extent of thinking about the message arguments presented when the elaboration likelihood was moderate (Puckett *et al.*, 1983).

If any one variable can influence persuasion by several means, it becomes critical to identify the general conditions under which the variable acts in each of the different roles. The ELM holds that when the elaboration likelihood is high (such as when personal relevance and knowledge are high, the message is easy to understand, no distractions are present, etc.), people typically know that they want and are able to evaluate the merits of the arguments presented and they do so. In high elaboration conditions, variables such as "attractiveness" have little direct impact on evaluations by serving as simple cues, but they may serve as persuasive arguments if relevant to the merits of the issue (such as when the attractiveness of a model serves as a relevant argument for a beauty product; or the physical beauty of a vacation destination serves as a compelling reason to visit that location). Alternatively, variables such as "attractiveness" may bias the nature of the ongoing cognitive activity when the elaboration likelihood is high. That is, when in a thinking mode, people may be especially motivated to find the good points in what a likable speaker has to say and the weak points in the message of a dislikable source. On the other hand, when the elaboration likelihood is low (e.g. low personal relevance or knowledge, complex message, many distractions, etc.), people know that they do not want and/or are not able to evaluate the merits of the arguments presented (or they do not even consider exerting effort to process the message). If any evaluation is formed under these conditions, it is likely to be the result of relatively simple associations or inferences. Finally, when the elaboration likelihood is moderate (e.g. uncertan personal relevance, moderate knowledge, moderate complexity, etc.), however, people may be uncertain as to whether or not the message warrants or needs scrutiny and whether or not they are capable of providing this analysis. In these situations they may examine the persuasion context for indications (e.g. is the source credible?) of whether or not they are interested in or should process the message.

Affective Processes in the ELM

As noted in beginning this chapter, the accumulated persuasion literature clearly suggests that reactions to a persuasive communication can be modified by pairing the message with an affect-eliciting stimulus (Petty and Cacioppo, 1981; McGuire, 1985). However, the direction of the effects observed have sometimes appeared puzzling, and the processes mediating these effects have not been clear.

The ELM suggests several roles for affect in persuasion and indicates the general conditions under which affect should assume each role. Specifically, the ELM holds that affect may serve as a persuasive argument, it may serve as a peripheral cue, or it may affect the extent or direction of argument processing (Petty *et al.*, 1988b). In the remainder of this section, each of these roles is explained.*

Affect under conditions of high elaboration likelihood

When the elaboration likelihood is high, people are motivated and able to process the merits of the issue-relevant arguments presented. Under these conditions, there are two possible roles for affect. First, affect could serve as an argument for the merits of the attitude object if it was relevant. For some people or in some situations or for certain attitude objects, a determination of the central merits of the object entails an analysis of one's *feelings* rather than (or in addition to) one's beliefs and behaviors. For example, attitudes toward a potential spouse might be based on the extent to which one feels love and warmth rather than disgust in his or her presence. In this instance, affect is serving as an argument (a relevant item of information) that is central to the merits of the object.†

In the example above, it was assumed that the affect was explicitly relevant to the merits of the attitude object under consideration and was therefore capable of serving as an item of issue-relevant information. *Irrelevant affect* may also have a role in persuasion under high elaboration conditions, however, if mood increases the accessibility of mood-congruent thoughts and ideas. Previous research is consistent with the view that positive moods cause other positive material in memory (e.g. thoughts, events, images) to come to mind, but negative moods increase the accessibility of negative material (Bower, 1981; Clark and Isen, 1982). Thus, when a person is actively processing a persuasive message while in a positive mood state, the ongoing elaboration should be positively biased, but when the person is in a negative mood, the elaboration should be biased in a negative manner. The biasing effects of mood should be especially strong if the message arguments are somewhat ambiguous and open to multiple interpretations, and the person does not have highly accessible attitudes and beliefs that are inconsistent with the induced affect. Some evidence for a rather general biasing property of affect was obtained by Johnson and Tversky (1983). In their research, the induction of negative affect produced a global

---

* It is important to note that our analysis applies to affect that is not associated with either very high (e.g. manic excitement) or very low (e.g. severe depression) levels of arousal. These extreme conditions are expected to disrupt information processing activity and performance in general (Easterbrook, 1959; Yerkes and Dodson, 1908).

† This does not mean that people carry this affect with them at all times. Rather it means that attitude change may require reconsideration of the affective properties of the stimulus (e.g. Do I still love you?; Cacioppo and Petty, 1982a).

decrease in the estimated frequency of negative events (e.g., fatalities due to heart disease), and positive affect produced a global decrease in estimates of these events. In short, the induced affect colored judgments.

Although no published persuasion research has been guided explicitly by this biased processing view, some research is consistent with it. For example, consider the abundant literature on the effects of fear arousing communications. The typical fear communication employed in social psychological research presents the noxious (fear arousing) consequences resulting from specific behaviors (e.g. smoking, failure to wear seatbelts, etc.; see Beck and Frankel, 1981). Interestingly, recent reviews of this literature have concluded that the arousal of fear has no direct effect on attitude change, "but only an indirect effect via the cognitive appraisal of the severity of the threat" (Rogers, 1983, p. 165; see also Leventhal, 1970). In short, the fear experienced by a message recipient may colour processing of the information provided. People in a fearful state may view the harmful consequences presented in the message as more serious than people who are less fearful and/or more likely to occur (see also Petty and Wegener, 1991; Schwarz *et al.*, 1985).* Similarly, people in a sad mood may be more susceptible to appeals relying on pity, and angry people to messages advocating punitiveness, because the thoughts triggered by the affect are consistent with the direction of the arguments in the message. On the other hand, a happy person who was processing a sad or a punitive message would have inconsistent thoughts, and the message might therefore be less effective (cf. Roseman *et al.*, 1985; Weiss and Fine, 1956).

Affect under conditions of moderate elaboration likelihood

When the elaboration likelihood is moderate, affect is postulated to have an effect on the extent of information processing activity. Recent studies by Worth and Mackie (1987), Mackie and Worth (1989), and Bless *et al.* (1990) have shown that people in a positive mood process a message less carefully than people in a neutral mood. That is, positive mood was associated with more persuasion mostly for a message containing weak arguments, because the flaws in the arguments were less likely to be processed when in a positive mood. On the other hand, a message with strong arguments was less effective when people were in a positive mood because the strengths of the arguments were not processed. In addition to finding that argument quality was a less important factor for people in a positive mood, Worth and Mackie (1987) found that subjects who experienced positive affect (winning $1) prior to a communication, reported attitudes that were based somewhat *more* on a simple expertise cue than subjects who were in a neutral mood.

---

*Fear should serve in this role most strongly when the elaboration likelihood is high and the fear is not so "arousing" as to disrupt information processing.

This finding is consistent with other research showing that positive affect is sometimes associated with attempts to reduce the load on working memory and the complexity of decisions, resulting in quicker judgments than when affect is neutral (e.g. Forgas and Bower, 1987; Isen and Means, 1983). One explanation for the disrupting effect of positive mood relies on the notion that positive mood increases the accessibility of positive material in memory, leaving less attention or capacity to process the message carefully. An alternative view holds that positive mood may make people less motivated to process a message, especially if processing it is likely to be difficult or unpleasant because such processing would be likely to attenuate the positive mood. Mackie and Worth (1989) reasoned that if the cognitive explanation was correct, giving subjects in a positive mood more time to process the message should remove the disrupting effect of mood. Bless *et al.* (1990) reasoned that if the motivational explanation was correct, increasing the importance of the task (without giving additional time) should remove the disrupting effect of mood. Because both the cognitive and motivational explanations received support when tested, it is possible that both explanations have some validity (see Mackie, this volume, for additional discussion). The motivational view also holds open the possibility that positive mood could increase information processing activity over a neutral mood if subjects expected the message to be especially pleasant, uplifting, agreeable, and/or interesting (cf. Murray *et al.*, 1990).

Affect under conditions of low elaboration likelihood

If people have relatively low motivation and ability to process a persuasive communication, then affect, to the extent that it has any effect at all, should serve as a simple peripheral cue. As a cue, affect would induce change that was consistent with its direction—the presence of positive affect should lead to more favorable attitudes than if positive affect was not present, but the presence of negative affect should lead to more unfavorable attitudes than if negative affect was not present.

In addition to the studies on classical conditioning of attitudes noted earlier, a number of other investigations are also consistent with the view that affect can serve as a relatively simple cue in a persuasion context when the elaboration likelihood is low. For example, Gorn (1982) manipulated the relevance of an advertisement for a pen by telling some subjects that they were serving as consultants to an advertising agency and that they would later get to choose a pack of pens as a gift (high likelihood of thinking about the pen), whereas other subjects were given little reason to process the target pen ad (low elaboration likelihood). All subjects were exposed to two different ads for a pen. One ad provided information relevant to evaluating the product, whereas the other ad featured pleasant music rather than information. About one hour after ad exposure, subjects were given a choice between the two brands of advertised pens. In the low elaboration likelihood condition, subjects favored the pen advertised with the pleasant music; however, under high elaboration conditions they favored the pen advertised with the informational campaign (see also Srull, 1983).

Summary

So far we have: (a) defined and distinguished the construct of "affect"; (b) presented a general conceptualization of the processes by which persuasive communications induce attitude change; and (c) highlighted the multiple roles for affect in this framework. In particular, it was argued that affect has much in common with other variables known to modify attitudes and is therefore capable of influencing attitudes in rather complex ways. In brief, when people are highly motivated and able to process issue-relevant arguments, affect will either serve as an argument, if it is relevant to a determination of the central merits of the issue, or it will bias the ongoing information processing activity. When people lack the requisite motivation and/or ability to process issue-relevant arguments, affect may serve as a simple peripheral cue. Finally, when people are uncertain as to whether the message warrants or needs scrutiny, affect will be especially important as a moderator of the route to persuasion (i.e. it will influence the extent of thinking about the object or issue under consideration).

Research on Multiple Roles for Affect in Persuasion

Several studies providing initial support for the ELM were described above. This research (reviewed in detail by Petty and Cacioppo, 1986a) has provided strong support for the idea that there is a tradeoff between argument processing and the operation of simple cues (see also reviews by Chaiken and Stangor, 1987; Cooper and Croyle, 1984; Sherman, 1987). That is, as the elaboration likelihood is increased, attitude change becomes more determined by the nature of the issue-relevant thoughts generated in response to the message arguments, but as the elaboration likelihood is decreased, attitude change becomes more determined by reactions to simple cues in the persuasion context. On the other hand, relatively little evidence exists to support the idea that any one variable can serve in multiple roles in different situations. Most of the available evidence comes from examinations across independent studies in which one variable appears to act in different roles in different experiments. Compelling evidence for the multiple roles postulate requires research in which one variable is shown to serve in multiple roles in a single study.

To provide some preliminary evidence about the plausibility of the hypothesis that affect can serve in multiple roles in persuasion situations, two studies were conducted (Petty *et al.*, 1991). In each study, the effects of positive affect that was irrelevant to the message topic were examined under conditions of high and low elaboration likelihood. The two studies were conceptually identical but employed different means of varying elaboration likelihood and affect. In addition, each study used very different types of persuasive messages.

Situational determinants of the use of affect

As explained earlier in this chapter, the ELM holds that irrelevant pleasant affect should serve as a positive peripheral cue when the elaboration likelihood is low. On the other hand, when the elaboration likelihood is high, irrelevant pleasant affect should bias the ongoing information processing activity, making positive thoughts and ideas more accessible.

In order to examine this hypothesis, college undergraduates were exposed to a persuasive message in the context of a relatively pleasant television program (an episode of a popular situation comedy) or a more neutral program (a segment from a documentary). The persuasive message was a commercial for a new pen that featured four strong or weak attributes of the product. The commercial lasted about 30 seconds and was surrounded by two other commercials for other products. In order to create the high and low elaboration conditions, high elaboration subjects were told that they would be allowed to select a free gift at the end of the experiment from a variety of brands of pens, whereas low elaboration subjects were told that they would be allowed to select their gift from a variety of brands of coffee (one of the ads presented during the program was for coffee). To amplify this manipulation, subjects in the high elaboration conditions were further told that the pen that they would see advertised would soon be test marketed in their city. Subjects in the low elaboration conditions were told that the pen to be advertised would be test marketed in a distant location. This manipulation had proven effective in varying the extent of thinking in previous research (Petty *et al.*, 1983; Schumann *et al.*, 1990).

In sum, the design of the study was a 2 (elaboration likelihood: low or high × 2 (affect: positive or neutral) × 2 (argument quality: strong or weak) between subjects factorial. Following exposure to the program and commercial, subjects reported on their mood states (e.g. happy–sad) and expressed their attitudes (e.g. favorable–unfavorable) and thoughts about several of the products featured. The thoughts were subsequently coded into the categories of positive, negative, and neutral (see Cacioppo and Petty, 1981, for a complete discussion of thought coding procedures). To control for individual differences in total thought production, the proportion of positive thoughts served as the primary dependent measure of biased thinking.

Manipulation checks revealed that subjects in the positive mood condition reported feeling more happy than those in the neutral mood condition. The

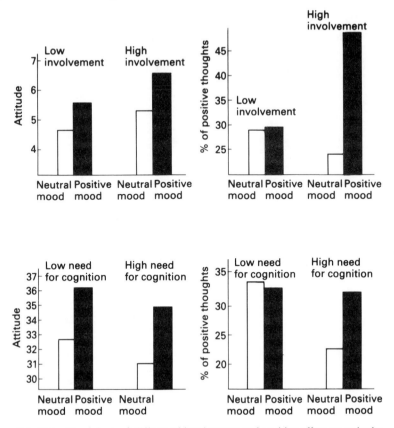

Fɪɢ 10.1   *Top left panel*: Effects of involvement and positive affect on attitudes toward a consumer product. *Top right panel*: Effects of involvement and positive affect on % of positive thoughts in response to a television commercial. *Bottom left panel*: Effects of need for cognition and positive affect on attitudes toward a social issue. *Bottom right panel*: Effects of need for cognition and positive affect on % of positive thoughts in response to a message on a social issue. Data are from Petty *et al.* (1991).

attitude and thought measures are presented in Figure 10.1. In the top left panel, it can be seen that positive affect led to more positive attitudes about the pen under both high and low elaboration conditions.* In the top right panel, it can be seen that affect interacted with elaboration condition in influencing thoughts. That is, the positive affect manipulation had no impact on thoughts under low elaboration conditions, but when subjects were motivated to think, positive affect increased the proportion of positive thoughts generated.

---

*In addition, a main effect for elaboration was observed. Subjects in the high elaboration condition reported more favorable attitudes than those in the low elaboration condition. Importantly, no interaction between elaboration condition and affect emerged.

To further explore the different processes induced by affect under high and low elaboration conditions, causal path analyses were conducted using LISREL VI (Joreskog and Sorbon, 1984) to simultaneously estimate the three paths between (a) self-reported mood and attitude toward the pen, (b) self-reported mood and proportion of positive thoughts generated, and (c) proportion of positive thoughts generated and attitude toward the pen. Separate analyses were conducted for high and low elaboration subjects. The top portion of Figure 10.2 presents the path coefficients resulting from these analyses. Under low elaboration conditions, mood had a direct effect on attitudes, but did not influence thoughts (see left panel). In contrast, under high elaboration conditions, mood had no direct effect on attitudes. Instead, mood influenced the production of positive thoughts, which in turn had an impact on attitudes (see right panel). In sum, both the experimental results (Figure 10.1) and the correlational results (Figure 10.2) are consistent with the view that although positive affect rendered attitudes more favorable under both high and low elaboration conditions, it did so by different processes. The fact that similar changes were induced by different processes is important because of the different consequences of these processes. That is, the more favorable attitudes induced by positive affect under high elaboration conditions should be more persistent, resistant, and

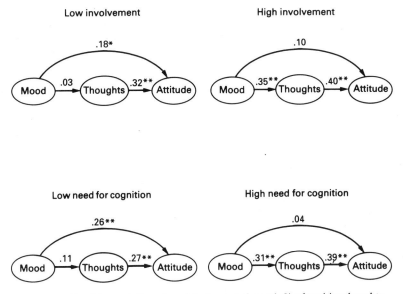

FIG 10.2   *Top left panel*: Causal model of reported mood, % of positive thoughts, and attitudes under low involvement conditions. *Top right panel*: Causal model under high involvement conditions. *Bottom left panel*: Causal model for individuals low in need for cognition. *Bottom right panel*: Causal model for individuals high in need for cognition. *Note.* * indicates p < .05; ** indicates p < .01. Data are from Petty *et al.* (1991).

predictive of behavior than the comparable changes induced by affect under low elaboration conditions.

Individual differences in the use of affect

In the previous study, a situational determinant of the role of affect in persuasion was examined. In a second study, an individual difference variable was investigated. Previous work on the ELM has shown that individuals differ in their tendencies to follow one route to persuasion or the other. People who enjoy thinking (those high in "need for cognition"; see Cacioppo and Petty, 1982b) tend to focus on the perceived quality of the arguments when they process a persuasive message, but people who do not enjoy thinking (those low in need for cognition) tend to rely on simple cues in the persuasion context (Haughtvedt et al., 1988). A reasonable hypothesis, then, is that affect will serve in different roles for people who characteristically do and do not like to think. For individuals with low need for cognition, pleasant affect should serve as a positive peripheral cue, but for individuals with high need for cognition, pleasant affect should bias the ongoing information processing activity.

In a study examining this hypothesis (Petty et al., 1991), individuals who scored above and below the median on the need-for-cognition scale were exposed to either a strong or a weak message arguing in favor of a new foster care system. Prior to message exposure, subjects engaged in a series of activities that placed them in either a relatively positive or a neutral mood. Specifically, upon entering the lab, subjects were told that they would participate in pretesting several tasks that might be used in future experiments. All subjects first engaged in completing some math problems, a word search puzzle, and an alphabetizing task. For the fourth task, subjects in the positive mood condition completed a "Life Event Survey" in which they were asked to recall a recent positive event in their lives which made them feel particularly good. They were asked to vividly recall the event and prepare a written description of it. This manipulation was adapted from Bless et al. (1990). Subjects in the neutral mood condition listened to neutral music during this time period.

In sum, the study was a 2 (need for cognition: low or high) $\times$ 2 (argument quality: strong or weak) $\times$ 2 (affect: positive or neutral) between subjects factorial. Following the mood induction and exposure to the message, subjects reported on their moods, expressed their attitudes toward the foster care program, and listed their thoughts about it. As in the previous study, the thoughts were subsequently coded into the categories of positive, negative, and neutral. Again, the proportion of positive thoughts served as the primary measure of biased thinking.

As expected, subjects in the positive mood condition indicated that they felt more "pleasant" during the message than subjects in the neutral mood condition. The attitude and thought measures are presented in Figure 10.1. In the bottom left panel, it can be seen that pleasant affect led to more positive attitudes about the foster care program for both high- and low-need-for-cognition individuals. In the bottom right panel, an interaction pattern between affect and thoughts can be observed. That it, positive affect had no impact on the thoughts of low-need-for-cognition individuals, but positive affect tended to increase the proportion of positive thoughts for people high in need for cognition.[*]

As in the first study, causal path analyses were conducted to explore the different effects of affect under high and low elaboration conditions. Separate analyses were conducted for high- and low-need-for-cognition individuals. The bottom portion of Figure 10.2 presents the path coefficients that resulted. For subjects low in need for cognition, mood had a direct effect on attitudes, but did not influence thoughts (see bottom left panel). On the other hand, for high-need-for-cognition individuals, mood influenced the production of positive thoughts, which in turn had an impact on attitudes (see bottom right panel). This study replicated the pattern observed in the previous experiment. Together, the studies provide strong support for the view that affect can serve in multiple roles in persuasion situations.

Future Research on the Role of Affect in Persuasion

Preliminary support is now available for the view that positive affect can serve in at least three roles in persuasion situations. In the research guided by the ELM and described above, positive affect was shown to serve as a simple cue when people were unmotivated to process the issue relevant arguments, but positive affect influenced the proportion of positive thoughts to the message when people were motivated to think about the communication. In research where no special attempt was made to enhance or reduce motivation or ability to process the message, positive mood was shown to disrupt information processing activity (see Mackie, this volume).

Even though the existing research provides a coherent though complex pattern of results, considerable additional work is needed before the multiple roles for affect in persuasion are understood. The conceptualization and evidence presented here have emphasized the "elaboration likelihood" of the persuasion context as an important determinant of the process

---

[*] Unlike the involvement study, however, the interaction between need for cognition and affect was not statistically significant. In addition, main effects for need for cognition and argument quality were present. Low-need-for-cognition subjects were more favorable toward the foster care program than high-need-for-cognition individuals and strong arguments produced more favorable attitudes than weak ones.

by which affect modifies attitudes.* Other variables also deserve attention as factors influencing the role of affect in persuasion. For example, it will probably be important to examine the extent to which the induced affect is congruent or incongruent with the affectivity of the arguments under consideration. For example, in our research, we found that positive affect increased positive thoughts and favorable attitudes when people were highly motivated to process unemotional arguments. If we had exposed recipients in a positive mood to emotional messages relying on clearly incongruent affect (e.g. arguments based on sympathy or pity) the enhanced positive thoughts elicited by the affect may have backfired! Under high elaboration conditions, affect may be most effective when it is consistent with (or at least not in conflict with) the type of arguments employed (e.g. fear would work better with danger arguments, but sadness would enhance sympathy appeals). Under low elaboration conditions, where affect is more likely to serve as a simple cue, the congruence of affect and arguments should be less important. Under moderate elaboration conditions, the nature of the message may interact with affect to determine how much processing takes place. For example, a person in a positive mood may be especially interested in processing a pleasant or agreeable message and avoiding unpleasant or disagreeable messages in order to maintain a positive mood. Alternatively, because of the spreading activation of mood-congruent material in memory, positive mood may allow a deeper processing of positive than negative communications (cf. Forgas and Bower, 1988).

In addition to the type of message presented, the nature of the attitude being challenged may also prove to be important. Edwards (1990) has argued that if the attitude under attack is based primarily on affect rather than cognitions, affective means of change should be especially powerful, but Millar and Millar (1990) have argued for the opposite conclusion. Whether it is better to "match" an affective persuasive appeal to affectively based attitudes or to provide a "mismatch" will probably depend on a number of factors. For example, if the persuasive attack is strong (i.e. it effectively undermines the basis of the attitude), then a match would seem better. If the attack is weak, then a mismatch might prove more persuasive, especially if the person has not experienced this type of challenge previously (cf., McGuire, 1964).

Finally, the basis of the affect itself may have important implications for information processing and persuasion. Some affect inductions require considerable cognitive activity (e.g. thinking of ways to spend a large sum of money) whereas others do not (e.g. listening to pleasant music). Will each be equally effective in biasing thoughts or serving as simple cues? Further-more, how does each type of affect modify thoughts? Does it influence how

---

*Existing research has also focused on positive rather than negative affect. Negative affect may have more complicated effects on judgments (cf. Isen, 1984).

"good" consequences appear, how "likely" they seem, or both (see Petty and Wegener, 1991)? It seems clear that researchers exploring the multiple roles for affect in persuasion will not run out of research questions in the near future.

Acknowledgments

Correspondence should be addressed to Richard E. Petty, Department of Psychology, Ohio State University, 1885 Neil Avenue Mall, Columbus, OH 43210, USA. This chapter was supported in part by NSF grant BNS 90-21647.

References

Allport, G. W. (1935). Attitudes. In C. Murchison (Eds), *Handbook of social psychology*, Vol. 2. Worchester, MA: Clark University Press.

Beck, K. H., and Frankel, A. (1981). A conceptualization of threat communications and preventive health behavior. *Social Psychology Quarterly*, **44**, 204–217.

Bem, D. J. (1972). Self-perception theory. In L. Berkowitz (Ed.), *Advances in experimental social psychology*, Vol. 6. New York: Academic Press.

Bless, H., Bohner, G., Schwarz, N., and Strack, F. (1990). Mood and persuasion: A cognitive response analysis. *Personality and Social Psychology Bulletin*, **16**, 332–346.

Bower, G. H. (1981). Mood and memory. *American Psychologist*, **36**, 129–148.

Breckler, S., and Wiggins, E. (1989). Affect versus evaluation in the structure of attitudes. *Journal of Experimental Social Psychology*, **25**, 253–271.

Cacioppo, J. T., and Petty, R. E. (1981). Electromyograms as measures of extent and affectivity of information processing. *American Psychologist*, **36**, 441–456.

Cacioppo, J. T., and Petty, R. E. (1982a). A biosocial model of attitude change. In J. T. Cacioppo and R. E. Petty (Eds), *Perspectives in cardiovascular psychophysiology*. New York: Guilford Press.

Cacioppo, J. T., and Petty, R. E. (1982b). The need for cognition. *Journal of Personality and Social Psychology*, **42**, 116–131.

Cacioppo, J. T., and Petty, R. E. (1987). Stalking rudimentary processes of social influence: A psychophysiological approach. In M. Zanna, J. Olson, and C. Herman (Eds), *Social influence: The Ontario symposium*, Vol. 5. Hillsdale, NJ: Erlbaum.

Cacioppo, J. T., and Petty, R. E. (1989). Effects of message repetition on argument processing, recall, and persuasion. *Basic and Applied Social Psychology*, **10**, 3–12.

Chaiken, S. (1987). The heuristic model of persuasion. In M. Zanna, J. Olson, and C. Herman (Eds), *Social influence: The Ontario symposium*, Vol. 5. Hillsdale, NJ: Erlbaum.

Chaiken, S., and Stangor, C. (1987). Attitudes and attitude change. *Annual Review of Psychology*, **38**, 575–630.

Clark, M. S. and Isen, A. M. (1982). Toward understanding the relationship between feeling states and social behavior. In A. H. Hastorf and A. M. Isen (Eds), *Cognitive social psychology*, New York: Elsevier/North Holland.

Cooper, J., and Croyle, R. (1984). Attitudes and attitude change. *Annual Review of Psychology*, **35**, 395–426.

Easterbrook, J. A. (1959). The effect of emotion on cue utilization and the organization of behavior. *Psychological Review*, **66**, 183–201.

Edwards, K. (1990). The interplay of affect and cognition in attitude formation and change. *Journal of Personality and Social Psychology*, **59**, 202–216.

Fazio, R. H. (1986). How do attitudes guide behavior? In R. Sorrentino and E. T. Higgins (Eds), *The handbook of motivation and cognition*. New York: Guilford Press.

Forgas, J. P. and Bower, G. H. (1987). Mood effects on person perception judgments. *Journal of Personality and Social Psychology*, **53**, 53–60.

Forgas, J. P. and Bower, G. H. (1988). Affect in social and personal judgments. In K. Fiedler, and J. Forgas (Eds), *Affect, cognition, and social behavior*. Toronto: Hogrefe.

Forgas, J. P., and Moylan, S. (1987). After the movies: Transient moods and social judgments. *Personality and Social Psychology Bulletin*, **13**, 467–477.

Gorn, G. (1982). The effects of music in advertising on choice behavior: A classical conditioning approach. *Journal of Marketing*, **46**, 94–101.

Griffitt, W. (1970). Environmental effects on interpersonal behavior: Ambient effective temperature and attraction. *Journal of Personality and Social Psychology*, **15**, 240–244.

Haugtvedt, C., Petty, R. E., Cacioppo, J. T., and Steidley, T. (1988). Personality and ad effectiveness. *Advances in Consumer Research*, **15**, 209–212.

Isen, A. M. (1984). Toward understanding the role of affect in cognition. In R. Wyer and T. Srull (Eds). *Handbook of social cognition*, Vol. 3. Hillsdale, NJ: Erlbaum.

Isen, A. M., and Means, B. (1983). The influence of positive affect on decision-making strategy. *Social Cognition*, **2**, 18– 31.

Janis, I. L., Kaye, D., and Kirschner, P. (1965). Facilitating effects of "eating while reading" on responsiveness to persuasive communications. *Journal of Personality and Social Psychology*, **1**, 181–186.

Johnson, E., and Tversky, A. (1983). Affect, generalization, and the perception of risk. *Journal of Personality and Social Psychology*, **45**, 20–31.

Joreskog, K. G., and Sorbon, D. (1984). *LISREL VI: Analysis of linear structural relationships by the method of maximum likelihood*. Chicago: International Educational Services.

Kelman, H. C. (1961). Processes of opinion change. *Public Opinion Quarterly*, **25**, 57–78.

Krugman, H. (1983). Television program interest and commercial interruption. *Journal of Advertising Research*, **23**, 21–23.

Lacey, J., Kagan, N., Lacey, B., and Moss, H. (1963). The visceral level. In P. Knapp (Ed.), *Expressions of the emotions in man*. New York: International Universities Press.

Leventhal, H. (1970). Findings and theory in the study of fear communications. In L. Berkowitz (Eds.), *Advances in experimental social psychology*, Vol. 5. New York: Academic Press.

Mackie, D. M., and Worth, L. (1989). Processing deficits and the mediation of positive affect in persuasion. *Journal of Personality and Social Psychology*, **57**, 27–40.

McGuire, W. J. (1964). Inducing resistance to persuasion: Some contemporary approaches. In L. Berkowitz (Ed.), *Advances in experimental social psychology*, Vol. 1. New York: Academic Press.

McGuire, W. J. (1969). The nature of attitudes and attitude change. In G. Lindzey and E. Aronson (Eds), *The handbook of social psychology*, 2nd edn, Vol. 3. Reading, MA: Addison-Wesley

McGuire, W. J. (1985). Attitudes and attitude change. In G. Lindzey and E. Aronson (Eds), *The handbook of social psychology*, 3rd edn, Vol. 2. New York: Random House.

Millar, M. G. and Tesser, A. (1986). Effects of affective and cognitive focus on the attitude–behavior relation. *Journal of Personality and Social Psychology*, **51**, 270–276.

Millar, M., and Millar, K. (1990). Attitude change as a function of attitude type and argument type. *Journal of Personality and Social Psychology*, **59**, 217–228.

Murray, N., Sujan, H., Hirt, E., and Sujan, M. (1990). The influence of mood on categorization: A cognitive flexibility interpretation. *Journal of Personality and Social Psychology*, **59**, 411–425.

Palmerino, M., Langer, E., and McGillis, D. (1984). Attitudes and attitude change: Mindlessness–mindfulness perspective. In J. Eiser (Ed.), *Attitudinal judgment*. New York: Springer.

Petty, R. E., and Cacioppo, J. T. (1979a). Effects of forewarning of persuasive intent and involvement on cognitive responses and persuasion. *Personality and Social Psychology Bulletin*, **5**, 173–176.

Petty, R. E., and Cacioppo, J. T. (1979b). Issue-involvement can increase or decrease persuasion by enhancing message-relevant cognitive responses. *Journal of Personality and Social Psychology*, **37**, 1915–1926.

Petty, R. E., and Cacioppo, J. T. (1980). Effects of issue involvement on attitudes in an advertising context. In G. Gorn and M. Goldberg (Eds), *Proceedings of the Division 23 program*. Montreal: American Psychological Association.

Petty, R. E., and Cacioppo, J. T. (1981). *Attitudes and persuasion: Classic and contemporary approaches.* Dubuque, IA: Wm. C. Brown.

Petty, R. E., and Cacioppo, J. T. (1986a). *Communication and persuasion: Central and peripheral routes to attitude change.* New York: Springer-Verlag.

Petty, R. E., and Cacioppo, J. T. (1986b). The Elaboration Likelihood Model of persuasion. In L. Berkowitz (Ed.), *Advances in experimental social psychology,* Vol. 19. New York: Academic Press.

Petty, R. E., and Cacioppo, J. T. (1990). Involvement and persuasion: Tradition versus integration. *Psychological Bulletin,* **107,** 367–374.

Petty, R. E., Cacioppo, J. T., and Kasmer, J. (1988a). The role of affect in the Elaboration Likelihood Model. In L. Donohew, H. Sypher, and E. T. Higgins (Eds), *Communication, social cognition, and affect.* Hillsdale, NJ: Erlbaum.

Petty, R. E., Cacioppo, J. T., and Schumann, D. (1983). Central and peripheral routes to advertising effectiveness: The moderating role of involvement. *Journal of Consumer Research,* **10,** 134–148.

Petty, R. E., Cacioppo, J. T., Sedikides, C., and Strathman, Al (1988b). Affect and persuasion: A contemporary perspective. *American Behavioral Scientist,* **31,** 355–371.

Petty, R. E., Harkins, S. G., and Williams, K. D. (1980). The effects of group diffusion of cognitive effort on attitudes: An information processing view. *Journal of Personality and Social Psychology,* **38,** 81–92.

Petty, R. E., Schumann, D., Richman, S., and Strathman, A. (1991). Multiple roles for positive affect in persuasion. Unpublished manuscript, Ohio State University, Columbus, OH.

Petty, R. E., and Wegener, D. (1991). Thought systems, argument quality and persuasion. In R. S. Wyer and T. K. Srull (Eds.), *Advances in Social Cognition* (Vol. 4). Hillsdale, NJ: Erlbaum.

Petty, R. E., Wells, G. L., and Brock, T. C. (1976). Distraction can enhance or reduce yielding to propaganda. *Journal of Personality and Social Psychology,* **34,** 874–884.

Puckett, J., Petty, R. E., Cacioppo, J. T., and Fisher, D. (1983). The relative impact of age and attractiveness stereotypes on persuasion. *Journal of Gerontology,* **38,** 340–343.

Razran, G. H. S. (1940). Conditioned response changes in rating and appraising sociopolitical slogans. *Psychological Bulletin,* **37,** 481.

Rogers, R. (1983). Cognitive and physiological processes in fear appeals and attitude change: A revised theory of protection motivation. In J. T. Cacioppo and R. E. Petty (Eds), *Social psychophysiology: A sourcebook.* New York: Guilford Press.

Roseman, I., Abelson, R. P., and Ewing, M. F. (1985). Emotion and political cognition: Emotional appeals in political communication. In R. Lau and D. Sears (Eds), *Cognition and political behavior.* Hillsdale, NJ: Erlbaum.

Schumann, D., Petty, R. E., and Clemons, S. (1990). Predicting the effectiveness of different strategies of advertising variation. *Journal of Consumer Research,* **17,** 192–202.

Schwarz, N., Servay, W., and Kumpf, M. (1985). Attribution of arousal as a mediator of fear-arousing communications. *Journal of Applied Social Psychology,* **15,** 178–188.

Sherman, S. J. (1987). Cognitive processes in the formation, change, and expression of attitudes. In M. Zanna, J. Olson, and C. Herman (Eds), *Social influence: The Ontario Symposium.* Hillsdale, NJ: Erlbaum.

Srull, T. K. (1983). The role of prior knowledge in the acquisition, retention, and use of new information. *Advances in Consumer Research,* **10,** 572–576.

Staats, A. W., and Staats, C. K. (1958). Attitudes established by classical conditioning. *Journal of Abnormal and Social Psychology,* **57,** 37–40.

Taylor, S. E. (1981). The interface of cognitive and social psychology. In J. H. Harvey (Ed.), *Cognition, social behavior, and the environment.* Hillsdale, NJ: Erlbaum.

Weiss, W., and Fine, B. J. (1956). The effect of induced aggressiveness on opinion change. *Journal of Abnormal and Social Psychology,* **52,** 109–114.

Wilson, T. D., Dunn, D., Kraft, D., and Lisle, D. (1989). Introspection, attitude change, and attitude-behavior consistency. The disruptive effects of explaining why we feel the way we do. *Advances in Experimental Social Psychology,* **22,** 287–343.

Worth, L. T., and Mackie, D. M. (1987). Cognitive mediation of positive affect in persuasion. *Social Cognition,* **5,** 76–94.

Yerkes, R. M., and Dodson, J. D. (1908). The relation of strength of stimulus to rapidity of habit formation. *Journal of Comparative and Neurological Psychology*, **18**, 459–482.

Zanna, M. P., Kiesler, C. A., and Pilkonis, P. A. (1970). Positive and negative attitudinal affect established by classical conditioning. *Journal of Personality and Social Psychology*, **14**, 321–328.

11

Feeling Good, But Not Thinking Straight: The Impact of Positive Mood on Persuasion

DIANE M. MACKIE

University of California, Santa Barbara

and

LEILA T. WORTH

Pennsylvania State University

Contents

Imagine that you want to ask your boss for a raise. Or convince a potential client that your product can outperform the competition's. Or persuade a voter to support a local zoning ordinance. If you could create the perfect conditions under which to make your appeal, what would they be? If you are like nine out of every ten students in our classes, you would want to have the target of your influence attempt in a good mood. "Wait until your boss is in a good mood and then ask for a raise," they tell us, or "Take your client to lunch, make your pitch when everyone's feeling fat and happy," and "If you can get voters feeling relaxed, maybe make them laugh, that's when they'll listen to you." In popular belief, then, a target who feels good is particularly receptive to persuasion. In this chapter, we refer to this subjective sense of feeling good or of pleasantness as being in a good mood or in a positive affective state (Isen, 1984; Fiske and Taylor, 1984). Our students believe that people in a good mood are more easily persuaded. Judging by the predominant use of humor, warmth, and attractive communicators in television and print commercials (Belch *et al.*, 1987; Holman, 1986), influence professionals share their views.

Early Efforts to Study the Effects of Mood on Persuasion

Is there any truth to this popular belief? What research has been done to date that bears on the idea that positive affect increases persuasion? Razran (1940) reported one of the earliest efforts to investigate the effects of positive affect on attitudes. He presented sociopolitical slogans to college student subjects either while the subjects enjoyed a free lunch or while putrid odors were released in the experimental room. Subjects later showed greater agreement with the slogans presented while food was present, whereas agreement with slogans presented with putrid odors decreased. Razran argued that the affect associated with the positive (food) or negative (odors) stimuli transferred to the contiguously presented slogans, increasing agreement with slogans seen while eating and decreasing agreement with slogans seen while smelling noxious odors. This associationist interpretation received further support from later studies demonstrating that repeated pairing of a word with a positive or negative stimulus influenced the word's evaluative rating (e.g. Staats *et al.*, 1962). Although critics appealed to the role of demand characteristics in these studies (Dabbs and Janis, 1965; Kahle and Page, 1976; Page and Kahle, 1976), more methodologically rigorous studies confirmed that affective responses can indeed be classically conditioned to words, short slogans, or objects (Kroeber-Riel, 1984; Zanna *et al.*, 1970).

Such classical conditioning effects do not, however, seem representative of the kinds of changes we usually think of as occurring when someone is persuaded. As the examples at the start of the chapter make clear, people believe that a good mood should facilitate the kind of persuasion that involves the give and take of information and argumentation, of reasons and evidence. And in fact, some early studies did confront subjects with more detailed persuasive communications. Janis *et al.* (1965), for example, found increased attitude change among subjects who read arguments on various issues while snacking on peanuts and sipping soda. Similar increases in acceptance were found when persuasive messages were accompanied by pleasant music (Galizio and Hendrick, 1972), or presented by a speaker portrayed in front of a very pleasant background (Biggers and Pryor, 1982).

Finally, Dribben and Brabender (1979) used the Velten mood induction technique (in which subjects are asked to study sentences designed to induce particular mood states) to create a positive mood in some recipients before exposure to counterattitudinal messages about motorcycle helmet laws. Those who read positive statements were more likely to adopt the advocated position than those who read neutral statements.

Consistent with the popular view, the results of these studies provided some evidence that conditions promoting a general state of feeling good might also promote persuasion. Although conditioning explanations of their results were implausible, these early studies provided little indication of how mood might enhance persuasion, what conditions might facilitate or inhibit such an effect, and whether, if at all, the results could be generalized. The program of research described in this chapter was designed to answer some of these questions. Our goal was to attain an understanding of the mechanisms through which positive mood might influence the *processing* or persuasive messages, permitting us to identify the situations in which positive affect might facilitate, and those in which it might hinder, persuasion. Our approach was thus to regard attitude change as a special type of social judgment, one that emerged after some exposure to and processing of attitude-relevant information.

Processing Approaches to Persuasion

Recent research on attitude change has investigated two different types of information processing strategies that people might adopt when they encounter persuasive communications (Chaiken, 1980, 1986; Chaiken *et al.*, 1989; Petty and Cacioppo, 1981, 1986). Each of these processing strategies culminates in a series of judgments about the validity of the persuasive message or its contents, judgments which in turn determine persuasion. One processing strategy involves relatively detailed, analytic, and effortful integration and evaluation of message content and of message-relevant thoughts. This kind of processing is referred to as systematic processing by Chaiken (1980) and as central route processing by Petty and Cacioppo (1981). When systematic processing occurs, message content becomes the primary determinant of the recipient's reaction to the influence attempt, and consequently the quality of message arguments determines persuasive success. Strong arguments engender thoughts favorable to the message and lead to persuasion, whereas weak arguments cause counterarguing and little persuasion (Chaiken, 1980; Petty and Cacioppo, 1979; Petty *et al.*, 1981). Thus, when message recipients are differentially persuaded by weak and strong arguments, it is typical to infer that the persuasive message was systematically processed. Because of the intensive and analytic nature of such systematic scrutiny of the message, both capacity and motivation are necessary for systematic processing to occur (see Chaikin *et al.*, 1989; Petty and Cacioppo, 1986, for reviews).

Systematic or central route processing has been contrasted with other strategies for dealing with persuasive communications. Heuristic processing, for example, allows message recipients to use cues in the persuasion context to judge the validity of the message without exhaustive processing of the message itself (see Chaiken, 1986; Petty and Cacioppo. 1986, for reviews). Persuasion can be produced via heuristic processing because some surface feature of the message (e.g. length or the use of statistics), the source (e.g. expertise or likability), or the communication context (e.g. audience reaction) is associated with or signals the validity of the advocated position. Because they do not rely on intensive examination of the persuasive message, heuristic strategies require less cognitive effort or motivation than systematic or central route processing.

Recent Research on Mood and Processing

What impact might positive mood have on the systematic or heuristic processing of a persuasive message? Although relatively few studies have investigated the effects of mood within a processing approach to persuasion, the literature regarding the effects of positive affect on cognitive processing in general is now voluminous (see Clark and Williamson, 1989; Fiedler, 1988; Forgas and Bower, 1988; Isen, 1984, 1987; Schwarz, 1990; and other chapter in this volume, for reviews). The evidence from many different studies now indicates that when faced with a problem to solve or a decision to make, people in a positive mood often simplify cognitive processing. They choose the quickest, least effortful way to arrive at a satisfactory answer (Isen, *et al.*, 1982). They rely more heavily on intuitive and heuristic strategies than on effortful algorithms (Isen *et al.*, 1982). They make decisions more quickly and based on less information (Isen and Means, 1983). Finally, they tend to be more confident about receiving positive outcomes (Johnson and Tversky, 1983; Wright and Bower, 1981) and about their ability to produce such outcomes (Kavanagh and Bower, 1985).

Why people feeling good show these effects is a matter of considerable debate, and we return to this issue below. With regard to the impact of positive mood on the processing of persuasive messages, however, these findings converge to suggest that for many reasons, we might expect people in a good mood to use heuristic, rather than systematic, processing when faced with a persuasive message. We tested this hypothesis in our first experiment (Worth and Mackie, 1987).

Experiment 1: How Does Positive Mood Affect Persuasive Processing?

Our strategy in this first experiment was to assess subjects' initial opinions, manipulate their affective state in a manner unrelated to the influence situation, present them with a persuasive message that could be processed either systematically or heuristically, and reassess their opinions to gauge the impact of mood on persuasive processing. After reporting their initial attitudes on the issue of controlling acid rain (among many others), our college student subjects participated in what they believed to be study on risk-taking. In reality, the procedures in this risk-taking study were intended to induce either a positive or no particular affective state. In the course of the study, subjects assigned to the positive mood conditions unexpectedly won a dollar in a lottery, an event we knew made people feel happy and pleased. In contrast, subjects assigned to the neutral mood conditions simply answered some questions about prior participation in lotteries. While ostensibly waiting for a risk questionnaire to be prepared, all subjects were then asked to participate in an unrelated study which required them to read and evaluate a speech about acid rain delivered by a delegate at a student environmental conference.

Before presenting the speech, we provided some of our subjects with a heuristic cue that potentially could be used to assess the validity of the speech without systematically processing its content. Some subjects in each mood condition were told that the delegate delivering the speech was an expert (an environmental studies major), whereas others were told that he was an equally intelligent (and therefore socially attractive) nonexpert (a mathematics major). If subjects agreed with the expert and rejected the nonexpert's position, regardless of the content of their speeches, we would be able to infer that heuristic, rather than systematic, processing of the message had taken place. As positive mood was expected to increase the use of heuristic processing, we expected elated subjects to show increased acceptance of the expert's speech and increased rejection of the nonexpert's speech.

After being told about the source, subjects saw either a proattitudinal or a counterattitudinal message about acid rain. Half the subjects read a speech composed of arguments we knew from pretesting to be strong and valid, whereas the rest of the subjects saw a speech comprising arguments pretested to be weak and specious. As noted above, differential reactions to strong and weak messages indicate systematic processing. If subjects were persuaded by strong messages and were unimpressed by weak messages, we could infer they had systematically processed the message. Although we expected this pattern of results from those in a neutral mood, we expected people in a good mood to do comparatively less systematic processing of the message.

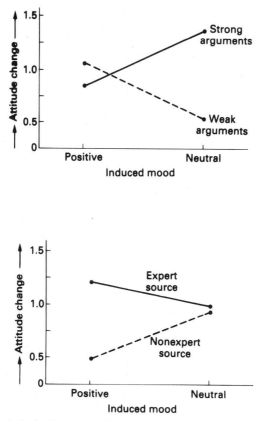

FIG 11.1   Attitude change toward the advocated position, as a function of mood, argument quality, and heuristic cue, Experiment 1.

After subjects read the persuasive message, we reassessed their attitudes on the acid rain issue, to see how the experimental manipulations had influenced acceptance of the advocated position. These results appear in Figure 11.1. The uppermost figure shows the impact of the manipulation of strong and weak messages on subjects in positive and neutral moods. As can be seen, subjects in a neutral mood were significantly more persuaded by strong arguments than by weak ones, whereas subjects in a good mood did not react differently to strong and weak messages. As predicted, subjects in a good mood engaged in less systematic processing of the message.

If subjects in a good mood were not systematically processing the message, how were they dealing with it? As can be seen in the lower graph in Figure 11.1, our hypothesis that subjects in a positive mood would engage in more heuristic processing in the persuasive situation also received support.

Subjects in a positive mood were more impressed by the expert's message than by the nonexpert's, whereas subjects in a neutral mood did not make this kind of differentiation.

Taken together, these findings provided the first evidence that subjects in a good mood engage in less systematic processing and more heuristic processing of persuasive messages than do subjects in a neutral mood. More recently, similar results with regard to positive mood have also been reported by Bless *et al.* (1990).

Our results are informative for several reasons. First, they suggest when the popular belief that feeling good increases persuasion is justified, and when the popular wisdom might not be so wise. When arguments used to advocate a position are weak, for example, our results suggest that mildly elated recipients will be more persuaded than neutral subjects who might scrutinize the available evidence more systematically. Elated subjects might also be more vulnerable to the persuasive power of heuristic cues. On the other hand, when strong arguments are presented, those in a good mood might be less persuaded than those in a neutral mood, perhaps because they do not process the strong arguments as carefully.

Second, the pattern of persuasion we produced was a function of the way in which mood influenced processing of the message, rather than a direct function of the mood state itself. Schwarz and Clore (1983, 1988) have suggested that in some complex processing situations, subjective feelings of mood may be used as a cue to making an evaluative judgment. From this perspective, message recipients who feel good (for reasons independent of the persuasive content) might decide a message is valid and accept it, because they misattribute their good feelings to the message or the position it advocates. Such a process would predict a persuasive advantage for positive mood, but was not supported by the interactional pattern of our results (nor by Bless *et al.*, 1990). Although perceivers may (correctly or incorrectly) use their feelings as a cue when involvement is low (Petty *et al.*, 1988) or when such information is in fact relevant to the judgment (when one is considering a potential lover, for example), persuasion in our study appeared to be mediated by the impact of mood on processing of the persuasive message.

The interactional nature of the results also rules out other mechanisms that would predict main effects for mood. Mood-congruency effects (Bower, 1981), for example, might lead one to expect that elated subjects would pay more attention to, encode more completely, and so be more impressed with positive aspects of a message (positive consequences of the advocated position, for example). Or, to the extent that a proattitudinal message can be thought of as congruent with feeling good, elated subjects might be expected to show more acceptance of an attitude-congruent rather than an attitude-incongruent message, compared with subjects in a neutral mood. As neither the processing nor recall of proattitudinal as compared with counterattitudinal messages was affected by induced mood, our results provided no sign of these kinds of effects.

Identifying the Underlying Mechanisms

The results of this initial experiment confirmed that mildly elated recipients are less likely to process a persuasive message systematically and more likely to process it heuristically. Our results do not, however, make clear *why* such effects might occur. As noted earlier, a multitude of possible mechanisms have been proposed to explain the impact of positive mood on processing. Most of these proposed explanations fall into two general classes of explanation, focusing on mood-induced reductions of either capacity or motivation to process.

According to the first view, positive mood may decrease systematic processing and increase satisficing strategies because, for a number of reasons, it disrupts attentional and processing allocation (Mackie and Worth, 1989; see also Isen, 1984; Isen *et al.*, 1982, for related views), thereby interfering with performance on other capacity-intensive processing tasks. Under conditions of positive affect, the strong cognitive links between items with (subjectively assigned) positive valence may produce a situation in which considerable amounts of material are activated in memory. The affective nature of some of this material might in turn automatically draw attention to itself, intruding upon other material also present in working memory (Mackie and Worth, in press). The presence of all this activated and preactivated material may provide both a complex and distracting cognitive context in terms of which incoming information must be interpreted. The simultaneous accessibility of this material might broaden or make diffuse the focus of attention, leading to a continual allocation and reallocation of processing capacity. If so, focusing attention in tasks that require sequential or analytic processing will be difficult. From this perspective, then, those in a positive mood may use judgment heuristics strategically because they are *unable* to maintain the disciplined attentional focus that is demanded by extensive and elaborate processing.

Alternatively, positive mood might also decrease systematic processing for motivational reasons related to the subjective experience of being in a good mood. Not surprisingly, being in a good mood is a positive and rewarding state. Individuals may well be motivated to maintain this positive state, selectively engaging in those activities that threaten to destroy it (Isen and Levin, 1972; Isen and Simmonds 1978; Mischel *et al.*, 1973). As extensive thinking about complex problems can be both effortful and stressful (Janis and Mann, 1977), the use of heuristics and satisficing strategies might provide an effective means for people in positive moods to avoid complex processing and maintain their positive mood. In this view, then, the use of judgment heuristics by people in a positive mood reflects a *lack of desire* to process extensively.

Experiment 2: Manipulating Capacity to Distinguish Mediators

The pattern of results found in our first experiment did not distinguish between these motivational and capacity explanations. We therefore conducted a study (Mackie and Worth, 1989, Experiment 2) that created experimental situations in which capacity and motivational explanations would make different predictions. Suppose, for example, that recipients were allowed to control their own exposure to a persuasive message. From the motivational perspective, this control gives people the perfect means by which to avoid lengthy and unpleasant processing of a counterattitudinal (and therefore mood-incongruent) message—they need consider the message only long enough to gain the information necessary to make some reasonable response (identifying a heuristic cue, for example). If motivational processes are at work, we might expect mildly elated recipients to look at the message for as brief a time as possible, and to rely on heuristic cues in determining message validity.

Quite different predictions would be made from the capacity perspective, however. If subjects are cognitively unable to systematically process when exposure to the message is limited, they could compensate by increasing their exposure time (Chaiken and Eagly, 1976). If cognitive constraints produce deficits in systematic processing, compensating for these cognitive constraints should eliminate processing deficits. From the capacity perspective, therefore, we might expect elated recipients to spend more time looking at the persuasive message, and when they do so, to show all the usual signs of systematic processing.

In this experiment, we again induced positive and neutral moods in a context unrelated to the main persuasion task after ascertaining our subjects' initial attitudinal positions. To provide converging evidence for the impact of affect, we used a different mood-induction technique and a different attitude issue. Before the experiment proper began, subjects were asked to view short video segments, supposedly to rate their suitability for use in a classroom project. Subjects saw either a humorous segment designed to induce positive mood, or a neutral piece on the corking of fine wines, intended to have no particular affective consequences. As the cover story involved asking subjects to rate the videos in various ways, we were able to ensure that the respective segments successfully induced the positive or neutral moods intended, without differing in their interest level.

With that task complete, subjects were again asked to read and evaluate a speech delivered by a delegate, this time to a conference on "Law and Society." The relevant issue in this study was handgun control. As before, we provided our subjects with a heuristic cue that they could use to judge the validity of the message if they wished. Half the subjects in each of the mood conditions were told that the delegate delivering the speech was an expert (a legal scholar) whereas the other half were told that he was not (merely a freshman interested in these issues). Half the subjects in each of these conditions saw a message comprising strong arguments (again, ascertained through extensive pretesting) whereas the other half saw a message composed of weak and specious arguments. Recall that the manipulation of argument strength provides a means of assessing whether systematic processing has occurred. All subjects saw a counterattitudinal message dealing with limits on handgun possession, presented on the monitor of a personal computer.

Of primary importance was the manipulation of exposure time. Half of the subjects in each mood condition were exposed to the message for a fixed amount of time, designed to be just enough time to read the message through once. These conditions thus replicated Experiment 1, and provided a comparison baseline of systematic processing of the message under limited exposure conditions. The other half of the subjects were exposed to an identical message but were told that they could look at the message for as long as they chose. The two dependent measures critical in distinguishing the capacity from the motivational explanations were acceptance of the message and the amount of time subjects spent viewing it.

The extent of attitude change toward the advocated position is represented in Figure 11.2. The two graphs on the left indicate the effect of the manipulation of source expertise and argument quality, respectively, on the

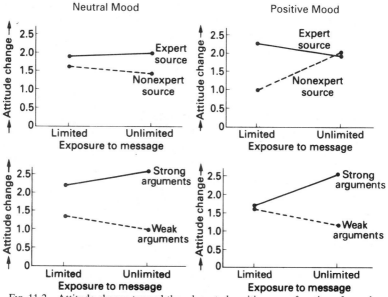

FIG 11.2   Attitude change toward the advocated position, as a function of mood, argument quality, heuristic cue, and exposure time, Experiment 2.

responses of neutral mood subjects given either limited or unlimited exposure to the message. As can be seen, neutral mood subjects were almost unaffected by the heuristic cue. As expected, these subjects instead processed the content of the message systematically, as indicated by their acceptance of the strong advocacy and rejection of the weak one. Both these effects were relatively uninfluenced by the manipulation of exposure time.

The results were quite different for those in a good mood, as can be seen in the two graphs on the right of Figure 11.2. The top panel shows the important impact that the exposure manipulation had on these subjects' use of the expertise heuristic. Mildly elated subjects given only limited exposure to the message accepted the expert's advocacy but rejected the nonexpert's message, showing the same reliance on heuristic cues as found in Experiment 1. When allowed to control their own exposure to the message, however, this reliance on the heuristic cue disappeared. At the same time, subjects in a good mood failed to differentiate between strong and weak arguments when exposure was limited, again replicating the results from Experiment 1. When allowed to control their own exposure to the message, however, elated subjects showed systematic processing comparable to that shown by subjects in a neutral mood, clearly differentiating between strong and weak arguments.

The exposure time manipulation thus had a substantial impact on the attitude change shown by subjects in a good mood. What was it about this manipulation that produced such dramatic differences? The key appears to lie in the amount of time subjects in the unlimited exposure condition chose to look at the message. Whereas subjects in a neutral mood looked at the message for only 74.87 s, subjects in a positive mood spent significantly longer doing so, $M = 85.15$ s. Subjects in a good mood not only looked at the message longer, but also systematically processed it when they did so (see also Mackie and Worth, 1989, Experiment 1).

As these results show, the motivational position fared rather badly in this experiment. The methodology we used—giving subjects control over their exposure time—allowed a clear test of whether good mood motivated people to minimize extensive processing as a means of preserving their pleasant mood state. Our results showed, however, that elated subjects looked at the message longer than did neutral mood subjects, a finding that is clearly incompatible with the motivational hypothesis. That these subjects chose to look at the message for fairly lengthy periods of time is especially compelling, given not only the counterattitudinal nature of the message but also the mildly negative connotations of the handgun issue itself.

In contrast, attentional allocation interpretations of the processing deficit shown by elated subjects were strengthened by these findings. When recipients in a positive mood were allowed to control their message exposure, they viewed the message for significantly longer than neutral mood subjects, and having done so, exhibited all the usual indications of systematic processing. These results support the idea that these subjects needed and used increased exposure time to compensate for reduced attentional capacity.

Experiment 3: Manipulating Motivation to Distinguish Mediators

Our first attempt to distinguish the cognitive and motivational mediators of positive mood focused on a manipulation of processing capacity. To provide a further test of the cognitive and motivational explanations, our next study (Worth, *et al.*, 1989) employed procedures designed to manipulate processing motivation. In this study, the critical conditions were ones in which incentives to process the message carefully were high, but the time in which the message could be viewed was limited. Finding that message recipients in a positive mood show processing decrements, even when incentives are high, would provide compelling evidence for the role of attentional allocation mediators. On the other hand, finding that elated subjects were perfectly capable of processing the message when the stakes were high enough would signal motivational deficits as the critical mediating variable.

Subjects again began the experimental session by reporting their attitude on acid rain, among other issues. Using the same two-experiment ruse as in Experiment 2, we then had subjects watch and rate a humorous or neutral video segment which successfully induced positive and neutral moods, respectively. A second experimenter then introduced the delegate evaluation task, which, as before, subjects completed at computer consoles.

All subjects were told that their task was to read and evaluate a speech, again ostensibly delivered by a delegate (whose expertise was not manipulated in this experiment). The critical manipulation in this study occurred in the initial instructions to the evaluation task. Half the subjects were given the standard instructions to read and evaluate the speech and the delegate's performance. The rest of the subjects, those in the high-incentive condition, were told in addition that it was very important that they do a thorough, accurate, and complete job of evaluating the delegate. To encourage them to do so, they were told that they would be paid monetary amounts that were proportional to the completeness and accuracy of their performance. It was stressed that the better the job they did, the more they would be paid.

All subjects saw a counterattitudinal message, comprising either strong or weak arguments, which appeared on the computer monitor for a limited amount of time. Subjects then answered several questions about the message and the issue. Responses on items designed to measure incentive indicated that as intended, subjects in the high-incentive condition thought the task was more important and put more effort into it than people in the low-incentive condition, $F(1,84)=6.87$, $P<0.01$. These differences were

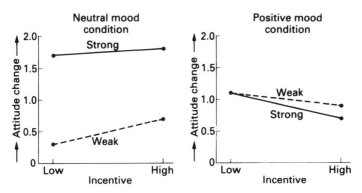

Fɪɢ 11.3   Attitude change toward the advocated position, as a function of mood, argument quality, and incentive, Experiment 3.

especially strong for those subjects in a good mood, and thus provided a good test of the incentive hypothesis in the crucial conditions. Given that we had successfully manipulated motivation to process, the critical dependent measure was acceptance of the advocated position as a function of the mood, incentive, and argument quality manipulations.

Attitude change toward the advocated position appears in Figure 11.3. As can be seen, subjects in a neutral mood processed the message systematically, and thus were significantly more impressed by the strong arguments than by the weak, $F(1,43)=6.51$, $P<0.01$. In contrast, those in a good mood failed to react differently to the strong and weak messages, $F(1,40)<1$. Even though the manipulation of incentives appeared particularly successful, and motivation to process the communication was high, subjects in a good mood failed to systematically process the content of the presented arguments. Like the data from Experiment 2, these results provide no support for the idea that motivational decrements contribute to elated recipients' failure to distinguish between strong and weak messages.

The Effects of Positive Mood on Persuasive Processing

Our strategy in these experiments was to apply a processing view of persuasion to help us understand the mechanisms that might underlie the popular view that positive mood increases persuasion. Approaching attitude change as a special form of social judgment makes clear the close and complementary nature of mood effects on persuasion and on social judgments in general (see other chapters in this book). Our program of research has shown that the picture is somewhat more complicated than the popular view leads us to believe—in fact, a positive mood may not always increase persuasion. The processing approach indicates that the extent and nature of persuasion will depend on how the persuasive message is processed, and the results of our studies indicate that mildly elated recipients do less systematic processing of messages than others. When arguments supporting an advocated position are somewhat weak, or when an obvious heuristic cue is present, this lack of systematic processing increases persuasion. When the arguments supporting a position are strong and valid, however, lack of systematic processing can reduce their persuasive impact.

What causes elated recipients to do less systematic processing? Although an extremely euphoric mood might lead recipients to avoid processing persuasive messages altogether, or make their careful consideration a very low priority, our subjects seemed perfectly willing to deal with the incoming persuasive material. They looked longer at the message when given the opportunity, and reacted appropriately to manipulations of increased incentive. Our findings thus seem inconsistent with the idea that elated subjects avoid processing because they believe it will undermine their mood (see also Schaller and Cialdini, 1990). Although our elated subjects were *motivated* to process, however, they seemed to have some *difficulty* in doing so, at least when message exposure was limited. This difficulty implicates some form of attentional constraint that affects extensive and analytic processing.

Why might being in a positive mood interfere with this particular kind of processing? Some of the apparent consequences of positive mood discussed earlier may well produce a cognitive context in which attentional and processing capacity was limited. For example, because positive material is thought to be more extensive and more interrelated (Isen *et al.*, 1983; Matlin and Stang, 1979), positive affect may lead to the simultaneous activation of a large amount of material, a diversity of associated thoughts and procedures, many of which might seem to be potentially related or relevant. In such a complex cognitive context, attention may be drawn to many different aspects of the material active in working memory, broadening and diffusing the attentional focus (Mackie and Worth, 1989). Such a situation may have several consequences for further processing. For example, incoming material might be interpreted in multiple and diverse ways, and from many different perspectives (Isen, 1987). Because of the activation of positively valenced material in memory, particular kinds of incoming information (mood-congruent items, for example) may be processed more deeply and more richly at many different levels (Forgas and Bower, 1987). Such effects might increase persuasion, for example, because perceivers can interpret attitude-relevant arguments—even silly or weak ones—in a multitude of ways, all of which have some bearing on the attitude judgment. Under such conditions, however, it may be difficult not only to decide which aspects of the persuasive context should receive attentional and processing capacity, but also to maintain attentional vigilance on any particular focus.

It is interesting to speculate that this diffuse allocation and reallocation of attention might be related in an adaptive way to the informational value of mood. Mildly positive mood states may signal release from the need to monitor either the environment or the self in any one particular way (Frijda, 1988). Positive mood may not only activate more material, but also make accessible many more ways in which to deal with this material, as well as make it more likely that we entertain the possibility of doing so (Isen, 1987). Thus a simultaneous activation of many diverse procedures for low-level monitoring of incoming information may also increase the cognitive flexibility with which such material is processed.

We have focused on the impact of positive mood on the processing of persuasive messages that comprise several arguments in support of a particular position. We have thus dealt primarily with persuasive situations in which a relatively complex informational base relevant to an idea, issue, or object is provided. To thoroughly ascertain the many implications of such information for a relevant attitude, recipients may need to extend, elaborate, and evaluate the provided information in some detail. We have suggested that in such cases, the diffusion of attention and simultaneous accessibility of diverse information induced by positive mood might be associated with decrements in elated subjects' performance of this kind of processing.

In other situations, affect may have different direct and indirect effects on evaluative judgments (see other chapters in this book). Such judgments might be made because a single factor in the persuasive situation, or because the attitude object made one feel good, regardless of its various and sundry other qualities. The accessibility of, and attention to, multiple categories and procedures that we have associated with positive mood may have little impact on the processing of such information (although it may affect its interpretation). Although we have focused on the way in which the diffusion of attention or the ready accessibility and appeal of multiple strategies for dealing with information might inhibit performance on sequential, analytic, and capacity-intensive processing, these same factors might well facilitate performance on tasks requiring creativity, idiosyncrasy, or dissociative solutions, for example (Isen 1987).

Guided by our interest in testing the popular notion that feeling good facilitates persuasion, we have focused on the processing consequences of positive mood. Yet comparing the impact of positive and negative might seem an elegantly simple way to test the motivational and cognitive explanations for the processing effects we have described. For example, it is often assumed that asymmetries in the effects of positive and negative mood provide evidence for motivational mediating processes, whereas symmetrical effects would support cognitive explanations of mood effects. As is often true of the subtle interplay between affect and cognition, however, the situation is not so simple. Some motivational theories do predict asymmetries, arguing that processing will be avoided to maintain a positive mood but engaged in to disrupt a negative mood (see Isen, 1984, for a review).

However, approaches that stress the informational value of mood states also predict asymmetries, since mild negative mood states might signal the need for increased attention to the environment (Frijda, 1988). At the same time, negative mood has also been seen as motivating initial attentional allocation to the self (Salovey, 1988), reducing, by implication, the attention paid to other aspects of the environment.

Nor is it clear that all cognitive models predict identical consequences for positive and negative moods. There is evidence for symmetrical congruency effects (Forgas and Bower, 1987), as well as for the fact that negative mood decreases performance on capacity-intensive tasks (Ellis and Ashbrook, 1988). Yet cognitive models need not predict such symmetrical effects. Because we try to distract ourselves from negative, but not from positive, moods, we may weaken the associative links between negative items much more than we do those between positive elements. At the same time, stimulus–procedure links may be much stronger when stimuli are negative rather than positive. Thus activation of positive material may have much more powerful effects on attentional allocation than activation of negative information.

Unfortunately, the data relevant to the impact of negative mood provide no clearer picture than do the competing theories. Evidence consistent with all of the positions described above exists in the judgment literature (see other chapters of this book). In the persuasion literature, Bless *et al.* (1990, Experiment 1) have demonstrated that an induced mood that was clearly more negative than an induced positive mood produced systematic processing of a persuasive appeal. More information about processing mediators is needed, however, before we know how to interpret these effects. The apparent inconsistency of the effects of negative mood highlights the conceptual and methodological difficulties encountered in working with negative mood. Because subjects try to resist the induction of negative moods, such manipulations are often less successful, less invariant in their consequences, and less longlasting. In addition, the differentiation and independence of negative mood states suggests that sadness, anger, anxiety, and dismay at unexpected failure may produce very different effects. This is not to say that such difficulties need not be considered when positive mood is investigated. However, their presence considerably complicates the attempt to learn about positive mood by simply comparing its effects to those of negative mood.

It is intriguing to speculate on the degree to which we might understand (if only implicitly) the relation between our moods and the kind of performances they facilitate and inhibit. If we do, we may well attempt to control a positive mood state so that we might process carefully. In our third experiment, we were careful to increase motivation while not eradicating positive mood. We suspect, however, that there are many cases in which careful processing of a message is of such importance that elated recipients might consciously "get out of a good mood" so that they might concentrate better. Just as our students believe they have more chance of persuading someone in a good mood, they believe they have more chance of concentrating, both on resisting persuasion and on other things, if they are not feeling too happy. As the subject who provided the title of our chapter expressed it, "You can be feeling good, but you're probably not thinking straight." The clear association our students see between positive mood and the inability to concentrate, between feeling good but not thinking straight, and the cognitive and motivational strategies they bring to bear because of this perceived association, seems likely to have many implications for persuasion (as well as other social phenomena), and is worthy of increased research attention. Our moods may not only signal us when and how we need to regulate our processing environment, but we might also regulate our moods in order to deal with that same environment.

Tracking the intricate interactions between the cognitive and motivational consequences of particular affective states and the cognitive and motivational requirements of particular processing operations that culminate in persuasion, offers both a challenge and a promise. The challenge, of course, is how difficult that task has proven, and will continue, to be. The promise, however, is better understanding of the many complex and subtle influences that mood has on our ability both to persuade and be persuaded.

Acknowledgment

The support of National Institute of Mental Health grant MH 43041 to Diane Mackie is gratefully acknowledged. Correspondence should be addressed to Diane M. Mackie, Department of Psychology, University of California, Santa Barbara, CA 93106, USA.

References

Belch, G. E., Belch, M. A., and Vilareal, A. (1987). Effects of advertising communications: Review of research. *Research in Marketing*, **9**, 59–117.

Biggers, T., and Pryor, B. (1982). Attitude change: A function of emotion-eliciting qualities of environment. *Personality and Social Psychology Bulletin*, **8**, 94–99.

Bless, H., Bohner, G., Schwarz, F., and Strack, F. (1990). Mood and persuasion: A cognitive response analysis. *Personality and Social Psychology Bulletin*, **16**, 331–345. Bower, G. H. (1981). Mood and memory. *American Psychologist*, **36**, 129–148.

Chaiken, S. (1980). Heuristic versus systematic information processing and the use of source versus message cues in persuasion. *Journal of Personality and Social Psychology*, **39**, 752–766.

Chaiken, S. (1986). The heuristic model of persuasion. In M. P. Zanna, J. M. Olson, and C. P. Herman (Eds), *Social influence: The Ontario Symposium*, Vol. 5, pp. 3–40. Hillsdale NJ: Erlbaum.

Chaiken, S., and Eagly, A. H. (1976). Communication modality as a determinant of message persuasiveness and message comperehensibility. *Journal of Personality and Social Psychology*, **34**, 605–614.

Chaiken, S., Liberman, A., and Eagly, A. H. (1989). Heuristic and systematic information processing within and beyond the persuasion context. In J. S. Uleman and J. A. Bargh (Eds), *Unintended thought: Limits of awareness, intention, and control*. pp. 212–252. New York: Guilford Press.

Clark, M. S. and Williamson, G. J. (1983). Moods and social judgments. In: H. L. Wagner and A. S. R. Manstead (Eds). *Handbook of Psychophysiology: Emotion and social behavior.* Chichester Wiley.

Dribben, E., and Brabender, V. (1979). The effect of mood inducement upon audience receptiveness. *Journal of Social Psychology,* **107,** 135–136.

Dabbs, J. M., and Janis, I. L. (1965). Why does eating while reading facilitate opinion change?—an experimental investigation. *Journal of Experimental Social Psychology,* **1,** 133–144.

Ellis, H. C., and Ashbrook, P. W. (1988). Resource allocation model of the effects of depressed mood states on memory. In K. Fiedler and J. Forgas (Eds), *Affect, cognition, and social behavior,* pp. 25–43. Toronto: Hogrefe.

Fiedler, K. (1988). Emotional mood, cognitive style, and behavior regulation. In K. Fiedler and J. Forgas (Eds), *Affect, cognition, and social behavior,* pp. 100–119. Toronto: Hogrefe.

Fiske, S., and Taylor, S. E. (1984). *Social cognition.* Reading: Addison-Wesley.

Forgas, J. P., and Bower, G. H. (1987). Mood effects on person perception judgments. *Journal of Personality and Social Psychology,* **53,** 53–60.

Forgas, J. P., and Bower, G. H. (1988). Affect in social and personal judgments. In K. Fiedler, and J. Forgas (Eds), *Affect, cognition and social behavior,* pp. 183–208. Toronto: Hogrefe.

Frijda, N. H. (1988). The laws of emotion. *American Psychologist,* **43,** 349–358.

Galizio, M., and Hendrick, C. (1972). Effect of musical accompaniment on attitude: The guitar as a prop for persuasion. *Journal of Applied Social Psychology,* **2,** 350–359.

Holman, R. H. (1986). Advertising and emotionality. In R. A. Peterson, W. D. Hoyer, and W. R. Wilson (Eds) *The Role of Affect in Consumer Behavior,* pp. 119–140. Lexington, MA: Lexington Books.

Isen, A. M. (1984). Toward understanding the role of affect in cognition. In R. Wyer and T. Srull (Eds), *Handbook of social cognition,* Vol. 3, pp. 179–236. Hillsdale, NJ: Erlbaum.

Isen, A. M. (1987). Positive affect, cognitive processes, and social behavior. *Advances in Experimental Social Psychology,* **20,** 203–253.

Isen, A. M., and Levin, P. F. (1972). The effect of feeling good on helping: Cookies and kindness. *Journal of Personality and Social Psychology,* **21,** 384–388.

Isen, A. M., and Means, B. (1983). The influence of positive affect on decision making strategy. *Social Cognition,* **2,** 18– 31.

Isen, A. M., Means, B., Patrick, R., and Nowicki, G. (1982). Some factors influencing decision-making strategy and risk taking. In M. S. Clark and S. T. Fiske (Eds), *Affect and cognition,* pp. 243–261. Hillsdale, NJ: Erlbaum.

Isen, A. M., and Simmonds, S. (1978). The effect of feeling good on a task that is incompatible with good mood. *Social Psychology Quarterly,* **41,** 346–349.

Janis, I. L., Kaye, D., and Kirschner, P. (1965). Facilitating effects of "eating while reading" on responsiveness to persuasive communications. *Journal of Personality and Social Psychology,* **1,** 181–186.

Janis, I. L., and Mann, L. (1977). *Decision making.* New York: Free Press.

Johnson, E. J., and Tversky, A. (1983). Affect, generalization, and the perception of risk. *Journal of Personality and Social Psychology,* **45,** 20–31.

Kahle, L. R., and Page, M. M. (1976). The deprivation–satiation effect in attitude conditioning without deprivation but with demand characteristics. *Personality and Social Psychology Bulletin,* **2,** 470–473.

Kavanagh, D. J., and Bower, G. H. (1985). Mood and self-efficacy: Impact of joy and sadness on perceived capabilites. *Cognitive Therapy and Research,* **9,** 507–525.

Kroeber-Riel, W. (1984). Emotional product differentiation by classical conditioning. In T. C. Kinnear (Ed.), *Advances in consumer research,* Vol. 11, pp. 538–543. Ann Arbor, MI: Association of Consumer Research.

Mackie, D. M., and Worth, L. T. (1989). Processing deficits and the mediation of positive affect in persuasion. *Journal of Personality and Social Psychology,* **57,** 1–14.

Mackie, D. M., and Worth, L. T. (in press). The impact of distraction on the processing and category-based and attribute-based evaluations. *Basic and Applied Social Psychology.*

Matlin; M. W., and Stang, D. (1979). *The Pollyanna Principle: Selectivity in language, memory, and thought.* Cambridge, MA: Schenkman.

Mischel, W., Ebbesen, E., and Zeiss, A. (1973). Selective attention to the self: Situational and dispositional determinants. *Journal of Personality and Social Psychology*, **27**, 129–142.

Page, M. M., and Kahle, L. R. (1976). Demand characteristics in the satiation–deprivation effect on attitude conditioning, *Journal of Personality and Social Psychology*, **33**, 553–562.

Petty, R. E., and Cacioppo, J. T. (1979). Issue-involvement can increase or decrease persuasion by enhancing message-relevant cognitve responses. *Personality and Social Psychology Bulletin*, **5**, 173–176.

Petty, R. E., and Cacioppo, J. T. (1981). *Attitudes and persuasion: Classic and contemporary approaches*. Dubuque, IA: Wm C. Brown.

Petty, R. E., and Cacioppo, J. T. (1986). The Elaboration Likelihood Model of Persuasion. In L. Berkowitz (Ed.), *Advances in experimental social psychology*, Vol. 19, pp.124–205. New York: Academic Press.

Petty, R. E., Cacioppo, J. T., and Goldman, R. (1981). Personal involvement and a determinant of argument-based persuasion. *Journal of Personality and Social Psychology*, **41**, 847–853.

Petty, R. E., Cacioppo, J. T., and Kasmer, J. A. (1988). The role of affect in the Elaboration Likelihood Model of persuasion. In L. Donohew, H. E. Sypher, and E. T. Higgins (Eds), *Communication, social cognition, and affect*, pp. 117–146. Hillsdale, NJ: Erlbaum.

Razran, G. H. S. (1940). Conditioned response changes in rating and appraising socio-political slogans. *Psychology Bulletin*, **37**, 481.

Salovey, P. (1988). The effects of mood and focus of attention on self-relevant thoughts and helping intention. *Dissertation Abstracts International*, **48**, 3121–3128.

Schaller, M., and Cialdini, R. B. (1990). Happiness, sadness, and helping: A motivational integration. In E. T. Higgins and R. M. Sorrentino (Eds), *Handbook of motivation and cognition: Foundations of social behavior*, Vol. 2. pp. 265–296. New York: Guilford Press.

Schwarz, N. (1990). Informational and motivational functions of affective states. In E. T. Higgins and R. M. Sorrentino (Eds), *Handbook of motivation and cognition: Foundations of social behavior*, Vol. 2. pp. 527–561. New York: Guilford Press.

Schwarz, N., and Clore, G. L. (1983). Mood, misattribution, and judgments of well-being. Informative and directive functions of affective states. *Journal of Personality and Social Psychology*, **45**, 513–523.

Schwarz, N., and Clore, G. L. (1988). How do I feel about it? Informative functions of affective states. In K. Fiedler and J. Forgas (Eds), *Affect, cognition, and social behavior*, pp. 44–62. Toronto: Hogrefe.

Staats, A. W., Staats, C. K., and Crawford, H. L. (1962). First-order conditioning of meaning and the parallel conditioning of a GSR. *Journal of General Psychology*, **67**, 159–167.

Worth, L. T., and Mackie, D. M. (1987). Cognitive mediation of positive affect in persuasion. *Social Cognition*, **5**, 76–94.

Worth, L. T., Mackie, D. M., and Asuncion, A. G. (1989). Distinguishing cognitive and motivational mediators of the impact of positive mood on persuasion. Unpublished manuscript, Pennsylvania State University, Pennsylvania.

Wright, W. F., and Bower, G. H. (1981). Mood effects on subjective probability assessment. Unpublished manuscript, Stanford University, California.

Zanna, M. P., Kiesler, C. A., and Pilkonis, P. A. (1970). Positive and negative attitudinal affect established by classical conditioning. *Journal of Personality and Social Psychology*, **14**, 321–328.

12

Positive Mood, Processing Goals and the Effects of Information on Evaluative Judgment

J. M. INNES and C. R. AHRENS

University of Adelaide

Contents

Introduction

This chapter is concerned with the examination of the influence of transient affective states upon the processing of information, which results in a change in an attitude held by the recipient of the information. It is necessary, first of all, in a volume concerned with social judgment, to make clear the relevance of such work to the issues considered in the other chapters.

The role of emotions and feelings in influencing the manner in which people view the world and their relations to the people around them has long been recognized as important. In the study of such judgments by psychologists, however, the role of affective processes was neglected for many years. The emphasis was placed upon cognition, the more or less rational processing of information, as central to an understanding of how people grow to make sense of their social environment.

This relative benign neglect has, however, in recent years been set aside. There is now a flurry of activity, both theoretical and empirical, to try to integrate how affective and cognitive processes may combine to influence the growth of social knowledge (e.g. Donohew *et al.*, 1988; Fiedler and Forgas, 1988; Izard *et al.*, 1984.)

The place of attitudes

Within the field of social psychology there has been a topic of interest which has, even if only implicitly, always been concerned with the interactions of cognition and affect in influencing social judgment. The concept of attitude has long held a central position, and for many years "attitude" was regarded as the key problem of study for social pyschologists (Allport, 1935). While a great deal of research has been conducted over the last 50 years into the development of attitudes (cf. McGuire, 1985), there has been confusion about the definition of the concept which has led, in turn, to a failure of attitude research to enlighten an understanding of the interaction of cognition and affect (Pratkanis and Greenwald, 1989).

A very common definition of "attitude" has viewed it as comprising three components, cognitive, affective, and behavioral (Rosenberg and Hovland, 1960), and the separate roles of these facets have been examined in numerous studies (e.g. Breckler, 1984). Another view has been more concerned with the evaluation of objects based upon cognition, and the theories of "reasoned" and "planned" action, for example, have been successful in predicting behavior from the beliefs that people hold about issues and events (Ajzen, 1988).

However, as Zanna and Rempel (1988) point out, there has been confusion at the very heart of the definition of attitude, one which is linked to the role of affect in judgment. Virtually all definitions regard an attitude as an *evaluative* judgment about an event or person or issue (Pratkanis and Greenwald, 1989). So the object of the attitude may be regarded, for example, as good, or evil or untrustworthy. Several theorists seem to include affect *necessarily* in this evaluation judgment, and this may be what has caused confusion. It is possible for a person to evaluate another person harshly or benignly in expressing their attitude, while being able, at the same time, either to experience a strong or a weak affective reaction, or even none at all. It is, theoretically at least, possible to evaluate a politician poorly while feeling quite happy about him or her and to judge people as evaluatively quite useful while intensely disliking them. Of course, intensive affect, if present, is likely to play an important part in determining both the valence (direction) of an evaluative judgment and the intensity of that judgment (Judd and Johnson, 1984). This is a matter for empirical investigation, however, and the theoretical distinction between presence of affect and the evaluative outcome needs to be maintained.

Abelson *et al.*, (1982) have shown that in the evaluation of politicians, affective and cognitive factors play separate roles in how people arrive at their judgments. Further work by us (Innes and Ahrens, submitted) has supported and extended this research by showing the subcomponents of affective reactions can play separate roles in evaluation. The major point to be drawn here is that an attitude, or evaluative social judgment, may have an affective component as well as a cognitive one. In that sense, therefore, attitudes may be regarded as prototypical evaluative social judgments for the study of the interaction of cognition and affect.

The affective state of the evaluator

As well as there being a structural affective component to an attitude, however, feelings can play another role in helping to determine the expression of an evaluation. The global affective state, or mood, experienced by a person can influence social judgments. A large proportion of the research which has been concerned with the interaction of affect and cognition has looked at, not the affect linked to the actual object of evaluation, but rather the influence of mood on the processes whereby judgments are made (e.g. Clark *et al.*, 1988; Forgas and Bower, 1988; Isen, 1987). Mood has been regarded as a possible means of priming, or making more accessible to recall, material thought likely to reside in long-term memory store that is relevant to the mood state. As Forgas and Bower (1988) state "mood states have a wide-ranging and persistent influence on many kinds of social judgments. Current mood-priming theories explain these biases as largely due to nonspecific interference in general cognitive processes, such as associations, attention, learning and memory" (p. 141).

When a person is making an attitudinal judgment, it is likely that the general mood which he or she is experiencing at the time may influence the form the judgment may take and also influence the reaction to information relevant to and upon which the judgment may be based. For example, Janis *et al.* (1965) showed that by inducing a positive mood state by allowing people to eat peanuts and drink Pepsi, they produced a more favourable attitude to issues in line with the contents of a persuasive message. The mediation of this effect, however, was not clear as it could be attributed either to cognitive biases in the processing of information or to some affective change induced through classical conditioning.

The investigation of the processes whereby attitudes are formed or changed has been clarified more recently by the development of a model for the persuasive process, the Elaboration Likelihood Model (ELM) (Petty and Cacioppo, 1986). This model enables us to consider the mood state of the recipient in the processing of attitude relevant information. The model provides for the prediction of different ways in which mood may affect processing, depending upon the presence of other variables in the setting.

The processing of persuasive messages

A central feature of the ELM is the distinction that is made between central versus peripheral routes to persuasion. By the former, Petty and Cacioppo (1986) mean that where an individual attends to the persuasive arguments that are presented, that is to the actual contents of the information, and where that individual is both motivated and has the capacity to respond to those arguments, either positively or negatively, then an enduring, structural change may occur in the cognitions held by that person. This change may then be expressed as an alteration in the attitude of the person towards the issue.

In the case of a peripheral route to persuasion, on the other hand, a lack of attention to the central features of the communication and more attention to incidental features—such as the source of the message (such that attractive people may gain more weight in deliberation than less attractive people) or how long (and therefore presumably how important) is the message—may lead to an attitude change. This change may be unstable and lacking in durability because no structural change has taken place. A similar, though not identical, model of the persuasive process has been proposed by Chaiken (Chaiken, 1987; Eagly and Chaiken 1984).

The particular role of affect in the ELM has recently been explored by Petty and his co-workers (Petty *et al.*, 1988a). The mood of the recipient of a message may play a role either in the central route to persuasion, and thereby produce an enduring change in social evaluation, or in the peripheral route, producing a relatively brief change. The effect will depend upon the central feature considered in the model, namely the likelihood that message elaboration will occur.

If the likelihood is low that a message will be processed so that, for example, the topic is uninteresting or the issue is irrelevant for the recipient, then mood may act as a peripheral cue and will enhance attention to, and the effect of, other peripheral factors, such as source of message. If elaboration likelihood is high, on the other hand, then mood may act as a central cue. In this sense, the arousal effect may act as an argument in itself. This may occur most clearly when the contents of a message are themselves emotional, as in a fear-arousal message, and a congruent mood state of the recipient can lead to greater attention and reaction to the arousal induced by the message (Petty *et al.*, 1988a).

The question arises as to what is the *direct* effect of mood on the form of thinking that is engaged in. Does a change in mood *itself* lead to simpler or to more elaborate thinking? If mood induces simpler thinking (or heuristic processing in Chaiken's, 1987, terms), will there be a greater likelihood of nonelaborate processing, with peripheral-route cues becoming important? On the other hand, if mood induces more complex thinking, then the probability of elaborative processing may be increased and central routes to attitude change may occur.

Mood effects upon thought processes

What is the evidence for the effect of mood on the quality or extension of thought? A good deal of research (cf. Isen, 1987) has suggested that an induced positive mood leads to less effortful means of processing information. So, for example, people make faster decisions by using less information (Isen and Means, 1983). It also appears that when presented with both positive and negative items of information, people in a good mood pay more attention to, and later recall more of, the positive material than they do the negative (Forgas and Bower, 1987). So there may be evidence of heuristic-based thought, with a simplification of issues congruent with the induced mood.

These results would suggest that induced mood may increase the likelihood of processing peripheral cues in a persuasion context. In support of this position, Worth and Mackie (1987) have found that individuals in a positive, compared with a neutral, mood state, were less influenced by whether the message was strong or weak in argument (i.e. in terms of the ELM they were less responsive to central-route cues). They were more influenced by whether the message source was presented as expert or nonexpert (i.e. they were more responsive to peripheral-route cues). This latter effect was particularly strong when supporting arguments were weak. This result has been supported by Bless *et al.*, (1990).

Not all of the literature on the cognitive effects of mood shows that simpler forms of processing are engaged, however. Isen *et al* (1985) have shown that positive mood induction can lead to the creation of a more diverse context of word association primes (Cramer, 1968; Innes, 1972). This leads to the production of more unusual, "creative" word associations compared with a neutral state. It may also be the case that when a person is in a positive mood, material in memory may be organized differently to result in a greater flexibility in attempting problems. Isen *et al.* (1987) have shown, for example, that positive affect facilitates creative problem solving which requires a formation of new associations. Positive mood may, therefore, reduce the elaboration of cognitive processing or enhance the creative utilization of that material. The question remains, under what circumstances will such outcomes of mood on cognitive elaboration occur during the processing of attitude-relevant persuasive information?

The work on the effect of mood upon social judgment has emphasized the role played in changing the accessibility of certain structures or associations to be used in making the judgments (e.g. Forgas and Bower, 1988). Mackie and Worth (1989) have shown that giving respondents more time to process a message reduces the impact of a mood manipulation. Thus instructional or situational manipulations may help to overcome the limiting cognitive effects of a positive mood induction. If mood does make certain thought processes more likely, then leading a person to think in that manner by, for example, specific instruction or goal direction may further facilitate the utilization of those processes under the influence of an induced mood.

Goals and social information processing

Processing goals are known to play a significant part in the acquisition and retrieval of social information (McCann and Higgins, 1988; Srull and Wyer, 1986). The expectations that people may have about the use to which they are to put information, or the strategies which they may adopt to enable them to process the material, can have a major impact upon the effect of the information. A major thread of research on such a topic includes, for example, the use of the "communication game" (Higgins *et al.*, 1982) stemming from earlier work by Zajonc (1960) (cf. Guerin and Innes, 1989, for a review) which showed that different role sets resulted in differences in the structures based upon information provided to subjects. The adoption of different roles has been shown to affect the expression of opinion (Innes, 1981).

The point is that if a person is given a particular expectation of how to deal with information, then this may result in a significantly different outcome than if no expectation is given. Bless *et al.* (1990) showed that when positive mood subjects were instructed to concentrate upon the arguments in a message, that is, to respond specifically to a central elaborative cue, then there was a response to message strength. In this sense, heuristic processing by people in a positive mood who followed instructions led to a form of systematic processing. Such evidence supports a motivational interpretation of the effects of positive mood induction (but see Mackie and Worth, this volume, for an alternative position). Positive mood may not necessarily reduce the cognitive capacity of the respondent. The person may merely be less motivated to work the material.

This may be extended further. If induced mood has an influence upon the motivational rather than the cognitive state of the individual, then it should be possible to change the motivation of the person to alter the amount of processing. Suppose recipients who are in a positive mood are instructed to respond to information naturally. Then the outcome may be very different from the case where subjects are motivated to perform in a mood-incongruent mode of thought.

In the studies of the effects of persuasive message, the ambient conditions usually emphasize the critical nature of the procedure, to evaluate and react to arguments. Such an ambient state may be incompatible with the processing state of the person in a positive mood. Isen *et al.* (1987) have shown positive mood subjects can act creatively. If the general instructions designed to motivate information processing emphasize creative and non-critical reactions, then such mood-congruent processing goals may result in outcomes very different from mood-incongruent processing goals.

In summary, the research into the role of affect in the structure and functioning of attitudes is held to be of relevance to the debate about the role of affect in social judgment. Affect in turn, according to the ELM (Petty *et al.*), is seen to have several different roles to play in influencing the ways in which attitude-relevant information is processed.

Affect may play a central or peripheral role in the processing of persuasive messages. Affect which is irrelevant to the content of a message will also play a part. The induction of positive mood has been shown to have both cognitive (reducing capacity for information processing) and motivational (reducing inducement to process) influences. The inducement to process information may, however, be rendered more or less compatible with the preferred state induced by the mood. If people are led to look at a persuasive message in a way that is congruent with how they would naturally examine the contents, then the outcome of the subsequent processing should be different from one resulting from incongruence.

We report here two studies. Both were designed to examine the influence of induced positive mood upon the processing of the contents of a persuasive message. They were designed to explore whether irrelevant affect may lead to central or peripheral routes to persuasion, as posited by the ELM (Petty *et al.*, 1988). The two experiments contained a manipulation designed to influence the motivational goal of the recipients, to see whether cognitive or motivational processes were altered as a function of mood. The two experiments differed in the variation of the messages used. In the first study the valence of the message, pro versus anti, was varied, with strength of message constant. In the second, strength was varied, with valence constant. The ELM posits the likelihood of elaboration as a central feature of the model, and this may vary with the perceived strength of the messages. Hence it is important, both for the ELM and for the question of the role of mood, to be concerned with strength.

Overview of the Two Studies

The two studies were very similar in structure. The similarities in procedure and measures will be described here, and the differences in the nature of the message manipulation will be presented separately for each. Both experiments were based on a two (mood condition) by two (instruction set) by two (nature of message) factorial design. All of the respondents were first year university students.

The rationale of both studies was to present subjects with a persuasive message concerned with an issue which had been previously rated as important, namely the concentration of media ownership in Australia. At the time of the first study there had been a series of take-overs of TV stations and newspapers so that the major electronic and print publishing companies were in the control of very few people. The issue was rated as important in pretests, but the respondents were only mildly in opposition to the take-overs. This changed over the course of the studies and influences the interpretation of the data between experiments, as will be shown later.

Prior to the presentation of the message, respondents were asked to describe how they felt at that moment via completion of the Depressive Adjective Check List (DACL), which comprised adjectives describing various moods and feelings (Ellis *et al.*, 1984). This provided a pretest of their mood state. In each study half of the respondents then were exposed to a tape recording designed to induce a positive mood. Twelve self-reference positive statements, taken from Teasdale and Russell (1983), were played, with 20 second pause after each statement, during which time the respondents were asked to try to adopt the kind of feelings implied by the statement. The tape lasted approximately six minutes. The other half of the subjects listened to a tape of similar form and length, except that the statements were designed to elicit minimum affect.

Immediately following exposure to the tapes, the respondents again completed the DACL. We thus obtained a change score as a measure of the success of the positive mood tape to induce in the respondents a happy mood.

In both studies the manipulation intended to influence the processing goal was the same. Half of the respondents were told to adopt a critical set, to read the message as if they had to present an appraisal of the contents to another group for class discussion and criticism, and possible assessment. This set is not the kind of analysis that is congruent with the mood literature presented by Isen and her co-workers. It may appear similar to the manipulation of Bless *et al.* (1990), but in this case a *critical* attention is emphasized.

The other half of the respondents were instructed to read the message and adopt a creative stance, one more congruent with a style of thinking associated with a positive mood. They were asked to imagine themselves in the situation of having been requested to lead a round-table discussion to introduce ideas on the issue in order to generate an atmosphere of "brainstorming," or creative debate.

The message was presented at this point (these manipulations are described later). In both experiments the messages were approximately equal in length and comprised four major arguments and a general conclusion. Following the message, respondents gave their evaluation of the issue, on an 11- point scale. They then completed two tasks which are critical for tests of the ELM. In the first, subjects were given time to write down their thoughts on the topic. These could be all on one side of the issue, or on both. The experimenter timed the task for three minutes. This measure of cognitive responding has been used extensively to assess the degree to which the respondents elaborate on the contents of the message. Although it is a retrospective measure of elaboration, it is less intrusive on comprehension of the message than any assessment that is made during the message presentation (Greenwald, 1981).

Following the cognitive response measure, subjects were asked to recall the arguments they had just read and to complete a multiple-choice questionnaire to assess comprehension and ensure that induced mood had not led to distraction from the message contents (McGuire, 1985).

We may now present the two experiments, identifying the nature of the message manipulation which distinguished them and considering the major results in turn.

Study 1

A variable which is clearly important in the ELM is the strength of arguments used. If the arguments in a message are strong, then any manipulation which increases the probability of elaboration will result in clear scrutiny of the arguments and therefore lead to attitude change in the direction advocated. If conditions reduce elaboration likelihood, however, then message scrutiny will be reduced and there should be less cognitive elaboration. Two messages were constructed, both strong in terms of supporting arguments, one arguing that media concentration was a good thing (the pro message), the other arguing for the opposite position (the anti message). Pretesting showed both messages to be equally strong and persuasive.

Success of mood manipulation

The mood manipulation was successful; positive mood condition subjects showed a significant increase in mood after listening to the induction tape, as measured by a change in DACL scores, while neutral mood condition subjects showed no change from the pretest, at which time they had been comparable in mood with the experimental group.

TABLE 12.1 *Interaction of mood, processing set, and message valence for evaluations: Study 1*

		Message valence			
		Anti media		Pro media	
Processing set		Critical	Creative	Critical	Creative
Positive mood	*M*	4.75	4.38	6.63	4.88
	SD	2.25	1.41	2.62	2.23
Neutral mood	*M*	4.29	3.63	4.13	6.75
	SD	0.95	1.60	2.23	1.49

Effects of messages on evaluative judgment

There was a significant interaction between mood manipulation, instruction and message valence [$F(1,56) = 5.70$, $P < 0.05$]. These data are shown in Table 12.1.

Mood and instructions interacted only in the pro-message condition. The anti message revealed no significant differences between instructions or mood, and no interaction. The pro message, however, resulted in a proattitude for positive mood subjects thinking critically but a more anticoncentration attitude for neutral subjects. Creative instructions tended to reverse the effect.

Number and direction of cognitive responses

There were no differences between any of the experimental groups in the total number of thoughts generated, nor in the number of neutral or irrelevant thoughts developed, so manipulated mood did not seem to result in any greater or lower expenditure of effort or thought. These data are not supportive, therefore, of a model of induced mood which predicts a general reduction in cognitive *capacity* (e.g. Isen, 1987). There were, however, differences with respect to the generation of pro- and anti-issue thoughts, and these give clues as to the nature of the mood manipulation upon the thought processes of the subjects.

Considering the generation of pro-issue thoughts, for neutral mood subjects there was no difference in the number of such thoughts between the pro- and anti-message conditions. There was a difference, however, for positive mood subjects. These subjects responded with more pro thoughts after the pro message, and fewer pro thoughts after the anti message (means 1.2 and 0.2, respectively). So positive mood subjects seemed to be more responsive to the *dominant* valence of the message, and did not generate contrary ideas. These data may suggest, therefore, that mood influences the motivational state of respondents, with a lowered desire to think in ways contrary to a message.

This interpretation is reinforced in the analysis of the number of anti-issue thoughts developed. In response to the pro message, neutral mood subjects produced significantly more anti-issue thoughts than did the positive mood subjects in the critical set condition; again positive mood seemed to induce a relatively noncritical reaction, even when respondents were instructed to think critically. The creative set manipulation did not produce differences between groups in the production of anti-issue thoughts.*

For the anti message, there were no differences between any of the groups in the production of anti thoughts, the overall average being about one-and-a-half anti thoughts. Thus the anti message may not have encouraged any particularly strong elaboration, as subjects were partially leaning in that direction anyway and so were not engaged by the arguments.

Such an interpretation is supported by analysis of the recall and comprehension data. There were higher comprehension scores and more correct recall for the pro than for the anti message and this points to all subjects paying less attention to the anti message, because that position was generally more congenial for them.

The results of the first experiment therefore suggest the following:

(a) Respondents were more likely to understand and recall, and hence engage elaboratively, with a message which was arguing for a position counter to the normative position in the population; in terms of the ELM, elaboration likelihood was low for previously normative positions.

(b) Positive mood seemed to be less likely than neutral mood to result in the development of systematic processing of message material. When positive mood subjects were asked to think critically about an issue, when presented with a message arguing against the normative position, they gave every indication of failing to do so. They produced pro-issue thoughts and few anti-issue thoughts, and their evaluation of the issue afterwards was significantly more in line with the message-advocated position, than was the case for neutral mood subjects.

(c) Instruction to think creatively about the issues presented did not seem to favor the elaborative processes of positive mood subjects. This failure of the creative instruction may support the conclusion in (b) above. Positive mood may reduce systematic processing and not merely induce a bias to agree with whatever the message suggests.

The data suggest therefore that positive mood acts as a peripheral

---

*It should be noted here, however, that the creative instruction set did produce a more even balance of pro-and anti-issue thoughts, an indication that the instruction was successful in inducing a more open-minded and creative approach to the message.

processing cue so that subjects in that condition are not likely to respond to the content or quality of the messages. The overall production of thoughts, with no differences in total production as a function of mood, suggests that affect is a cue to change motivation to process and not to lower capacity to function. The first study, however, with the manipulation of an anti-issue message, arguing for an extreme stance on the normative position, had failed properly to contrast manipulations which would test the ability of the ELM to account for the role of affect in the processing of persuasive messages. A second study was therefore conducted.

Study 2

According to the ELM, strong arguments are likely to have a more persuasive effect than weak arguments. Any additional variable which reduces the engagement of central-route, or systematic, processing, however, should reduce the likelihood of a scrutiny of the argument used in a message. Therefore, strong and weak arguments may have essentially the same effect upon processing and expressed evaluation. If positive mood does reduce systematic processing, then people in such a state should show little difference in reaction to messages of differing strength.

Study 2 therefore contrasted messages of different quality of argument. In order to ensure that elaboration likelihood would be moderate to high, the pro-issue side was chosen. The message used in Study 1 which advocated media concentration was contrasted with a weak message arguing for the same case. Both messages were of the same format, with four arguments and a final conclusion. The other variables were manipulated as in Study 1.

Success of mood manipulation

As in Study 1, the mood induction was successful, with a change in mood occurring for the positive group in the predicted direction and no change in the neutral condition.

Effects of message on evaluation

Two significant effects were found. First of all, message strength affected evaluation. Those who were exposed to the strong arguments were significantly more in favor of the concentration of media (i.e. in the direction of the

TABLE 12.2   *Interaction of mood, processing set and message strength for evaluations: Study 2*

Processing set		Message strength			
		Weak		Strong	
		Critical	Creative	Critical	Creative
Positive mood	M	5.00	4.63	5.25	6.29
	SD	2.83	1.60	0.96	2.75
Neutral mood	M	3.50	6.00	8.86	7.57
	SD	0.71	2.45	1.46	1.90

arguments) than were those who read the weak arguments [means 7.20 and 5.00, respectively, $F(1,40) = 8.94$, $P < 0.01$].

This effect was, however, modified by an interaction of mood, message, and the instruction set which was very close to conventional levels of significance [$F(1.40) = 3.74$, $P = 0.06$]. The means are shown in Table 12.2.

Examination of these means shows a pattern which can be readily related to the expectations derived from the ELM (Petty *et al.*, 1988a). Under the critical instruction set, the subjects in the neutral mood condition responded very much in line with the contents of the message; strong arguments produced significantly more agreement than weak arguments. In the positive mood condition, on the other hand, there was little difference between the two conditions. This suggests, therefore, that the induction of a positive mood *reduces* the objective or systematic processing of the arguments [cf. Panel 111(b) of Figure 7.2, Petty *et al.* (1988a)].

In the creative instruction condition, however, the mood manipulation acted as a negative peripheral route cue. The strong message still had an effect, but a very much weaker one compared with the weak message, while at the same time the positive mood reduced the impact of the messages overall; there is an inhibition of opinion change [cf. Panel 11(b) of Figure 7.2, Petty *et al.*, (1988a)].

These opinion data suggest that a positive mood may, under some conditions (critical set), inhibit processing while under others (creative set) act as a negative cue. It seems that positive mood does not interact with a processing goal that is likely to be congruent with a natural effect of the mood (the creative set). At the same time, in this study, it seems at first sight that positive mood does *not* act merely to produce a peripheral, heuristic acquiescence to the contents of a message, unlike the studies of Worth and Mackie (1987) and of Bless *et al.* (1990).

The reasons for initially considering that heuristic acquiescence does not occur comes from an analysis of the cognitive responses generated by the subjects. The responses generated were coded as pro concentration (i.e. in the direction of the message), anti concentration or neutral/irrelevant. Approximately equal numbers of pro- and anti-concentration thoughts were generated in response to the strong message, indicating elaboration and processing. Significantly more anti-concentration thoughts were also generated in response to the weak message, also an indication of elaboration in refuting poor argumentation. A problematic finding, however, was that positive mood subjects were more likely to generate anti-concentration thoughts than were those in the neutral mood condition. This result might suggest that the positive mood subjects are not mindlessly reflecting the tone of the message; rather they are engaging in counter-message thinking. This supports a conclusion drawn from the results of Study 1.

However, the pattern of opinion data suggests consistently that positive mood, in Study 2, inhibits a change in the direction of the position advocated in the messages. Furthermore, the cognitive response data overall suggests that a positive mood renders a person less able to respond *differently* to the manipulation of message strength and instruction set.

The position may be, therefore, that cognitive response data do not necessarily reflect elaboration of material. Apparent effort of elaboration, in producing counter-message thoughts in response protocols, may be the result of "top-of-the-head" thinking. In both studies, positive affect may result in the same processes, but the content upon which those processes engage may be different.

In Study 1, positive mood was associated with thought production in line with message valence; certainly *not* thinking that is evidence of strong elaboration. In Study 2, positive mood was associated with anti-message thinking; apparently *evidence* of elaboration. However, a change had occurred in consensual thinking between the times when the two studies were conducted. At the time of the first experiment, the prevalent mood was mild opposition, but at the time of the second, the prevalent opinion was much more strongly opposed. A person in a positive mood, therefore, when presented with a message advocating a position contrary to the prevailing opinion, could argue, *apparently* elaboratively, with anti-message thoughts. But these thoughts could be merely "top-of-the-head" and not be used in any cognitively elaborative sense to influence opinion.

Any apparent contradiction between the studies in outcome can therefore be explained by an examination of the broader social context in which the opinion issue could be placed. The consideration of opinion issues which are current and dynamic is important in social psychological research. There are dangers for the control of internal validity of an experiment in that the nature of the issue may change over the course of a series of studies, but there are also benefits for external validity in that the opinions are properly embedded in the social fabric.

Such data, incidentally, point to the importance of considering attitudes not merely as predispositions of individuals, but as shared social expressions with which individuals are in contact. The European notion of "social representations" may be of value in helping to understand the dynamics of opinion change (cf. Augoustinos and Innes, 1987; Jaspers and Fraser, 1984).

Summary

The data from these two experiments point to the conclusion that positive mood acts to reduce elaborative processing of attitude-relevant material. The influence of mood does not seem to be via a reduction in the cognitive capacity of respondents. Positive mood subjects seem to be able to retrieve as many thoughts in total as neutral mood subjects and, in Study 2, are more likely to generate anti thoughts. The effect is more likely to be mediated by a reduction in the motivation to think critically about message content. There is an increase in "top-of-the-head" thinking. Whether the thoughts that are produced are coded as pro or anti the issue need not indicate critical thought. What needs to be taken into context is the normative thinking on the issues. The subjects in a positive mood were more likely to respond to message content in terms of what were the more prevalent thoughts on the issues at the times the studies were conducted.

The results of Study two do seem to give strong support to the ELM (Petty *et al.*, 1988b). Positive induced mood, irrelevant to the content of the persuasive message, may act in different ways dependent upon the instructional set that it provided for respondents. The interesting question remains as to what may be the interaction between the induction of mood and the affect which may be engendered by the content of the message. Happy-inducing or fear-inducing messages will have cue value, according to the ELM. Induced mood may, depending upon instructions, facilitate or inhibit the attention paid to the affective cue content. Any outcome will be complicated by the degree to which induced moods are congruent or incongruent with the affect induced by the message.

The instructional sets provided for the respondents, in Study 2, influenced the impact of mood upon the form of processing. There was little or no suppport, however, for the idea that positive mood respondents would be able to deal more effectively with information under some (creative) sets than others. A similar conclusion may be drawn from the work of Bassili and Smith (1986) with respect to the influence of induced sets on the processing of attributional information.

It may be, of course, that the provision of more extensive help to participants to acquire the necessary set may achieve some increase in the ability of a person to engaged in elaborative processing while in a positive mood.* Research into the polarisation of opinion (Tesser, 1984) suggests that a schema needs to be present in order for any thought processes to influence the expression of opinion. Recent work indicates that the structure of the schema needs to be taken into account (Millar and Tesser, 1986). Further research needs to ensure that, when investigating the effects of mood on processing, participants have the capacity to engage in the form of thought conducive to the schemata.

Mackie and Worth (this volume) consider the influence that positive mood may have upon the processing of information in different modes. Their data suggest that mood interferes with the sequential and analytic processing while it may facilitate creative solutions. Our data suggest that there may be a further variable that needs to be studied. That is, the degree of knowledge, or skepticism, held by the respondent. The topic used by Mackie and Worth, the effects of acid rain, may have a wider array of scientific and socially relevant information associated with it than is the case with the topic used in our experiments. Until we have some idea about the knowledge structures held by recipients we may not be able to make clear predictions of when mood may facilitate or interfere. It seems clear in other areas that the cognitive structure maintained by individuals can lead to very different outcomes, as a results of experimental manipulations (cf. Judd and Lusk, 1984; Millar and Tesser, 1986).

Individual differences in structure of schema may not be the only variable that needs to be examined. Petty *et al.* (this volume) have shown that "need for cognition" has a moderating effect upon the relationship between induced mood and attitude. Those with a high need for cognition show a relationship between mood and attitude via the number of thoughts generated. The presence of a strong schema would be likely to strengthen such as association.

The results of the Petty *et al.* experiment, however, are difficult to relate to those reported in this chapter. The issue used in the present studies seems likely to be more linked with ongoing social issues, generating greater numbers of positive and negative thoughts relevant to the issue of perhaps more central thoughts. What will be important in any research which is concerned with the investigation of mood and its relationship to attitude and attitude change, will be to establish the social importance of the issue and the

---

*Research into the influence of positive mood on interpersonal communication, with a model of communication based upon associative responding (Rosenberg and Cohen, 1966), has also shown that mood does not result in creative responding but rather leads to an increase in the number of dominant, primary, associations to cue words, to facilitate communication (Innes, 1986; Innes and Ahrens, in preparation). So task specification, requiring communicative accuracy, leads to an inhibition of creativity, even in a situation much more close to the task used by Isen *et al.* (1965) to investigate the influence of mood on associative responding. It may be noted that Fiedler and Stroehm (1986) found somewhat similar effects, whereby induced mood effects upon memory were overcome by the structural constraints of the task. This serves to remind us that social influences upon task performance may be a figure upon a background of characteristics (Innes, 1982; Zajonc, 1965).

personal importance of the issue. This is not just to vary the response involvement of the individual with respect to the topic. The function that the attitude plays for the individual, be it expressive, social, or value-expressive, will have important influences upon how that person deals with the affective reactions to the issue.

As Zanna and Rempel (1988) point out, the relation of affect to the evaluative reaction we call attitude has not been clearly delineated to date. Pratkanis and Greenwald (1989) make an important statement that the functions of an attitude be considered, and clearly point to the importance of the evaluative dimension. They do not adequately distinguish between affect and evaluation. The study of the interaction of transient mood state with the valence and intensity of the affective component of an attitude may afford a vital entry into our understanding of the structural nature of attitudes. It may also enable us to understand further the interaction of cognition and affect

Acknowledgment

Some portions of the date presented in this chapter were presented at the XXIV International Congress of Psychology, Sydney, 1988, and appear in the Proceedings of the Congress. The research reported here was supported by a grant from the Australian Research Council, Dr J. M. Innes, Principal Investigator.

Correspondence should be addressed to Dr J. M. Innes, Department of Psychology, University of Adelaide, Adelaide, South Australia 5001.

References

Abelson, R. P., Kinder, D. R., Peters, M. D., and Fiske, S. T. (1982). Affective and semantic components in political person perception. *Journal of Personality and Social Psychology*, **42**, 619–630.

Ajzen, I. (1988). *Attitudes, personality and behavior*. Milton Keynes, Open University Press.

Allport, G. W. (1935). Attitudes. In C. Murchison (Eds.), *A handbook of social psychology*. Worcester, MA: Clark University Press.

Augoustinos, M., and Innes, J. M. (1987). Social representations and social schema. Presented at the 16th Meeting of Australian Social Psychologists, Australian National University.

Bassili, J. M., and Smith, M. C. (1986). On the spontaneity of trait attribution: Converging evidence for the role of cognitive strategy. *Journal of Personality and Social Psychology*, **50**, 239–245.

Bless, H., Bohner, G., Schwarz, N., and Strack, F. (1990). Happy and mindless? Moods and the processing of persuasive communications. *Personality and Social Psychology Bulletin*, **16**, 331–345

Breckler, S. J. (1984). Empirical evaluation of affect, behavior and cognition as distinct components of attitude. *Journal of Personality and Social Psychology*, **47**, 1191–1205.

Chaiken, S. (1987). The heuristic model of persuasion. In M. P. Zanna, J. M. Olson, and C. P. Herman (Eds), *Social influence: the Ontario Symposium*, Vol. 5. Hillsdale, NJ: Erlbaum.

Clark, M. S., Milberg, S., and Erber, R. (1988). Arousal-state-dependent memory: Evidence and implications for understanding social judgments and social behavior. In K. Fiedler and J. Forgas (Eds), *Affect, Cognition, and social behavior*. Toronto: Hogrefe.

Cramer, P. (1968). *Word association*. New York: Academic Press.

Donohew, L., Sypher, H. E., and Higgins, E. T. (Eds), (1988). *communication, social cognition, and affect*. Hillsdale, NJ: Erlbaum.

Eagly, A. H., and Chaiken, S. (1984). Cognitive theories of persuasion. In L. Berkowitz (Ed.), *Advances in experimental social psychology*, Vol. 17, pp. 267–359. New York: Academic Press.

Ellis, H. C., Thomas, R. L., and Rodriguez, I. A. (1984). Emotional mood states and memory: Elaborative encoding, semantic processing and cognitive effort. *Journal of Experimental Psychology: Learning, Memory and Cognition*, **10**, 470–482.

Fiedler, K., and Forgas, J. (Eds) (1988). *Affect, cognition, and social behavior*. Toronto: Hogrefe.

Fiedler, Z., and Stroehm, W. (1986). What kind of mood influences what kind of memory: The role of arousal and information structure. *Memory and Cognition*, **14**, 181–188.

Forgas, J. P., and Bower, G. H. (1988). Affect in social judgments. *Australian Journal of Psychology*, **40**, 125–145.

Forgas, J. P., and Bower, G. H. (1987). Mood effects on person perception judgments. *Journal of Personality and Social Psychology*, **53**, 53–60.

Greenwald, A. G. (1981). Cognitive response analysis: An appraisal. In R. E. Petty, T. M. Ostrom, and T. C. Brock (Eds), *Cognitive responses in persuasion*. Hillsdale, NJ: Erlbaum.

Guerin, B., and Innes, J. M. (1989). Cognitive tuning sets: The consequences of anticipated communication. *Current Psychological Research and Review*, **8**, 234–249.

Higgins E. T., McCann, C. D., and Fondacaro, R. (1982). The "communication game": Goal-directed encoding and cognitive consequences. *Social Cognition*, **1**, 21–37.

Innes, J. M. (1972). Word association response commonality and the generation of associative structures. *British Journal of Psychology*, **63**, 63–72.

Innes, J. M. (1981). Polarization of response as a function of cognitive tuning sets and individual differences. *Social Behavior and Personality*, **9**, 213–218.

Innes, J. M. (1982). The next-in-line effect and the recall of structured and unstructured material. *British Journal of Social Psychology*, **21**, 1–5.

Innes, J. M. (1986). Induction of mood and communication strategy. Presented at the 15th Meeting of Australian Social Psychologists, Townsville, Australia.

Innes, J. M., and Ahrens, C. (submitted) Political perception in Australian: Affective versus cognitive appraisal.

Innes, J. M., and Ahrens, C. (in preparation). The effect of induced mood upon the accuracy of dyadic communication.

Isen, A. M. (1987). Positive affect, cognitive processes and social behavior. In L. Berkowitz (Ed.), *Advances in experimental social psychology*, Vol. 20, pp. 203–253. New York: Academic Press.

Isen, A. M., Daubman, K. A., and Nowicki, G. P. (1987). Positive affect facilitates creative problem solving. *Journal of Personality and Social Psychology*, **52**, 1122–1131.

Isen, A. M., Johnson, M. M. S., Mertz, E., and Robinson, G. (1985). The influence of positive affect on the unusualness of word associations. *Journal of Personality and Social Psychology*, **48**, 1413–1426.

Isen, A. M., and Means, B. (1983). The influence of positive affect on decision-making strategy. *Social Cognition*, **2**, 18–31.

Izard, C. E., Kagan, J., and Zajonc, R. B. (Eds) (1984). *Emotions, cognition and behavior*. Cambridge University Press.

Janis, I. L., Kaye, D., and Kirschner, P. (1965). Facilitating effects of "eating while reading" on responsiveness to persuasive communications. *Journal of Personality and Social Psychology*, **1**, 181–186.

Jaspers, J., and Fraser, C. (1984). Attitudes and social representations. In R. M. Farr and S. Moscovici (Eds), *Social representations*. Cambridge: Cambridge University Press.

Judd, C. M., and Johnson, J. T. (1984). The polarizing effects of affective intensity. In J. R. Eiser (Ed.), *Attitudinal judgment*. New York: Springer.

Judd, C. M., and Lusk, C. M. (1984). Knowledge structures and evaluation judgments: Effects of structural variables in judgment extremity. *Journal of Personality and Social Psychology*, **46**, 1193–1207.

McCann, C. D., and Higgins, E. T. (1988). Motivation and affect in interpersonal relations: The role of personal orientations and discrepancies. In L. Donohew, H. E. Sypher, and E. T. Higgins (Eds), *Communication, social cognition, and affect*. Hillsdale, NJ: Erlbaum.

McGuire, W. J. (1985). Attitudes and attitude change. In G. Lindzey and E. Arousou (Eds), *Handbook of social psychology*, 3rd edn, Vol. 2. New York: Random House.

Mackie, D. M., and Worth, L. T. (1989). Processing deficits and the mediation of positive affect in persuasion. *Journal of Personality and Social Psychology*, **57**, 1–14.

Millar, M. G., and Tesser, A. (1986). Thought-induced attitude change: The effects of schema structure and commitment. *Journal of Personality and Social Psychology*, **51**, 259–269.

Petty, R. E., and Cacioppo, J. T. (1986). *Communication and persuasion: Central and peripheral routes to attitude change*. New York: Springer.

Petty, R. E., Cacioppo, J. T., and Kasmer, J. A. (1988a). The role of affect in the Elaboration Likelihood Model of persuasion. In L. Donohew, H. E. Sypher, and E. T. Higgins (Eds), *Communication, social cognition and affect*. Hillsdale, NJ: Erlbaum.

Petty, R. E., Cacioppo, J. T., Sedikides, C., and Strathman, A. J. (1988b). Affect and persuasion: A contemporary perspective. *American Behavioral Scientist*, **31**, 355–371.

Pratkanis, A. R., and Greenwald, A. G. (1989). A sociocognitive model of attitude structure and function. In L. Berkowitz (Ed.), *Advances in experimental social psychology*, Vol 22, pp. 245– 285. New York: Academic Press.

Rosenberg, M. J., and Hovland, C. I. (1960). Cognitive, affective and behavioral components of attitude. In M. J. Rosenberg, C. I. Hovland, W. J. McGuire, R. P. Abelson, and J. W. Brehm. (Eds), *Attitude organization and change*. New Haven CT: Yale University Press.

Rosenberg, S., and Cohen, B. D. (1966). Referential processes of speakers and listeners. *Psychological Review*, **73**, 208–231.

Srull, T. K., and Wyer, R. S. (1986). The role of chronic and temporary goals in social information processing. In R. M. Sorrentino and E. T. Higgins, (Eds), *Handbook of motivation and cognition*. New York: Guilford Press.

Teasdale, J. D., and Russell, M. L. (1983). Differential effects of induced mood on the recall of positive, negative and neutral words. *British Journal of Clinical Psychology*, **22**, 163–171.

Tesser, A. (1980). Self-generated attitude change. In L. Berkowitz (Ed.), *Advances in experimental social psychology*, Vol. 11. New York: Academic Press.

Worth, L. T., and Mackie, D. M. (1987). Cognitive mediation of positive affect in persuasion. *Social Cognition*, **5**, 76–94.

Zajonc, R. B. (1960). The process of cognitive tuning and communication. *Journal of Abnormal and Social Psychology*, **61**, 159–167.

Zajonc, R. B. (1965). Social Facilitation. *Science*, **149**, 269– 274.

Zanna, M. P., and Rempel, J. K. (1988). Attitudes: a new look at an old concept. In D. Bar-Tal and A. W. Kruglanski (Eds), *The social psychology of knowledge*. Cambridge: Cambridge University Press.

13

Influence of Mood on Judgments About Health and Illness

PETER SALOVEY

Yale University

ANN O'LEARY

Rutgers University

and

MARTHA S. STRETTON, STEPHANIE A. FISHKIN and CHLOÉ A. DRAKE

Yale University

Contents

Recently, one of us had the following experience. He woke up in the morning feeling a bit under the weather, draggy, and had little appetite for breakfast. Heading for work anyway, he recalled the journal article that had been rejected the day before, the fight with his mother on the telephone last weekend, and the editor nagging him for a chapter that was now holding up production on a book to which he had agreed to contribute. These ruminations left him feeling quite depressed by the time he reached the office. Once sad, he especially noticed the aching feelings in his stomach and the tug-of-war in his intestinal tract. He also became aware of the aching in the back of his legs—not enough exercise—and that his hair was slowly but surely turning grey. He recalled the 214 serum cholesterol count reported to him by his physician the week before and cogitated on how his "borderline" high cholesterol was certainly going to send him to an early grave, if his GI tract didn't quit on him first. In this instance, a sad mood facilitated negative evaluations of physical symptoms and health information.

Imagine, however, that our hero had woken up with similar physical symptoms, but on his drive to the office, he thought about the close game that his softball team had just won (he pitched), the grant proposal for which he had received promising feedback, and the dear friend from childhood who was visiting the next weekend. Perhaps his mood state would be characterized by joyful contentment upon reaching work. Perhaps in such a blissful mood, he would not notice the rumblings in his stomach—or if he did, just dismiss them as mere "butterflies." Thinking back, in his happy mood, to the results of his cholesterol test—the 214—he might contemplate how lucky he was that his cholesterol was only "borderline" high, after all, he has never been careful about what he eats. After 10 years of daily cheese-steak sandwiches, he actually felt remarkably lucky. "Yes," he might think to himself, "I'm going to live until a ripe old age." In this instance, happiness promoted a more positive interpretation of physical symptoms and health information.

In this chapter, we are going to discuss how mood influences the appraisal of physical symptoms and judgments about health and illness. Health information is often ambiguous; its meaning is not always well understood (e.g., how should one understand a 214 cholesterol level?), and hence contextual cues such as mood are likely to influence its interpretation. After describing some recent experiments demonstrating the systematic effects of mood on the experience of physical symptoms and health beliefs, we will then describe three mechanisms that might explain the associations between mood and health-related judgments. The first mechanism concerns mood-congruent recall, the proposal that memories consistent in emotional tone with an ongoing mood state are more likely to come to mind than are memories with a different affective valence. The second mechanism is mood-induced shifts in focus of attention, in particular, the tendency for individuals experiencing sadness to attend selectively to themselves rather than the external environment. Switching levels of analysis from the cognitive to the physiological, the third mechanism to be discussed is the notion that changes in mood lead to actual alterations in endocrine and immunological functioning causing real (not just appraised) changes in health status. We will conclude this chapter with a discussion of the implications of this work for discovering biases in health survey data and understanding hypochondriasis.

Why Study Links Between Mood and Health?

The ancient Greek humoral system of medicine incorporated personal factors thought to be associated with excessive quantities of each of the four essential humors, and was thus perhaps the first systematic (if erroneous) description of personality–health interactions. During the 1940s and 1950s, investigation into this topic was restricted to speculation concerning the role of unconscious conflict in determining the specific symptomatology of the classic "psychosomatic" diseases, such as asthma, rheumatoid arthritis, and ulcer, but these formulations have fallen out of favor in recent years. Scientific research on the topic of psychological influences on health gained momentum with the advent of interest in "stress," thanks largely to the work of Hans Selye (1956). Much of the early work in this area concerned the stresses associated with the accumulation of "life change" (reviewed in Minter and Kimball, 1978). In these studies, subjects reported which of the common life events provided in a checklist had occurred in their lives within the recent past, and the prevalence of these events was related to subsequent health outcomes. Methodological criticisms concerning the use of retrospective self-report, the failure of the stress measure to account for the appraisal of events by individuals and to assess chronic and minor stressors, and confounding of stressor and outcome assessments in these studies ultimately resulted in the waning of interest in research on global stressors.

For many years, psychotherapists and practicing physicians have noticed that individuals suffering from psychological distress, such as depression and anxiety, often also report various physical symptoms—typically back pain, headaches, dizziness, bowel and bladder irregularities, gastric distress, and the like. A challenge for both practitioners is to disentangle the psychological versus physiological roots of somatic complaints. At times, patients need care both for psychological and physical complaints. In other cases, however, the relief of psychological distresses, such as depression, eliminates the need for more expensive medical care.

In a review of the literature on mood and physical symptoms, Katon (1984) noted that depressed individuals do report somatic ailments in greater numbers than nondepressed individuals. Similarly, health status is appraised less positively among the depressed (Maddox, 1962; Tessler and Mechanic, 1978). And when hospitals offer psychological services, by which individuals presumably can have their psychological distresses attended to, utilization of medical services for relief of physical symptoms is reduced (Cummings and Follette, 1976; Follette and Cummings, 1967; Jones and Vischi, 1979).

Although it has not been difficult to document the comorbidity of depressed mood and increased reports of physical complaints, the direction of causality is less certain. Intuitively, it seems obvious that the onset of physical illnesses with debilitating symptoms that interfere with pleasurable daily activities or cause considerable pain should result in depressed mood. Findings supporting an association between illness and depression have been obtained in correlational and time-series analyses of physical symptoms and mood (Hancock, 1987; Persson and Sjoberg, 1987), in clinical studies of pain patients who develop depressive disorders (Keefe *et al.*, 1986; Turk *et al.*, 1987), and in observation of individuals with other medical problems (Rodin and Voshart, 1986).

However, the more interesting direction of causality that has not been explored as systematically is the hypothesis that changes in ongoing moods produce changes in the evaluation of physical symptoms and in subsequent judgments about health and illness. Consistent with this view are theories that various physical health problems are the manifestation of underlying depressive disorders. Such an argument has been made for various conditions, especially chronic pain (Blumer and Heilbronn, 1982; but see Turk and Salovey, 1984).

The direction of causality in understanding links between mood and physical symptoms, however, is not easily addressed by existing research. Most studies reported in the literature have used cross-sectional, correlational designs. Longitudinal studies are virtually nonexistent. One promising line of research concerns the laboratory induction of mood states followed by opportunities for subjects to report upon beliefs about their physical health. The random assignment of subjects to mood inductions allows for a direct test of the hypothesis that mood shifts have consequences for health-related cognitions. In an experiment involving the induction of moods, Croyle and Uretsky (1987) found that perceived health status varied in a mood-congruent direction, and that subjects who experienced sad moods reported more physical symptoms than those induced to experience happy moods. Of course, increased symptom reporting may reflect biased reporting, vigilance, or, in fact, the actual experience of more symptoms. Several mood-induction studies in this tradition were reported by Salovey and Birnbaum (1989), and it is to these findings we now turn.

Some Findings from Laboratory Studies of Mood and Health-related Cognitions

In a recent series of experiments, Salovey and Birnbaum (1989) asked college students who were experiencing the flu (but nonetheless had to complete their Introductory Psychology subject pool requirement) to participate in a study in which moods would be induced in the laboratory. In several different experiments, subjects were randomly assigned to happy, sad, or neutral mood-induction conditions. Moods were produced by using an Autobiographical Recollections Method (ARM) developed by Wright and Mischel (1982) and refined by Salovey and Singer (1989) (this procedure has also been termed Self-Generated Imagery). In a darkened room, subjects listened to a tape recording over headphones that instructed them to relax, close their eyes, and to imagine vividly incidents from their past that would produce the requisite mood. After about five minutes, the subjects were instructed by the tape to complete various measures of health status located on the desk in front of them. Subjects' moods were verified using brief scales at several points during the experimental session. At the end of the session, subjects were debriefed, and those in the sad condition were offered the opportunity to participate in a happy mood induction.

Mood and symptom appraisal

In the first experiment (Salovey and Birnbaum, 1989, Experiment 1), 66 subjects suffering from the flu (or flu-like symptoms) were induced to feel happy, sad, or neutral moods. They completed a standard physical symptom questionnaire (Wahler, 1968) and mood scales (McNair *et al.*, 1971) both prior to and after the mood-induction procedure. These scales were included among a large variety of tasks in order to minimize experimental demand. The cover story for the experiment did not mention mood. Rather, the study was described as an investigation of imagination in college students. As expected, since subjects were randomly assigned to mood-induction conditions, there were no differences in mood or symptom reports prior to mood induction. However, after subjects experienced happy, sad, or neutral moods (which were verified using the mood scale), they reported symptoms of differing intensity and frequency.

As illustrated in Figure 13.1, subjects assigned to the sad mood condition reported nearly twice as many aches and pains, a subset of items from the symptom checklist, as subjects assigned to the happy condition (even though both groups reported the same level of physical symptoms just prior to mood induction). Moreover, sad subjects reported more physical symptoms from

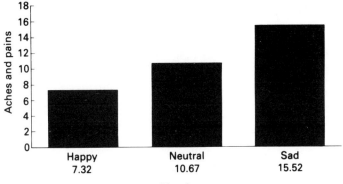

FIG 13.1   Influence of mood on reporting of physical symptoms among subjects experiencing the flu (data from Salovey and Birnbaum, 1989).

the previous week than happy subjects, and they attributed greater discomfort to these symptoms.

The differences among the mood-induction conditions were confirmed by correlating symptom reports and mood scales after mood induction. Indeed, the saddest subjects reported the greatest number of aches and pains ($r = -.46$, $p < 0.0001$), the most frequent symptoms of any kind, from nasal congestion to fatigue ($r = -.30$, $p < 0.01$), and the most discomfort due to their symptoms ($r - .30$, $p < .01$).

Mood and judgments of health efficacy

The presence of physical symptoms is but one factor in motivating individuals to attend to their health. Perhaps more important than perceptions of physical symptoms in determining illness behaviors, such as treatment-seeking, are beliefs about one's capacity to engage successfully in salubrious behaviors and expectations that such behaviors will alleviate illness or maintain health. We termed the former set of beliefs *health self-efficacy* and the latter *health outcome efficacy* (after Bandura, 1977). Self-efficacy beliefs are important predictors of diverse health behaviors such as smoking cessation, eating a healthy diet, and engaging in safe sex (McKusick *et al.*, 1986; O'Leary, 1985). Individuals are unlikely to engage in health behaviors that they feel incapable of carrying out. Similarly, individuals are reluctant to engage in behaviors that they do not believe are health enhancing (Turk *et al.*, 1984).

Salovey and Birnbaum (1989) constructed two 26-item scales to measure health self-efficacy and outcome efficacy among our subjects with the flu. Each scale presented subjects with behaviors in which they might engage in order to relieve their symptoms (e.g., visit the health center, stay in bed, drink fluids). Subjects rated how able they were to carry out each behavior and how likely each was to improve their health. Ratings from 0 to 100 were solicited for each item, and a mean across the 26 items was calculated for each scale.

Once again, subjects were randomly assigned to happy, sad, and neutral mood-induction conditions and their efficacy ratings requested after the mood-induction procedure was administered. As depicted in Figure 13.2, these judgments varied as a function of mood state. Sad subjects perceived themselves as considerably less able to carry out health-promoting behaviors, and they were somewhat less likely to believe that these behaviors would relieve their illness.

Thus, it appears that mood influences expectations that are thought to be closely linked to performing health behaviors (Bandura, 1986). These connections between mood and efficacy expectations are consistent with findings in other behavioral domains, from romance and athletics (Kavanagh and Bower, 1985) to altruism (Salovey, 1986; Salovey and Rosenhan,

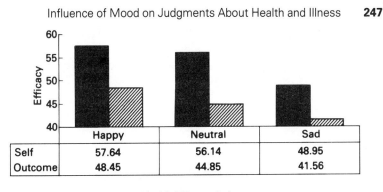

	Happy	Neutral	Sad
Self	57.64	56.14	48.95
Outcome	48.45	44.85	41.56

Health Efficacy Judgment
■ Self   ▨ Outcome

FIG 13.2 Influence of mood on judgments of health efficacy among subjects experiencing the flu (data from Salovey and Birnbaum, 1989).

1989). When individuals experience sadness, they feel less capable of carrying out required behaviors (Kanfer and Zeiss, 1983). And even if they perceive themselves as capable, they are not especially confident that such behaviors would relieve their illnesses.

Individuals experiencing sad moods who are ill may thus be caught in a bit of a bind. On the one hand, they experience their symptoms as more frequent, intense, and discomforting. On the other, they believe there is little they could actually do to make themselves feel better. Such malaise may make the sad individual especially unlikely to adhere to treatment recommendations. "Why bother taking these pills, getting extra rest, or drinking fluids," our sad, sick friend may think to him or herself, "I couldn't do it, and it wouldn't matter anyway."

Mood and judgments of risks and vulnerabilities

Other important health-related beliefs that appear to be precursors of health behavior are perceptions of vulnerability to future illnesses. Beliefs about risk likelihood and severity have been found to contribute to interest in risk-reducing behaviors such as seeking medical treatment when sick (Becker *et al.*, 1977; Cummings *et al.*, 1979; Kulik and Mahler, 1987; Weinstein, 1982, 1983). Individuals appear to be unlikely to take health protective actions when they do not perceive themselves to be vulnerable to future illnesses (Janz and Becker, 1984). The cheese-steak sandwich lover among us is unlikely to stop eating them for lunch every day if he continues to believe that contracting heart disease is an extremely low probability event for him.

Estimates of the likelihood of future positive and negative events have generally been among the most mood sensitive of all judgments (e.g., Forgas and Moylan, 1987; Johnson and Tverksy, 1983; Mayer and Volanth, 1985). In a recent study, Salovey and Birnbaum, (1989, Experiment 3), asked 33

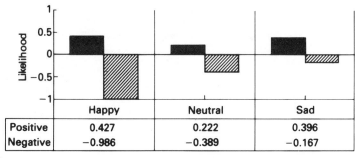

	Happy	Neutral	Sad
Positive	0.427	0.222	0.396
Negative	−0.986	−0.389	−0.167

Future outcome
■ Positive   ▨ Negative

FIG 13.3   Influence of mood on judgments of risk and vulnerability in the health
domain (data from Salovey and Birnbaum, 1989).

healthy undergraduates to submit to a happy, sad, or neutral mood induction. They then were administered a 14-item scale containing health-related outcomes, and requested to estimate the likelihood that each might happen (a) in the average Yale student's lifetime and (b) in their own lifetime. The items reflected both positive (e.g., regularly maintain an exercise program) and negative (e.g., develop high blood pressure) health outcomes. Perceived vulnerability was operationalized as the difference between subjects' estimates for the average Yale student and for themselves. Thus, a positive score indicated that the subjects felt the event was more likely to happen to him or her than to other students. A negative score indicated that the subject felt the event was less likely to happen to him or her relative to the peer group. Separate scores were calculated for the positive and negative items.

The most noticeable trend in these data, which are displayed in Figure 13.3, is that subjects, no matter what mood they were induced to experience, always believed that negative health events were less likely to befall them than their peers, and that positive outcomes were more likely to come their way. This tendency to believe that one must be "above average" in future health has been referred to as *unrealistic optimism* or *perceived invulnerability* (Perloff and Fetzer, 1986; Weinstein, 1982, 1983, 1984, 1987), and may be included among the biased self-beliefs that help individuals to maintain a positive self-regard (see Taylor, 1989; Taylor and Brown, 1988, for reviews).

Moreover, for negative health outcomes (future diseases) but not positive health outcomes (maintaining good health), mood had a systematic and linear influence on probability estimates. Happy individuals thought that future diseases were considerably less likely to befall them than their classmates. This bias was almost completely eliminated among subjects made to feel sad.

It seems reasonable to ask why mood had a strong impact on estimates of negative health events, such as contracting some form of cancer or developing arthritis, but not positive health events, such as being in great physical shape or maintaining a well-balanced diet. There is probably something fundamentally different about these sets of items. The positive items asked subjects to make estimates about events for which they had current self-knowledge (e.g., their diet or exercise regimen). Negative items, on the other hand, involved speculation about future events for which little relevant self-knowledge could be marshalled (e.g., will I ever have a stroke, heart disease, cancer?). Mood seems to have a stronger impact on judgments that are not well anchored in preexisting knowledge (Forgas and Bower, 1987). Hypothetical judgments are more sensitive to contextual variables such as mood, since moods are likely to be more informative in such judgments—there are few competing sources of information on which to base these inferences (see Salovey and Mayer, 1990; Schwarz, 1989; see also the chapters by Schwarz and Bless, and Clore and Parrott in this volume). Likewise, we could expect mood to be more likely to influence the perception of ambiguous physical symptoms, such as back pain, than those less open to subjective interpretation, such as coughing up blood.

Three Possible Mechanisms

Moods clearly affect judgments about one's health. In the studies just reviewed, subjects who experienced sad mood inductions were more likely to report physical symptoms, less likely to feel capable of carrying out health-protective behaviors, more pessimistic about improving their health, and more likely to believe that they would be victims of future diseases than subjects who experienced happy mood inductions. In the next section of this chapter, we would like to discuss three mechanisms by which mood might influence these effects on health judgments: (1) by influencing the memories most easily brought to mind, (2) by affecting the focus of attention, and (3) by altering physiological processes directly, especially the immune system, and, therefore, actually influencing health. In addition, a fourth mechanism is possible whereby mood influences behaviors (e.g., care-seeking, smoking, exercising) that have health ramifications. This sequence, however, is not discussed explicitly in what follows, but is alluded to in each of the three sections below. Because the first two mechanisms have been discussed elsewhere (Salovey and Birnbaum, 1989; Salovey and Rodin, 1985; Salovey *et al.*, 1991), they will be given less attention here than the third one.

Mood-congruent recall

Mood may affect beliefs about health and illness by influencing the memories most easily brought to mind. A fairly robust finding in the mood–

memory literature is that individuals can more easily recall material from memory that is congruent in valence with an ongoing mood state (for reviews of the mood-congruent recall literature see Blaney, 1986; Gilligan and Bower, 1984; Isen, 1987; Mayer and Salovey, 1988; Singer and Salovey, 1988). Perhaps the earliest investigation of mood-congruent recall was conducted by Fisher and Marrow (1934), who hypnotically induced seven subjects to experience either happy or sad moods. Subjects were then provided with stimulus words and asked to free associate to them. They generated mood-congruent associates more quickly than incongruent ones. Autobiographical memories have been especially sensitive to mood-congruent recall, whether the moods are induced in the laboratory (Salovey and Singer, 1989; Snyder and White, 1982; or occur naturally (Lloyd and Lishman, 1975). The basic finding is that mood-congruent memories are more likely to be recalled than incongruent ones, and they are recalled more quickly than incongruent memories (Teasdale and Fogarty, 1979; Teasdale and Taylor, 1981).

When individuals are asked to make judgments about their health, they often base these judgments on what is most easily brought to mind (Tversky and Kahneman, 1973). And what comes to mind when the sad person thinks about health? Most likely, sadness recruits memories about the death of close friends and relatives, previous experiences with illness, images of sick people, and the like. When individuals think about such things, they believe that they are more likely to occur (Anderson, 1983; Carroll, 1978). For example, in one study (Sherman *et al.*, 1985), subjects imagined contracting a disease described either with easily imagined symptoms or symptoms that were hard to conjure up. Subjects then rated their likelihood of contracting the disease, and easily imagined diseases were rated as more likely. In our experiments, mood may create a context in which memories about health or illness can be easily brought to mind and vividly imagined. These fantasies may subsequently influence judgments about present health status and future health-relevant events. Moreover, mood may color the interpretation of ambiguous information (such as some symptoms) rendering it affectively charged. This information may then serve as a cue for the recall of similarly valenced health-related thoughts. In turn, the availability of these thoughts collectively can influence judgments about health and illness.

Changes in attentional focus

Moods may also influence perceptions of physical symptoms and beliefs about health because changes in mood are associated with shifts in attentional focus on to or away from oneself. Salovey and Rodin (1985) proposed that during all strong emotional experiences, but especially when they are negative, there is a tendency for individuals to focus their attention onto themselves rather than on the external environment. In a variety of correlational studies, increased attentional focus onto the self has been associated with depressed moods (e.g., Ingram and Smith, 1984; Smith and Greenberg, 1981; see also a recent review of this literature by Ingram, 1990). Sadness-induced self-focusing has also been demonstrated experimentally (Salovey, submitted; Wood *et al.*, 1990). Pyszczynski and Greenberg (1987) have proposed that there is a self-focusing style that plays a role in the onset, maintenance, and exacerbation of depression. This theory builds on earlier work (Carver and Scheier, 1981; Duval and Wicklund, 1972) suggesting that allocation of attention onto the self serves a regulatory function and helps the individual to maintain goal-directed behavior. The depressive self-focusing style may in fact help to explain some of the more unusual effects that sadness has on judgments, such as increasing the accuracy of beliefs about the self, reducing self-inflating biases, and eliminating illusions of control (cf. Taylor and Brown, 1988).

Focusing attention on the body increases perceptions of symptoms and sensations (Pennebaker, 1982). For example, individuals who live in un-stimulating environments—which presumably do not provide enough competition for internal cues—report more physical symptoms than individuals in stimulating environments. In experimental research, when subjects are instructed to exercise while attending to bodily cues (heartbeat or breathing), they are more likely to report symptoms (Pennebaker and Lightner, 1980). And every jogger knows that the pain associated with running seems lessened if one can focus attention externally by listening to music tapes during the run (see Fillingim and Fine, 1986, on this point).

The comorbidity of depression and physical symptoms, described at the outset of this paper, may be understood because both appear to be related to self-focused attention. Of course, when one is self-focused, attention may be directed toward the mood-congruent ruminations of the conscious mind, or to the experiences of the body, or to both. We would expect, however, that when sad moods produce body-oriented self-focused attention, symptoms should be more likely noticed, and indeed, experienced more intensely. The greater salience of somatic cues may subsequently influence judgments about present and future health status as well.

Mood-induced changes in immune system functioning

Although it could not be studied in the experiments described earlier, mood may also have direct effects on the physiological processes upon which symptom reports are based, and may even lead to illness by lowering resistance to effects of pathogens like bacteria and viruses. Although this notion has been popular wisdom for many centuries, the effects of distress on the functioning of the immune system have been studied only for the last 15 years or so, a period during which increasingly sophisticated tests for immunologic assessment have been developed. This endeavor, christened "psychoneuroimmunology" by Robert Ader in his 1981 book by that title (and mercifully abbreviated to PNI in more recent years) has resulted in the accumulation of considerable evidence for effects of a variety of psychosocial factors on immune functioning (reviewed by O'Leary, 1990). Although many of the stressors studied in the early period of inquiry were extreme and unusual (for example, space splashdown), more recent studies have revealed significant immune effects even of relatively minor, everyday events and resulting mood states.

Psychological influences on immune function. As noted above, early psychoimmunologic research focused on the effects of severe stressors. For example, in several investigations, bereavement was demonstrated to lower immune functioning (Bartrop *et al.*, 1977; Irwin *et al.*, 1987; Schleifer *et al.*, 1983). A more frequently experienced form of social disruption—marital separation and divorce—is, however, also capable of reducing immune competence, and this is true both for women (Kiecolt-Glaser *et al.*, 1987) and men (Kiecolt-Glaser, *et al.*, 1988). These papers also reported psychological correlates of immune function indicating that, among divorced people, high levels of attachment to the lost spouse and the spouse (rather than the subject) having initiated the divorce were associated with depressed immunity, while among married subjects, lower reported marital quality was associated with reduced immune competence. Even commonly observed levels of loneliness in the absence of recent loss have been found to be associated with reduced immune function in such disparate populations as medical students (Glaser *et al.*, 1985; Kiecolt-Glaser *et al.*, 1984a) and psychiatric inpatients (Kiecolt-Glaser *et al.*, 1984b).

Depression and depressed mood, psychological states that presumably accompany the stress of social disruption, have been examined in their own right, and here too effects have been observed across a wide gradient of severity. Patients hospitalized with major depressive disorder have been shown to have impaired immunity (Schleifer *et al.*, 1984), and the effects are not due to the stress of hospitalization (Schleifer *et al.*, 1985). Although these studies employed standard clinical assessments of functional immune status, another study has demonstrated impairment of the ability of lymphocytes to repair DNA damaged by irradiation in depressed psychiatric inpatients (Kiecolt-Glaser *et al.*, 1985). This finding may have important implications for the development of cancers.

Even naturally occurring, nonclinical fluctuations in daily mood may have immunologic correlates. One recent study examined mood as it related to salivary immunoglobulin-A antibody, which is the first line of defense against bacteria and viruses entering the body (Stone *et al.*, 1987). In this study, salivary antibody response to stimulation with a rabbit albumin antigen was measured three times each week for eight weeks. Mood was measured with a standard mood adjective checklist. In a within-subjects analysis, secretion of salivary antibody was found to be significantly greater on days when more positive mood was reported, and lower when more negative mood was reported. Since daily fluctuations in mood are related to daily events (Stone, 1987), one would expect that everyday stressors might produce immunologic changes. Indeed, a number of studies have reported reductions in immune function accompanying the very common stress of academic examination (see Kiecolt-Glaser and Glaser, 1987).

Methodological issues in PNI research. Among the criticisms of psycho-immunologic research employing healthy subjects is the claim that the observed fluctuations in immune function may not be of sufficient magnitude to result in illness. A few studies have assessed self-reported health and found it to be related to psychological factors (Glaser *et al.*, 1987; Kiecolt-Glaser *et al.*, 1988); however, it is clearly not the case that illness invariably accompanies strong negative mood (of course, the presence of a pathogen is necessary for illness to occur). It may be reasonable to think of mood-related immunologic effects as constituting risk factors for illness, much as elevated blood pressure or serum lipids increase risk for myocardial infarction. A number of studies have utilized specific illness models and demonstrated psychoimmunologic effects of relevance to the disease under consideration (reviewed by O'Leary, 1990); these studies are less vulnerable to this criticism.

Another criticism of psychoimmunologic research is that apparent relationships between psychological stress and immune function may be mediated by stress-induced changes in behaviors, such as diet, sleep, use of psychotropic substances, or exercise. Since each of these behaviors has immunologic effects, it is possible that stress is exerting only indirect, behavioral effects rather than direct, affect-mediated ones. Some of the studies reported above have attempted to assess these behavioral factors; however, a comprehensive assessment would be difficult, if not impossible, to conduct.

One final note: although the predominant finding obtained in PNI studies to date has been suppressed immune function in connection with negative mood, this is not always the case. Some stressors, particularly those activating the sympathetic nervous system, may have some immune enhancing effects, at least in the short run (e.g., Wiedenfeld *et al.*, submitted). The literature concerning the "cancer-prone personality"—and cancer is an immune-related disease—would suggest that low levels of distress may be associated with unfavorable outcome (reviewed by Contrada *et al.*, 1990). The interactions between the nervous, endocrine, and immune systems are very complex (e.g., Blalock, 1989), and it would be unwise to draw simplistic conclusions at this point.

Some Implications

So far, we have discussed some of the ways moods influence the perception of physical symptoms and judgments about health and illness. We have argued that these mood effects might be explained by three (not mutually exclusive) mechanisms, mood-congruent recall, mood-induced shifts in attentional focus, and actual changes in the functioning of the immune system brought on by mood shifts. In this final section of the chapter, we shall describe two implications of this connection between moods and health that reflect two lines of research that we are currently conducting. The first concerns the accuracy of health information reported in health surveys. In particular, we are investigating whether ongoing moods bias memory for previous physical symptoms, especially complaints about pain. The second implication concerns the understanding of hypochondriasis. We propose that depressed mood (and consequent self-focused attention) accounts, in part, for the abnormal reporting of physical symptoms and consequent fear and worry that characterize the hypochondriac.

Memory biases on health surveys

If mood influences the reporting of physical symptoms and beliefs about health, can we trust the data obtained from large-scale health surveys, such as the National Center for Health Statistics' Health Interview Survey? Under a contract from NCHS, Salovey and his colleagues are presently investigating how mood (and other variables) affect memory for past health-related events (Salovey *et al.*, 1990). We have focused much of this research on the reporting of physical pain. Because physical pain is especially focused on the self, judgments about it can be expected to be highly mood sensitive.

The quality of survey data on experiences with pain is threatened by a variety of sources of error in the recall of painful episodes as well as biases in judgments about the nature of present and past pain. Results of the studies reported in this chapter suggest that one source of error is the respondent's mood at the time of the survey. Mood has an especially strong impact on the processing of affectively laden information, as described earlier. Painful experiences are certainly affectively charged events, and memories about them may be organized around their affective qualities.

The role of moods and emotions in the accuracy of judgments about and recall of painful experiences has not been studied directly, despite the fact that it is suggested as the key variable mediating the accuracy of pain recall by many researchers (e.g., Eich *et al.*, 1985; Hunter *et al.*, 1979; Kent, 1985; Norvell *et al.*, 1987; Roche and Gijsbers, 1986). For example, respondents who experienced fear of going to the dentist remembered dental pain as more severe than it actually was. Kent (1985) asked dental patients to rate pain expected prior to the dental procedure, actual pain experienced as a result of the procedure, and then, three months later, to recall the amount of pain they had experienced. Only modest correlations between recalled and actual pain were obtained ($r = .42$), indicating that factors other than the initial pain experience accounted for most of the variance in pain recall after 3 months. Interestingly, among individuals who were not anxious about dental work, the recalled/experienced correlation was much higher ($r = .79$), but there was virtually no correlation between the two among highly anxious individuals ($r = -.11$). In general, recall drifted in the direction of anxiety; that is, highly anxious individuals remembered the pain experience as much more severe than it actually was. These results are only suggestive, however, as the small sample size (fifteen low-anxious and eight high-anxious subjects) probably produced unstable correlations, the differences among which could not be evaluated statistically.

Another example is provided by mothers experiencing labor and childbirth. They tend to underreport the intense pains of labor after the baby is born. Guerra (1986) noted that "the parturient will tolerate much more pain and discomfort than will other surgical patients" (p. 77). In fact, Norvell *et al.* (1987) found that pain ratings on visual analogue scales made during the three phases of labor revealed considerably more intense pain than retrospective ratings made two days postpartum. The affective state of the mother during labor (fear, anxiety) and her affective state after the birth of the child (joy, relief) are so incongruent that there may be considerable interference with recall of material in the latter state that was encoded during the former (i.e., there will be no mood state-dependent memory facilitation; Bower, 1981).

Each of these situations exemplifies the important role played by affect in the recall of pain. Despite its common endorsement as an important factor resulting in inaccurate pain reporting, survey researchers have given scant attention to affect in the design of surveys and in the interpretation of their results. Recently, we completed several studies in which subjects recruited from the local community answered questions like those found on health surveys after experiencing a happy, a sad, or a neutral mood induction (Salovey, *et al.*, 1990). One set of questions asked subjects to recall the number of days during the previous year on which they experienced each of seven different kinds of pain (e.g., headache, dental, stomach). We then summed these days into a pain recall index. As can be seen in Figure 13.4, this index was mood sensitive. Consistent with the previous work reported in this chapter relating mood to the report of physical symptoms, women experiencing sad moods reported having experienced more pain than did women who experienced happy moods. However, an unusual pattern of pain reporting was found among men; more days of pain were recalled in both the happy and sad conditions as compared with the neutral control group, although none of these differences were statistically significant. Additional studies of affective biases in the reporting of pain and physical symptoms are now underway in order to understand this unpredicted mood by gender interaction.

Understanding hypochondriasis

Hypochondriasis is characterized by (a) the experience of physical symptoms and (b) worry and fear about one's health (DSM–IIIR, American Psychiatric Association, 1987). Some ongoing work suggests that these two components, although correlated, are indeed separable (Stretton *et al.*, submitted). Recently, Stretton and Salovey (1990) proposed that both of these dimensions of hypochondriasis may be augmented by depressed moods and by subsequent shifts in attentional focus on to the self. The apparently frequent comorbidity of clinical hypochondriasis and depression is consistent with this hypothesis (Diamond, 1985; Kellner *et al.*, 1983–84; Kenyon, 1964).

Stretton (1990) recruited a sample of 250 healthy adults in order to study the relationship between sad mood, self-focused attention, and the two

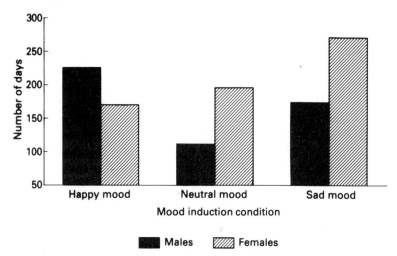

Fig 13.4   Influence of mood on recall of physical pain during past year (data from Salovey *et al.* 1990).

dimensions of hypochondriasis—physical symptom reporting and unjusti-fied fear and worry. Sadness and self-attending made significant and inde-pendent contributions to accounting for the variance in symptom reporting and fear and worry, controlling for subjects' prior health history. Of six different personality variables measured reliably by Stretton, sad mood was the one most strongly associated with hypochondriasis.

Although these results provide support for a view of hypochondriacal concerns that emphasizes the importance of depressed moods and self-focused attention, we are mindful that some investigators have argued against the utility of separating somatic and psychological complaints. For instance, Costa and McCrae (1985, 1987), Watson and Pennebaker (1989), and Watson (1988) have argued that neuroticism or negative affectivity (the tendency to *kvetch* about most anything) may be a "third variable" that accounts for observed associations between dysphoric moods and reported health problems. Although we do not discount this possibility, we are encouraged (from the standpoint of understanding hypochondriasis) by the repeated observation that individuals experiencing psychological distress are more likely than others to report physical symptoms and seek treatment for them (Mechanic, 1976, 1978, 1980).

Summary

Moods clearly affect perceptions of physical symptoms and judgments about health. When sad, individuals report more symptoms than when they are happy. Likewise, they believe they are less capable of carrying out behaviors that will alleviate their ills, and they are more pessimistic that any actions they might choose to take will relieve their symptoms. Sad indi-viduals also believe that they are more vulnerable to future illness—heart disease, cancer, arthritis—than when happy. These links between mood and health beliefs can be understood by examining underlying mechanisms at two different levels of analysis. At a cognitive level, mood facilitates the recall of memories congruent with the mood. When sad, individuals may be more likely to call to mind previous experiences with illness. Subsequent judgments may then be based on the ease with which these autobiographical memories flood consciousness. Also at the cognitive level, sad individuals are more likely to focus their attentions on to themselves rather than on the external environment. The sad person may thus become acutely aware of internally generated symptoms and sensations and be less likely to be distracted by engaging stimuli from the environment. At the physiological level, recent research suggests that sad moods may be associated with immune system changes that can produce vulnerability to real illness. This chapter concluded with two implications of this line of research. One concerns the accuracy of symptom reporting—especially physical pain—on health surveys, and the other, a view of hypochondriasis emphasizing the role of depressed mood and self-focused attention.

Acknowledgments

We would like to thank Joseph P. Forgas, Paula M. Niedenthal and William J. Sieber for their comments on earlier drafts of this chapter. Preparation of this manuscript was facilitated by the following grants to Peter Salovey: National Institute of Health Biomedical Research Support Grant S07 RR07015, National Cancer Institute grant CA42101, National Center for Health Statistics contract 200-88-7001, and a Presidential Young Investigator Award from the National Science Foundation (9058020). The experiments reported in this chapter were funded by the John D. and Catherine T. MacArthur Foundation Mental Health Network on Determinants and Consequences of Health-Promoting and Health-Damaging Behavior. Ann O'Leary is supported by grant MH45238 from the National Institute of Mental Health. Please address all correspondence to Peter Salovey, Department of Psychology, Yale University, Box 11A Yale Station, New Haven, CT 06520-7447, USA.

References

Ader, R. (Ed.) (1981). *Psychoneuroimmunology*. New York: Academic Press.

American Psychiatric Association (1987). *Diagnostic and Statistical Manual of the Mental Disorders*, 3rd ed., rev. Washington, DC: American Psychiatric Association.

Anderson, C. A. (1983). Imagination and expectation: The effect of imagining behavioral scripts on personal intentions. *Journal of Personality and Social Psychology*, **45**, 293–305.

Bandura, A. (1977). Self-efficacy: Toward a unifying theory of behavioral change. *Psychological Review*, **84**, 191–215.

Bandura, A. (1986). *Social foundations of thought and action*. Englewood Cliffs, NJ: Prentice-Hall.

Bartrop, R., Lazarus, L., Luckhurst, E., Kiloh, L. G., and Penny, R. (1977). Depressed lymphocyte function after bereavement. *Lancet*, **1**, 834–836.

Becker, M. H., Haefner, D. P., Kasl, S. V., Kirscht, J. P., Maiman, L. H., and Rosenstock, I. M. (1977). Selected psychosocial models and correlates of individual health-related behaviors. *Medical Care*, **15**, 27–46.

Blalock, J. E. (1989). A molecular basis for bidirectional communication between the immune and the neuroendocrine systems. *Physiological Reviews*, **69**, 1–32.

Blaney, P. H. (1986). Affect and memory: A review. *Psychological Bulletin*, **99**, 229–246.

Blumer, D., and Heilbronn, M. (1982). Chronic pain as a variant of depressive disease: The pain-prone disorder. *Journal of Nervous and Mental Disease*, **170**, 381–406.

Bower, G. H. (1981). Mood and memory. *American Psychologist*, **36**, 129–148.

Carroll, J. S. (1978). The effect of imagining an event on expectations for the event: An interpretation in terms of the availability heuristic. *Journal of Personality and Social Psychology*, **36**, 1501–1511.

Carver, C. S., and Scheier, M. F. (1981). *Attention and self-regulation: A control-theory approach to human behavior*. New York: Springer.

Contrada, R. J., Leventhal, H., and O'Leary, A. (1990). Personality and health. In L. A. Pervin (Ed.), *Handbook of personality: Theory and research*. pp. 638–669. New York: Guilford Press.

Costa, P. T., and McCrae, R. R. (1985). Hypochondriasis, neuroticism, and aging: When are somatic complaints unfounded? *American Psychologist*, **40**, 19–28.

Costa, P. T., and McCrae, R. R. (1987). Neuroticism, somatic complaints, and disease: Is the bark worse than the bite? *Journal of Personality*, **55**, 299–316.

Croyle, R. T., and Uretsky, M. D. (1987). Effects of mood on self-appraisal of health status. *Health Psychology*, **6**, 239–253.

Cummings, K. M., Jette, A. M., Brock, B. M., and Haefner, D. P. (1979). Psychosocial determinants of immunization behavior in a swine influenza campaign. *Medical Care*, **17**, 639–649.

Cummings, N. A., and Follette, W. T. (1976). Brief psychotherapy and medical utilization. In H. Darken (Ed.), *The professional psychologist today*, pp. 165–174. San Francisco: Jossey-Bass.

Diamond, D. B. (1985). Panic attacks, hypochondriasis, and agoraphobia: A self-psychology formulation. *American Journal of Psychotherapy*, **34**, 114–125.

Duval, S., and Wicklund, R. A. (1972). *A theory of objective self-awareness*. New York: Academic Press.

Eich, E., Reeves, J. L., Jaeger, B., and Graff-Redford, S. B. (1985). Memory for pain: Relation between past and present pain intensity. *Pain*, **23**, 375–380.

Fillingim, R. B., and Fine, M. A. (1986). The effects of internal vs. external information processing on symptom perception in an exercise setting. *Health Psychology*, **5**, 115–123.

Fisher, V. E. and Marrow, A. J. (1934). Experimental study of moods. *Character and Personality*, **2**, 181–188.

Follette, W. F., and Cummings, N. A. (1967). Psychiatric services and medical utilization in a prepaid health setting. *Medical Care*, **5**, 25–35.

Forgas, J. P., and Bower, G. H. (1987). Mood effects on person-perception judgments. *Journal of Personality and Social Psychology*, **53**, 53–60.

Forgas, J. P., and Moylan, S. (1987). After the movies: Transient mood and social judgments. *Personality and Social Psychology Bulletin*, **13**, 467–477.

Gilligan, S. G., and Bower, G. H. (1984). Cognitive consequences of emotional arousal. In C. E. Izard, J. Kagan, and R. Zajonc (Eds.), *Emotions, cognition, and behavior*. pp. 547–588. New York: Cambridge University Press.

Glaser, R., Kiecolt-Glaser, J. K., Speicher, C. E., and Holliday, J. E. (1985). Stress, loneliness, and changes in herpes virus latency. *Journal of Behavioral Medicine*, **8**, 249–260.

Glaser, R., Rice, J., Shendon, J., Fertel, R., Stout, J., Speicher, C., Pinsky, D., Kotur, M., Post, A., Beck, M., and Kiecolt-Glaser, J. K. (1987). Stress-related immune suppression: Health implications. *Brain, Behavior and Immunity*, **1**, 7–20.

Guerra, F. (1986). Awareness and recall. *International Anesthesiology Clinics*, **24**, 75–99.

Hancock, M. (1987). Depression and symptom reporting. Unpublished Senior Essay, Yale University, New Haven, CT.

Hunter, M., Philips, C., and Rachman, S. (1979). Memory for pain. *Pain*, **6**, 35–46.

Ingram, R. E. (1990). Self-focused attention in clinical disorders: Review and a conceptual model. *Psychological Bulletin*, **107**, 156–176.

Ingram, R. E., and Smith, T. W. (1984). Depression and internal versus external focus of attention. *Cognitive Therapy and Research*, **8**, 139–152.

Irwin, M., Daniels, M., Smith, T. L., Bloom, E., and Weiner, H. (1987). Impaired natural killer cell activity during bereavement. *Brain, Behavior and Immunity*, **1**, 98–104.

Isen, A. M. (1987). Positive affect, cognitive processes, and social behavior. In L. Berkowitz (Ed.), *Advances in experimental social psychology*, Vol. 20, pp. 203–253. San Diego: Academic Press.

Janz, N. K., and Becker, M. H. (1984). The health beliefs model: A decade later. *Health Education Quarterly*, **11**, 1–47.

Johnson, E. J., and Tversky, A. (1983). Affect, generalization, and the perception of risk. *Journal of Personality and Social Psychology*, **45**, 20–33.

Jones, K., and Vischi, T. (1979). Impact of alcohol, drug abuse, and mental health treatment on medical care utilization: Review of the research literature. *Medical Care*, **17** (Suppl. 12), 1–82.

Kanfer, R., and Zeiss, A. M., (1983). Depression, interpersonal standard setting, and judgments of self-efficacy. *Journal of Abnormal Psychology*, **92**, 319–329.

Katon, W. (1984). Depression: Relationship to somatization and chronic medical illness. *Journal of Clinical Psychiatry*, **45**, 4–11.

Kavanagh, D. J., and Bower, G. H. (1985). Mood and self-efficacy: Impact of joy and sadness on perceived capabilities. *Cognitive Therapy and Research*, **9**, 507–525.

Keefe, F. J., Wilkins, R. H., Cook, W. A., Crisson, J. E., and Muhlbaier, J. H. (1986). Depression, pain, and pain behavior. *Journal of Consulting and Clinical Psychology*, **54**, 665–669.

Kellner, R., Abbott, P., Pathak, D., Winslow, W. W., and Umland, B. E. (1983–84).

Hypochondriacal beliefs and attitudes in family practice and psychiatric patients. *International Journal of Psychiatry in Medicine*, **13**, 127–139.

Kent, G. (1985). Memory for dental pain. *Pain*, **21**, 187–194.

Kenyon, F. E. (1964). Hypochondriasis: A clinical study. *British Journal of Psychiatry*, **129**, 1–14.

Kiecolt-Glaser, J. K., Fisher, L. D., Ogrocki, P., Stout, J. C., Speicher, C. E., and Glaser, R. (1987). Marital quality, marital disruption, and immune function. *Psychosomatic Medicine*, **49**, 13–34.

Kiecolt-Glaser, J. K., Garner, W., Speicher, C. E., Penn, G., and Glaser, R. (1984a). Psychosocial modifiers of immunocompetence in medical students. *Psychosomatic Medicine*, **46**, 7–14.

Kiecolt-Glaser, J. K., and Glaser, R. (1987). Psychosocial moderators of immune function. *Annals of Behavioral Medicine*, **9**, 16–20.

Kiecolt-Glaser, J. K., Kennedy, S., Malkoff, S., Fisher, L., Speicher, C. E., and Glaser, R. (1988). Marital discord and immunity in males. *Psychosomatic Medicine*, **50**, 213–229.

Kiecolt-Glaser, J. K., Ricker, D., George, J., Messick, G., Speicher, C. E., Garner, W., and Glaser, R. (1984b). Urinary cortisol levels, cellular immunocompetency, and loneliness in psychiatric inpatients. *Psychosomatic Medicine*, **46**, 15–23.

Kiecolt-Glaser, J. K., Stephens, R. E., Lipetz, P. D., Speicher, C. E., and Glaser, R. (1985). Distress and DNA repair in human lymphocytes. *Journal of Behavioral Medicine*, **8**, 311–320.

Kulik, J. A., and Mahler, H. I. M. (1987). Health status, perceptions of risk, and prevention interest for health and nonhealth problems. *Health Psychology*, **6**, 15–27.

Lloyd, G. G., and Lishman, W. A. (1975). Effect of depression on the speed of recall of pleasant and unpleasant experiences. *Psychological Medicine*, **5**, 173–180.

Maddox, G. L. (1962). Some correlates of differences in self-assessment of health status among the elderly. *Journal of Gerontology*, **17**, 180–185.

Mayer, J. D., and Salovey, P. (1988). Personality moderates the interaction of mood and cognition. In D. Fiedler and J. Forgas (Eds.), *Affect, cognition, and social behavior*, pp. 87–99. Toronto: Hogrefe.

Mayer, J. D., and Volanth, A. J. (1985). Cognitive involvement in the emotional response system. *Motivation and Emotion*, **9**, 261–275.

McKusick, L., Wiley, J., Coates, T. J., and Morin, S. F. (1986). Predictors of AIDS behavioral risk reduction: The AIDS behavioral research project. Paper presented at the New Zealand AIDS Foundation Prevention Education Planning Workshop, Auckland, New Zealand.

McNair, D., Lorr, M., and Droppleman, L. (1971). *EDITS manual for the Profile of Mood States*. San Diego, CA: Educational and Industrial Testing Service.

Mechanic, D. (1976). The effect of psychological distress on physician utilization: A prospective study. *Journal of Health and Social Behavior*, **17**, 353–364.

Mechanic, D. (1978). Effects of psychological distress on perceptions of physical health and use of medical and psychiatric facilities. *Journal of Human Stress*, **4**, 26–32.

Mechanic, D. (1980). The experience and reporting of common physical complaints. *Journal of Health and Social Behavior*, **21**, 146–155.

Minter, R. E., and Kimball, C. P. (1978). Life events and illness onset: A review. *Psychosomatics*, **19**, 334–339.

Norvell, K. T., Gaston-Johansson, F., and Fridh, G. (1987). Remembrance of labor pain: How valid are retrospective pain measurements? *Pain*, **31**, 77–86.

O'Leary, A. (1985). Self-efficacy and health. *Behavior Research and Therapy*, **23**, 437–451.

O'Leary, A. (1990). Stress, emotion, and human immune function. *Psychological Bulletin*, **108**, 363–382.

Pennebaker, J. W. (1982). *The psychology of physical symptoms*. New York: Springer.

Pennebaker, J. W., and Lightner, J. M. (1980). Competition of internal and external information in an exercise setting. *Journal of Personality and Social Psychology*, **35**, 167–174.

Perloff, L. S., and Fetzer, B. K. (1986). Self–other judgments and perceived vulnerability to victimization. *Journal of Personality and Social Psychology*, **50**, 502–510.

Persson, L-O., and Sjoberg, L. (1987). Mood and somatic symptoms. *Journal of Psychosomatic Research*, **31**, 499–511.

Pyszczynski, T., and Greenberg, J. (1987). Self-regulatory perseveration and the depressive self-focusing style: A self-awareness theory of depression. *Psychological Bulletin*, **102**, 122–138.

Roche, P. A., and Gijsbers, K. (1986). A comparison of memory for induced ischemic pain and chronic rheumatoid pain. *Pain*, **14**, 393–398.

Rodin, G., and Voshart, K. (1986). Depression in the medically ill: An overview. *American Journal of Psychiatry*, **143**, 696– 705.

Salovey, P. (1986). The effects of mood and focus of attention on self-relevant thoughts and helping intention. Unpublished doctoral dissertation, Yale University, New Haven, CT.

Salovey, P. (submitted). Mood-induced self-focused attention.

Salovey, P., and Birnbaum, D. (1989). Influence of mood on health-relevant cognitions. *Journal of Personality and Social Psychology*, **57**, 539–551.

Salovey, P., Jobe, J. B., Willis, G. B., Sieber, W. J., van der Sleesen, S., Turk, D. C., and Smith, A. F. (1990). Response errors and bias in recall of chronic pain. *Proceedings of the American Statistical Association, Section on Survey Research Methods*, 413–420.

Salovey, P., and Mayer, J. D. (1990). Emotional intelligence. *Imagination, Cognition, and Personality*, **9**, 185–211.

Salovey, P., Mayer, J. D., and Rosenhan, D. L. (1991). Helping and the regulation of mood. In M. S. Clark (Ed.), *Review of Personality and Social Psychology*, Vol. 12, pp. 215–237. Beverly Hills: Sage.

Salovey, P., and Rodin, J. (1985). Cognitions about the self: Connecting feeling states and social behavior. In P. Shaver (Ed.), *Self, situations and social behavior: Review of personality and social psychology*, Vol. 6, pp. 143–166. Beverly Hills, CA: Sage.

Salovey, P., and Rosenhan, D. L. (1989). Mood and prosocial behavior. In H. L. Wagner and A. S. R. Manstead (Eds.), *Handbook of social psychophysiology*, pp. 371–391. Chichester: Wiley.

Salovey, P., and Singer, J. A. (1989). Mood congruency effects in recall of childhood versus recent memories. *Journal of Social Behavior and Personality*, **4**, 99–120.

Schleifer, S. J., Keller, S. E., Camarino, E., Thronton, J. C., and Stein, M. (1983). Suppression of lymphocyte stimulation following bereavement. *Journal of the American Medical Association*, **250**, 374–377.

Schleifer, S. J., Keller, S. E., Meyerson, A. T., Raskin, M. J., Davis, K. L., and Stein, M. (1984). Lymphocyte function in major depressive disorder. *Archives of General Psychiatry*, **41**, 484– 486.

Schleifer, S. J., Keller, S. E., Siris, S. G., Davis, K. L., and Stein, M. (1985). Depression and immunity: Lymphocyte function in ambulatory depressed, hospitalized schizophrenic, and herniorrhaphy patients. *Archives of General Psychiatry*, **42**, 129–133.

Schwarz, N. (1989). Feelings as information. Technical Report of the Zentrum fur Umfragen, Methoden und Analysen, Mannheim, Germany, ZUMA-Arbeitsverich Nr. 89/03. To appear in E. T. Higgins (Eds.), *Handbook of motivation and cognition: Foundation of Social Behavior*, Vol 2. New York: Guilford Press.

Selye, H. (1956). *The stress of life*. New York: McGraw-Hill.

Sherman, S. J., Cialdini, R. B., Schwartzman, D. F., and Reynolds, K. D. (1985). Imagining can heighten or lower the perceived likelihood of contracting a disease: The mediation effect of ease of imagery. *Personality and Social Psychology Bulletin*, **11**, 118–127.

Singer, J. A., and Salovey, P. (1988). Mood and memory: Evaluating the network theory of affect. *Clinical Psychology Review*, **8**, 211–251.

Smith, T. W., and Greenberg, J. (1981). Depression and self-focused attention. *Motivation and Emotion*, **5**, 323–331.

Snyder, M., and White, P. (1982). Moods and memories: Elation, depression, and the remembering of events in one's life. *Journal of Personality and Social Psychology*, **49**, 1076–1085.

Stone, A. A. (1987). Event content in a daily survey is differentially associated with concurrent mood. *Journal of Personality and Social Psychology*, **52**, 56–58.

Stone, A. A., Cox, D. S., Valdimarsdottir, H., Jandorf, L., and Neale, J. M. (1987). Evidence that secretory IgA antibody is associated with daily mood. *Journal of Personality and Social Psychology*, **52**, 988–993.

Stretton, M. S. (1990). Predicting health concerns. Unpublished doctoral dissertation, Yale University, New Haven, CT.

Stretton, M., and Salovey, P. (1990). Cognitive and affective components of hypochondriacal concerns. Unpublished manuscript, Yale University, New Haven, CT.

Stretton, M., Salovey, P., and Mayer, J. D. (submitted). Assessing hypochondriacal concerns.

Taylor, S. E. (1989). *Positive illusions: Creative self-deception and the healthy mind*. New York: Basic Books.

Taylor, S. E., and Brown, J. (1988). Illusion and well-being: A social psychological perspective on mental health. *Psychological Bulletin*, **103**, 193–210.

Teasdale, J. D., and Fogarty, J. (1979). Differential effects of induced mood in retrieval of pleasant and unpleasant events from episodic memory. *Journal of Abnormal Psychology*, **88**, 248–257.

Teasdale, J. D., and Taylor, R. (1981). Induced mood and accessibility of memories: An effect of mood state or of mood induction procedure? *British Journal of Clinical Psychology*, **20**, 39–48.

Tessler, R., and Mechanic, D. (1978). Psychological distress and perceived health status. *Journal of Health and Social Behavior*, **19**, 254–262.

Turk, D. C., Rudy, T. E., and Salovey, P. (1984). Health protection: Attitudes and behaviors of LPN's, teachers, and college students. *Health Psychology*, **3**, 189–210.

Turk, D. C., Rudy, T. E., and Stieg, R. L. (1987). Pain and depression: 1. "Facts." *Pain Management*, **1**, 17–26.

Turk, D. C., and Salovey, P. (1984). "Chronic pain as a variant of depressive disease": A critical reappraisal. *Journal of Nervous and Mental Disease*, **172**, 398–404.

Tversky, A., and Kahneman, D. (1973). Availability: A heuristic for judging frequency and probability. *Cognitive Psychology*, **5**, 207–232.

Wahler, H. J. (1968). The Physical Symptoms Inventory: Measuring levels of somatic complaining behavior. *Journal of Clinical Psychology*, **24**, 207–211.

Watson, D. (1988). Intraindividual and interindividual analysis of positive and negative affect: Their relations to health complaints, perceived stress, and daily activities. *Journal of Personality and Social Psychology*, **54**, 1020–1030.

Watson, D., and Pennebaker, J. W. (1989). Health complaints, stress, and distress: Exploring the central role of negative affectivity. *Psychological Review*, **96**, 234–254.

Weinstein, N. D. (1982). Unrealistic optimism about susceptibility to health problems. *Journal of Behavioral Medicine*, **5**, 441–460.

Weinstein, N. D. (1983). Reducing unrealistic optimism about illness susceptibility. *Health Psychology*, **2**, 11–20.

Weinstein, N. D. (1984). Why it won't happen to me: Perceptions of risk factors and susceptibility. *Health Psychology*, **3**, 431–437.

Weinstein, N. D. (1987). Unrealistic optimism about susceptibility to health problems: Conclusions from a community-wide sample. *Journal of Behavioral Medicine*, **10**, 481-500.

Wiedenfeld, S., O'Leary, A., Bandura, A., Brown, S., Levin, S., and Raska, K. (submitted). Impact of perceived self-efficacy in coping with stressors on components of the immune system.

Wood, J. V., Saltzberg, J. A., and Goldsamt, L. A. (1990). Does affect induce self-focused attention? *Journal of Personality and Social Psychology*, **58**, 899–908.

Wright, J., and Mischel, W. (1982). Influence of affect on cognitive social learning person variables. *Journal of Personality and Social Psychology*, **43**, 901–914.

14

Affect and Person Perception

JOSEPH P. FORGAS

University of New South Wales

Contents

Perceiving another person is one of the most common, yet at the same time most complex and demanding tasks we face in everyday life. Unlike physical perception, social perception usually involves highly elaborated judgments about characteristics which are not directly observable, but must be inferred, requiring the use of high-level cognitive processes. Affect can play an important role in person perception both through influencing the particular kind of information processing strategy adopted by judges, and through its influence on the way social information about another person is attended to, selected, interpreted, learned, remembered, and evaluated in judgments. This chapter describes the general conceptual and historical background to studying affective influences on person perception judgments, and a multiprocess approach to the understanding of such effects is developed. In the second half of the chapter, a series of our empirical studies illustrating various aspects of affective influences on person perception judgments are described.

The Background to Research on Affect in Person Perception

Since the earliest experimental investigations of person perception phenomena, it has been clearly recognized that person perception is inevitably a constructive process, although the role of affect in that process has not received much attention until quite recently. Asch's (1946) seminal work in this field showed that even the analysis of the simplest kind of person stimuli, consisting of brief lists of adjectives, is subject to the constructive perceptual biases of the perceiver, seeking to impose shape, form or "Gestalt" on the disparate characteristics of the stimulus person. Later work provided additional evidence for the major role played by the perceiver's expectations, construals, and implicit representations in the person perception process. Kelly's (1955) work on personal constructs offered strong arguments for taking the phenomenology of the perceiver seriously, and later extensive research on implicit personality theories provided hard empirical evidence for the role of constructive processes in person perception (Rosenberg and Sedlak, 1972; Schneider, 1973).

Despite the strong tradition of constructivist approaches to person perception, there is also a second, perhaps more atomistic and mechanistic, view that has had a major influence on research in the field. Anderson's (1974) work on "cognitive algebra", although essentially rooted in the psychophysical measurement tradition, nevertheless did conceptualize social perception judgments as the predictable outcome of simple, arithmetically derived information integration processes. Within this framework the characteristics of the perceiver, including affective states, are of peripheral interest only, although affective information could in principle be considered as part of the information integration process. This view assumes that the traits and characteristics of the judgmental target (another person) may be treated as in a sense "given" or readily available to the perceiver, and once identified, this information retains permanent, enduring meanings not affected by other information units or the phenomenology of the judge. The information integration approach has been extremely useful in providing a sound basis for studying complex judgmental processes, and its applicability clearly extends to contemporary research on mood effects on social judgments (see Kaplan, this volume). Nevertheless, its underlying metaphor of the social perceiver as a passive information processor falls short of a realistic understanding of the selective and constructive aspects of person perception (cf. Argyle, this volume). Indeed, it may be argued that the information in person perception is almost never "given." What influences the selection and interpretation of information about a person is usually the single most crucial question in person perception research. Nor is the assumption of the "invariable meaning" of personality characteristics required by information integration analysis plausible or supported by the available evidence. Instead, as Asch argued, personality traits do seem to live an intensely social life, their meanings forever shifting and changing depending on whatever other information becomes available to the perceiver.

Interestingly, these two conflicting traditions of person perception research, the holistic, constructivist, and phenomenological approach, and the atomistic, mechanistic, and reductionist approach, continue to exert considerable influence on contemporary research. The relative decline of information integration research gave rise to the emergence of the currently dominant paradigm, the information processing model of person perception. "Person memory" is the study of the cognitive processes involved in the encoding, retrieval and combination of information about other people (Hastie *et al.*, 1980). In these terms, social perception may be thought of as a process of semantic categorization, which requires the translation of observed information about people into semantic representations, leading to the activation of relevant prior experiences and knowledge structures (Wyer and Srull, 1981). It is the process of activation of representational structures that allows perceivers to "go beyond the information given," by making inferences and attributions about their target based on their prior experiences with people. This model of person perception has some important advantages as well as disadvantages. One advantage is that it links person perception, clearly a high-level cognitive process, with established information processing paradigms and, in particular, cognitive research on memory and representational structures. It also has the benefit of drawing together two previously distinct fields in person perception research: information integration and implicit personality theory. Person memory as a concept allows the simultaneous explanation of both the assimilation of novel information, and the impact of "old" knowledge on impression formation. However, the paradigm is essentially still an atomistic one, assuming "cold" cognition on the part of the perceivers where feelings, evaluations, and preferences play a role only insofar as they become components in a cognitive representational system. This currently dominant information processing metaphor continues to be criticized because of its lack of attention to the role of affect in judgments (Forgas, 1981), and its focus on the isolated, lonely perceiver separated from the social and cultural context as its focus of attention (Argyle, this volume).

Affect in Person Perception: A Multiprocess Approach

Affective, evaluative reactions to others are clearly an essential part of the person perception process. As Zajonc (1980) argued, affect is likely to be the primary medium of interpersonal behavior, and affective reactions often precede or inform subsequent cognitive elaborations (cf. Clore and Parrott; Niedenthal and Showers; Schwarz and Bless, this volume). Although the recent debate about the primacy of affect or cognition remained rather inconclusive (Lazarus, 1984; Zajonc, 1984), it helped to focus attention once again on the emotional aspects of interpersonal judgments and behavior. Reactions to other people in particular are often affective. Such spontaneous affective responses may often lead to the direct activation of relevant past experiences (Niedenthal and Showers, this volume) and may also inform perceptions and judgments (Clore and Parrott; Schwarz and Bless, this volume). The encoding and retrieval of affective reactions to others may constitute a distinct and separate representational system from the kind of semantic representations studied by person memory researchers. If such affective reactions in person perception are as common and spontaneous as they appear to be, with simple cues such as a facial expression, a tone of voice, or a nonverbal gesture directly triggering evaluative reactions (cf. Forgas, 1988; Forgas *et al.*, 1983; Niedenthal and Showers, this volume), it is of particular importance to study the influence of affective states on interpersonal judgments. This chapter describes a general theoretical framework assuming a multiprocess approach in the study of affective influences on person perception judgments, and later, the main findings of our continuing research project on mood effects on person perception and judgments will be summarized.

In conceptualizing mood effects on person perception judgments, it is first necessary to consider the various alternative ways a judge might approach a task of person perception. Many contemporary models are based on a "single-process" assumption—that is, they implicitly or even explicitly suggest that there is one particular information processing strategy that is universally used in making person perception judgments. It is proposed here that, in reality, people have multiple information processing strategies available to them when making judgments about others. One of the most critical questions in person perception research concerns the variables that influence the selection of a particular strategy. Affect can play a role in determining (a) which of several possible processing strategies is selected in a given situation and (b) how information is dealt with once a particular processing strategy is adopted.

There is considerable cumulative evidence suggesting that in making many kinds of decisions and judgments about others, people have at least four, and possibly more, alternative kinds of processing strategies available to them. How affective states will influence person perception judgments will largely depend on which of these possible processing strategies is adopted in a given situation.

(1) A *direct-access strategy* is likely to be adopted by perceivers when the target is familiar or closely related to previous targets, and preexisting crystallized judgments are available. In such instances, the direct retrieval of the preformed assessment or evaluation is all that is required for a judgment to be made. Although this is the simplest person perception strategy, as it does not require the online computation of a new impression, it is likely that a large proportion of our everyday person perception judgments are made in this way. This strategy is available only if the problem or judgment is not novel and has already been exhaustively processed in the past. As the judgment or decision simply requires the retrieval of an already formed,

crystallized reaction stored in memory, the potential for mood-based biases in such judgments at the retrieval stage is rather limited. There is some evidence that such stored perceptions and evaluations about others may be surprisingly powerful and even resistant to disconfirming evidence (Snyder, 1984). Once a perception and judgment about a person is computed, subsequent encounters will presumably strongly cue the retrieval of pre-formed evaluation. This retrieval process may be relatively robust and resistant to change, due to the strong cueing provided by the judgmental target.

(2) A *substantive processing strategy* is likely to be adopted when no preformed judgment is available, and judges need to select, interpret and integrate novel information about a person in computing a judgment. It is this kind of online information processing strategy and the sort of judgmental process it involves that traditional models of person perception have taken as their model. Most of the cognitive processes involved are assumed to be automatic and uncontrolled, although this need not always be the case. This strategy, by definition, involves dealing with the substance of the information available in seeking to construct a new judgment. Contemporary social–cognitive models of person perception address and analyze this process mainly in terms of memory theories, seeking to account for the information processing principles involved in assimilating novel information into a preexisting category system (Hastie *et al.*, 1980). Much of the earlier work on person perception also falls into this category, assuming that person perception judgments are substantive and information-driven, although there may be significant differences between the models as to their assumptions about the nature of the combinatorial rule used by judges (cf. Anderson, 1974; Asch, 1946). It is when employing the substantive process-ing strategy that affective influences can play a major role in person perception judgments. The kind of memory-based models proposed by Bower (1981), Isen (1984), and others also implicitly assume the adoption of a substantive processing strategy.

(3) A *motivated processing strategy* may be employed when a perceiver has no prior crystallized judgment to fall back on, and there are motivational pressures for a particular judgmental outcome to be achieved. For example, in a dysphoric mood judgments may be oriented towards controlling the negative mood state. Motivated processing usually involves more controlled and less automatic processing in search of a desired judgmental outcome. This distinction was first proposed by Clark and Isen (1982) to apply to mood effects on social judgments, although much work remains to be done in specifying the exact nature of controlled processing and the circumstances that lead to it. Affective states probably play a major role in eliciting such motivated processing strategies, and in our research negative affect in particular was repeatedly found to have such motivational consequences (cf. Forgas, 1989).

(4) The *heuristic processing strategy* is the fourth alternative, likely to be adopted when the judge has the possibility to bypass or eliminate the stage of substantive processing altogether, to arrive at a judgmental outcome without the detailed consideration of the available information. Just as in the direct-access strategy, person perception in this case does not involve the substantive consideration of relevant information. The assumption is that judges, for whatever reason, choose to avoid or shortcircuit the detailed processing of the available information, and try instead to arrive at a judgment by the simplest and least effortful means. For example, judgment of a person may be based on irrelevant associations with extraneous variables (Griffitt, 1970), his or her superficial similarity to an already familiar other, or may be simply inferred from the perceiver's prevailing affective state (cf. Clore and Parrott, this volume). Affect has been shown to play a very important role in heuristic processing strategies (Schwarz and Bless, this volume).

Distinguishing between these alternative person perception strategies has considerable benefits. In particular, the influence of affective states on person perception judgments may largely depend on which of the various strategies is adopted by a judge. The direct-access strategy, relying as it does on the retrieval of preformed judgments may be most impervious to the influence of affective states on judgments. The substantive processing strategy in turn may be subject to affect-based distortions in the selection, learning, interpretation and retrieval of information about people. There is now extensive evidence supporting the existence of strong and reliable affect-based distortions in the substantive processing of person perception judgments, to be considered later in this chapter (cf. Forgas and Bower, 1987, 1988). The third, motivated processing strategy has received relatively less attention to date, and motivational processes are often invoked in *posthoc* analyses of results that do not readily fit the predictions of automatic processing models. However, there is now growing evidence that motivation plays a role not only in interpersonal preferences (Schachter, 1959), but also in the perceptual and judgmental processes underlying such choices (Forgas, 1989). Finally, the outcome of judgments based on the heuristic strategy may be influenced by the affective state of the judge more directly, as moods themselves may be mistakenly interpreted as a source of heuristic information about reactions to a target (Schwarz and Bless, this volume).

An important remaining question concerns the variables that influence which of the different processing strategies will be adopted in a given situation. The affective state of the judge may again play a role in that decision, and there is some evidence suggesting that positive affective states are more likely to be associated with heuristic and direct access strategies rather than with substantive processing strategies, while dysphoric moods often seem to be linked to motivated processing strategies.

The distinction between the processing strategies suggested here is also consistent with other theoretical formulations in the social judgmental literature and should help to systematize the differences between them. For example, Petty and Cacioppo's (1986) influential Elaboration Likelihood Model postulates two processing strategies when judging persuasive messages, central-route processing and peripheral-route processing, which in important respects mirror the distinction between substantive processing and heuristic processing proposed here (see also Petty *et al.*, this volume). Fiedler (this volume) also proposed a dual-process formulation, in which the alternative strategies of constructive versus reconstructive processing have some of the features of substantive versus heuristic and direct-access processing strategies described here. Schwarz and Bless (this volume) devote considerable attention to the informative functions of affective states, and their role in selectively activating careful, analytic, or effort-minimizing, heuristic processing styles. In conjunction, these contributions offer the basis for an integrated consideration of how affective states might selectively lead to different kinds of information processing strategies in person perception judgments.

Affect and Cognition in Person Perception

Perceptions and judgments of other people always involve an element of interpretation and construction, as we have seen above. In cognitive terms, this means that person perception is essentially a top-down process: the assumptions and expectations we start out with will influence the evidence that we find, the interpretations that we make and ultimately, the judgments we arrive at. Most social behaviors are inherently ambiguous, open to alternative, and often conflicting, interpretations, and often there are few real criteria for deciding the accuracy of such inferential judgments.

Short-term affective states, quite often automatically elicited by the judgmental target, may in turn influence later perceptions and interpretations. Through the automatic priming and activation of cognitive constructs and representations that were experienced in a similar affective state, the top-down interpretation of subsequent inputs is likely to be biased in an affect-consistent direction. Various information-retrieval models have been proposed to account for such effects (cf. Bower, 1981; Isen, 1984). The associative network model by Bower (1981), described in some detail in Chapter 1, is one of the more influential and parsimonious of such accounts. The model assumes that mood states are represented in a memory system similar to other information units, and are linked to other knowledge structures by associative pathways formed in the course of prior experiences involving that mood. Whenever a mood is experienced, its representational node is activated, and this in turn will spread activation to other constructs associated with that mood, facilitating their retrieval and use in cognitive processing. Bower's semantic network model proposes that each distinctive emotion, such as joy, depression, or fear has a specific node or unit in memory that collects together many other aspects of the emotion that are connected to it by associative pointers . . . each emotion unit is also linked with propositions describing events from one's life during which that emotion was aroused . . . Activation of an emotion node also spreads activation throughout the memory structures to which it is connected.

(1981, p. 135).

Whenever an affective state is experienced, information associated with that state in the past becomes primed, and is more likely to be recalled and used in information processing. Although this is essentially a memory model, dealing with the role of affect in information storage and retrieval, the predicted superior availability of affect-related information does have widespread implications.

The model implies that the experience of a mood state will (a) facilitate the *learning* of mood-congruent information because of the availability of a richer mood-congruent associative base; (b) selectively focus *attention* on mood-congruent information; (c) selectively help the *retrieval* of mood-consistent information; and (d) selectively facilitate mood-consistent *associations* and the *interpretation* of ambiguous information in a mood-consistent manner. All of these processes should have a cumulative effect on person perception judgments, particularly when a substantive processing strategy is adopted.

These mood effects on cognition are particularly important in social perception and judgments. It seems to be an inherent feature of social perception that it is a highly selective and interpretive process (Heider, 1958; Kelly, 1955). As we have seen the information for the social perceiver is rarely "given," but must be selected from an often exceedingly complex and ambiguous stimulus array, such as is represented by another person, and then must be further processed and interpreted. Affective states may influence not only what we see and pay attention to, but also what we remember, the associations we form, and the way we interpret the available information. We have known for some time that the enduring expectations, cognitive representations and "implicit theories of personality" of a perceiver are often more important in social judgments than the actual characteristics of the target (Asch, 1946; Kelly, 1955; Schneider, 1973). What the affect-priming model of Bower (1981) suggests is that much more transient, insubstantial variables, such as a perceiver's current mood state, may have equally important effects on social perception.

Affect-priming formulations imply that feelings have an indirect and automatic effect on cognitive processes and, ultimately, social judgments. Other models assume a much more direct, informational role for affective states. The most comprehensive account of the informational role of mood states in the heuristic processing of social information is offered by Clore and Parrott (this volume) and by Schwarz and Bless (this volume). Both of these accounts emphasize that moods themselves have informational value that can influence social judgments without the necessary intermediary of a cognitive representational system. Clore and Parrott in particular argue for a broad and general conceptualization that helps to establish links between affect-as-information theories and various other models of heuristic judgmental processes. Schwarz and Bless in their chapter make the additional point that affective states are not only influential in informing qualitative judgments, but may also be effective in triggering alternative processing strategies. In terms of this approach, we may think of the choice by a judge to rely on substantive or heuristic processing as itself affectively mediated. To the extent that positive moods may inform us that an environment is nonthreatening, such states are more likely to result in heuristic rather than substantive processing strategies (cf. Forgas, 1989).

Affect and the Choice of Processing Strategy

One of the determinants of whether a person perception judgment will be based on direct-access, motivated, heuristic, or substantive processing strategies is how the person feels about the target. Much debate in the person perception literature is due to the implicit assumption by many researchers about the existence of a single processing strategy to deal with a variety of judgments. Research on person prototypes provides a good illustration. For example, Cantor and Mischel (1979) proposed that prototypicality is a critical feature of person stimuli with predictable facilitatory effects on person memory and judgments. According to such a single-process model, highly prototypical targets should always be more memorable and more informative leading to more confident person perception judgments than less prototypical targets. Targets low in prototypicality, or composed of the features of several prototypes, should be more difficult to encode and remember and, consequently, to judge. Evidence from these authors suggested that prototypicality was indeed positively related to both memory and judgmental measures: characters composed of a single prototype (extroverts or introverts) were easier to remember and judge than characters composed of a variety of features.

How would persons with unusual, nontypical characteristics be remembered and judged? While Cantor and Mischel (1979) assume that prototypicality is a helpful feature when dealing with social information, other evidence suggests exactly the opposite: unusual, inconsistent or atypical stimuli are easier to encode and remember than are consistent ones, according to Hastie and Kumar (1979) and others. Clearly, being prototypical is sometimes helpful and sometimes not, in the person perception process, suggesting at least two alternative processing strategies available to judges when dealing with such information. Assimilating information to a preexisting prototype is the easier, less effortful strategy, not unlike the heuristic processing style described earlier. Dealing with inconsistent information, in contrast, requires more effort and attention to actual information and deeper processing, consistent with the substantive processing strategy described above.

When are these two alternative strategies likely to be employed? Affective variables may well play an important role in determining which of the two approaches, heuristic or substantive processing, is likely to be adopted in a given situation. Person categories are not merely cognitive abstractions but are profoundly social and cultural products impregnated with evaluative and normative characteristics and affective valence. It may be expected that the stronger the affective and normative reaction to the target, the more likely it is that a heuristic rather than a substantive processing strategy should be used. We investigated this possibility in two experiments (Forgas, 1983, 1985). In the first study, it was hypothesized that salient, affectively loaded prototypes should "dominate impressions, leading to the poor processing of prototype inconsistent characters. In the case of low salient prototypes the opposite effect was expected, with novel and prototype-inconsistent information . . . leading to superior recall and predictions" (1983, p. 156).

The prototypes were elicited in a separate study using a representative sample of student judges who were asked to list the most familiar types of people in their social environment. The 16 most commonly nominated types and their defining characteristics were identified, and a multidimensional scaling analysis of these prototypes was undertaken. These prototypes included the usual array of student types, such as "intellectuals," "surfies," "medical students," "radicals," "bludgers," and the like (cf. Forgas, 1983). The affective salience of each of these prototypes was assessed through separate judgments about "how strongly people would react to this type of person" by a group of judges. In addition, the location of each prototype in the multidimensional representations was also used as an index of affective salience. Of the sixteen prototypes, the four most and four least affectively salient types were identified, and features of these types were combined into prototype-consistent and prototype-inconsistent descriptions. In essence, the study involves a 2 × 2 design, with two levels of prototypicality (high versus low) factorially combined with two levels of affective salience (high versus low).

We found a significant interaction between prototypicality and affective salience, with people remembering a high-salient prototypical target and a low-salient non-prototypical target better than other combinations. As expected, "these data show that subjects followed different information processing strategies depending on whether the target character was culturally salient or not" (p. 166), with affectively salient prototypes more likely to receive heuristic processing. Essentially, with affectively salient characters, subjects choose to disregard inconsistent characteristics, making their judgments in accordance with the prototype-assimilation model illustrated by

Cantor and Mischel (1979). It almost seems as if the salient prototype was "too dominant, vivid and normatively loaded for inconsistent characteristics to be associated with it" (p. 167).

In contrast, targets that were composed of low-salient prototypes were apparently processed using a different, more elaborate and substantive processing strategy, with inconsistent combinations remembered better than consistent combinations. In terms of memory models, superior memory for these characters was probably due to the deeper and more detailed processing that the inconsistent characterstics received. Evaluative person perception judgments and predictions about future behavior were also influenced by the interaction of prototypicality and salience. However, judgments of self-confidence did not show a similar pattern, with judges being more confident in rating inconsistent and salient targets than others. This apparently inconsistent finding is supported by research in person perception and attributions, showing that unusual, unexpected, or atypical features are often particularly informative and increase a judge's confidence. Overall, these results suggest that the affective quality and salience of the target may selectively trigger substantive or heuristic information processing strategies, with prototype-inconsistent information likely to be ignored in the heuristic processing mode, but receiving detailed attention in the substantive processing mode (Figure 14.1).

This study was later repeated with some improvements and modifications, yielding essentially similar results. Highly affectively salient and prototype-consistent characters, and low-salient inconsistent characters were better remembered, were predicted in more detail, and were evaluated more positively than were other combinations, suggesting the operation of two distinct processing strategies (Forgas, 1985). These studies are strongly suggestive of the role of affective variables in generating different information processing strategies. In subsequent experiments, we sought to investigate more exactly the processes whereby temporary mood states come to influence substantive processing strategies.

Affect in Person Perception: Empirical Investigations

There is now a growing literature looking at the role of affective and mood states on thinking about, remembering, and processing information about social stimuli, including other people (e.g. Bower, 1981, this volume; Forgas and Bower, 1987, 1988). During the past several years, we have been engaged in a series of studies investigating the role of low-intensity, transient mood states in a variety of social perception and judgmental tasks. The affective states we looked at are similar to the mild, nonspecific experiences of feeling "good" or feeling "bad" that are a common feature of everyday life.

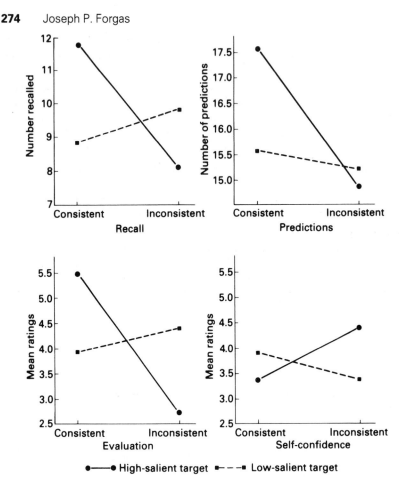

Fig 14.1   The effects of affective salience (high versus low) and prototypicality (consistent versus inconsistent) on the recall, evaluation, prediction, and confidence-rating of person stimuli: affective salience facilitates the heuristic processing of prototypical characters (after Forgas, 1983).

Affect and the perception of interactive behaviors

The perception of interactive behaviors is one of the most common person perception tasks. In one of our studies, we (Forgas *et al.*, 1984) looked at the role of affective states in how people perceive and interpret their own social behaviors, and the behaviors of others. Affective biases in this process may be a feature of depression (Roth and Rehm, 1980). Subjects were induced to feel happy or sad using a hypnotic mood-induction technique, and were then asked to look at a video recording of a social interaction they engaged in with another, previously known, person during the previous day. The interactions were constructed in such a way that four different kinds of encounters were created: formal–intimate, formal–nonintimate, informal–

intimate, and informal–nonintimate. Subjects were asked to identify and score positive, skilled, and negative, unskilled, behaviors both for themselves and for their partner as they observed it on the videotape. We found (see Figure 14.2) a strong and unexpected bias in how the behaviors recorded on the videotape were perceived and interpreted, indicating the strong influence of the temporary mood state of the judge. Happy subjects tended to identify far more positive skilled behaviors than negative unskilled behaviors both in themselves and in their partners than did sad subjects. There was one exception to this strong and consistent mood-induced bias in perceptions. Sad subjects were more critical of themselves than of their partners, a pattern similar to the self-deprecating bias often found in judgments by persons suffering from depression (Roth and Rehm, 1980). We may account for these target-specific differences in at least two ways. In terms of an affect-priming conceptualization, it is likely that dysphoric moods selectively prime information that is self-depracatory. Alternatively, in terms of a dual-process model, it could be argued that self-relevant

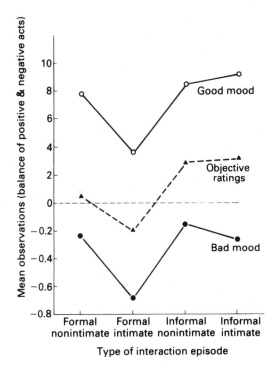

FIG 14.2   The effects of mood on perceptions of interactive behaviors in four different encounters: positive mood subjects perceive more positive and fewer negative behaviors than objective raters, while negative mood subjects see more negative and fewer positive behaviors in the same videotapes (after Forgas *et al.*, 1984).

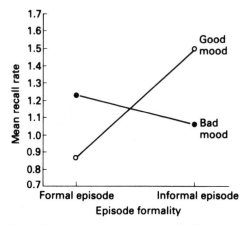

Fɪɢ 14.3   Mood effects of memory: good mood facilitates the recall of details of
easy, informal episodes (after Forgas *et al.*, 1984).

judgments in dysphoria are more susceptible to mood-consistent distortions because of the greater complexity and degree of elaboration involved in the substantive processing of such information.

The present experimental design presents a particularly challenging test of mood effects on substantive social perception judgments. Everyday social judgments not based on the objective evidence of a video recording may be more likely to be influenced by a person's temporary mood than judgments of videotaped encounters. The significant differences between judgments of the self and judgments of others found here are consistent with other experiments, as well as clinical research (Forgas and Bower, 1988; Ottaviani and Beck, 1988). There was also some indirect evidence in this study for the role of memory biases in these judgmental effects. When asked to recall details of the interactions they participated in during the previous day, subjects in a happy mood tended to recall more details about easy, informal episodes, while people in a sad mood remembered more about difficult, formal interaction episodes (Figure 14.3).

Affective influences on learning and judgmental latency

Further investigations of mood effects on the substantive processing of information about persons helped to specify the nature of the strategies involved. In one of our experiments (Forgas and Bower, 1987), subjects participated in an impression formation task, which required them to read about a variety of other persons on a computer screen. Later, they were asked to make social judgments about these targets. In fact, the computer was programmed to record accurately how long each subject took to read each piece of information about a person, and how long they took to make each impression formation judgment. Consistent with the implications of affect-priming formulations, we found that people tended to spend more time reading, and learning information about a target when that information matched their mood state. This finding provided direct evidence for the kind of processing bias assumed to operate in the substantive processing of social information; namely, that people do pay selective attention to, and learn more thoroughly, mood-consistent rather than mood-inconsistent information (see Figure 14.4).

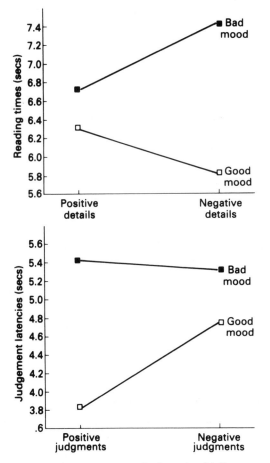

Fig 14.4   Affective influences on processing latencies. (a) Greater processing times when reading mood-consistent rather than inconsistent information. (b) Shorter processing times when making mood-consistent rather than inconsistent judgments (after Forgas and Bower, 1987).

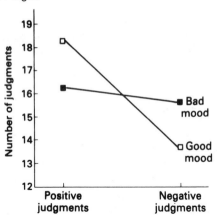

F<small>IG</small> 14.5   The influence of affect on the number of positive and negative person
perception judgments (after Forgas and Bower, 1987).

How far did these selective attention and learning biases influence the outcome of person perception judgments? The analysis of impression formation judgments in our study revealed the now familiar mood-bias effect: happy people made more positive, lenient judgments while sad people were far more likely to be critical in their perception of the target character. These data support the prediction that in social judgments involving substantive processing strategies, mood states will bias judgments in a mood-consistent direction through their influence on information storage and retrieval processes (Figure 14.5). Next, we also looked at the time taken by subjects to make positive or negative person perception judgments. Remarkably, the latency to make each judgment was also influenced by mood. Mood-consistent judgments took less time to make than inconsistent judgments. This pattern once again supports the mood-priming model, which assumes that when engaged in substantive processing, the superior activation and availability of mood-related constructs should be reflected in mood-consistent judgments requiring less time to make than do inconsistent judgments (Figure 14.4).

This experiment then provides clear support for the prediction of priming models than by "spreading activation, a dominant emotion will enhance the availability of emotion-congruent interpretations and salience of congruent stimulus materials for learning." (Bower, 1981, p.451). A richer associative base in turn may lead to the slower and more detailed processing of mood-consistent details in a learning task (Craik and Tulving, 1975), but the faster retrieval of mood-relevant details in a judgmental task. Mood-consistent details may also have the effect of enhancing the intensity of existing moods, further motivating judges to give such information greater attention. Mood states may also act to selectively remind subjects of congruent episodes from their past, again resulting in the slower and more detailed processing of such materials in learning tasks. This latter effect is also predicted by most affect-as-information formulations.

Affective influences on memory and judgments in children

What role do moods play in the way young children, as against adults, learn, remember, and use information in their substantive social judgments about others? Such mood-based distortions in interpersonal perceptions and evaluations may have important consequences for emerging patterns of friendship and social adjustment in childhood. Once again, we found evidence for significant mood-based differences in cognitive processing (Forgas *et al.*, 1988), although the results were in some respects quite different from the adult data. In this study, schoolchildren received an audiovisual mood manipulation, followed by exposure to two target characters, both children of their own age. One day later, a matching or nonmatching mood state was induced, and their memory and person perception judgments for the targets seen on the previous day were assessed. Results showed evidence for mood-state dependent memory. Characters seen in matching encoding and retrieval moods were remembered better. Learning about the two targets in different mood also helped to improve memory for both. Children also demonstrated a significant negativity bias in their memory and judgments about others, something that is rarely found with adult subjects. This possibly reflects the weak emotional socialization in children and the lack of suppression of negativity biases. To the extent that children have a more restricted repertoire of emotional experiences, and may not have fully internalized adult norms of politeness, these differences were not entirely surprising.

Despite the overall support in our studies for the kind of mood-induced perceptual biases predicted by the associative network model when a substantive processing strategy is adopted, there are several remaining questions that have also been identified. Negative mood effects were found to be less consistent and enduring than positive mood effects. There are several possible explanations for this. A critical part of socialization is to learn to control and deal with negative emotional states. It may be that the rules and norms pertaining to negative affect and its expression are superimposed on the kind of mood-priming processes predicted by the network model. If this were the case, we would expect young children to be more likely to give free expression to the kind of cognitive distortions associated with negative moods than adults do, and indeed, there is some evidence for such a difference from our research (Forgas *et al.*, 1988). The relative volatility of negative mood effects on social perception and judgments may also be due to the greater likelihood that controlled, motivated information processing strategies may be superimposed on the kind of automatic processes assumed by network models.

A related possibility is that positive and negative moods not only influence memory processes, but also selectively trigger different information processing strategies. Negative moods in particular may be related to a slower, more detailed, and analytic kind of information processing strategy typically employed when using a substantive processing strategy, while positive moods lead to faster, more open, creative but also less analytic processing typical of heuristic processing strategies (Fiedler, this volume). Motivational as well as cognitive principles may be involved, as people are presumably motivated to control and escape from an aversive mood state, and this may lead them to consciously and selectively focus on potentially rewarding information. Some of these possibilities were considered in several of our recent experiments, looking at the effects of positive and negative moods on social decisions, choices, and attributions (Forgas *et al.*, in press).

Praise or blame? Affective influences on achievement attributions

Mood may influence not only information storage and retrieval, but also the way information, once available, is used. In some recent experiments, we looked at the role of moods in how people make substantive attributions and inferences about success and failure, both for themselves and for others. In the first study in this series, subjects made to feel happy or sad were given the task of making attributions for the success or failure of a stimulus person facing a typical "life dilemma." Targets were described as succeeding or failing in a job, or winning or losing on an investment. These descriptions were based on the Choice Dilemmas Questionnaire extensively used in group judgmental research, and specially modified and validated for the present purposes. We found that, on the whole, subjects in a good mood were likely to make positive, lenient attributions, preferentially identifying internal, stable causes for success, and external, unstable causes for failure (Figure 14.6).

Follow-up experiments expanded these findings by also looking at real-life rather than hypothetical outcomes, and assessing the role of cognitive as against motivational processes in the attribution outcome. In the next experiment, attributions were made for a real-life event, doing well or badly at an exam, and this time actor–observer differences were also investigated, by assessing attributions to the self, as against others. Results again showed that positive mood resulted in more favorable attributions to both self and other. In negative mood, instead of displaying an increased self-serving bias, as predicted by motivational accounts, subjects were particularly critical of themselves, blaming stable and internal causes for their failure, and crediting unstable, external causes for their successes. This bias did not generalize

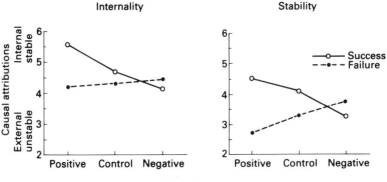

Fɪɢ 14.6   The effects of mood on attributions for success and failure in hypothetical life dilemmas: more internal and stable attributions for success than failure in positive mood (after Forgas *et al.*, in press).

to others, however, who continued to be given credit for succeeding, and little blame for failing (see Figure 14.7).

These results do not support motivational explanations of attributional biases, which imply that subjects should be most likely to engage in self-serving attributions when they need it most, i.e. in a negative mood. We may better account for this pattern of results in terms of the influence of affective states on preferred information processing strategies. Affect may inform a person that cognitive vigilance is required (when in a bad mood), or not required (when in a good mood). In a good mood, people are more likely to engage in open, effortless, and relatively careless information processing (Isen, 1984), using heuristic processing and the superior availability of affect-consistent cognitions from their memory system.

Negative mood, in contrast, seems to lead to slow, detailed, and analytic processing of the available information, and the imposition of controlled information processing strategies, and particular focus on the self. This mode of processing may tend to result in conscious information processing strategies which can counterbalance the effects of the greater availability of affect-consistent cognitions, and may lead to particularly negative assessments of the self, without similar consequences for judgments of others.

Once again, the kind of self–partner differences we found are matched by evidence from the clinical literature dealing with depressive affect and cognition. Clinically depressed patients exhibit a similar pattern to that found in several of our studies (Forgas *et al.*, 1984; Forgas and Bower, 1987, 1988). Depressed people are often more critical of themselves than they are of others, tend to selectively blame themselves for negative outcomes, and are more likely to remember unpleasant or negative events than others do (Ottaviani and Beck, 1988; Roth and Rehm, 1980).

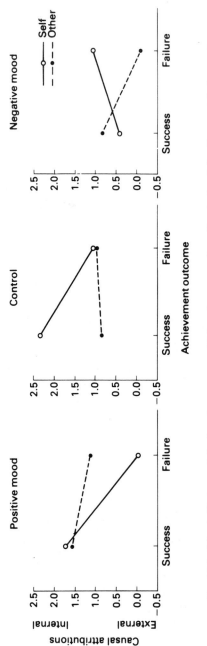

FIG 14.7 Mood effects on attributions for success and failure in an exam for self and other (after Forgas *et al.*, in press).

Affect and interpersonal choices

We next looked at the role of emotional influences in such complex and elusive cognitive tasks as interpersonal decisions and choices. Pioneering work by Schachter (1959) suggests that a person's emotional state may have significant influences on interpersonal choices. It seems that people who are in a negative mood as a result of being made anxious not only prefer the company of others, but most prefer the company of those who are in a similar predicament, presumably because they assume that such partners may potentially be a source of comfort to them. It is intriguing to consider whether negative moods may also trigger specific, motivated information processing strategies targeted to achieve rewarding outcomes, a process that may underlie the kind of personal preferences demonstrated by Schachter and others.

In a series of investigations, we looked at interpersonal decisions made by subjects who were experimentally induced to experience a mild positive or negative affective state, as a result of succeeding or failing on a bogus test. Unlike in Schachter's early studies, we were not only interested in the kind of interpersonal choices subject make (the decision outcome), but also in the kind of information they selected, and the decision-making strategies they adopted (Forgas, 1989). Subjects who were made to feel happy or sad were asked to select a partner for an anticipated cooperative task for themselves or another person from a number of potential candidates. The candidates were described in a "personal file" in terms of large number of relevant personal qualities, each recorded on a separate card. Some information dealt with interpersonal skills and personality, other details related to intelligence and task competence. Subjects were told to sequentially number every card (information unit) as they looked at it, and also rate their perception of the relevance or lack of relevance of the information it contained. This way, we obtained a step-by-step record of the decision processes adopted by happy and sad subjects, and their evaluation of the information they dealt with.

Results showed that happy subjects reached a decision faster, were more efficient in dealing with information and eliminating irrelevant details, focused more on the task-related qualities of the potential partners, and ultimately made choices that preferred competent rather than merely rewarding partners. In other words, in a positive mood subjects adopted an efficient and reasonably appropriate strategy by focusing on task-related features (Figure 14.8). In contrast, sad subjects were slower, less efficient, and paid more attention to the personality and social skills of potential partners. Ultimately, they preferred partners who were socially rewarding rather than competent. As far as the actual decision-making strategy is concerned, happy subjects were more likely to adopt a more efficient, "comparison-by-features" type strategy in their decisions than were sad

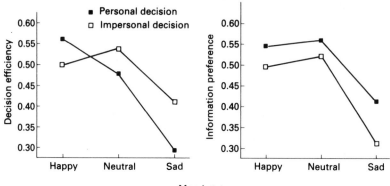

FIG 14.8   The effects of mood on interpersonal decisions. (a) Decision efficiency. (b) Information preference. (Higher values indicate preference for more social rather than task information, and more efficient decision strategies.) (After Forgas, 1989.)

subjects. A summary of the results is shown in Figure 14.8. The findings of this study are consistent with our expectation that happy moods are more likely to trigger heuristic processing strategies, while sad moods induce motivated processing. Indeed, it seems that dysphoria may often generate intentional, motivated strategies specifically designed to eliminate the unpleasant affective state. Motivated processing is a common and as yet little researched strategy in person perception that probably plays an important role in interpersonal judgments both by normal and by depressed populations.

Mood effects in individual versus group judgments

Not all social judgments are made by individuals. Often, important decisions involving person perception tasks are entrusted to groups or committees in the belief that their decision-making processes will be less biased and more representative than individual decisions. Yet we know from research on group judgments that group discussion *per se* may be the source of significant bias in the decision-making process. In one of our recently completed studies (Forgas, in press) we analyzed the influence of transient positive and negative moods on person perception by individuals, as against groups. We relied on the repeated-measures design well known from group research, when individual and group judgments are performed by the same people on two different occasions, in this instance separated by a two-week interval. Judgmental targets were a number of person categories, each judged on a range of bipolar scales measuring three underlying judgmental dimensions: evaluation, competence, and confidence. Before both individual and group judgments, positive, negative, or neutral mood

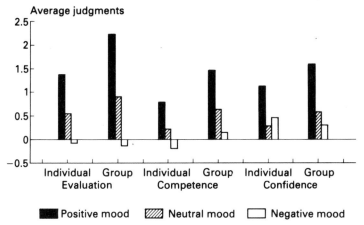

Fɪɢ 14.9   Mood effects on individual and group judgments on three judgmental dimensions: group discussion polarizes positive affective distortions, but eliminates negative affective distortion by individuals (Judgments are on a 6-point $-3/+3$ scale.) (After Forgas, in press.)

was induced in subjects in a factorial design, using films as the induction medium. Results showed that judgments of the person targets by individual judges were more positive in a happy mood, and more negative in a sad mood than judgments by controls. This pattern is consistent with data from previous experiments, and supports the affect-priming model as an account of mood-induced judgmental biases when substantive processing of information is likely (Figure 14.9).

Mood had a somewhat different effect on group judgments. In a positive mood, groups made even more positive judgments than individuals, as would be predicted by group extremity shift theories. In a negative mood, however, exactly the opposite occurred. The negativity of individual judgments was not enhanced, but instead attenuated as a consequence of group discussion (Figure 14.9). The most likely explanation of this effect can again be found in the kind of processing strategy groups are likely to adopt under these circumstances. Exposure to the opinions of others in a group is likely to trigger a more controlled, motivated processing strategy, as well as highlighting the undesirable aspects of extreme negative judgments of others. We are currently involved in follow-up investigations focusing on the actual interactive strategies adopted by people when performing group judgments in different mood states.

Evidence from field studies

In addition to the extensive laboratory evidence for mood effects on person perception judgments summarized above, we have also attempted to show that similar judgmental distortions also reliably occur in field settings.

We used a variety of naturally occurring events as mood manipulations. Supporters of winning or losing rugby teams, people who won or lost money in a betting shop, or received a small gift or a sweet in a shopping center were our subjects, answering a variety of questions dealing with social judgments. In one study, almost 1000 visitors to happy, sad, or aggressive films were interviewed immediately after leaving a movie theatre (Forgas and Moylan, 1987). They were asked to answer public opinion survey type questions about their perception of political leaders, and parties, as well as about their life satisfaction and expectations about the future. On all questions, subjects in a good mood after a happy film gave significantly more positive and lenient judgments and attribution than subjects who just saw a sad or aggressive film, suggesting that mood-based distortions in social judgments are a common—and probably underestimated—feature of everyday life.

Summary and Conclusions

The evidence outlined in this chapter has important and relatively clearcut implications for research on mood effects on social judgments. Feelings have a crucial influence on many cognitive processes (cf. Forgas and Bower, 1988), yet the precise nature of this influence is still far from clearly understood. Person perception, by definition, involves high-level, abstract cognitive processes necessarily requiring the selection, learning, retrieval, and interpretation of information about the characteristics of people that are usually not directly observable. In the first part of this chapter we surveyed some of the traditional approaches to person perception research, and suggested that historically, at least two alternative conceptualizations can be identified. The first, constructivist approach assumes that person perception is an active, even creative, process where the characteristics of the judge are almost as important to the judgmental outcome as the characteristics of the target. The second view is more mechanistic, assuming that information about people is "given", with permanent, enduring meanings, and that the study of person perception therefore involves the analysis of the combinatorial, information integration strategies used by people.

Most traditional, as well as contemporary, approaches to person perception are based on a single-process assumption—that is, the belief that there is one enduring way of processing information about people. In contrast, in this chapter a multiprocess approach was outlined, proposing that there are multiple information processing strategies available to judges when forming impressions, and that the decision as to which process to adopt in a particular situation is one of the more interesting issues in person perception research. Affective states may be among the more important variables determining the choice of a particular person perception strategy.

On the basis of past research as well as our own empirical work, it was suggested that at least four distinct information processing strategies may be identified in person perception: (1) the *direct access strategy*, when preexisting, crystallized judgments are simply retrieved from memory; (2) the *substantive processing strategy*, when the available information about a target is selectively processed, involving learning, associative, and memory processes, in order to arrive at a novel judgment about a person; (3) the *motivated processing strategy*, when the motivation to achieve a particular judgmental outcome overrides the usual processing alternatives; and (4) *the heuristic processing strategy*, when judges choose to ignore or bypass relevant information in order to simplify the judgmental task and form an impression using various shortcuts. Figure 14.10 illustrates such a multi-process model and the factors influencing which processing alternative is adopted in given situations.

In the second half of the chapter, a number of our empirical studies illustrating affective influences on person perception judgments were briefly summarized. The evidence surveyed here is generally consistent with the

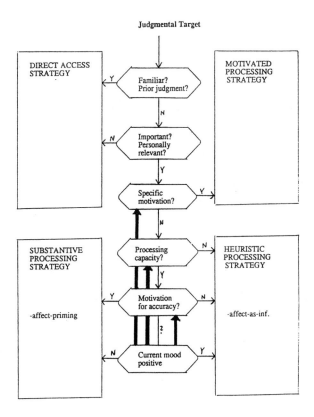

FIG 14.10   A multiprocess model of mood effects on social judgments.

multiprocess approach. In some studies, we found evidence for the operation of affective influences on substantive processing strategies, leading to
the selective learning, interpretation, and recall of valenced information
and, ultimately, the distortion of the ensuing person perception judgments
in an affect-consistent direction (cf. Forgas *et al.*, 1984; Forgas and Bower,
1987). Actual differences in processing times, and judgmental latencies in
particular, support the various mood-priming formulations. Other studies
produced evidence indicating that judges relied on motivated, controlled
processing strategies in reaching a judgment. This was particularly the case
when dysphoric subjects had the task of making person perception judgments about people they actually expected to meet. Under these circumstances, the motivation to obtain rewarding, pleasant partners was apparently paramount in the judgmental processes adopted (Forgas, 1989).

At the most general level, these results suggest that there is a broad and
pervasive tendency for people to perceive and interpret others in terms of
their feelings at the time, and to adopt different information processing
strategies when dealing with information about people depending on their
temporary affective state. Mood-induced differences in information selection, retrieval, and interpretation of the kind demonstrated here may have
particularly important consequences for interpersonal decisions and judgments. There is some recent evidence suggesting that mood effects on
cognition and judgments are most likely to be significant when the information base is complex and elaborate, selective and constructive processing
is required, and the evidence is capable of supporting alternative interpretations (cf. Forgas *et al.*, in press). This is precisely the case in person
perception judgments.

This conclusion must be tempered by a number of important qualifi-
cations, however. There is growing evidence suggesting that positive and
negative moods are not equally effective in influencing information processing and judgments. Negative mood effects are typically less robust, and
more dependent on a variety of situational and contextual factors. Moreover, not all judgments are equally influenced by mood; we have seen that
negative moods in particular are far more likely to influence self-relevant
judgments and cognitions than judgments of others, at least when the targets
are not intimately known. These exceptions suggest that in addition to the
affect-priming principles proposed by Bower (1981), a variety of other
factors, social, motivational, or personal in character, also influence how
affective states influence cognition and, ultimately, perceptions and judgments. More detailed attention as to how affect influences the different
information processing strategies available to judges remains one of the
more important tasks for future research.

This chapter began by emphasizing the complex, constructive character of
person perception judgments. We may conclude by observing that although
much has already been discovered about the information processing and

representation functions of affective states, not enough is known about how affect triggers and influences different processing strategies. A multipurpose framework for studying person perception may be useful in focusing attention on this important and as yet insufficiently understood question.

Acknowledgements

Financial assistance from the Australian Research Council and help by Ms Sandy Morrison in the preparation of this chapter is greatly acknowledged. Requests for reprints should be sent to Joseph P. Forgas, School of Psychology, University of New South Wales, P.O. Box 1, Kensington 2033, Sydney, Australia.

References

Anderson, N. H. (1974). Cognitive algebra: integration theory applied to social attribution. In L. Berkowitz (Ed.), *Advances in experimental social psychology*, Vol. 7, pp. 1–101. New York: Academic Press.

Asch, S. E. (1946). Forming impressions of personality. *Journal of Abnormal and Social Psychology*, **41**, 258–290.

Bower, G. H. (1981). Mood and memory. *American Psychologist*, **36**, 129–148.

Cantor, N., and Mischel, W. (1979). Prototypes in person perception. In L. Berkowitz (Ed.), *Advances in experimental social psychology*, Vol. 12. New York: Academic Press.

Clark, M. S., and Isen, A. M. (1982). Towards understanding the relationship between feeling states and social behavior. In A. H. Hastorf and A. M. Isen (Eds), *Cognitive social psychology*. New York: Elsevier–North Holland.

Craik, F. I. M., and Tulving, E. (1975). Depth of processing and the retention of words in episodic memory. *Journal of Experimental Psychology: General*, **104**, 268–294.

Forgas, J. P. (Ed.). (1981). *Social cognition: Perspectives on everyday understanding*. London: Academic Press.

Forgas, J. P. (1983). The effects of prototypicality and cultural salience on perceptions of people. *Journal of Research in Personality*, **17**, 153–173.

Forgas, J. P. (1985). Person prototypes and cultural salience: the role of cognitive and cultural factors in impression formation. *British Journal of Social Psychology*, **24**, 3–17.

Forgas, J. P. (1988). The role of physical attractiveness in the interpretation of facial expression cues. *Personality and Social Psychology Bulletin*, **13**, 478–489.

Forgas, J. P. (1989). Mood effects on decision-making strategies. *Australian Journal of Psychology*, **41**, 197–214.

Forgas, J. P. (in press). Affective influences on individual and group judgements. *European Journal of Social Psychology*.

Forgas, J. P., and Bower, G. H. (1987). Mood effects on person perception judgements. *Journal of Personality and Social Psychology*, **53** 53–60.

Forgas, J. P., and Bower, G. H. (1988). Affect in social and personal judgments. In K. Fiedler and J. P. Forgas (Eds), *Affect, cognition and social behavior*. Toronto: Hogrefe International.

Forgas, J. P., Bower, G. H., and Krantz, S. (1984). The influence of mood on perceptions of social interactions. *Journal of Experimental Social Psychology*, **20**, 497–513.

Forgas, J. P., Bower, G. H., and Moyland, S. J. (in press). Praise or blame? Affective influences on attributions for achievement. *Journal of Personality and Social Psychology*.

Forgas, J. P., Burnham, D., and Trimboli, C. (1988). Mood, memory and social judgements in children. *Journal of Personality and Social Psychology*, **54**, 697–703.

Forgas, J. P., and Moylan, S. J. (1987). After the movies: Mood effects on social judgments. *Personality and Social Psychology Bulletin*, **12**, 467–478.

Forgas, J. P., O'Connor, K., and Morris, S. L. (1983). Smile and punishment: the effects of facial expression on responsibility attribution by groups and individuals. *Personality and Social Psychology Bulletin*, **9**, 587–596.

Griffitt, W. (1970). Environmental effects on interpersonal behavior: Ambient effective temperature and attraction. *Journal of Personality and Social Psychology*, **15**, 240–244.

Hastie, R., and Kumar, P. A. (1979). Person memory: Personality traits as organizing principles in memory for behavior. *Journal of Personality and Social Psychology*, **37**, 25–38.

Hastie, R., Ostrom, T. M., Ebbesen, E. B., Wyer, R. S., Hamilton, D. L., and Carlston, D. E. (Eds) (1980). *Person memory: The cognitive basis of social perception*. Hillsdale, NJ: Erlbaum.

Heider, F. (1958). *The psychology of interpersonal relations*. New York: Wiley.

Isen, A. M. (1984). Towards understanding the role of affect in cognition. In R. S. Wyer and T. K. Srull (Eds), *Handbook of social cognition*, Vol. 3. Hillsdale, NJ: Erlbaum.

Kelly, G. A. (1955). *The psychology of personal constructs*. New York: W. W. Norton.

Lazarus, R. S. (1984). On the primacy of cognition. *American Psychologist*, **39**, 124–129.

Ottaviani, R., and Beck, A. T. (1988). Cognitive theory of depression. In K. Fiedler and J. Forgas (Eds), *Affect, cognition and social behavior*. Toronto: Hogrefe.

Petty, R. E., and Cacioppo, J. T. (1986). *Communication and persuasion: Central and peripheral routes to attitude change*. New York: Springer.

Rosenberg, S., and Sedlak, A. (1972). Structural representations of implicit personality theory. In L. Berkowitz (Ed.), *Advances in experimental social psychology*. New York: Academic Press.

Roth, D., and Rehm, L. P. (1980). Relationships among self-monitoring processes, memory, and depression. *Cognitive Therapy and Research*, **4**, 149–157.

Schachter, S. (1959). *The psychology of affiliation*. Stanford, CA: Stanford University Press.

Schneider, D. J. (1973). Implicit personality theory: A review. *Psychological Bulletin*, **79**, 294–309.

Snyder, M. (1984). When belief creates reality. In L. Berkowitz (Ed.), *Advances in experimental social psychology*, Vol. 18. Orlando, FL: Academic Press.

Wyer, R. S., and Srull, T. K. (1981). Category accessibility: Some theoretical and empirical issues concerning the processing of social stimulus information. In E. T. Higgins, C. P. Herman, and M. P. Zanna (Eds), *Social cognition: The Ontario Symposium*, Vol 1. Hillsdale, NJ: Erlbaum.

Zajonc, R. B. (1980). Feeling and thinking: Preferences need no inferences. *American Psychologist*, **35**, 151–175.

Zajonc, R. B. (1984). On the primacy of affect. *American Psychologist*, **39**, 117–123.

Name Index

Subject Index